EVOLUTION OF BRITISH ECONOMY AND SOCIETY
1870–1979

JAMES HADFIELD

B.A. Hons., Dip.Ed., M.A., Ph.D. (Sheffield)
B.Sc.(Econ), Hons., External (London)

CHURCHMAN PUBLISHING LIMITED

Evolution of British Economy and Society, 1870–1979

by

James Hadfield
was first published in 1990 by
Churchman Publishing Limited
117 Broomfield Avenue
Worthing, West Sussex BN14 7SF

Publisher: Peter Smith

Copyright © James Hadfield 1990

Represented in
Dublin; Sydney; Wellington;
Kingston, Ontario and Wilton, Connecticut

Distributed to the book trade by
Bailey Book Distribution Limited
(*a division of the Bailey and Swinfen Holdings Group*)
Warner House, Wear Bay Road
Folkestone, Kent CT19 6PH

ISBN 1 85093 126 7

Typeset by Columns of Reading
Printed in Great Britain by Bourne Press Ltd.

1 Day

University of Plymouth Library

Subject to status this item may be renewed
via your Voyager account

http://voyager.plymouth.ac.uk

Exeter tel: (01392) 475049
Exmouth tel: (01395) 255331
Plymouth tel: (01752) 232323

CONTENTS

LIST OF TABLES

"All the prizes . . . . go to specialisation. Hence far too much of the time, both of teachers and students, is spent dealing with what is new, and not what is important".

R.H. Tawney, quoted in G. Chapman, *A Kind of Survivor*, Gollancz, 1975. p 207

"What can the England of 1940 have in common with the England of 1840? But then, what have you in common with the child of five whose photograph your mother keeps on the mantelpiece? Nothing, except that you happen to be the same person".

G. Orwell, "The Lion and the Unicorn", in *Collected Essays* etc., 2, Penguin, 1970, p 71

"As so often happens in economic history, nothing is simple and, in terms of the groundswell of the community's material existence, few changes are sufficiently spectacular to blot out the influence of the customary, the commonplace, and the ordinary".

B.E. Supple, "Income and demand 1860–1914", in ed. R. Floud and D. McCloskey, *Economic History of Britain since 1700*, 2, p 143

". . . . there is the fact that it is literally impossible to give, in linear prose, an account of any complex event or situation which does not distort its subject in one way or another".

J. Naughton, *The Listener*, 24.9.1981 p 349

"In literature truth about life cannot be attempted without truth about society, which is where much post-war fiction and drama is shaky . . . ."

Roy Fuller, *Souvenirs*, London Magazine Editions, 1980, p 177

PREFACE

"Disinterested intellectual curiosity is the life-blood of real civilisation."[1] While this remains a major justification of social history, many have more utilitarian aims. To some, the health of Britain's economy and society in the late 20th century is a source of concern.

Such concern has been expressed throughout the period covered in this work and it will be shown that the roots of the country's major economic problems – relatively low economic growth and productivity, for example – can be unearthed by the end of the 19th century. Indeed, it is quite impossible to understand modern society without a knowledge of the past.

For British institutions and attitudes have evolved over generations. We simply do not start with a clean blackboard[2] on which we can draw a tidy plan, however perfect that may appear. There is already much on the board and it is not easy to rub off, for it consists of deep-rooted feelings, attitudes, stances, institutions. Nations, like individuals are much influenced by, though they are not prisoners of, their past.

Nor are the advantages brought by a knowledge of Britain's past limited to native Britons. British history is of interest because Britain was the first country to industrialise, and because the English language and some British institutions were exported to wide areas in the days when the Empire embraced roughly a quarter of the earth.

Further, it is frequently asserted that the early specialisation inherent in our educational system divides us into scientists and technologists on the one side and arts and social science specialists on the other. Obviously, a modern society needs technical experts, but it also needs people with a broad understanding who can communicate. While avoiding the folly of extravagant claims, a study of social and economic evolution should help towards an understanding of attitudes and beliefs.

Modern societies are immensely complicated and complex. Often it is quite impossible to give a simple answer to a question. Why has Britain's once dominant economy suffered a serious relative decline in efficiency? Why and how did people limit the size of their families? Answers are of course possible and are later attempted, but to pretend that they are clear cut would be foolish. Anyone attempting to tell the story of Britain over the past 100 years surely deserves sympathy. A selection has to be made from the billions of facts and opinions concerning millions of people. It is possible for decent, educated, intelligent participants or witnesses to present utterly contradictory accounts of an occurrence – a fact well known to marriage guidance counsellors! Preparing her biography, J. Harris was told that William Beveridge was "a man who would not give a penny to a blind beggar" and "one of the kindest men who ever walked the earth".[3]

Further, in these times of detailed research and deep specialisation each conclusion in a general work may well be scorned and rejected. Yet there is a place for such works since not all students have time or opportunity to devour a vast mass of reading.

To help fill their buckets of knowledge drawn from the ocean, this wide introduction is presented.

Woodnewton,
Peterborough.
1988.

PART I: SETTING THE SCENE

---

1. HISTORY

1.1 Importance

The central relevance of modern British history is this. Britain was the first country to industrialise and to break out of the constraints of a rural, agricultural, traditional, society. With her Industrial Revolution of around 1760–1840, this country was the first to embark on that process of self-sustaining economic growth which up to 1979 was regarded as needed and natural throughout the world. "This world, which has never before been ready to accept universally any of the universal faiths offered for its salvation, is apparently prepared to embrace the religion of science and technology without reservation".[1] Certainly, in the 19th century, Europe avowedly followed Britain's lead.[2]

Being first brought great advantages. Early 19th century Britain was essentially without world competitors. "The workshop of the world" became the leading industrial, commercial, naval, imperial, power.

Now that "all our pomp of yesterday" is indeed "one with Nineveh and Tyre" it is possible to dwell, surely without fear of accusation of jingoism, on the amazing story of how a small group of islands off the coast of Europe came to rule an Empire embracing about a quarter of the human race. Effects remain wide, deep and great. For example, English has become an international language, with all that that implies for the reception of English literature and ideas.

1.2 Tradition and change

Modern Britons have inherited very much from the past: structures, institutions, beliefs, attitudes, systems.

Most obvious, are the structures, the castles and churches, stately homes, cottages, barns, colleges, hospitals and so on. The past is there, in a visible form which is absent from American or African grasslands.

Of institutions the most basic and important is the family, its utility proved by its almost universal existence. For some centuries before the 19th, English and other West European families had developed characteristics which differentiated them from families in some other world cultures. The family was nuclear – father, mother, children.[3] The extended family had not the power and importance accorded to it in some societies. Marriage was undertaken by adults. Shakespeare had his Juliet married in her early teens but he was not describing a common state of affairs in his day or in later centuries. In the 16th and later centuries, marriages were normally entered into by people in their twenties – the man commonly around 3–5 years older than the woman. Certainly by the 19th century marriages were not normally arranged by parents, though pressures might well be brought, especially in those numerous cases when a baby was on the way. It was not common in Britain, as it was in some societies, for much older men to marry young girls. Age differences between spouses were not vast and companionship was therefore easier.[4]

Family, Church, School, formed a trio of institutions which maintained and fostered culture and tradition.

The churches were Christian. Pre-eminent in England after the 16th century was the Established Church of England with the Monarch at its head. Protestant non-adherents, or Dissenters, gained a large addition of numbers around the early 19th century when Methodism gained a hold, particularly in the new manufacturing districts. Roman Catholicism also gained ground in the 19th century, there being less than 1000 priests in 1837, 2,500 in 1887.[5]

It is quite impossible to understand Victorian Britain without the realisation that to many – to Lord Shaftesbury[6] and others less famous – religion was the most important issue in life. Throughout England the "parochial system of the Church – its clergy resident in every village . . . . . has struck its fibres too deep into the soil of English life to be rooted out . . ."[7] Fascinating records of Norfolk clergymen reveal the breadth and depth of parochial activity.[8] It was different in urban working class districts, but even there Chapel or Church might be the main centre of leisure activity.

There were ancient Universities and many schools founded over previous centuries. Particularly in England, most passed through a bad time in the 18th century before being reformed and augmented in the 19th. In general, Scotland's educational system was more alive, successful and democratic than that of England – so a procession of better educated Scots took over key positions in England and the Empire. By the 19th century, until the State took over in 1870, Church charitable organisations were providing schooling for very large numbers of English children. Boys from wealthy English families were sent to public schools where main subjects of study were the Classics. Study of the life and literature of ancient Greece and Rome had deep effects on 19th century English literature and thought.

Main British political institutions clearly reveal the retention of tradition plus implementation of change through centuries of evolution. Could they return, 1870 Radicals would note with surprise that the Monarchy survives and enjoys massive popular support. But the near autocracy of a Henry VIII has evolved into the constitutional monarchy of Elizabeth II. The English Parliament dates back to the 13th century, but only in this 20th century has it become fully representative. Similarly, very important local government has seen much history and great changes. English and Scottish legal systems, trial by jury, Magna Carta, habeas corpus have come down to us from long-past centuries.

This is all very relevant and significant. By, say, 1800 when the Industrial Revolution was changing Britain, there was already a strong tradition of the "free-born Englishman". In spite of poverty, hardship, awful gaps between rich and poor, the real power of landed magistrates, repression and transportation, Britons enjoyed valuable inherited rights which were – and indeed still are – sadly lacking in many other countries. "The Englishman's home was his castle". Government officers could not normally enter a house and make arbitrary arrests without cause shown. In serious cases, an accused person, presumed innocent until proved guilty, was entitled to be tried by 12 other citizens who might not bring in a verdict desired by the Authorities. Parliament always provided a privileged forum for discussion of grievances and attacks on the executive. In the direst days of early 19th century economic depression, social suffering and Government repression, a brilliant journalist, William Cobbett, could get his popular views over to hundreds of thousands.

Success in 18th century wars culminating in Nelson's and Wellington's victories, led to colonial and naval hegemony and to a century of "Pax Britannica", (or British peace), from 1815–1914. There was much national pride and bombast – the spirit of "Rule Britannia" and "Hearts of Oak". In the 19th century, foreigners noted Britons' nationalism and feelings of superiority.[9] Self-satisfaction and pride had been growing over modern centuries, since Shakespeare wrote of "this blessed plot". Confident national cohesion handed down into the 20th century helped to carry Britons through the cruel blizzards of 1914–45.

Radicalism

Pre-industrial developments generally strengthened individual-istic as opposed to communal forces in British in contrast to other societies where communal ownership of land and/or the large extended family were the rule.[10] Yet there was a persistent, important, indigenous radical strain running through centuries. In English peasant upheavals of the 14th century, men asked the fundamental question:

> "When Adam delved and Eve span,
> Who was then the gentleman?"

The 16th century Reformation when Britain broke away from the Roman Catholic Church, certainly stimulated freer, scientific, rational, thinking, which in those days was all too often stifled by Catholic Church and priests. In the great Puritan Revolution of the 17th century, thousands of pamphlets were written and read in a vast surge of religious, political, social challenge, as Diggers and Levellers propounded and attempted to realise ideals of equality, when the proposition was advanced that "the poorest he that is in England hath a life to live as the greatest he".

True, Puritans suffered eclipse, but their ideas lived on in a myriad spheres. The Puritan Sabbath became the strictly observed Sunday of the 19th and 20th centuries – by no means entirely dead in 1979. Puritan emphasis on individual salvation, decency, responsibility, work, hard choices, plus considerable slices of Puritan democratic Church government survived in Nonconformist chapels.[11]

In Scotland, Calvinism had a more powerful and lasting effect than in England. One beneficial effect was an emphasis on education.

British culture is part of that Western civilisation which owes much to the religion of Judaea and the learning of Greece and Rome. Britons have exported aspects of their culture, particularly to former Empire countries.

But cultural flows have not been all one way. Back in the middle Ages, Europe learned much from the nearby Moslems.[12] Centuries later many Indian words passed into English: bungalow, shampoo, pyjamas and many others.[13] One of the most typical of British activities – tea drinking – came from the East.

In this 20th century the large import of American and other films has affected language and attitudes. Mass foreign travel has led to the adoption of Mediterranean foods.

Such are a few glimpses into the vast field – increasingly worldwide – of cultural exchange.

The pre-industrial economic and social system

At the end of the 17th century, three-quarters of English people lived in the countryside and worked on the land, though they might well have a subsidiary occupation such as cloth-making. But 18th century Britain had advanced far beyond the limits of mere subsistence production. There was considerable market exchange, it was a money economy with trade at home and abroad. There were towns, (London had about half a million people by 1700), banks, brewers, capitalists, bills of exchange professions, learning.

Much of traditional England survived into the 20th century. In 1933, Priestley wrote of "old England, the country of the cathedrals and minsters and manor houses and inns, of Parson and Squire, guide-book and quaint highways and byways England".[14]

In the 18th as in the 20th century, the land was privately owned. Indeed much of it had passed into the hands of the very few, with resulting great inequalities. By the 18th century, some 300 landed aristocrats owned much of Britain which they effectively ruled. Grandees, such as Dukes of Bedford, Devonshire, Northumberland, had incomes of over £50,000 a year.[15] Britain was very different from, say, Africa, when, up to this century, much land was vested in the tribe to be used, not owned, by the cultivator, and even from neighbouring France where, after 1789, much land was owned by a large number of peasant cultivators.

Much British land was let out by landlords to tenant farmers who might hire labourers who, until the 19th century, often lived as servants in the farm-house.

True, not all landlords were great aristocrats. There was a considerable class of 3 to 4 thousand squires owning land. Also, farmers might still own their own farms.

Nor was it just the land which was privately owned. The large number of enterprises in commerce, trade, finance, domestic industry, was owned by individuals, partnerships or companies. The latter included the famous East India and Hudson's Bay companies and the Bank of England. There were joint-stock commercial banks. But, following much speculation, the "Bubble Act" of 1720 restricted company formation. In 1800, the British economy was what it had been for centuries and was to remain, with great changes, a private enterprise, capitalist, economy.

Clearly, the above were developments of great significance.

Society

Society was hierarchical. In each local area, people took their place, determined by birth, on a vertical mountain of power, privilege and responsibility with the landed lord at the peak, squires, clergy, farmers, traders, labourers below. In the main, this order of precedence was accepted like day and night, winter and summer. Into the 20th century, in many, (but not all), rural areas, it was accepted that local aristocrats were natural leaders.

The upper class was not a caste: it was possible – but difficult – to rise into it. Women might climb up the social scale through marriage.[16] There were huge class differences, injustice, exploitation in rural Britain. The Game Laws provided an example of class legislation of a very selfish kind. But the best of the landlords took their duties very seriously.[17] They, their agents (an early example of a professional body) and the landscape gardeners and others they employed bequeathed a productive agriculture and very beautiful countryside.

But it is very necessary to give strong emphasis to the hierarchical social system. Though by then great inroads had been made into its power bases, the aristocracy still ruled Britain when Lord Salisbury formed his Cabinet in 1895 of 2 marquesses, 2 dukes, one earl, one viscount, three barons, two squires, one director of the Bank of England, and one rich ex-businessman.[18]

In the second half of the 20th century, even supporters of the aristocracy could be surprised by its ability to survive.[19]

Change

One modern scholar sees modern history as a "long revolution" which includes three great changes: the democratic revolution, meaning the determination of people to govern themselves; the industrial revolution; the cultural revolution, meaning the aspiration to widen and extend the active process of learning.[20]

In all three fields, modern Britain took great steps forward but by 1870 it was the Industrial Revolution which had had the most far-reaching effects. Already by 1870, Britain had become a mainly urban, industrial nation.

Industrialisation

Machines took over from humans and animals. They have continued to do so and have become vastly more powerful and intricate. Self-sustaining economic growth began and continued as part of current income was ploughed back into the real investment in buildings and plant which added to output.

It must be stressed that industrialisation enabled 19th century Britain to support much increased numbers and (over the whole century) to give that increased population a higher standard of living. Pre-industrial Britain was not without problems. There could be sheer want. On his visit to Western Scotland in 1773, Dr. Johnson noted: "In Mull the disappointment of a harvest, or a murrain among the cattle, cuts off the regular provision; and they who have not manufactures can purchase no part of the superfluities of other countries. The consequence of a bad season is here not scarcity but emptiness; and they whose plenty was barely a supply of natural and present need when that slender stock fails, must perish with hunger".[21]

The family

Many institutions survived the bombardment of industrialisation with remarkable resilience. Again the most important was the family. For example, mid 19th century Preston "was predominantly a familistic society"[22] in which in 1851 73 per cent of families were nuclear, consisting of a married couple or widowed person with (or rarely without) children. Nearly three quarters of homes were occupied by a married couple family.

Just over half Preston's 1851 resident population were migrants, though most came from within 20 miles of the town. Great efforts were made to find jobs for relatives who often lived near to each other. Pre-welfare state generations were heavily dependent on kin in times of sickness, worklessness, old age. Grannies were useful when young mothers wanted to continue at work, so old women were less likely to be on poor relief in Lancashire than elsewhere.

Women and the young worked for wages and a consequent degree of independence denied on village farms. Indeed one historian was convinced that the Industrial Revolution widened economic opportunities available to women.[23]

On farms and in domestic industry, the whole family had worked together. Now in mill towns, men, women and children went out to paid work, perhaps in separate establishments. Here was a vast change.

Suffering

Early industrialisation brought cruel exploitation and much suffering, very fully described.[24] Some main evils – long hours, child labour, appalling housing and sanitary conditions – were not new. Among what was new and resented were the imposed discipline and regular hours of the factories.[25]

In the mills and streets of Manchester – Salford, evils were far more obvious than they had been in the cottages and roads of rural Suffolk. Wrongs were exposed and slowly remedied through the efforts of reformers and trade unionists and by Government legislation and inspection. By 1870 labour of young children in factories and of women down mines had been stopped, hours of work in factories of women and juveniles were regulated, safety measures were enforced. As production grew so standards of living improved. Enforcement of sanitary legislation removed the worst health hazards.

But it was a harsh age, lambasted by Dickens and by later historians.[26] The Rev. Malthus, a benevolent clergyman and teacher in private life, summed up much early 19th century opinion when he stated: "A man who is born into a world already possessed if he cannot get subsistence from his parents . . . and, if the society do not want his labour, he has no claim of *right* to the smallest portion of food, and, in fact, has no business to be where he is. . ."[27]

A century later, Malthus's ruthless analysis was no longer given expression but hard attitudes to the unfortunate lingered. Down and out in 1930s Liverpool, formerly middle-class Helen Forrester found: "The studied rudeness with which every member of the family was faced whenever dealing with officialdom, as personified by the public assistance committee, by the labour exchanges, by the voluntary agencies working in the city, was a revelation to us".[28]

Some other consequences of industrialisation

The Industrial Revolution bequeathed to modern Britain some main continuing problems including regional imbalance, urban ugliness, class relationships.

Industrialisation was a regional rather than an overall national development. East Anglia, (which, indeed, lost its clothing industry), Wessex, Scottish and Welsh Highlands were among areas which saw no dark satanic mills. Acute differences arose between the industrial areas of North, Midlands and Wales on the one hand and the south-east on the other. Industrial areas, it might be said "colonised" or "exploited" non-industrial, taking their vigorous young, ruining their home industries.

Over the 19th century, Britons became a mainly urban, propertyless, wage-earning people. Numbers in both urban and rural areas grew to around 1820, then between 1821 and 51 many English villages lost population.[29] Industrial towns grew: Bradford had 29,000 people in 1801, 77,000 in 1851. Mainly built without deliberate planning and with a desire merely to house workers near their work, 19th century industrial towns were often quite horribly ugly and depressing. New industrial areas housed very large proportions of propertyless workers. For example, social structure in 1861 Oldham has been thus analysed.[30]

Percentages of total

Magnate, Professional, Tradesman	Small master, Clerical, Shopkeeper	Craft	Semi-Skilled	Labourer. pauper
2	15	20	44	19

Whereas, in the village, Hall and poor man's cottage were a few hundred yards apart, in the towns classes were segregated in appropriate districts. Differences between Fulwood and Attercliffe, (in Sheffield), became very marked. Here was another vast change of continuing relevance.

Why was the victory of urbanisation, industrialisation, proletarianisation so complete in Britain? After all, just across the Channel numbers of peasants and small businessmen were much greater in France. The British agrarian system of landlords, farmers, labourers has been noted. Effects were strengthened by enclosure of commons and open fields around 1760–1830. Denied economic opportunities in their villages, the landless went to towns where pay was often better. A jaundiced contemporary comment was: "Who will work for 1s 6d or 2s a day in a ditch when we can get 3s 6d or 5s a day in a cotton works, and be drunk four days out of seven?"[31]

Class

Over the decades of the Industrial Revolution, writers named, and many Britons came to feel they belonged to, one of three layers – upper, middle, working classes, reaping main rewards from the three sources of income described by the classical economists – rent, profit, wages.

Modern class relationships developed. As one observer of the Lancashire scene wrote in 1832: "Between the manufacturers of the country and the labouring classes subjects of controversy have arisen . . . The bargain for the wages of labour develops organised associations of the working classes, for the purpose of carrying on the contest with the capitalist . . . . a gloomy spirit of discontent is engendered and the public are not unfrequently alarmed. . ."[32] Marx developed the thesis that conflict between capitalists and workers was the most central and crucial of all conflicts in society.

Though we have entered upon a path with a myriad mazes and by-ways, it is folly to ignore the lasting significance of such developments.

Growth with increased employment and rising living standards

By 1870 the economy had definitely "taken off". There was increased employment, real wages and standards of life of the majority were rising.

In a book of perhaps dreadfully perennial application, Malthus had forecast in his "Essay on Population" 1798, that unchecked population rose faster than food supplies until famine slashed numbers. But Malthus, working at Cambridge and Haileybury, knew little of the Northern industries which were to provide work and income and enable Britain to import food for growing numbers.

It is true that the upward line of growth was not dead straight. There were ups and downs – booms and slumps. Two main types of trade cycle are here mentioned: the Kondratieff and the best-known, the Juglar, which is the one often simply called the Trade cycle. Kondratieff wrote of long cycles of around 50 years each: prices rose 1789–1814, and fell 1815–49, rose 1850–73 and fell 1873–96, rose 1896–1924 fell 1921–33, then rose to 1970. After 1970, economic activity but not prices faltered.

In the Juglar cycle, boom and slump occupied some nine years. There were serious slumps about every decade from 1878 to 1918. The worst depression over the century to 1979 came in 1929.

Overseas dimension

In the 19th century Britain became the main industrial, trading, imperial, investing country in the world. We cannot and shall not ignore the deep significance of overseas relations.

Free Trade[33]

19th century Britain took the deliberate, almost unique, step, of concentrating on growth and efficiency as a manufacturing and commercial economy and allowing agriculture and industry to be exposed to the uninterrupted winds of foreign competition. By 1860, Free Trade had been almost completely achieved. It was immensely significant that the British Empire – about a quarter of the World in 1914 – was, in the main, a huge Free Trade area, though self-governing colonies such as Canada and Australia did impose their own tariffs.

19th century liberals much extolled Free Trade which they regarded as one of the main causes of Britain's propserity. But from a selfish, national, point-of-view it can be maintained that Britain was unwise to abandon tariffs.[34] Mid 19th century Britain enjoyed almost a world monopoly in the supply of machine-made cotton goods and modern engineering products. She could have exploited that monopoly position by retaining tariffs on goods coming into Britain even though this would have meant higher British costs and prices. The dangers of a high degree of specialisation could have been avoided had Britain protected her arable farming and her industries of the late 19th century which began to suffer from foreign competition. Agricultural protection would have slowed migration to the towns and overseas and would have slowed down that massive switch to urban and industrial life which caused such hardship in the ugly, sprawling conurbations.

On the other hand, Free Trade stimulated much efficiency and led to the cheap imports which pushed up British real wages.

Free Trade was regarded as the cornerstone of 19th century economic policy and staunch defenders still mustered when it came under attack in the less confident early 20th century. 14 economists wrote to "The Times" in 1903 to support it.

By 1840 an estimated third of exports of the rest of the World came to Britain. This proportion was still 17 per cent in 1913.[35] Mid 19th century Britain was easily the world's main supplier of industrial goods – cotton, coal, iron, engines. Even in 1913, Britain was still the world's leading exporter of manufactures, though the lead over Germany had become relatively small.[36]

London became the centre of a world financial and trading system which aided commerce through the wide adoption of known exchange rates determined by an international gold standard. Currencies were linked to a common denominator, gold, so clearly had a fixed relationship to each other. If A equals 2B and 4C, then B equals 2C. Up to the Great War, this Gold Standard worked reasonably successfully.

Other aspects of modernisation

The above comments on change have concentrated mainly on the effects of the Industrial Revolution. but the vast subject of modernisation of a traditional society demands some mention of the growth of bureaucracy, of rationalism and professionalism.

As central and local government administration and inspection increased so the bureaucracy grew. Professions – doctoring, nursing, engineering, teaching and so on – greatly expanded. Science and efficiency were needed. Increasingly officials and professionals were selected not because of who they were but because of what they knew. Rational enquiry and action much replaced customary ways of doing things.

Year after year, science discovered explanations of phenomena and causes of diseases and calamities. Superstition remained and remains widespread but it is not as wild and dangerous as pre-industrial rural superstition. In 1847 it was rumoured in Norfolk that the Queen had ordered all children under 5 to be killed, (in fact the Poor Law authorities had had workhouse children vaccinated). In the previous year, a woman wounded an alleged witch so that she might be cured by the drawing of her blood.[37] Mass media and education eradicated much of such nonsense.

Yet much of "Old England" survived the floods of industrial-isation and modernisation. The "workshop of the world" was never fully captivated by the charms of commercial success. Indeed, in influential elite circles, industry and commerce lacked the esteem and prestige of aristocracy, land, top professions, classical scholarship. Through the 19th century, birth much determined social standing. When, in the Great War, Mrs. Helen Gwynne-Vaughan was appointed Commander of the Women's Army Corps in France, the fact that she was niece to a Lord seems to have been of more significance than her University qualifications.[38] Landed aristocracy and their life-styles remained influential and enticing throughout the century. Successful middle-class businessmen acquired country properties. One view is that rapid economic growth was dampened down because Britain never fully became an industrial and commercial society.[39] Such deep-seated cultural factors are important. Of course, many have rejoiced at and supported such stances, without perhaps counting their costs.

Britain in 1870

In brief outline, by 1870, Britain was already a much industrialised, urbanised country which had travelled some way on the journey of modern economic growth and was successfully providing growing numbers with work and rising living standards; was the main trading, colonising, society in the World, with easily the most powerful Navy and with vast overseas interests; had a private enterprise, capitalist, free market, competitive economy; was, politically, a Limited Monarchy with effective power exercised by Ministers who had to command majority support in an elected House of Commons; enjoyed inherited, valuable, civil rights which much safeguarded individual liberty; had also inherited grave inequalities in a marked class system which gravely reduced equality of opportunity; reaped from continuing industrialisation not only benefits but also huge costs including heavy environmental disasters, some quite appalling social conditions and the continuing sundering of communities along class lines.

These short statements of complex realities later receive expansion and clarification. It is here emphasised that a distinctive society had evolved by 1870 and that this reality was clear to observers in the 20th century. Orwell thought that: "when you come back to England from any foreign country, you have immediately the sensation of breathing a different air. . . Yes, there *is* something distinctive and recognisable in English civilisation. It is a culture as individual as that of Spain."[40] In the 1970s, Melvyn Bragg wrote: "For though cheap and easy tags about England and the English must be shown for what they are, there is in any country with a tradition, a culture and energy, a recognisable face."[41]

In key respects, British society differed even from societies of nearby Continental Europe. Until 1916, general conscription was unknown in Britain. There was none of that glorification of the Army which featured in 19th century Prussia or France.

2. LAND AND PEOPLE[1]

2.1 Some basic geographic determinants

Compared with many countries in what can be a very harsh world, Great Britain offers an environment well suited to economic development. Great natural disasters, such as earthquakes, are unknown or rare. On most days of a normal year, outside work is possible. The land is not baked by seven months of rainless days, as are the vast tropical grasslands, nor is it frozen hard for a similar period like the hinterlands of Canada or the U.S.S.R. Indeed a country more than 50 degrees North of the Equator normally has a surprisingly mild climate.

Britain is a group of islands off the coast of Europe. The fact that the country is surrounded by sea has been of the greatest historical significance. In modern centuries the Royal Navy dominated the seas so the country was safe from the invasions which smote continental countries with traumatic effects. As late as 1940, the existence of 20 miles of far from still waters was vital. It may be added that the seas have been an important source of food. In 1976 fish worth some £220 million were landed. Later, the importance of the overseas commerce carried on over the seas receives much attention. Here it may be noted that physical separation from Europe contributed to separate development and insular pride.

Geologically, Britain can be roughly divided by a line running from York to Exeter. North and West of this are the old, hard rocks of the Highlands and Southern Uplands of Scotland, the Lake District and Pennines, Wales, and the South-West peninsula. South and East, with extensions into areas such as Cheshire, are the newer sedimentary rocks and the lower-lying, flatter areas. These, particularly over the drier East, are the traditional arable lands, where until the 18th century advent of industrialisation based on coal, lived much of the population. These areas are still highly farmed, (over 90 per cent of the Holland Division of Lincolnshire is cultivated farmland), with intensity and scientific success. Successive generations have so worked upon and changed the natural land that the fields of modern Britain could be included with man-made capital rather than among gifts of nature in any enumeration of factors of production.

Industrialisation needs energy. In Britain this came from coal. In 1865 Jevons wrote that coal "commands this age".[2] Up to 1914, the coal industry expanded vastly and on, or near, the coalfields were located the main industrial areas – Central Scotland, Northumberland and Durham, Lancashire and Yorkshire, the Midlands, South Wales. Coal plus an estuary – Clyde or Tyne – meant shipbuilding and vast coal exports. Coal plus iron-ore, (e.g. County Durham and Cleveland), meant steelmaking midway at Middlesbrough.

In this 20th century, up to 1980, coal has been much replaced by other forms of energy such as oil, natural gas, electricity, (though in Britain the latter is mainly produced in coal-fired power stations), and nuclear power. But leaps in the oil price, plus certainty that the life of North Sea oil and gas fields is limited and some difficulties and fears concerning the nuclear programmes, led to an upsurge of interest in coal and to large new developments as at Selby in Yorkshire.

Britain's modern iron and steel industry was based not only on coal but also on large domestic supplies of iron-ore. In 1885 main ore producing areas with their output were: Cleveland, nearly 6 million tons, Cumberland and Lancashire, 2½ million tons; Scotland 1.8 million; Staffs 1.8 million; and Lincolnshire and Northants 2.3 million. In 1966, some 13 million tons were still being mined.

In the second half of the 19th century, falling quantities of copper, tin and lead were still raised. In the mid 1880s copper, tin and lead mines employed 41,000 workers.[3]

Enormous quantities of sand and gravel, salt, limestone, slate, timber, are among other gifts of nature. Nor must it be omitted that in the age of mass travel, millions of foreign visitors (over 12 million in 1978), came to see Britain's heritage, shops, countryside and contribute handsomely to domestic income and the receipts of the Balance of Payments.

This brief summary of major resources would be incomplete without a mention of that great boon which, (quite unexpectedly to most Britons), came in the 1960s and 1970s in the form of North Sea natural gas and oil. Measured in millions of therms, total natural gas available for U.K. consumption rose from 15 in 1960 to 12,568 in 1975.[4]

In 1969 came the discovery of oil in the British sector of the North Sea. The first oil to come ashore was landed by tanker in 1975. The importance of the new industry is very obvious when it is noted that in 1975, Britain imported 85.8 million tons of crude oil worth £3,371 millions. By 1978, the Balance of Payments contribution of North Sea oil and gas, (what it would have cost to have imported them) was £4.6 billion.[5] By 1980, Britain was nearly self-sufficient in oil in the sense that total production (some of which was exported) was little short of total consumption. Truly here was an enormous, but temporary, bonus.

Yet, though Britons are fortunate in many respects, the following dominant facts remain: first, Britain (especially England) is a relatively very crowded land; second throughout the century covered in this work, it has had to import quite vital, large scale, supplies of food and raw materials.

In 1978, practically 56 million people lived in the 94,000 square miles of the United Kingdom. The overall density of population (about 594 per square mile) is not as high as in say, Holland, but, as often, averages are misleading. Long stretches of Scotland, Wales, the North are nearly empty. A famous war-time pilot noted: "Many people think it's a small place and that we are overcrowded in our little island, but it's amazing how unpopulated the country really is. In the Western Isles, for instance, you can fly for miles without seeing any sign of habitation".[6] True, but England itself, with around 923 people to the square mile, is one of the most densely populated countries in the world, while the millions of Greater London live at 11,664 to the square mile. As will be detailed later, of 48½ million in England and Wales in 1971 nearly 16 lived in the conurbations, 12 in largish towns of over 50,000 each, 10 in small towns. The sensible planning and ordering of a densely packed, mainly urban people continue to pose a vast challenge partly, but certainly not entirely met.[7]

Victorian observers commented on the beauty of the country-side. Escott wrote; "It is the month of June; every feature in the peaceful landscape is in the perfection of its beauty; the fresh deep green of the English foliage – the freshest and deepest in all the world – has yet lost nothing of its depth or freshness. . ."[8] Kilvert described: "a lovely May morning and the beauty of the river and green meadows, the woods, hills and blossoming orchards was indescribable."[9]

The countryside was a source of cohesion, pleasure and pride to Victorian, and later generations. Beatrice Potter wrote in 1881: "The English country looks perfectly enchanting clothed in its spring loveliness. No foreign land, however exquisite it may be, can have the same power of calling out the sympathy and affection of the beholder as the native country".[10]

Alas, within the beautiful rural stretches were some appalling housing conditions, while many square miles were utterly blasted, ruined, changed by unplanned industrialisation. Around St. Helens chemicals killed off vegetation.[11] The squalid and deplorable homes[12] of the Black Country, the iron works of once rural Brightside and Salmon Pastures in then smoky Sheffield, the miles of houses, shipyards, works along once rural Tyne or Clyde, the pit villages of Durham, and London's East End, all provided an ugly depressing stage on which millions of lives were lived out. The environmental costs of industrialisation and urbanisation were heavy and lasting and must be set against the undoubted rise in living standards which certainly came in the later 19th century. In England's North in 1933, Priestley condemned the quite appalling environments he encountered.[13]

Rising densities of population obviously meant that many Britons lacked space and this strong reality has sometimes inhibited economic development and has heightened social tensions.

In particular, since the domestic stock of resources is insufficient to sustain the mainly self-sufficient economy of the U.S.A. or U.S.S.R., Britain has been, and is, a major trading country.

2.2   Demography: main trends.

Three changes of vast significance differentiated 1979 Britain from 1870 Britain:

1.   On average, people lived much longer;
2.   Families were much smaller;
3.   Population was no longer rising at anything like the 1870 rate.

After centuries of slow and fluctuating growth, Britain's population entered upon a sustained rise in the 18th century. Earlier marriages, leading to a higher birth-rate, plus a falling death-rate, were responsible. In 1870, birth and death-rates were still high, with the birth-rate well above the death-rate and numbers therefore rising. In the 1870s, the birth-rate began a long, heavy fall which did not end until the mid 20th century when, particularly in the 1960s, there was a temporary rise before a heavy slump in the 1970s. The death rate fell throughout the century following 1870, but saving of life (particularly infant life) was particularly striking over the early decades of this 20th century.

By the 1970s low birth and death-rates were holding population roughly stationary. An average couple marrying in 1890 had about 6 children: their successors marrying around 1930 had 2. People lived longer: percentages of British population aged over 65 were 5 in 1901, 12 in 1951, 18 in 1981 (the last figure includes women over their retirement age of 60).

So, before the 18th century, birth and death-rates were both high and population grew very slowly. In 1979, birth and death dates were both low and population was again roughly stationary.

Details, plus consideration of additional factors such as migration follow.

2.3   Health and mortality

"Man that is born of woman hath but a short time to live . . . . He cometh up and is cut down like a flower. . ." The beautiful language of the Anglican Prayer Book, heard over generations by millions, conveyed the particular truth that, before the 20th century, the lives of the departed had indeed often been short.[14] One of the greatest differences between former and modern times is that today people, on average, live much longer. In 1840, given prevailing death-rates of the time, the average Briton could expect to live for around 40 years. By 1977–79, expectation of life at birth was, for males 70.0, for females 76.1 years.

If an adult aged 79, and a baby aged one, die, then the average age of death is, of course, 40. It was the terrible slaughter of infants, vulnerable to infectious diseases, which was a major cause of short life up to the 20th century. Around 1730–49 three of four infants born in London died aged under 5. The loss of beloved children caused heavy grief.[15] In earlier generations, death took the place of modern divorce as the agency producing broken homes and one-parent families.

As late as 1898, in one of the world's richest and most advanced countries, in Gateshead 209 and in Sunderland 202, per 1,000 babies born died before their first birthday.

Chronicles of the famous exemplify the remorseless ravages of early death. Patrick Bronte married in 1812. In 1821, his wife died aged 38. His 6 children died at ages ranging from 10 to 38.

The infant mortality rate (death rate in the first year of life per 1,000 born), is reasonably assumed to be one of the surest guides to a country's health and welfare, since infants are particularly susceptible to want and infection.

In England and Wales, infant death rates collapsed as follows:

1870–72	156	1930–32	64
1890–92	149	1960–62	22
1910–12	110	1970–72	18

20th century industrial depression retarded the fall in Scotland's rate. It was 127 in 1870–92 compared with 156 in England and Wales, but 84 in 1930–32 compared with England and Wales's 64. However, by 1970–72 the Scottish rate, at 19, was practically down to that of England.[16]

The crude general death-rate in England and Wales fell from 22 per 1000 in 1871–5 to 12 just before the Second World War.

Perhaps it could be argued that a reduction in the death rate does not imply an improvement in health. A 19th century statistician, Farr, in 1874, held that: "There is relation between death and sickness, and to every death from every cause there is an average number of attacks of sickness, and a specific number of persons incapacitated for work".[17] In days when infections, not heart diseases and cancer, were the main killers, this was a reasonable finding.

On future pages, it will be made abundantly clear that behind the national averages lay very significant variations in class and regional infant and general mortality statistics.

Reasons for falling death-rates

Why did health improve and death-rates fall? From a mass of interlocking factors the following are disentangled.

The major factor accounting for better health and longer life was the rising standard of living. Over the decades people were better housed, better clothed, washed and (most important of all) better fed. So they could resist disease. Sometimes, disease germs lost much of their violence for unexplained reasons. This seems to have happened to scarlet fever. In Darlington, the scarlet fever mortality rate among school age children fell from 14 per 1000 in 1850 to 0.05 in 1928.[18] However, improvement could have resulted from the better health of the hosts, or from natural selection of a stock with greater immunity.

Improved feeding was a main cause in the steady fall in the tuberculosis death-rate in the late 19th and early 20th centuries, for there was no effective drug until the 1940s. Higher living standards meant not only better food, but also shorter hours of work, more holidays, more soap and water, a better environment, and more knowledge of elementary health science.

Environmental improvement destroyed many dangerous organisms. Thus the great boon of pure water in the towns slashed cholera deaths. The important work of the local authorities in their fight against germ-laden filth will be later detailed, when it will also be emphasised that among health-giving advances in the environment was better housing.

To the environment health services of the 19th, were added the personal health services of the 20th, century. Included were provision of health visitors, of clinics for mothers and babies, for sufferers from tuberculosis or venereal diseases.

Personal health services were part of the provision of better social services which provided the safety net which broke the fall of many into dire poverty and disease: Old Age Pensions, National Insurance and the rest.

By no means all the improvements followed action by the Authorities. People did much for themselves. Not only did they dress more sensibly, wash more frequently, clean their teeth, drink less alcohol, (in the early decades of the 20th as compared with the 19th century), but, most important of all, they limited the size of their families. Members of small families, could receive more food, more room, more attention than members of large families.

Quantity and quality of medical care improved. Numbers and skills of doctors, nurses, midwives, health visitors, ancillary staffs, plus hospital provision, vastly increased and improved. As will be shown, this was particularly true after the introduction of National Health Insurance in 1912 and of the National Health Service in 1948.

The march of medical science enabled 19th century health officers to recognise and destroy disease-carrying organisms and 20th century doctors to destroy organisms within the body which were causing pneumonia and a host of former slaughterers. In particular, the sulphonamide drugs and penicillin, introduced around the late 1930s and early 1940s often rapidly cleared up what had previously been lethal conditions.

2.4 Birth-rate

The birth-rate per 1,000 population reached a modern peak in the 1870s. It then fell to 1940 with perhaps temporary post-Second World War recovery, as follows:

England and Wales

1871–80	35.5	1906–10	26.3	1946–50	18.0
1881–90	32.5	1929–30	16.7	1956–60	16.4
1891–1900	29.2	1936–40	14.7	1961–65	18.1
				1966–70	16.8
				1977	11.6

This decline in the birth-rate has led to what is arguably the most important change in British society since 1870 – the fall in average family size. In the 1870s and 1880s over half the Victorians (in England and Wales) grew up in families with 6 or more children. Ten per cent of women marrying around 1870 had over 10 children. By World War II, only around 0.3 per cent of wives married about 1925 had had more than 10 children, only just over 7 per cent had had 6 or more children, two-thirds had 2 children or less.

It would be difficult to exaggerate the importance of the change on the lives of women, children and the whole family. Women were most affected since they bore and cared for the children. 43 per cent of British women, married in the 1870s, but only 2 per cent of those married between 1925 and 1929 had seven or more children. From clear evidence it is obvious that many births before the widespread adoption of birth control were unplanned and bitterly resented.[19]

Family limitation was a very important social revolution. Health improved because childbirth itself was weakening and dangerous, because infant mortality in large families was higher than in small, because overcrowding and risks of infection were reduced, because there were more food and attention available to each member of a small than of a large poor family.

Family standard of living rose, for large families were a major cause of poverty. Family income per head slumped while children were young, then often rose again when children went out to work and gave much of their earnings to parents.[20]

2.5 Migration

From 1870 to 1914 there was heavy migration from the U.K., particularly to North America and Australia. From 1876 to 1914 the net movement from U.K. ports was 5,205,000. The exodus was very heavy in the 1880s, (net migration from England and Wales alone was 601,000), but reached its peak in 1906–14 when, from the U.K., 511,000 went to the U.S., 845,000 to Canada, 311,000 to Australia and New Zealand. In 1913 alone, 470,000 left the U.K., mainly to N. America and Australia.[21] In those years just before 1914, the Irish did not fill a large proportion of the emigrant berths: in 1913, 31,000 Irish left their country. This was in sharp contrast to what had happened in the tragic mid 19th century decades. Between 1820 and 1910 nearly 5 million Irish emigrated: by the 1880s two-thirds of persons born in Ireland were living outside the country.[22]

The migrants left Britain to seek opportunities lacking in the villages and crowded cities of their native country. Their going significantly reduced population pressure: on the other hand it entailed the loss of thousands of vigorous young people and increased the proportion of females in the population (56 per cent of emigrants in 1921 to 1925 were males).

After the 1914–18 War, migration resumed on a much reduced scale. From 1921 to 1925 the average net outward movement was over 100,000: from 1919 to 1926 British arrivals in Canada averaged 51,000 a year. For the whole period 1901 to 1931 British net emigration was over 2,000,000.

The great slump of the early thirties changed all this. Work was about as difficult to find in Sydney as in Birmingham. Indeed movement was reversed. From 1931–39 the net annual inward balance was around 60,000 and from 1931 to 1951 England and Wales registered a net gain from migration of 757,000.

Scotland, with a mid 20th century population of some 5 million, continued to suffer a continuing drain of human resources.

Table 1 *Estimates of net loss by migration, Britain, 1871-1970 (thousands)*[23]

		England & Wales	Scotland
1871–80		164	93
81–90		601	217
91–1900		69	53
1901–10		501	254
1911–20	includes war deaths	620	239
1921–30		172	392
1931–50		− 758 (Gain)	320
1951–60		− 352 (Gain)	255
1961–70		106	298

In the austere post Second World War years of 1946–50, 720,000 people left the U.K.: around a third to a half of them were professional and skilled workers. But there was also considerable immigration as, for example, well over 100,000 Poles were allowed to settle in the country. "Displaced persons" – refugees from war-shattered Europe – were also recruited for Britain's booming industries.

From about 1954 to 1962–3 there was a large influx of Commonwealth immigrants from the West Indies, India, Pakistan. By 1966 nearly a million residents in England and Wales had been born in the Commonwealth. After the Commonwealth Immigration Act of 1964, entry of dependants and others continued at a reduced rate. However, each year, 1964 to 1977, more people left the U.K. than entered as migrants. In 1965 the net loss was 58,000 and in 1971, 39,000. Such are the official figures, concerning the accuracy of which much doubt must be held.

2.6 Population figures

The effects on population of excess of births over deaths and of net movement of migrants are made clear in the following table.

Table 2 *British Population 1871–1981 (thousands)*

Year	England and Wales	Scotland
1871	22,712.3	3,360.0
81	25,974.4	3,735.6
91	29,002.5	4,025.6
1901	32,527.8	4,472.1
11	36,070.5	4,760.9
21	37,886.7	4,882.5
31	39,952.4	4,843.0
51	43,757.9	5,096.4
61	46,104.5	5,179.3
71	48,603.9	5,227.7
81	Great Britain 54,129.	

Compared with 20th century experience in less developed countries, where rates of natural increase of some three per cent per year, with doubling of numbers in around 20 years, are fairly commonplace, Britain's population growth was never very rapid. Percentage increase in the population of England and Wales was 81 from 1851 to 1901, 34 from 1902–51. The average annual growth rate fell from 1.48 (1831–51) to 0.47 (1931–51), rose slightly to 0.54 (1951–61) before again falling in the 1970s when the U.K. population became roughly stationary.

2.7 Balance of population

Within overall population growth, changes have occurred in balances between male and female, single and married, young and old.

More boy than girl babies are born. In 1871, in England and Wales, 104,811 males were born to each 100,000 females. Over the 25 years following the Second World War, about 106 boys were born to every 100 girls.

But when infant death rates were very high, boys were particularly at risk. As late as 1930–32, the England and Wales mortality rates in the first years of life was 0.07186 for males, 0.05455 for females. Dangerous occupations, emigration, slaughter in 1914–18, removed more men than women. In 1921, for every 1,000 males in England and Wales, there were 1,096 females. Women lived longer than men – on average. This has long been the case. A girl born in 1910–12 could expect to live for 55.4, a boy for 51.5 years.

Yet, the vast saving of infant and young lives resulting from medical and general advances has meant that, as the 20th century advanced, males came to outnumber females in the younger age groups. In 1901, females predominated in every major age division. By 1931 there were more males than females in the 0–14 age group. By 1966, there were more males than females in all groups under age 40. By the later 20th century, at the ages at which people usually marry, there were more men than women, more bachelors than spinsters.

Females per 1000 males: England and Wales

Year	At all ages	Age 15–19	Age 20–39
1901	1068	1019	1107
1966	1064	968	986

Bachelors per 1000 spinsters aged 15–44 in Gt. Britain:
1901 981   1931 979   1951 1154   1971 1376

Clearly girls wishing to marry were in a far more favourable position in 1971 than were their grandmothers in 1931.

In 1901, in England and Wales, per 1000 people aged 15–19, 3 males and 15 females were married: by 1966, corresponding figures were 17 and 79. Per 1000 aged 20–24 173 males and 272 females were married in 1901: 330 males and 584 females in 1966. In Scotland, the trend towards earlier marriage was only slightly less marked: by 1966 per 1000 aged 20–24, 321 men and 537 women were married. Marriage certainly remained very popular. Per 1000 unmarried males, the marriage rate in England and Wales rose from 52.3 in 1901–5 to 74.4 in 1968. The married and widowed came to form a much higher proportion of total population.

Marital status of population (per cent)

		Single	Married	Widowed and divorced	
England & Wales					
	1901	59.7	34.8	5.3	
	1966	41.1	51.2	7.0	0.7
Scotland					
	1901	63.9	30.6	5.5	
	1966	45.9	46.7	7.0	0.4

Of marked relevance to the fall in the average age of marriage has been the fall over the past two centuries in the age of the onset of puberty among girls. In the 1870s this was around 14 years 3 months for upper and middle class girls, about 16 for many working-class girls, overworked in mills and on poor diets. By the 1970s, class differences had largely disappeared. Upper and middle class girls started to menstruate at around 12.9 years, working class girls at just over 13.[24]

It seems clear that better nourishment has been one key factor in accounting for this significant development. Here, too, is quite dramatic evidence of rising living standards and reduction of class differences in adequacy of diet.

In many less developed countries today, around half the population is under 21. In 1871, in England and Wales, 45 per cent of people were aged under 20: by 1951 ths proportion was down to 28 per cent. In 1871, high birth and death rates meant a rapid fall in numbers as one went up the pyramid of age-groups. There were 7 times as many people aged 0–4 as there were aged 65–69.

But in 1951, owing to the low birth-rate of the thirties, there were 600,000 more people aged 40–44 than there were aged 5–19, while there were twice as many people aged 0–4 as there were 65–69.

In 1871, also in England and Wales, 149,900 males and 174,100 females were aged 70–74: by 1951 corresponding figures were 591,200 and 836,000.

By 1971, over 10 million Britons were aged over 60. Women outnumbered men in this group by 1,916,000. Aged under 20, there were 17,400,000 people: males outnumbered females by 454,000.

3. SOME MAIN STRANDS OF EVOLUTION
1870–1979

3.1 Relative national decline

In absolute terms Britain's economy improved between 1870 and 1979. She produced far, far more goods and services and distributed them more equitably in the latter year than in the former. But, relative to the economies of other countries, that of Britain has declined. National power and influence, particularly imperial and naval, has greatly lessened in absolute terms. It is not clear that this has had harmful effects on the ordinary members of British society.

In 1870, the United Kingdom was very easily the leading industrial, financial, imperial, naval, maritime, country in the World. Her people were the very richest: on average they enjoyed the highest income per head. However income was very unevenly divided. By 1970 apart from a few scattered colonies, all of the former Empire was independent. The Royal Navy which in the 19th century was normally equal to at least two other navies had now a fraction of the might of American or Soviet navies. The average standard of living, judged by national income statistics, was higher in North America, Australia, all West European countries (except Italy and Ireland) and booming oil states in the Middle East.

True, much of this was completely predictable. Perhaps, the strange fact is that a small island off the coast of Europe should ever have arisen to such a position of world-wide power as that occupied by Britain in 1913. Clearly the U.S.A. and U.S.S.R. with their size and resources were almost bound to overtake Britain. Much more disturbing, however, is that, in industrial out-put, countries of a similar size and resources, e.g. West

Germany, should have overtaken Britain by so great a margin.

The transition from colonies to independence was foreseen and indeed worked for by many Britons. Practically all the former dependencies have voluntarily remained within a loose association – the Commonwealth. In Britain, it seems certain that the average citizen was quite unconcerned about the loss of her or his country's former imperial might.

Britain's central economic weakness through much of the period covered by this work has been her relatively low rate of economic growth, i.e. growth of output of goods and services. For "compound interest is a remorseless arbiter"[1] the gap between lines rising at 5 per cent and 2 per cent per annum continues to widen more and more markedly. In 1950, Britain (with the possible exception of Denmark), was the richest of all the nine countries which became E.E.C. members by the 1970s. By 1975 she was the poorest with the exception of Italy and Ireland. Expressed in U.S. dollars, for purposes of comparison, 1975 incomes per head were 6,026 in West Germany, 3,703 in the U.K. Admittedly, comparisons of national incomes are notoriously difficult and inexact but there is much evidence that the general picture offered by these figures is correct.

Does it matter that the rate of growth has been relatively low? Again, according to published national income statistics, Britain was still, compared with most, a rich country in 1979. Problems often resulted from affluence: road congestion, overeating leading to obesity, alcoholism, heavy smoking, crowded airports and holiday beaches – and so on.

In economic, as in other fields of endeavour, success or failure strongly tend to be cumulative. Nothing succeeds like success: nothing fails like failure. High output and income make possible high capital formation, research and development, training. All lead to still higher output. Technological advance is cumulative. New machinery leads to new methods of production, change in one line of production leads to change in another. Growing industries present, stagnant industries deny, opportunities to the most able and thrusting. In the late 20th century, only rich economies can afford the massive costs of modern infrastructure, (roads, airports, ports, services, water supplies and so on), education, research, health, and social services which form the essential apparatus of a modern, advanced economy.

The psychological impact of constantly observing the greater economic success of some other nations may be injurious to general morale.

In the case of Britain, perhaps the strongest argument against any feeling of complacency concerning relative decline is the repeated, but vital fact that hers is an open economy. Exports shrink, imports rise, if efficiency and competitiveness are not maintained.

3.2 Absolute rise in output, standard of living, welfare

In 1957, Prime Minister Harold Macmillan said: "Most of our people have never had it so good. Go around the country, go to the industrial towns, go to the farms, and you will see a state of prosperity such as we have never had in my lifetime – nor indeed ever in the history of this country".[2]

Statistics relating to income and standards of living proved him correct. The century following 1870 which saw an enormous fall in Britain's political and economic power also saw major improvements in the real income, standard of living, welfare services of the great mass of the people. On average, Britons in 1970 were better off in material terms than they had been in their long history, though there are exceptions, (e.g. Church of England clergy) to the general trend.

In years leading up to 1979, most Britons enjoyed a standard of living higher than that of previous generations in their own, and of contemporaries in most other countries. Except for minorities in formerly prosperous groups, it simply was not true of the 20th century that (as a Nevil Shute character put it): "The standard of living had slipped imperceptibly in England as year succeeded year, as war succeeded war".[3]

Immensely scholarly modern analysis[4] finds that the growth of gross domestic product, (output of goods and services in the home economy), gross domestic product per head, and real disposable income per head was as follows:

Table 3 *Growth of G.D.P., G.D.P. per head, Real disposable income per head, 1856–1973*

Period	G.D.P.	G.D.P. per head	Real disposable income per head	(Annual percentage growth rates)
1856–1973	1.9	1.2	1.3	
1873–1913	1.8	0.9	1.0	
1913–1924	−0.1	−0.6	−0.4	
1924–1937	2.2	1.8	2.0	
1937–1951	1.8	1.3	0.7	
1951–1973	2.8	2.3	2.5	

Already slow growth before 1914, the devastating effects of World Wars (particularly the first) the, (in British experience) success of the post-Second War period are very clear.

So it must be emphasised that the ranges of goods, services, opportunities, available to the great majority of Britons in 1979 were vastly greater than those available in 1870.

Further the normal working week required to produce greater real income was dramatically shortened. Full-time manual workers worked the following "normal" and "actual" hours ("actual" hours included overtime).[5]

	Actual	Normal	Overtime	
1856	65.0	63.0	2.0	
1873	56.0	54.0	2.0	
1924	45.8	47.0	−1.2	(Many on short time)
1951	46.3	44.4	1.9	
1973	43.9	40.0	3.9	

By 1931, 100 firms at least had adopted a five-day week[6] but this practice was not generally adopted in industry and offices until after the 1939–45 war. To shorter hours was added the boon of increasingly longer paid holidays: Bank holidays plus a week between the Wars, a fortnight after 1945, three to four weeks by the 1970s.

It is impossible to be equally clear about the diminution of strain for the later 20th century economy still imposes great stress on some participants. What is clear is that very much of the sweaty toil of previous centuries has been handed over to the machines. Costs of economic growth – including human strain, pollution, overcrowded and dangerous roads, production, and exchange of unnecessary goods – have been described in many works.[7] On the other hand, growth has made possible immense benefits for the great mass of Britons – including a more health-sustaining diet, better clothing, warmer houses with water, sanitation, and much equipment which frequently serves to make life easier and more comfortable. Growth has also made possible vast public expenditure. Neither large private consumption nor heavy public expenditure is possible in a poor country.

One limited example only will here be considered to illustrate general improvement. Healthy sleep is a fundamental require-ment of human – particularly young human beings. Sadly, up to the late 19th and early 20th centuries, sleeping arrangement of many babies were not only unhealthy but downright dangerous. They slept with their parents and were sometimes overlaid by heavy adults. In 1928, a coroner in a London working-class borough commented that the decrease in deaths of infants suffocating while in bed with their parents "may be explained by the greater user of cots."[8] Poor children in early 20th century Britain crowded into one poorly covered bed with parents.[9] A child at one of Newcastle's excellent evening play centres in the nineteen-thirties, having asked for five dolls, arranged them in a doll's bed with the comment: "That is how we sleep at home".[10] As standards of living rose and family size fell, separate cots and beds with adequate covers, and – increasingly – separate rooms could be provided.

Higher standards of living and welfare among the mass of the people resulted from: first, greater production generated by more machines and knowledge and improved organisation; second, vastly improved public social care operating through govern-mental supervision of workplaces and of the general environ-ment, plus provision of social services; third, the work of collective organisations such as trade unions and co-operative societies; fourth, the efforts of millions of people to improve their own lot in life through education, work and saving, moving into better paid occupations and so on.

To end this section, two columns of figures vividly portray (a) the relative decline of Britain as an exporter of manufactures (b) the marked growth in quantity of British exports.

U.K. Exports 1899–1975[11]

	U.K. share in world exports of manufactures	Volume of U.K. exports (1958=100)
1899	34.0	33
1913	30.9	91
1929	22.9	74
1937	21.3	59
1950	25.3	91
1975	9.3	221

3.3   Determining role of science and technology

20th century life has been vastly changed by science. A fundamental contemporary problem is this: science has advanced very rapidly, but, essentially human nature has perhaps not changed. A fascinating account of a Shropshire village in 17th century England was prefaced by a modern editor's view that: "Perhaps the final impression we retain upon putting down the book is that while our way of life has changed almost out of recognition over the past three hundred years, human nature has remained the same."[12]

In what must be an inadequate section for whole libraries could be filled with writings on this subject – through a selection of examples, an attempt is here made to indicate the overriding determination of trends in economy and society by the march of science and technology.

During the First Industrial Revolution, individuals in Britain, often men with little book learning, had invented machines and initiated processes. By the second half of the 19th century, advance in new industries demanded the existence of numbers of highly trained specialists. By the 20th century, change and progress had been built in into the economic system. In Universities and in firms which maintained Research and Development departments, scientists strove to extend the boundaries of knowledge, to discover new products and processes. While it is true that many 20th century inventions have been made by individuals,[13] much industrial advance now stems from the research departments of institutions and firms.

Birth, life, death

To mother and child, birth became far less risky. In England and Wales, the maternal mortality rate per 1000 births fell from around 4 early in the century to 0.26 in 1961. By 1979, the overwhelming majority of babies were born in hospitals among the equipment and drugs of a modern labour ward. Controversies surround this change from home deliveries, but in any dangerous condition advantages are clear. That the child has an expectation of much longer life than was the case in previous centuries has been made abundantly obvious. Medical science can claim some of the credit.

Among the most important 19th and 20th century advances have been the following. In the 19th century, Pasteur and others showed that germs – and not bad air – caused some diseases. This knowledge – re-inforcing empirical observation – led to attacks on dangerous organisms in water and milk. In the 20th century, organisms attacking the human body were destroyed by chemical agents. Ehrlich coined the term chemotherapy to describe such treatment. He introduced salvarsan as an unpleasant, but effective treatment for horrible syphilis. But the great advances here came in the 1930s. In 1935, prontosil was introduced, followed in 1938 by sulphapyradine, widely known as M and B, (May and Baker) 693. In the treatment of meningitis, puerperal sepsis, pneumonia, results were dramatic. Pneumonia had been a massive killer, not only of the old. At one Newcastle hospital M and B was used in the last 3 months of 1938, with the following results:[14]

	Cases	Deaths
To Sept.	120	37
Oct.–Dec.	32	3

During the Second War, penicillin, discovered in the 1920s by Alexander Fleming and later developed as a therapeutic agent by D. Florey, E.B. Chain and their team at Oxford,[15] was a most valuable addition to the physician's armoury. As late as the 1930s, a rusty nail in the thumb could be fatal.

Similarly, advances in surgery saved many lives and much suffering. Anaesthetics and antiseptics reduced death-rates following amputations. Surgery saved victims of appendicitis and restored sight to those with cataracts without imposing great pain.[16]

Medicine reaped benefits from a host of international scientific and technological advances. From the host, a mere few examples must suffice: X-rays (discovered in 1895);[17] discovery of blood-groups, blood transfusion;[17a] the electrocardiograph and electron microscope; kidney machines; those whole batteries of advanced equipment shown on television films of heart operations and the life-saving machines of intensive care units to which many owe their lives.

Here in medicine are surely some of the most beneficial of scientific advances. For most people, life is longer with the possibility of years of active and fruitful retirement.[18]

Food, clothing, shelter

Knowledge, production, preservation and distribution of food have been vastly changed as a result of modern advances. Before 1914 the importance in diet of proteins and vitamins was discovered. Active research continued over the inter-war period.[19] Later in the century, much emphasis was switched from description of diets to avoid malnutrition, to diets to avoid overweight, heart diseases and strokes.

Food production

Over the past century, science and technology have revolution-ised farming with mechanisation, fertilisers, chemicals to control weeds and pests, advances in breeding, factory farming.

While the 19th century saw the adoption of important machines such as McCormick's reaper, men and horses still cultivated most British farms in 1939. During and after the Second War, tractors, (which had been in use since the First War), combine-harvesters, milking-machines, bailers, and a host of other machines led to the virtual disappearance of the horse as a working farm animal[20] and to a great reduction in human labour.

To the natural fertilisers of the 19th century – manure and, for example, sodium nitrate imported from Chile – 20th century chemical industry added vast quantities of synthetic fertiliser. Just before the First War, Haber in Germany produced nitrogen synthetically.

The weeds, insects, viruses, fungi, which had for centuries wrecked havoc among man's crops were brought under control by sprayed chemicals. Not all were happy with the results.

Plant breeders were much helped by the re-discovery in 1900 of the work of G. Mendel, published in Germany in 1866 but neglected. Mendel had expounded principles of the inheritance of genes. R.H. Biffen, of Cambridge, corroborated Mendel's findings and before the First War produced a valuable strain of wheat – Little Jos.

Following the discovery in 1949 of a method of freezing semen which enabled it to be kept over a period, artificial insemination of cattle and sheep became universal. The farmer had the benefit of mating his cows with the best bulls at low cost. Veterinary science[21] and animal husbandry benefited from those advances in 20th century chemotherapy and nutritional science which have already been mentioned. After the Second War battery cages for laying hens were widely adopted in Britain. Pigs were also housed in large numbers in confined spaces.

There is criticism of modern farming methods. Sales in health food shops rose sharply after the 1960s. But defenders of new techniques and systems point out that huge concentrations of urban dwellers, such as exist in Britain, can only be fed at reasonable cost through the adoption of modern farming methods.

For many centuries before the 19th, foods and drinks had been preserved and sometimes fundamentally changed by drying, salt-curing, smoking, pickling, preservation in sugar or fermentation. Bread-making and cooking were ancient arts in which the best of pre-industrial millers and housewives were very proficient. Science and technology again added knowledge, instruction, mechanisation, new products and far better methods of preservation and distribution.

By the 20th century, food firms and organisations had their laboratories. Food science was taught in Colleges and Universities. Increasingly after 1860, with the enactment of the Adulteration of Food and Drink Act, the Authorities clamped down on the addition of harmful additions to food.

Perhaps the best-known of new products was margarine, first produced in France, 1868–70. It is emphasised elsewhere that world-wide transport facilities brought vast quantities of foods to Britain after around 1870. Canning and refrigeration vastly aided this import trade. By this 20th century, largescale production of bread and confectionery had been mechanised. After the Second War, prepacked meals and a whole host of convenience foods were sold in supermarkets and stored in the refrigerators and freezers which greatly grew in numbers in home kitchens. Sliced loaves reduced the work of sandwich preparation. Dried milk, instant coffee, preservatives in foods were among the achievements of the food chemists.

There have been losses and gains. The stone milling of 1850 preserved more of the vitamins in flour than did later milling. Repeated worries arise from chemical additives to food. On the other hand, the justifiably real 19th century fear of tuberculosis from milk has gone and there is far tighter control by Authorities and firms of food standards than there was in 1870.

New products and modern distribution have brought great changes to the clothing worn by the mass of the population. For example, to the traditional materials have been added the products of modern chemistry. Already by 1913 Britain was a leader in the world's limited production of rayon and artificial silk. By 1951, British production was 174,000 tonnes. Other important man-made fibres, such as nylon, discovered in 1937, and the polyesters developed after the Second War, and plastics such as poly vinyl acetate (PVC), a substitute for leather, came into widespread use.

As much emphasised elsewhere, modern production, distribution and retailing brought ready-made clothes to all. Mass-survey techniques helped. In the 1950s, British women's sizes were ascertained.[22] Clothes could be produced on the ubiquitous sewing machine, patented in the U.S.A. by Singer in 1851, which "effectively ended the traditional bondage of women to the needle".[23]

Similarly, the typical British home was much changed by modern technology. Gas or electric lamps, cookers, and fires, flush toilets, bath-rooms, hot and cold water, central heating, were great boons. Again, the products of chemistry brought great changes to the home. In the typical kitchen of 1860, floor and wall coverings, working surfaces, equipment and containers were all made of traditional materials. By 1960, all or part of surfaces, containers and equipment were likely to consist of the products of modern chemical industry such as plastics.[24]

Work

Technology has brought about a massive replacement of manual by machine work – in homes, fields, ditches, roads, building-sites, mines, foundries, ports, factories and a host of other work-places. It is terrible to contemplate the prodigious quantities of utterly exhausting, drink demanding, strength and life curtailing, manual toil that went into the building of the Victorian economy. In the steel works at the end of the 19th century, four men, each charging about 3.4 tons per hour, loaded an open-hearth furnace which demanded 48 tons of materials in about 3½ hours.

The "great physical and constitutional strength" needed "in the face of a furnace radiating a considerable amount of heat" is very obvious.[25] A contemporary drawing of 1861[26] shows a 20-ton armour plate being dragged from a flaming and smoking furnace by dozens of men with chains and pincers. In pre-1914 years, well over 200 million tons of coal a year was being hacked out of the ground by men working with picks and shovels. Over the first half of the 20th century, the percentage of coal cut out by machine rose from 1½ to nearly 80 and the percentage moved underground on conveyors went up from nil to 80.[27] In industry after industry, machines could produce more and quicker than men. Thus, an expert has commented that before 1850 the ancient glass industry "was a craft" but that by 1900 craftsmen were being "replaced by chemical control and mechanical methods of manufacture". In the last two decades of the 19th century, bottle-making machines were introduced. Far fewer men could produce far more bottles per hour: 2500 with a machine compared with 150 an hour produced by hand by a team of five.[28]

In farming, changes have been dramatic. A century ago, workers cut, tied, stooked, carted, stacked, threshed the corn. Now a combine harvester worked by one man doing the work done a century ago by about ten, executes these tasks.

Of course, not all changes have been to the total benefit of labour. Henry Ford was not the first but he was the best-known originator of the assembly-line technique copied in many mass production industries. Production went up but the deadly boredom of much of the work in such factories is a major problem of modern times.

For good or ill, it seems very likely that much of such work will in future be performed by robots controlled by computers. In the 19th century, C. Babbage, sadly born a century before his time, had designed and worked on an analytical engine. The first modern general-purpose digital computer was presented to Harvard University in 1944. By 1953, a British computer was handling confectionery orders for J. Lyons & Co.

By the 1970s, vastly improved, small computers could take over more and more tasks formerly performed by people. A new phrase, "the collapse of work"[29] had an ominous ring.

Yet it is necessary to again emphasise the great benefits that technology has brought to many whose grandparents had to wear themselves out with manual toil. Combined with smaller families, and probably much more help from husbands, availability of modern equipment has, for example, vastly improved the lot of women. In ordinary homes, the traditional Monday wash-day (particularly if the family was large and/or the men were engaged in dirty work), was very unpleasant and arduous. Piles of dirty clothing were rubbed with soap and swirled round in a tub. They were then squeezed in a mangle turned by hand to remove the worst of the wet and, with often ill-founded optimism, strung out in garden, yard, road, to dry. Clothes steaming round a coal-fire greeted many a' doctor or nurse visiting a bronchial child stretched on a sofa a few feet from them. What a vast benefit it was when the whole filthy load could be pushed into a washing machine, detergent loaded, a knob pulled and clean clothes taken out in about an hour!

A range of electric gadgetry has lightened house-work and improved homes: vacuum cleaners, (developed, for example by W. Hoover in the U.S. in 1907), electric fires, water-heaters, cookers, refrigerators.

Education

By 1979, knowledge had become the central economic resource. Growing industries such as electronics had a science base. Hence the emphasis in recruitment on qualifications and, often, the preference for younger people with relevant new knowledge and the sad rejection of older workers with only experience to offer. So educational provision has been vastly expanded and curricula changed to provide the nation with needed scientists and technologists.

England came late to this important development. In 1839, professors of chemistry and other sciences petitioned Oxford University to be excused lecturing since there were so few students. It must be added that Cambridge, Glasgow and the new University College, London, already had strong science courses and that in the industrial districts thousands of work-men studied in the evenings at Mechanics' Institutes. In the main, the public schools placed vast emphasis on the Classics. True the new Universities of the 20th century had excellent technology departments – (glass and metallurgy at Sheffield, for example), – and by 1926, over 21,000 pupils offered chemistry and over 13,000 Physics in School Certificate, (O Level), examination. But the great expansion of higher scientific education came after the Second War. Though figures are not completely comparable, on science courses at British Universities there were 5815 men and 1846 women in 1938–39, 45,910 men and 17,766 women in 1977–78.

In this brief section, emphasis has been placed on the physical and natural sciences and the technology which have revolutionised life-styles. However, it would be folly to forget the vast expansion in knowledge and in numbers studying the social sciences – economics, sociology, psychology and so on. As late as 1939, economics and sociology were rarely studied in schools and – particularly in the case of sociology – by but small numbers in Universities. Vast expansion followed in the 1950s.

Over the 19th and 20th century, advances in knowledge have fundamentally altered the ways in which educated people regard the World, their environment, people. From a fascinating story of enormous and continuing leaps in discovery one may perhaps select Darwin's evolutionary thesis, Pasteur's discovery of germs, Mendel's findings about heredity, Einstein's theories of energy, space and time, the penetration of the atom's secrets, Freud's writings on the human mind, discoveries of the chemical composition of human cells, continuing additions to our knowledge of the universe around us.

Leisure

In the 19th century, many workers had very little leisure. Typically, the young Joseph Chamberlain, entering his family's old cordwaining business in London in 1852: "worked strict hours . . ; the business only closed during weekdays on Good Friday and Christmas Day, and even then letters were brought round to the family residence by an old employee."[30] A great change of the 20th century has been that the leisure which was previously a benefit enjoyed in amplitude by the few has been extended to the many. "This is the revolution – that leisure brings fulfilment. The majority of people in this country have, over the past three generations, approached the area of demands once cordoned off for the exclusive use of the well-born and wealthy. . ."[31]

Technological advances – bicycle, car, film, radio, television, and so on – very greatly changed leisure use.

Travel and communication

By 1870, Britons could travel the length and breadth of the country on the very comprehensive railway system. In later 19th century novels and autobiographies, train journeys often figure prominently. Those who could afford, (there were 21,282 grooms and 16,174 coachmen in England and Wales in 1871), covered short distances in horse-drawn vehicles.

Between 1870 and 1914, the bicycle, the tram and the London Underground brought the great boon of mobility to millions of ordinary citizens. The very important modern bicycle appeared in Britain in numbers by the 1880s. The Rover of 1885 was "the first commercially successful bicycle. . . It employed all the elements of the modern machine".[32] To many, the cycle widened what has been very narrow horizons. "How little and cramped seems the life before the cycle came into it",[33] wrote a correspondent to "Lady Cyclist" in 1895.

By 1900, heavy-duty electric motors for tram-line and railway use were available. "The introduction of all-electric tramcars in British provincial cities during the first years of the century profoundly influenced the lives of the common people. . . For the first time in history the undermass enjoyed the benefits of cheap urban travel", wrote one urban resident.[34]

In 1887–90, the first of the London "tubes", the City and South London line, was built. Such was its success that by the end of the century, three more lines were built.

Railways, plus cycles, trams and tubes enabled growing numbers to live at a distance from work-places. Suburbs grew.

In this 20th century, the motor vehicle has become the main means of transport. The first car to be owned in mass was the famous Ford Model "T" of the U.S.A., more than 15 million of which were sold between 1908 and 1927. By 1976, 57 per cent of British households had a car. Collectively, motor vehicles are a curse, polluting the environment with noise and dangerous fumes, killing and maiming thousands each year, (6,600 killed, 82,000 seriously injured on the roads in 1977). To the individual owning one, a car has brought convenience and pleasure. Leonard Woolf, (husband to Virginia), wrote: "Certainly nothing ever changed so profoundly my material existence, the mechanism and range of my everyday life, as the possession of a motor-car. . ."[35]

In 1903, in the U.S.A. the Wright brothers made the first short powered flight in an aeroplane. In 1909, Bleriot flew over the English Channel. In and between two World Wars, aircraft were vastly improved: jet propulsion, (in Britain the invention of F. Whittle), was introduced during the Second. By the 1960s, millions of Britons flew abroad each year on business or pleasure. A benefit of fast, easy travel was that relatives could renew contact with emigrants. Over previous generations, a sad feature of sometimes hard-hit regions was that young people left for the Dominions and were often never seen again. "I have heard so many women say, 'If only I could see him again – just once' ",[36] wrote one Scot of a mining area in the inter-war period.

Over the 19th and 20th centuries, national and international communications were revolutionised by the telegraph, telephone, wireless and television. 1839 saw the opening of the first telegraph line from Paddington to West Drayton. Railways made much use of this new method of sending fast messages which were tapped out – usually in Morse code – and transmitted along the lines. In the 1850s and 60s, submarine cables connected Britain to France, Ireland, the United States. By the end of the century there was a very comprehensive national system plus a world-wide network of submarine cables and national lines over which messages could be sent to all parts of the world. Benefits accruing to international traders and rulers of far-flung empires were clearly great. At home, before the widespread advent of the telephone, sudden news that one was catching the 10.12 and would arrive at 4.20 was sent by telegraph.

In 1876, in the U.S., Alexander Graham Bell and Elisha Gray invented the telephone. By 1885 there were 10,000 telephones in Britain: 1879 had seen the first telephone exchange in London. By 1896, though Britain lagged behind some other advanced countries, the country had a network of trunk lines connecting major centres of population. The 20th century saw vast technical developments such as automatic exchanges and direct dialling. By 1976, over half British households had a telephone – with all its costs and benefits. It is not easy to envisage modern administration or business deprived of the telephone.

After fundamental 19th century scientific work by Maxwell, Hertz and others, in the first year of the 20th century, Marconi sent wireless messages over long distances. Soon it was found that the human voice could be transmitted. By 1928 there was a global radio-telegraph communication between the main centres of the then British Empire. Radio-telephone contact between Britain, the U.S. and other countries was established in the 1920s.

To millions of listeners at home and abroad, from the 1920s the B.B.C. sent out radio programmes. By 1939 B.B.C. television had arrived, but the War interrupted developments and the almost universal provision of television had to wait until the decades following 1950.

War

Tragically, science which has brought such great benefits has also given man the means to inflict immense slaughter and destruction.

Two World Wars were fought with weapons devised by modern technology and mass-produced in the factories of industrial states.

Britain survived in 1940 because, among other reasons, she had radar and radio communication to excellent fighter planes. Modern scientific devices played key roles, for example, in aiding navigation in bomber planes and in hunting U-boats in the crucial Atlantic battle.

But the very nature of war was fundamentally changed when

atom bombs were dropped on Japan in 1945. The Germans had used rockets packed with high explosive against England in the closing stages of the war. Such rockets were vastly developed in the U.S.S.R. and U.S.A. over the decades after 1945. Rockets – or missiles – loaded with nuclear explosives, became terrible weapons of mass-destruction.

Atomic energy

Pupils learning science in the 19th century were taught that the atom was the basic unit of matter. Over the first four decades of the 20th century, scientists discovered that the atom had a central nucleus round which particles called electrons moved. By 1939, "every physicist in the world could know the basic theory of atomic energy."[36a] In December 1942 the first nuclear reactor was successfully operating at Chicago University. The atom bomb was produced in 1945: the hydrogen bomb by 1952.

Since the Second War, Britain has developed atomic energy plants, which have fed power into the Central Electricity Board's networks.

But the discovery of nuclear energy which could have brought vast benefits to mankind, now poses a terrible threat which led in the 1960s and again after 1980 to a mass movement – the Campaign for Nuclear Disarmament.

Conclusion

It is repeated that this brief section on science and technology must be incomplete. The impact of technology is all-pervasive. Consider, for example, some basic benefits brought to the student. Joseph Swan, (1828–1914), one inventor of the electric lamp, wrote: "The days of my youth extend backwards to the dark ages, for I was born when the rushlight, the tallow dip or solitary blaze of the hearth were the common means of indoor lighting. . . . . In the chambers of the great, the wax candle, or exceptionally a multiplicity of them, relieved the gloom on state occasions; but as a rule, the common people, wanting the inducement of indoor brightness such as we enjoy, went to bed soon after sunset".[37]

Mass-produced books receive mention later. Here one may

note the universal use after the Second War of biros. In the 1930s students still needed fountain-pens or pencils.

Again, of vast significance has been the creation of mass societies[38] in which individual, class, regional differences have come under increasing pressure from central institutions, mass media, mass advertising and so on. Technology has clearly played a leading role here. By this 20th century, for the first time in world history, all classes in advanced countries were considerably wearing the same kind of clothes, travelling in similar vehicles, going to the same cinemas, listening to and watching the same programme on radio or T.V. Compared with any previous age, the impact of society on the individual was vastly greater. Some are sure that in this "age of the masses" high culture is in decline. But advantages of decent living and our cultural heritage are more widely available to all than ever before.

3.4   From individualism to collectivism and corporatism

From 1870 to 1979, in Britain, there was a vast growth in size of the typical business firm, of Trade Union membership and power, of Government activity, taxing and spending. There has been a great shift away from the Victorian individualist, laissezfaire economy to the more collectivist, corporatist, socialist society of the later 20th century. Here is a truly major development.

There were some large firms in 1870: as early as 1849 probably the largest iron plant – Dowlais – employed 7000. There was Central and Local Government activity, there were Trade Unions and Co-operative Societies. But the productive economic structure erected by the Industrial Revolution and the early Victorians was predominantly one of individual proprietorships or partnerships, and of small enterprises. In the mid 19th century decades, however, English company law recognised the principle of limited liability. The liability of an investor was limited to the extent of the shares he held – he could lose their value but no more. Monies accumulated by the growing affluent classes were invested in companies – the railways were early examples. The share-holders owned – but did not control – these enterprises. The latter were directed by Boards of Directors, members of which might collectively own but a very small proportion of the shares. Day-to-day management was exercised by salaried professional managers.

Here was one of the most fundamental and far-reaching development of the modern economy. 19th century economist, Alfred Marshall, believed that "perhaps nearly half" of the older men controlling industry in 1850 had been born in a cottage and worked their way up. Such men, "were the most complete individualists, owing nothing, so they supposed, either to society or to education".[39] They operated in conditions of strong competition. While small firms remained, and indeed remain, an important segment of the economy, yet facts concerning the growth of large firms are indeed startling. Thus, from 1909–70 the percentage share of the hundred largest enterprises in U.K. net manufacturing output increased from about 16 in 1909 to 40 in 1970. True, this overall average concealed very great variations between industries: 73 per cent in vehicles: one per cent in leather, leather goods, furniture in 1968. But in 1972, the hundred largest manufacturing enterprises had an average of 31,000 employees.[40] Similarly, English banking came to be dominated by the "Big Five" which dwindled to Four – Barclays, Lloyds, Midland, National Westminster. Retailing provided another clear example of the movement to large-scale enterprise. In 1870, over most of Britain, the only retail outlets were the local general or specialist shops. Thus, in Northampton in the 1870s 260 shopkeepers were listed plus numerous specialists such as 63 bakers and 16 booksellers.[41] None of the well-known national names of the succeeding century appear. Co-ops were already growing and around the 1870s the multiple shop firms began to expand in the main consumer goods trades. By 1950, 638 multiples each with ten or more branches had a total of 44,800 branches.[42] To many British (and indeed foreign) shoppers, shopping now means a visit to one of a large chain of supermarkets or stores. Yet, very large numbers of small shops do survive.

To those who campaigned for Real Ale, the disappearance of local breweries and increasing control of public house outlets by a relatively few large brewing firms was a cause of concern. In 1869–70 the British Isles had 33,840 commercial breweries: by the 1970s seven brewing groups were said to account for 80 per cent of beer output.

Most certainly, the growth in size has not stopped at the coast-line of Britain for in this century, enormous multi-national corporations (such as Shell, I.C.I., Unilever, Ford, Barclays International) have vastly increased their international output, trade, influence and investment.

As usual, change has brought gains and losses. The evolution of large concerns has often meant more investment, research, welfare provision, greater ability to compete with foreign giants. In retailing, the emphasis on standardised high quality at reasonable price which has characterised some large retailers has benefited millions.

In the 1880s, young George Sturt took over the family workshop and learned the trade of wheelwright from his skilled workmen: eight skilled workmen or apprentices, eight "friends of the family",[43] worked with him. By 1968, one calculation was that a typical employee in manufacturing industry was in a plant employing 480 and in vehicles, nearly 3000 people.[44]

In contrast to the 1880s situation, a majority of employees in 1980 were in trade unions. Certainly, in the past century, growth in numbers, influence and power of trade unionists, has been among the oustandingly important developments in Britain. In 1868, at the first officially recognised Trade Union Congress, 34 delegates represented some 118,000 members.[45] In 1979 delegates represented 12 million members.

In 1912, Sir Edward Grey, Liberal Foreign Secretary, wrote: "This coal strike is the beginning of a revolution. We shall, I suppose, make it an orderly and gradual revolution, but labour intends to have a larger share and has laid hold of power. Power . . . is passing from the House of Commons to the Trade Unions. . ."[46]

While his views may be challenged, (the unions have consistently maintained that they are not attempting to usurp the role of Government and Parliament), yet Grey's comment, like his more famous evening utterance of Aug. 3rd, 1914,[46a] deserves remembrance.

While most certainly there never was a time when laissezfaire principles were a complete guide to governmental action in Britain, yet, compared with 1979, economy and society in 1870 were remarkably free from state intervention. True, responsibilities of Government were already considerable, including:

relations with foreign states; government of dependencies; defence; law and order; management of public debt; legislation to control banking and the money supply, railways and companies; limited financial aid to, and consequent inspection of elementary schools; inspection of factories and mines covered by legislation; Poor Law provision for paupers; and, in a growing number of local areas – supervision of environmental health through control of sanitation and provision of water.

In the 19th century, an important facet of progress was the development of an efficient civil service recruited on merit through examination – though it must be admitted that those receiving the Oxford and Cambridge education normally necessary for entrance to top posts mainly belonged to the wealthy classes.

But growing numbers of enfranchised citizens were not satisfied with existing public provision: they constantly demanded much more and politicians seeking votes gave ear to their pleas. Apart from the obvious, and sometimes very vast, expenditure on war and defence, public spending rose to meet the cost of education, health, school meals, pensions, national insurance, inspection and control of environment and work-places and (in post-World War II decades), to control and support the economy. Details occupy many subsequent pages.

In the decades following 1940 the public sector played a role of dominating importance in the British economy. The phrase "public sector" means central government, local government, nationalised industries. Public ownership of industries became significant in the 20th century. Industries such as naval dock-yards, ordnance factories and the Post Office had long been controlled by Government and Civil Service. In the present century, however, normally an industry was taken into public ownership through the formation of a public corporation directed by a chairman and board appointed by the relevant Government Minister. Existing owners of the industry were bought out. By 1940, the Port of London Authority, B.B.C., the new airlines, were examples of such nationalised undertakings. After the Second War, the Labour Government nationalised a number of important basic industries. After 1951, additions to the list included the Post Office, (which has become another public corporation and no longer directly controlled government department), and the shipbuilding industry.

Central and local government do not themselves generate the income needed for their vast outlay. They tax citizens and increasingly such taxes have become onerous and unpopular. Tax avoidance and evasion were reported widespread by the late nineteen-seventies. Not that they were new. Smuggling was a considerable industry up to the 19th century, while one episode in the mid-Victorian period with its great reputation for business honesty, (no doubt in some respects deserved), revealed 28 persons claiming compensation for loss of one year's profits totalling £48,159, and obtaining £26,973, following demolition work. "They had returned their profits to the Income Tax at £9,000".[47] Since in 1870 the standard rate of tax was 2½ per cent, while in 1970 it was 41 per cent, there was then less cause for evasion.

By the 1970s it was alleged that heavy taxation and generous social services had so removed both incentives and sanctions that the will to take the risks and to work hard have been sapped. The Labour Government in the late seventies set firm limits to the growth of state spending while, in 1979, Conservative commitments to cut taxation and Government spending received support from the electorate. Yet by 1983 after four years in office, the Conservative administration had failed to reduce total public spending.

Over the century surveyed in this work, the overall picture is very clear. Government activity, spending and taxing markedly increased with great effects on economy and society.

Victorian society was strongly individualist. A leading Liberal thinker, Morley, thus summed up much current orthodoxy: society, he explained, is "only a name for other people". The individual should not "lay the blame on society" but should be encouraged to develop "a sense of responsibility for his own character".[48] Liberalism accomplished much but failed to significantly lessen by 1914 the yawning, indefensible gulf between rich and poor. It was therefore considerably replaced by socialism.

3.5   Urbanisation

Of his Wessex, Hardy wrote: "A depopulation was also going on . . . the process, humorously designated by statisticians as 'the tendency of the rural population towards the large towns' being really the tendency of water to flow uphill when forced by machinery".[49]

The census of 1851 was the first to reveal a predominantly urban nation. In England and Wales, 49.8 per cent of the people then lived in rural areas, a percentage which was to fall to 28 by 1891. As already indicated, absolute decline in numbers in many rural communities was obvious in the period 1821–51. In others falls were postponed until the second half of the 19th century. Thus, in Northamptonshire villages, decline in numbers was clear after 1861. Populations fell from 1861 to 1871: Woodnewton's from 529 to 491, and so on. But local towns continued their growth: Northampton from 7020 in 1801 to 41,1568 in 1871.[50]

From 1851 to 1951 urbanisation continued. Not only did towns grow, in some areas they so merged as to form extended built-up urban areas to which the name "conurbation", (Latin "urbs" = city, "con" = together), was applied. A sociologist, Weber, considered the growth of these "sprawling conglomerations of humanity" to have been the most marked social phenomenon of the 19th century.[51] Certainly, we are here concerned with very major social developments.

In 1851, over a third of the English and Welsh lived in towns of over 20,000, and over a fifth in towns of over 100,000 people: by 1891 the corresponding proportions were a half and nearly a third. By 1907, London had 4½ million people, 8 other towns over 250,000, 24 over 100,000 and another 42 (75 in all) over 50,000.[52]

The English conurbations, (Greater London, South-east Lancashire, West Midlands, West Yorkshire, Merseyside and Tyneside), held 8,345,000 people in 1871 and 16,794,000 in 1951.[53] The next twenty years saw outward movement and their 1971 population was 15,928,000. Numbers in towns continued to grow, though in the case of large English towns with over 100,000 people, percentage growth in numbers 1951–71 was less than the percentage growth of total English and Welsh population. The complete picture in 1971 was as follows: the population of England and Wales was 48,593,700: 15,928,000 lived in conurbations, 6,754,100 in towns of over 100,000, 5,392,200 in towns of 50,000, and 9,961,200 in towns of under 50,000 people. Over 10½ million lived in rural districts.

In Scotland, of 5,227,700 people, 1,731,000 lived in the vast Clydeside conurbation; 1,491,800 in large and 994,800 in small burghs, leaving just over a million in districts or counties.

By 1951, 80 per cent of the population of the United Kingdom lived in urban areas. For England and Wales, the definition of "urban" here used is that provided by local government administration. Following legislation of 1888, and 1894, boroughs (large towns), urban districts (small towns), and rural districts had their own councils. It seemed reasonable to designate as "rural" areas under the control of rural district councils. The line of demaraction was inexact. Thus in Easington Rural District of County Durham, with 75,642 people in 1921, no less than 655 of every 1000 males aged 12 and over worked for collieries.[54]

So, in 1951, a more sophisticated definition of "urban" was attempted: the criterion became a density of more than 10 persons to the acre. By such a definition 31½ million (72 per cent) in England and Wales lived in "urban" areas.[55]

Whatever definition is employed, the very significant fact emerges that some three-quarters to four-fifths of Britons lived in towns in the middle of the twentieth-century. The average employed British citizen was now a factory or office worker in a town: not a farmer, farm-worker or craftsman as had been the case two centuries earlier.

The main reason for urban growth is very clear: lack of employment opportunities in the villages. It was not simply a matter of declining farm employment, (overriding though that factor was), urban industries and services deposed many local crafts.

The second half of the 20th century has seen some reversal of a previous massive migration. The advent of mass car ownership enabled many to combine the benefits of rural living with urban work. The population of English and Welsh rural districts increased by over 9 per cent from 1951 to 1961 and 18 per cent from 1961 to 1971. Moreover, in more than a third of rural districts in 1966, over 40 per cent of those in employment travelled to towns to work.[56]

Urbanisation brought profound changes in attitudes and behaviour. For: "the traditional culture and morality of England were based on the patriarchal village family of all degrees: the father worked, the mother saw to the house, the food and clothes: from the parents the children learnt the crafts and industries necessary for their livelihood, and on Sundays, they went together, great and small, to worship in the village church".[57] Strong elements of such a society remain in rural, farming areas.

There were economic and social gains from industrialisation and urbanisation. Particularly for the poor who were youngish, able, energetic and ambitious, rural life could be choking in its frustrations. As Kipling wrote of the man who had seen service in South Africa:[58]

> " 'Ow can I ever take on
> With awful old England again
> An' 'ouses both sides of the street,
> An' 'edges two sides of the lane,
> And the parson an' gentry between,
> An' touchin' my 'at when we meet – . . . .
> Me that 'ave watched 'arf a world. . . .
> An' I'm rollin' 'is lawns for the Squire, Me!"

Again, it must be stressed that it is folly to romanticise rural life. An early introduction to farm work inculcated in one American economist "an enduring knowledge" of the unpleasantness of manual labour and convinced him that "all other work was easy".[59] As late as the 1920s Harold Owen, brother to the famous Wilfred, after starving in London, had to work on farms. He hated "the whole beastly business of earning a pittance on these slave-driving farms . . . with heart-breaking hours of monotonous work". A cottage he lived in was "shockingly damp".[60]

Of course farms varied greatly, but that there were rural slums in England became painfully obvious to the many who were evacuated to them in 1940.

3.6 From oligarchy to democracy and greater social justice

In the 18th and through very much of the 19th centuries, British central and local government were under the control of landowners. By 1979 Britain was an effective mass representative democracy: M.P.s and local councillors were elected by all citizens aged 18 and over listed on electoral rolls who took the trouble to vote.

It is frequently assumed that Britain is an old political democracy. The fact is that, in the literal sense of the word, (Ancient Greek "demos" = people, "kratos" = rule), democracy is a twentieth century development. Only since 1918 has a majority of adults had the vote. In 1969, the minimum voting age was lowered from 21 to 18 years and the total electorate which has been about 3 millions before, and 5 millions after, the 1884 Reform Act was over 40 millions by 1974.

Given the great importance of local government as provider, (under central governmental supervision and control), of sanitary, environmental, educational and social services of direct significance to citizens, then the democratisation of local government deserves emphasis. Already by 1870, governing bodies of the towns and the Poor Law Guardians, were elected. Major reforms came with Acts of 1888 and 1894 which set up County, County Borough, Urban and Rural District and Parish Councils.

With changes such as increasing democratisation, this local government system remained in operation until the 1970s, when major change re-defined administrative boundaries and powers. By the 1930s, at the zenith of their power, (before, for example, they lost their hospitals to the National Health Service and their energy undertakings to nationalised industries), major Local Authorities exercised very important functions, including control of schools, hospitals and clinics, local roads, parks, sanitation, public health control, public assistance (successor to the Poor Law), and so on. Of course, many of these functions remain largely under local control.

Around 1870, republicanism was proclaimed by leading Radicals and some believed that monarchy would not survive for very long. Yet in 1979, Queen Elizabeth was esteemed by the great majority of her subjects.

Also surviving in 1979 was the House of Lords, though it had lost very much power over the 20th century and had mainly become an amending and debating second chamber, increasingly composed of Life Peers.

Britain's voting system favours two main parties – until the

Great War, these were Conservatives and Liberals; the latter were replaced by Labour. Advocates of proportional representation believe it to be a fairer system which would have destroyed that dominance of two main factions which (they hold) has helped entrench outworn class divisions and confrontation.

In 1870, Gladstone and Disraeli headed the opposing parties and had already enunciated ideas still much worthy of study, the implementation of which helps account for the relatively peaceful nature of Britain's modern evolution.

"In a progressive country" said Disraeli in 1868, "change is constant, and the great question is not whether you should resist change which is inevitable, but whether that change should be carried out in deference to the manners, customs, laws and traditions of a people, or whether it should be carried out in deference to abstract principle and arbitrary and general doctrines. The one is a national system, the other . . . a philosophic system. I have always considered that the Tory Party was the national party of England".[61]

The continuing survival and success to 1979 of the Conservative Party is a fact. Around 1906 there must have been many who thought the days numbered of a political party dominated by landowners and businessmen asking for the votes of predominantly urban, propertyless workers. Yet in 1979, some 30 per cent of voting Trade Unionists helped Mrs. Thatcher to victory. This surely is additional proof of the sheer strength of conservatism and of tradition in British history.

Also in the 1860s, Gladstone said: "Please to remember that we have got to govern millions of hard hands; that it must be done by force, fraud or good will; that the latter has been tried and is answering".[62]

In 1870 Britain's government existed with the consent of the governed, and, roughly, that essential attribute of democracy has been present ever since. By mid-Victorian decades, the military cowing of discontent which had featured so prominently in years around 1819 seemed quite unnecessary. Unlike most continental nations, Britons were not subject to military conscription. Half the small regular army was normally over-seas. The Navy was ill suited to suppressing disorder in Sheffield. In 1870, Police Forces were still a relatively new feature of British life, (the Metropolitan Police date from 1829). Their advent had been much opposed – as a threat to traditional liberties – by Radicals and many working people. They were unarmed and had to slowly win popular support sufficient for the acquisition of information and reasonably successful functioning. Police Forces are, of course, manned by human beings who are imperfect and open to criticism. But, one reason for Britain's relatively peaceful evolution into a modern democracy has been the existence, (outside -Ulster), of a normally unarmed police relying upon considerable co-operation with the public.

By the 1870s, there was very much freedom of speech and writing in the political sphere. J.S. Mill's "On Liberty", (1859), is still a classic statement of the value of individual freedom and the dangers of suppression, since for example, "the opinion which it is attempted to suppress by authority may possibly be true".[63] It is the great glory of the Victorians that, in and out of Parliament, in Reports of official enquiries, in many writings of fact and fiction, they ruthlessly exposed the evils of factory labour, insanitary towns, some work-houses, child prostitution and a host of abuses. Indeed, a leading authority on the age could only think of two institutions – Representative government and the Family – which were not assailed by Victorians.[64] Very often the Victorians had the will, the confidence and the energy to carry through the needed reforms. For the majority of Britons, life was better in 1901 than in 1837. Some credit must go to the country's political institutions which permitted widespread free debate.

Credit for the successful building of a democratic society in Britain must go to a host of reformers of varying beliefs and in diverse camps. Not to be forgotten is the important fact that the ruling classes of 1870 did surrender much power and privilege without the armed struggle or bloody revolution which some considered inevitable.

In modern Britain, mass democracy – with all its imperfections – is a considerable reality. Each week, thousands of opinions pass upwards from the people in the form of letters or phone calls to representatives and the media, of suggestions or complaints made at meetings, M.P.s' "surgeries" and the like. There are always openings through which the erupting lava may flow: normally it need not build up until there is a vast explosion as in Russia in 1917 or Iran in 1979.

It was, and indeed still is, the consistent hope of many

reformers that political would be followed by economic democracy. The latter is hard to define but its advocates have stressed greater equality of income and of living and working conditions often to be attained through some form of socialism.

Not all developments have favoured them. As enterprises grow in size, so they become more hierarchical. A modern large-scale company, like the Army, has very many grades from private to Field Marshal. Executive grades in huge multi-national companies are now sometimes recruited solely from graduates. So in certain, though not all, respects it has become harder for a manual worker to rise.

In huge modern enterprises, personal contact between those at the top with shop-floor workers is minimal. True, 1870 relationships between say, a farmer and his men could be harsh and very unpleasant, as labourers found when they joined the Agricultural Labourers' Union and were sacked. But some recollections[65] do tell of mutual respect and harmony in small enterprises.

Future pages detail much conflict between Capital and Labour over the century under review. Most certainly, too, in 1979, problems of industrial relations and of income distribution were still very much with us. But the following advances may appear clear:

First, though some consider them to be far too great, gaps between classes in 1979 were far, far less than in 1870 or 1910. No longer did large sections of the population live in absolute, grinding poverty while a minority enjoyed huge, largely tax-free incomes in their vast houses staffed by numerous servants. It is impossible to reasonably deny that the majority had moved upwards in standards of living and welfare;

Second, educational provision had enabled growing numbers to move up into salaried occupations in an expanded economy;

Third, welfare provision, and taxes to pay for it, had reduced class differences;

Fourth much technological progress had levelled the classes. Members of all social groups could and did buy Marks and Spencers' shirts or watch "The Forsyte Saga" on T.V.;

Fifth, the public sector and many private companies in Britain in 1979, did make serious and consistent efforts to recruit and promote on merit.

No attempt is made over subsequent pages to hide continuing inequalities. Here a brief note on the evolution of methods of recruitment of army officers will throw some light on changes and continuing problems.

In 1870, Army commissions were still bought, mainly by rich landowners. Gladstone's Government abolished such purchase but, (apart from good results following removal of the ability of rich, but possibly incompetent, men to buy promotion), change was very limited. In prestigious Regiments, officers could not live on the pay and had to have private incomes.[66] The Great War slaughter of officers led to large scale promotion from the ranks and in the Second War a systematic system of War Office Selection Boards, with intelligence tests and psychiatrists, was established.

After the Second War, the son of a farm labourer, if he had the requisite qualifications and personality, could get to Sandhurst and become an army officer. Yet Sandhurst still recruited considerably from the public schools, partly because public school boys were the ones who applied, partly because they were judged by expert panels to be the ones best suited to lead men in a crisis. By 1980, however, it was clear that Sandhurst was taking cadets from a wide range of schools.

Here is another example of evolution at work. The modern Army does make serious, systematic attempts, through the use of scientific testing devices, to find the best officers. On the other hand, the social groups wich supplied the top officers of 1930 still supplied most of those of 1970.[67]

Further, in the great 20th century wars, it became very obvious to many that gulfs between officers and men in the British Army remained vastly greater than in, say, the Australian Army which was certainly not less successful while managing to be far more egalitarian in key respects.

Finally, however, in this brief survey, it cannot be denied that the power and influence of organised workers was enormously greater in 1979 than in 1870. Some unions were very strong; workers are far better protected from danger or instant dismissal. Attempts have been made to legislate for equal opportunities for people of both sexes and of all racial origins.

Yet, as 1979 ended, there were the clearest signs that powerful sections of the Labour Party, for example, were quite dissatisfied with existing progress towards equality and intended to speed up movements towards greater economic democracy.

Over the past century, that majority of Britons which is female has benefited from advances.

First, like men of course, they have gained much from medical improvements. In their cases, advances in gynaecology and surgery have been significant. In the 20th century, tuberculosis has ceased to be the scourge it was in the days of the Brontes, sulphonamide drugs have cut down death-rate from puerperal fever, and so on;

Second, for millions of women, the greatest change has been that they have gone out to and continued with work, (often with an interruption for childbearing and rearing). By 1976, 10 million women went out to work: 6.7 million of these were married. Advantages and disadvantages have been much considered. But in the early years of this century women were quite convinced they were blazing a fine pioneering trail: "To no man, I think, can the world be quite so wonderful as it is to the woman now alive who has fought free. Those who come after her will enter by right of birth upon what she attains by right of conquest . . . the independence that was to be as Dead Sea ashes in our mouth tastes very sweet indeed."[68] Previously marriage had been the only honourable trade open to very many women;

Third, while marriage has been voluntarily entered into by the vast majority of women, it became far, far easier to end an unhappy partnership through divorce in which in 1979, the wife's right to a house and income was strongly protected;

Fourth, women gained effective choice whether or not to have children. Again, here was a change of clear importance;

Fifth, most houses in which many women still spend much of their lives have been made vastly more comfortable and easier to run. Horizons and contacts have been much widened by wireless, television, the phone;

Sixth, like men, women have benefited (and suffered), from other technological advances. By 1975, well over 40 per cent of women aged 27–39 had a car driving licence;

Seventh, women have won political rights, (admittedly with some disappointing results);

Eighth, particularly, over recent decades, women have gained much legal protection. Earlier advances are mentioned elsewhere, here it is added that the Equal Pay Act (1970) and Sex Discrimination Act (1975) stipulated equal pay for like work and attempted to end the segregation of women into less skilled, lowly paid jobs. An Equal Opportunities Commission was established to supervise implementation of these Acts. The Employment Protection Act (1975) included provision for paid maternity leave and the right to return to work after childbirth. The Domestic Violence and Matrimonial Proceedings Act (1976) enabled a married woman to ask for an injunction against her violent husband. The Sexual Offences (Amendment) Act, 1976, gave the right to anonymity to a rapist's victim. The Social Security Pensions Act (1975) ended some sex discrimination in the social security system: a married woman was to receive the common level of sickness and unemployment benefit.

Ninth, women have gained immensely from the state provision described elsewhere in this work, from education, health service, pensions. In the 1870s very many young girls went from school into domestic service. In 1980, their descendants often went into VIth forms and to higher education.

Staunch supporters of women's liberation counter much of the above, pointing, for example, to continuing discrimination in employment and pay; to disadvantages endured by married women, dependent on husbands' hand-outs; to feeble participation in Parliament and many leading professions; to difficulties in bringing up children in an age when – they say – more is demanded of mothers, and so on.

Certainly, in key respects, women's anticipated and chosen lot remains much the same as it was a century ago. In the late 1960s, a group of London schoolgirls outlined their expectations: "apart from one notable exception . . . the essays were monotonously similar. The great majority of the girls saw themselves married by the time they were twenty years old. A year or two later all the young marrieds had started a family of two or three children". "Teaching hours suited both of us", wrote one girl, (they were asked to look back on their lives from their 80th birthday), "as I was always back home before five o'clock to do the housework and cook a meal".[69]

Yet it is impossible to believe that an extremely able young woman could be driven to write a century later what Florence Nightingale despairingly uttered in 1851 when convention and family opposition was preventing her from entering the then very unfashionable career of nursing: "O weary days – oh evenings that seem never to end – for how many years have I watched that drawing-room clock and thought I never would reach the ten! and for twenty, thirty years more to do this!" Her natural bitterness boiled over into: "Women don't consider themselves as human beings at all. There is absolutely no God, no country, no duty to them at all except family . . . I have known a good deal of convents. . . But I know nothing like the petty grinding tyranny of a good English family".[70]

A life-span later, Vera Brittain, summoned from war-time nursing by a sick mother, was furious at finding the latter out of bed: "Forgetting that parents who had been brought up by their own forbears to regard young women as perpetually at the disposal of husbands or fathers. . ."[71]

On subsequent pages, the uneven but persistent and considerable steps towards greater economic and social equality between classes and the sexes are further examined.

3.7   Changes in beliefs and ideas

The following leading developments are given some coverage:

1. Decline of Christianity
2. Waning of a belief in progress
3. Imperialism
4. Socialism
5. Growth of humanitarianism and of tolerance
6. Great change 1950–70

Decline of Christianity

There has been in Britain a marked decline in religious observance and in the influence and power of Christian churches in general and of Protestant churches in particular. True, even in the 19th century Christianity never gained much influence over huddled masses of the very poorest in the large cities, particularly London. They did not attend church. In Dickens's Coketown: "the perplexing mystery of the place was, who belonged to the eighteen denominations? Because, whoever did, the labouring people did not".[72] However, the great majority of large groups –

country people, middle and upper classes, respectable Methodist working class folk – did. Indeed, by 1980s standards, Victorian religious observance was remarkably great. Church attendances on 30/3/1851 were recorded. In England and Wales 40 per cent were worshippers, (nearly 20 per cent Anglican, just over 20 per cent non-Anglican). In London, the percentage was down to a quarter and in 8 large towns to 27 per cent. Yet it was truly "an astonishing scale of religious activity."[73] In a typical 19th century English village, practically all except infants, the very old and a few rebels attended church or chapel every Sunday, sometimes two or three times. Church building, (between 1801 and 1873, 4,210 new Anglican and some 20,000 non-Anglican places of worship were opened),[74] charitable and overseas missionary endeavour were on a vast scale.[75] It is indeed impossible to ignore the obvious fact that, ranging from Lord Shaftesbury to many cotton operatives, very many Victorians firmly believed in the Christian religion, and that this life, being merely a preparation for the next, was best spent in eschewing pleasure and concentrating on work and worship. A leading authority held that 19th century evangelical religion was "the greatest binding force in a nation which without it might have broken up".[76]

Change gradually came after about 1870. Christianity declined in importance in face of desertion and attack by agnostics, pleasure-seekers and socialists. In his "Origin of Species" (1859) and "Descent of Man" (1871), Darwin set out his theories of evolution. These, together with advances in geology which proved that rocks and species had existed for millions of years, dealt great blows at those who believed every word of the Bible to be the truth. After about the 1880s, the plutocracy of Victorian and Edwardian Britain, headed by the Prince of Wales, later Edward VII, turned from the Sunday School teaching which had occupied hours of three Victorian Lord Chancellors[77] to more hedonistic, if less worthy, pursuits. The idealism of young Northern working and professional people was often channelled not into the Methodist Church as in earlier decades, but into the Independent Labour Party.

One of the most famous autobiographical accounts of a desertion of evangelical religion is that provided by Edmund Gosse.

Gosse's father was a Puritan of the old school, devoted to

personal salvation, bible-reading and Sundays of "unbroken servitude" to worship and prayer. The son rebelled, turned to literature for pleasure and relief and denied that "evangelical religion . . . . . . is a wholesome or valuable or desirable adjunct to human life. It divides heart from heart . . . . . it invents virtues which are sterile and cruel; it invents sins which are no sins at all. . . ."[78]

By early years of the twentieth century, Church attendance was less regular than in the Victorian hey-day. Two counts of Sunday attendance at places of worship in London in 1886 and 1902–3 showed a fall from 1,167,312 to 1,003,361. The net number of worshippers in 1902–3 was 832,051 out of a population of 4,470,000.[79] In the 20th century the decline in religious observance continued. About 35 per cent of adults (aged 17 and over) in York attended Sunday service in 1901, a proportion which fell to some 18 per cent in 1935 and 13 per cent in 1948.[80]

Even in Scotland, by the end of the 19th century there was clear evidence that the Churches' hold on the population had weakened. In mining and industrial towns, growing Socialism had often replaced Christianity as a main belief held by idealistic youth.

Yet while there has been change and decline, Christianity is still a potent force among a section of British society. In 1980, there was over 1.8 million communicants at Christmas in the Church of England alone, while in the same year, 266,000 infants were baptised into that Church.

There have been some gains from the decline in the power of the Established Church and its clergy, particularly in rural areas, where in the 19th and early 20th centuries they still had much authority and wealth – not always well used. The Rev. Francis Kilvert was appalled to hear that a fellow clergyman, ordering a schoolmistress to have windows and doors of the schoolroom open in harsh weather, had said "This is my school and I will have my word attended to".[81] In the 1920s a well-informed observer was very critical of the rural clergy: "The blunt fireside judgment of the mass of agricultural labouring families on many a parson is that he is witless and lazy, a self-satisfied drone, who, by the advantage of his social position, has secured a soft job. . . ."[82]

By 1979, much had radically changed. Incomes of the clergy

were relatively low, parishes had merged, only those with a sincere vocation would be likely to enter the profession.

Waning of a belief in progress

Belief in the certainty of progress was never universal, but it was widespread over the century which ended in 1913. True, writers such as Richard Jefferies, around the 1870s, considered that "men only look to the day and live fast. There is a sense of uncertainty in the atmosphere of the age: no one can be sure that the acorns he plants will be permitted to reach their prime, the hoofs of the 'iron horse' may trample them down as fresh populations grow".[83]

Yet in many respects, the Victorian was a confident, self-assured, vigorous age:

> "Oh, our manhood's prime vigour! no spirit feels waste,
> Not a muscle is stopped in its playing, nor sinew unbraced,–
> Oh, the wild joys of living! the leaping from rock up to rock. . . . . . "[84]

Expressions of faith in social advance seem naive to disillusioned modern minds. "Virtue is the child of knowlege: Vice of Ignorance: therefore education, periodical literature, railroad travelling, ventilation, and the arts of life . . . serve to make a population moral and happy"[85] wrote Newman, a religious leader. "The objects of this Society are the moral and intellectual advancement of its members. It provides them with groceries, butcher's meat, drapery goods, clothes and clogs",[86] said the Prospectus of the Rochdale Co-operative Pioneers. Later in the century, the great economist Marshall was still quite convinced that the poor were not to be for ever with us. – "I regard all this problem of poverty as a mere passing evil in the progress of man upwards; and I should not like any institution started which did not contain in itself the causes which make it shrivel up, as the causes of poverty itself shrivelled up".[87]

When Marshall thus wrote in 1895, Victorian certainties were already under much attack, yet nearly 20 years later in 1914 the confident youth of the nation volunteered for war in what now seems an amazing surge of patriotism and self-sacrifice (combined, of course, with other reasons). The Great War was a turning point: "Never such innocence again".[88] The vast chasm between those in the water-filled trenches and their fellow-nationals who often prospered, the utter blunderings – all created a mood of cynicism, re-inforced by the failure to create after the War a "land fit for heroes to live in". Changes in attitudes to authority resulting from the Great War were great. Any surviving nineteenth century certainty of progress and continuing inevitable advances towards civilisation and humanity received hammer blows from the world-wide depression of 1929–1933 and (perhaps the most horrible shocks of all) from the revelations of what happened in Hitler's and Stalin's camps.

Imperialism

Although for much of the period covered by this work the British Empire was vast, although it had some marked effects on the home country and huge stretches of the World, yet only of a limited period (around 1872 to 1902) can it be said with confidence that imperialism, (meaning here a belief in the value of Empire), was a powerful force in Britain and even then many were indifferent or hostile to it.

In 1872 Disraeli made imperialism one of the planks of the popular Conservative platform and in 1876 he persuaded a reluctant Parliament to grant a pleased Queen the title of Empress of India. Some liberals such as Dilke and even a few socialists such as Robert Blatchford supported the movement. Academic backing came from writings such as Seeley's "Expansion of England" (1883). Some of the newly enfranchised working class were won over by offers of a powerful combination of imperialism and social reform.

Yet some always did deplore imperialism: W.S. Blunt[89] denounced it with the vigour of an Old Testament prophet, some liberals were never supporters and in general it was opposed by the new Labour movement. The bloody nose inflicted on Britain by the Boers (1899–1902) revealed the possible dire costs of imperialism.[90] Growing nationalist movements in Ireland, Egypt and India showed that the sun of Empire was setting. Nationalist leaders on visits to Britain had no difficulty in finding friends and supporters in London. After the Second World War the end came quite quickly.

At its peak around 1919 the British Empire could be divided into two distinct parts. There were the self-governing dominions, (virtually independent after 1926), of Canada, Newfoundland, Australia, New Zealand, South Africa. Apart from the last named these were mainly peopled by European emigrants.

Second, there was the large, dependent Empire, far and away the most important constitutent of which was India. To this Empire, vast additions were made between 1870 amd 1919, particularly in Africa and the Middle East. Motives for acquisition were many and complex: each British dependency had its own history. As often, economic motives were important, though, most certainly, they were not the only ones.

Later, the difficult task of evaluating benefits and costs of Empire will be briefly attempted. Here another question is put: did the acquisition and loss of Empire have much effect on British society?

To the mainly white dominions went many thousands of British emigrants. Painstaking modern research has revealed that of emigrants from England and Wales, from the 1870s to 1914, about 40 per cent returned to their homeland: D. Baines, *Migration in a mature economy*, C.U.P. 1985, p 279. Australia and New Zealand, peopled by largely working class emigrants from Britain's villages and towns (some of whom had not departed voluntarily), were among the most democratic and egalitarian societies in the world. In the late 19th century, agitators such as Tom Mann worked in both Britain and Australia, while £30,000 of Australian money did much to win victory for the London dockers in the famous strike of 1889.[91] In two World Wars these countries fought alongside Britain and very many British came into contact with their forces. Throughout the period covered in this work, strong economic and social ties – much weakened it is true by factors such as Britain's membership of the E.E.C. – have been maintained. In 1978, Australia took £856 million of British exports.

To the dependent territories went limited numbers of administrators and traders plus (often on five-year postings) British soldiers. At the end of the 19th century, "the great mass of the imperial service like the officer corps of the colonial forces, was pre-eminently upper middle class".[92]

To such people the Empire meant very much – though they

regarded Britain as home. Their children were often sent back at an early age and, (if they survived), they generally retired to Britain. They found that even their own class had little interest in their doings. In the 20th century a lady from India remarked on "the total disinterest of the people in England to Indian affairs. I don't think any of us ever spoke about India for the six months or so we spent in England".[93]

Tens of thousands saw Regular Army service abroad, particularly in India. In 1897, of a British army of 212,00 men, about 72,000 were in India, and 32,000 in colonial postings. The latter could be pleasant (as in Malta) or quite horrible (as in Aden where an 1890s traveller commented on the faces of the British soldiers – "shrivelled up – a pathetic sight to see").[94] In India especially in the hot season, a soldier's life could be indescribably boring. Kipling's Mulvaney asked in a work of fiction what many must have thought in real life: "Mary, Mother of Mercy, fwhat the divil possist us to take an' kape this melancholious counthry?".[95]

To the great mass of the British working class at home their Empire meant little. To one who lived in a Salford slum it seemed that: "What the undermass got materially from empire . . . . it is hard to see unless it was the banana . . . which . . . began to appear increasingly in slum greengrocers' shops during the later years of the nineteenth century". But the writer does concede that there was "propagation of the imperialistic idea" and that "the indigent remained staunchly patriotic".[96]

While a few deeply regretted and some positively welcomed it, most 20th century Britons seemed quite unconcerned at the 20th century loss of Empire: among public developments and happenings (which to most people are of far less important than personal successes or failings) it caused far less concern than employment prospects, rising prices and other domestic problems.

Socialism

In British politics in 1870, socialism was of practically no importance: in 1979 it was the avowed faith of many and, for sixty years, had been the stated programme of one of the main political parties.

British socialism had British origins which can be traced back to 17th century Levellers and earlier radicals. But modern socialism arose as a response to the obvious inequalities, sufferings and ugliness resulting from industrialisation. In the 1880s Socialism first became an important political and social force in this country. Ben Tillett, Tom Mann and John Burns helped build up the New Unionism of unskilled workers amid an atmosphere of militancy new to that generation. In 1881 was founded the Social Democratic Federation, the first modern socialist organisation of national importance in Britain.[97]

Much better known was the Fabian Society, which at the peak of its influence in the late 19th and 20th centuries, included among its members Sidney and Beatrice Webb, Bernard Shaw and H.G. Wells. Some modern scholarship diminishes the importance of the Fabians: "those who can blow their own trumpet not only sound louder than those who cannot, but automatically provide material for music critics".[98] But all are likely to gasp in admiration at the sheer volume of work accomplished by, say, the Webbs. On top of writing "monuments to scholarship" such as "Industrial Democracy",[99] one or both founded the London School of Economics, toiled away on London's education committees, served on the 1905–9 Poor Law Commission, took a leading role in drafting the 1918 constitution of the Labour Party.

By 1890, Beatrice Potter (later Webb) was writing in her diary: "*I* mean by socialism not a vague and sentimental desire to 'ameliorate the condition of the masses', but a definite economic form; a peculiar industrial organisation – the communal or state ownership of Capital and Land".[100] Many rising politicians and their supporters were not as clear-sighted.

1893 saw the foundation of the Independent Labour Party, which particularly in industrial belts of Clydeside and Northern England, attracted idealists who gave to this new movement the devotion given by their grandparents to Methodism. On Clydeside the party was strong until the period between the wars. In more disillusioned times a member in those days recalled that – "Our vision was simple and good. We wanted to create a different social order and saw it as our first task to prepare ourselves intellectually and spiritually".[101] Not only in Glasgow, but in English towns such as Bradford, the I.L.P. worked for socialism in general and for practical advances in local social fields such as education and child care.

Currents moving along the new socialism included William Morris's work and writings, Henry George's "Progress and Poverty" (1879) and Robert Blatchford's "Merrie England" (1894) which sold the best part of a million copies in a year.[102]

Of far, far greater international importance than George Blatchford or the Webbs, was Karl Marx. The first part of "Das Kapital" appeared in German, in 1867. Yet, it is extremely doubtful whether, through the period covered in this work, Marx had any great influence on the country in which he wrote. Writing around 1932, one authority held that: "Marx, even at second hand, has had little influence on English thought; on English action, almost none".[103] He might not have been so certain in the slump years which followed his pronouncement, for Marxist publications, for example by the Left Book Club, had a wide readership. In 1979, professed Marxists formed a strong minority in many academic institutions, their interpretations of economic history and social organisation (for example) were influential, they formed a penetrating minority in a number of Unions and Constituency Labour Parties.

In 1900, the Trade Unions, I.L.P., S.D.F., and Fabian Society formed the Labour Representative Committee soon to be called the Labour Party. After 1918 this became one of the two main political parties. The 1918 Constitution stated the Party's objectives to be: "to secure for the producers by hand and by brain the full fruits of their industry and the most equitable distribution thereof that may be possible upon the basis of the common ownership of the means of production and the best obtainable system of popular administration and control of each industry and service".

Later chapters will examine to what extent such aims were realised.

Growth of humanitarianism, tolerance and aspects of freedom

The young H.H. Asquith: "Walking up Ludgate Hill to school one morning in 1864 . . . came upon the bodies of five murderers, hanging with white caps over their heads, outside Newgate. Half an hour before they had been publicly executed. . ."[104] Late 19th and 20th century British schoolboys were spared such sights, for public executions ceased after 1868, while, of the 220 capital offences of 1800, only two (murder and treason) survived in 1870.

Flogging in the peace-time Regular Army ceased at the start of the period covered in this work but judicial "whippings" were administered until well into this century. Around 1900 numbers were large: 3,278 were "whipped" in 1900 and 1,632 in 1911–12, (presumably, many of these were boys who were birched). In his Salford slum, Roberts noted cases of brutal punishments of children: "Among the fathers administering such punishments were men who in childhood had themselves received forty-eight strokes of the birch – a common sentence – at the local prison".[105]

In 1911–12, for example, 31 persons were sentenced to death, though in 13 cases the sentence was commuted to penal servitude for life.

Imprisonment in the 19th century was rigorous punishment imposed by magistrates and judges in far higher proportions of sentences than was the case by 1980.

By the 1970s, capital and corporal punishment were no longer imposed by Britain's courts. In spite of all the imperfections and problems, treatment of offenders in 1980 was far more humane than in 1870. It must be added that sometimes change has come in face of massive public opposition voiced in favour of retention of, for example, hanging.

Humanitarianism, tolerance and freedom have grown in other spheres. However, it must be admitted that by no means all regard such changes as good: toleration may mean the toleration of evil, freedom may be abused.

An early 19th century visitor to Britain considered it to be "the classic land of liberty and religious toleration, the two greatest blessings which men can enjoy".[106] But in their personal daily lives in family and community many were subjected to restriction of freedon and of individual self-expression.

Victorian society was very firmly based on the family and it is folly to deny the vast benefits brought to society by stable, caring family life. Very often, respectability triumphed: the children did not become vandals or criminals.

But by no means all families were happy. Drink, unemployment, bad housing, strain, poverty, human failings and perversities, all helped to turn some homes into little hells.

Only for the few (and they mainly among the rich) was there an escape in divorce. In 1870 divorce was rare, difficult and very much frowned upon. Involvement in a case could ruin a career, as Parnell and Dilke found. In 1980 divorce is far easier, commoner and (by many) accepted as far preferable to the continued unhappiness of a broken-down marriage. Some (including strict Catholics) do not normally countenance it. Here, however, is another vast change between 1870 and 1980.

Victorian society could be very intolerant of those who did not conform to its norms. J.S. Mill wrote of "The despotism of custom". Most people he thought "have no tastes or wishes strong enough to incline them to do anything unusual and they consequently do not understand those who have, and class all such with the wild and intemperate. . ."[107] The Victorians did not agree with "doing one's own thing." In addition, they could be quite incredibly prudish, and downright hypocritical.

In 1896, Hardy's "Jude the Obscure" aroused a storm of criticism and, wrote the author, was "burnt by a bishop – probably in his despair at not being able to burn me".[108] Late 20th century readers of this novel must be amazed at the reaction of so many of Hardy's critics. In the early decades of this century, D.H. Lawrence could not get some of his works published.[109] Earlier, others had suffered more severely from pressures which many might call bigotry. Kilvert recorded how a pregnant barmaid ended her life in the local river.[110] Gifted author, and homosexual Oscar Wilde had his life shattered by a stiff prison sentence. In 1903, famous soldier, Hector Mcdonald, a Highland crofter's son, who rose from private to Major-General, shot himself following accusations of homosexual behaviour.[111]

Great Change 1950–70

With melodramatic effect, extent of change is often exaggerated. Thus much emphasis is often given to the advent of the "permissive society" around the 1960s. Certainly there was change. By 1979, an unmarried couple could live together even in an English village and arouse little comment: it was different a century before. But not all was so new. Before 1914, in times of Victorian morality, church-going, male domination, and high imperialism we know that some lived far from moral lives, denounced Christianity and imperialism, and so on.[112] Two World Wars much changed prevailing attitudes and orthodoxies. In the inter-war period an avalanche of left-wing writings harassed majority opinion.

Yet, when every exception and qualification has been entered, it must be agreed that around 1955–70 a great change surged over expression, belief, behaviour, in this, as in other similar, countries. From the mid-1950s onwards came the Suez fiasco, Osborne's "Look back in Anger", free publication of "Lady Chatterley's Lover", satire and frankness on T.V., student unrest, the Beatles, mini-skirts, Women's lib., the pill, upturning of class barriers by North Country writers and the young, drugs, vandalism and more crime.

Under such blows it seemed to many that the fabric of national consensus and unity was coming apart at the seams. The perennial generation gap assumed more than normal proportions. Duty and respectability no long commanded.

Importantly, now that there was no longer a widely accepted code, each individual felt free to do his or her own thing and each group felt obliged to push its own interests and demand higher pay, pensions, subsidies, grants, allowances, perks. By the 1970s sad results of the weakening of cohesion were very apparent.

Perhaps the scale of change has been exaggerated. Conservative victory in 1979, patriotic support for Falkland recovery by force in 1982, showed the strength of continuing tradition. Some ignored the gains, others the costs, of change. In 1979, a woman would not have suffered as Catherine Cookson's mother did, when she bore an illegitimate child some 70 years earlier in a North-eastern Catholic, working-class home.[113] On the other hand, it is folly to ignore the suffering brought by the utter irresponsibility, the broken families, drugs, V.D., vandalism and increased crime which accompanied emancipation.

Shattered beliefs of proven value have not been replaced. A modern writer[114] has quoted with effect this poem on the demise of 19th century certainty:

"Those – dying then,
Knew where they went –
They went to God's Right Hand
That Hand is amputated now
And God cannot be found –

The abidication of Belief
Makes the Behaviour small –
Better an ignis fatuus
Than no illume at all –"

4. OUTLINE OF THE PERIOD

In 1865 the American Civil War ended and a united nation entered upon a period of breakneck economic expansion; in 1871 a unified Germany came into being and with the vigour of new nationhood soon challenged Britain's industrial lead; in the 1870s Japan launched itself upon a successful programme of modernisation. The modern world was rapidly taking shape.

Apart from conflicts which were relatively minor in 20th century terms, there was peace from 1871 to 1914 and world scientific, technological and economic progress was rapid. The tragedy of the 20th century had begun: xenophobic nationalism was boiling over at the very time when the railway, steamship, cable, telephone and wireless were uniting mankind.

1871 saw Stanley's famous encounter with Livingstone in Central Africa. Over the next thirty years, European states partitioned that Continent. In 1913 European power in the World was at its peak.

In Britain, Queen Victoria reigned until 1901, Edward VII from 1901 to 1910 and George V from 1910 to 1936. In 1870, Gladstone was well into his first great reforming Liberal ministry of 1868–74. Disraeli's Conservatives appealed to the new electorate with a popular programme of defence of existing institutions, imperialism and social reform and were in power from 1874–80 when they enacted factory and health measures of direct benefit to the working class. Gladstone split his party in 1886 because he was determined to give Home Rule to Ireland. He presented the Conservatives with 20 years, (1886–1905) of nearly continuous rule. The very able Lord Salisbury was Prime Minister for most of the period: his undoubted conservatism at a time when many of his countrymen were demanding much-needed change may have been harmful to Britain's long-term prospects.

Imperialism boiled up into the South African War of 1899–1902. At roughly the same time, a growing lack of confidence in Britain's ability to stand alone and in the lead, led to a fateful seeking of alliances and agreements which was so soon to entangle the country in European conflict. It also led to a move to abandon Free Trade and to seek tariff barriers.

It was now the turn of the Conservatives to be divided – in their case over tariffs. This great Tory handicap helped the Liberals to sweeping victory at the polls in 1906. With the support of a contingent from the emergent Labour Party and of the Irish Nationalists, Liberals ruled until the Great War coalition was formed.

It was their last Ministry and one of their most productive in terms of reforms. Unfortunately, these were also years of dangerous international strife and domestic division.

In 1914, in very important respects, the 19th century decisively ended and this violent 20th century began. Here was one of the clearest and most dramatic of turning points.

5. THE ECONOMY

5.1 The economic system

In 1870 Britain's was very distinctly a capitalist, free enterprise, market economy, not planned, directed, controlled by the State.

Adam Smith, in his "Wealth of Nations", 1776, had advanced the "pregnant consideration that under certain social arrangements, which we would describe as perfect competition, private interests are indeed harmonised with social interests".[1] He argued that the operation of the "invisible hand" of the price or market system helped all: consumers needed bread for which they were prepared to pay, bakers made and sold the bread because they could make a profit. Competition in the 19th century was not perfect but it was very strong. 63 bakers were operating in Northampton in the 1870s.[2] Certainly in the distribution trades there were many small outlets: selling coal to Londoners was "an open fighting trade" and there were many such.[3] Even the largish companies which had grown to run the railways, iron and steel, shipbuilding, engineering plants were often in strong competition. Prices of imports and exports fluctuated much in the trade cycle. Profits rose and fell with the weakest going to the wall. In the great basic industries there were many firms: just over 2000 in Lancashire cotton in 1914. As late as 1925–6 there were still 1,400 colliery undertakings operating 2500 pits. In 1913, factory inspectors knew of 113,000 factories and 148,000 workshops. Even the railway companies might be in neighbourhood competition: there were two main lines from London to Birmingham and so on. In the mid 1880s there were 120 joint-stock and about 250 private banks.

After studying a detailed portrayal of mid-Victorian business, a modern economist wrote of her "impression that the main factor shaping entrepreneurial behaviour in this period was the existence of persistently strong and often intensifying competitive pressures. . . This seems to have been the classic era of the expanding, competitive capitalist economy".[4]

There was still much individual private enterprise – farms, shops, building, import and export services, the myriad small businesses in and around Birmingham, and so on. But companies and the modern capitalist system were growing. Finance for the companies came from ploughing back of profits, local borrowing, selling of shares. There were some 170,000 rentiers, receiving dividends in 1871.[5] Investors provided businessmen with the money to buy their new sheds, cranes, machines. Keynes looked back: "For a hundred years the system worked . . . with an extraordinary success and facilitated the growth of wealth on an unprecedented scale. . . The morals, the politics, the literature and the religion of the age, joined in a grand conspiracy for the promotion of saving. . ."[6]

A crucial difference between the 19th and the 20th centuries is that in the former wages took a much smaller, and profits a much greater, share of the national cake. Wages were and are mainly spent on consumption. Much of profit then went into investment: into buying new machines and structures. Many 19th century profits "do not by any means represent the gains of passive shareholders: they are mainly the fruit of the efforts of hardworking men and are in no sense fortuitous."[7]

The competitive economic system – like all systems – had its good and bad points.

Employment, income, standard of living, rose. In 1913 a more numerous British people were living better than their grand-parents in 1870. Though the vast gaps between those well up and those well down the ladder did not narrow, most people moved up a rung or two. Details follow later.

Competition kept down prices and normally ensured service. Prices were relatively stable from 1815 to 1914, (compared with 20th century experience). There were rises and falls but prices in 1913 were lower than in 1815: (the latter year did come at the end of an inflationary war period). One index, that of Phelps Brown and Sheila Hopkins,[8] (1451–75 = 100), reads:

1815–1467   1893– 914
1873–1437   1913–1021

Prices fell from 1873 to 1896 and rose from 1896 to 1913.

For fortunate classes this was a golden age. Son of a doctor and grandson of a famous scientist, G. Huxley, born 1894, wrote when old: "Few indeed, of the human race in any era can have been so fortunate in their youth as were I and my contemporaries of my nationality and class".[9]

Keynes thus summed up pre-1914 benefits: from the working class, he asserted, "escape was possible for any man of capacity or character at all exceeding the average into the middle and upper classes, for whom life offered, at a low cost and with the least trouble, conveniences, comforts and amenities beyond the compass of the richest and most powerful monarchs of other ages. The inhabitant of London could order by telephone, sipping his morning tea in bed, the various products of the whole earth, in such quantity as he might see fit, and reasonably expect their early delivery on his doorstep. . ."[10]

Alas, not all Britons shared the good fortune and ability to take rosy views of Huxley and Keynes. As described on future pages, poverty remained widespread and income and wealth differentials vast. The Duke of Westminster had an income of £1,000 a *day* in 1914,[11] (mainly from his London rents): very many families had to manage on around a pound a week.[12] Continuing poverty plus gross inequality was the major reason for the superseding by collectivism of 19th century liberalism and laissezfaire. Here was the first major fault in 19th century capitalism.

Second, growth was considerable but not consistent. Booms peaked in 1873, 1882, 1890, 1899–1900, 1907. Troughs were at their deepest in 1879, 1886, 1893, 1904, 1908–9. From the trend line of output, national product was over 5 per cent higher in the booms, over 5 per cent lower in the slumps.[13] In those pre-dole days, the up to 10% unemployment among trade unionists in the worst recessions caused great hardship.

Third, a considerable section of workers – domestics, plus dress, or saddle, or carriage makers, producers and sellers of luxuries – catered mainly for needs of the wealthy when they could have been producing sometimes much needed necessities. True, however, consumption of food, clothes, coal did much increase.

Fourth, the market system was not geared to provide essential services – for example, education and medical services – to those people who could not afford to pay.

Fifth, increasingly producers sought to avoid the rigours of strong competition by making amalgamations, trusts, arrangements.

Sixth, in their search for profits, 19th century industrialists often quite failed to meet certain costs which were thrust on the community. Thus air and water were polluted, countryside ruined.

Seventh, 19th century capitalism was based on the simple rule of buying in the cheapest, selling in the dearest, market. Workers learned this rule and combined to get the highest rate they could for their labour. 20th century industrial relations problems took root.

It must be added that, first, up to 1914, the British economy was, in the main, still successful. Second, economic systems are operated by human beings not by dogma–directed robots. Paternalism, custom, desire to stand well in the neighbourhood, concern to do the decent thing, anxiety to retain skilled labour, pride in craft, all still guided decisions, relationships, work-practices. In a village, a large farmer might consider himself under an obligation to offer work to village boys: "Boys leaving school were taken on at the farm as a matter of course, and no time expired soldier or settler on marriage was ever refused a job".[14] Young George Sturt unexpectedly took over the family wheelwright's shop on his father's sudden death. Competitors and commercial travellers were considerate. "The steadiness of the men was doubtless what saved me from ruin. . . They possibly (and properly) exaggerated the respect for good workmanship and material".[15]

Even in domestic service, unpopular employers might find it hard to recruit. "I have known houses where a servant was wanted, and when telling the caller of the vacancy, received in reply, 'Thank you, but I don't think I should care to go there'. . . I quite understood. . ."[16]

At least to the skilled, an expanding economy gave some

choice and protection. "Many a Monday when father didn't appear on the job the foreman a notorious 'ale can' himself, arrived at the house in mid-morning. . . 'We're stuck, Bob, lad'. . . ."[17]

On subsequent pages, no attempt is made to hide the exploitation and sufferings endured by many. But it is a complex story.

5.2   Still around the top of Division I

Industry

A classic portrayal of Britain's economy over the period 1850–1886 states that: "Indisputably, Britain still led the world's industrial motion. Still the only true 'industry state', she had her immense accumulations of mechanical productive power; her cotton industry; her coal industry; with a dozen others supreme in mechanism; and she had large exports of every kind of machine. . . The basic engineering inventions had been nearly all British, the great steel inventions all. Single-handed, Britain had created modern shipbuilding. . ."[18]

Certainly, in the industrial race Britain set off well before other competitors and in the century 1770 to 1870 she built up a commanding lead. Her industrial prosperity was based on the great basic industries: textiles (particularly cotton), coal, iron and steel, engineering, shipbuilding. These continued to expand and flourish, (though here and there disconcerting cracks could be traced), until the Great War. True, they ran into increasing competition. Cotton manufacture has often taken a leading role in the transformation from an agrarian to an industrial economy. The industry grew; in the United States and India which grew the lint, in Japan and in European countries which did not. Later, a host of emergent countries were to follow suit. By 1913 in coal production, iron and steel and in the volume and value of manufacturing output, Britain was well overtaken by the United States – as was entirely predictable. In iron and steel, in important new industries such as chemicals and electrical goods and in total manufacturing output Britain was also overtaken in the late 19th and early 20th centuries by Germany, which was not so certainly predictable. In 1913 Britain was still the leading exporter and importer, the main financial centre, easily the leading shipbuilding and carrying country, far and away the main investor overseas, and the chief naval and imperial power.

Difficulties – competition, tariffs, slumps, financial crises – there were, but it is also necessary to mention the advantages brought by world economic development. Leading industrial states were – and indeed still are – each other's customers. Thus, in 1912 Germany bought cottons worth £8.3 million, woollens worth £6.6 million, coal and coke to the value of £4.4 million and £4.2 million worth of ironwork and machinery from Britain.[19] Germany exported cheap steel which British firms used profitably to build ships. The vast world-wide economic development often benefited British industry and trade. After all, was not Britain as the chief exporter of capital, main trader and Empire-builder, in a unique position to profit? In the 30 years before 1870, 125,000 miles of railway were laid down in the World; in the 30 years after 1870 360,000 miles were constructed.[20] Clearly, builders of railway locomotives, makers of steel, importers and exporters, stood to gain. It was certainly not an entirely unfavourable economic environment in which to operate.

"Whoever says Industrial Revolution says cotton".[21] In 1850 statistics of raw cotton consumption (in metric tons) in the West European countries were: Britain 222,046, France 59,273, Belgium 7,222, German Customs Union 17,117. By 1851 there were 255,000 male and 272,000 female cotton workers. Britain's lead to cotton manufacture was great and continued until 1913. Statistics of cotton spindlage in major countries (in thousands) were:

	1867	1913		1867	1913
Great Britain	34,000	55,576	France	6,800	7,400
U.S.A.	8,000	30,579	Germany	2,000	10,920

Very large reserves of knowledge and skill were built up in the Lancashire mill towns as workers taught young girls and boys alongside them. In the 1860s and 70s: "Other things equal . . . it would appear that English power looms ran faster and wasted less; while the English weaver minded more machines – generally twice as many as his French or German counterparts."[22]

In the other great textile industry, wool, Britain's lead was less but still there. She had just over 2 million worsted spindles in 1867, as compared with some 1,750,000 in France, and 320,000 in Germany, her 71,500 worsted looms greatly exceeded the 20–25,000 of France and 10,000 of Germany.[23]

Total U:K. coal output (millions of tons) rose from around 50 in 1850 to 110.4 in 1870, 189.7 in 1895 and 287.4 in 1913.[24] Later it will be shown that with this imposing growth came a disturbing fall in productivity per man. As late as 1870, half the world's known coal output was raised in Britain.[25] It could not and did not last. By 1900, the U.S.A. had overhauled Britain and was producing 240 million tons as against Britain's 225 and Germany's 107.

In the period 1870–1914, Britain's iron and steel industry expanded but foreign industries expanded much faster. In this respect, iron and steel was to be the forerunner of a range of British industries in the 20th century. Incredible though it now seems, in 1870 Britain was still producing half the world's pig-iron, three and a half times as much as the United States, more than four times as much as Germany.[26] Much development was still to come: British pig-iron production went up from nearly 6 million tons in 1870 to over 10 million in 1913 while steel output climbed from 220,000 in 1870 to 7,666,000 in 1913. But by 1913 Germany was producing over 17 and the United States over 31 million tons of steel.[27] Britain had been left far behind.

Engineering was a very wide-ranging industry in which achievement was almost bound to, and did, vary. In 1870, main products included textile machinery, steam engines for many purposes, railway rolling stock and machine tools. In the early 20th century, to the above list must be added cycles, motor cycles, motor vehicles and parts, agricultural machinery, internal combustion engines and hydraulic machinery.

As usual, conflicting views are possible on British achievement. One is that technological decline in the engineering industries could be seen "very early . . . somewhere between 1851 and 1867".[28] Another authority considers such pessimism "entirely mistaken".[29] The record of achievement is, indeed, a very mixed one.

By 1870 machinery had been introduced to produce standardised arms and parts – British bayonets cost much more than

American so Gladstone had machines installed to cut costs,[30] and
by the 1850s rifles were being assembled from interchangeable
parts. The period 1870 to 1914 saw the widespread diffusion of
mass-produced machines which eased labour in home and factory
and aided the travel of many thousands on the roads. Domestic
sewing machines were produced at Clydebank before 1870.
Derivatives transformed much of the making of footwear from a
domestic to a factory industry. Cycles, motor cycles and, (to a
small extent by 1914), cars, revolutionised travel. These new
machines were increasingly mass-produced with standard interchangeable parts which were themselves shaped in their
thousands by machine tools – turret lathes and milling machines –
which cut and shaped pieces of metal into any required form.

In general, in this new technology, America took the lead.
There were many reasons, perhaps the most obvious was that
relative shortage of, and consequent high reward to, labour,
induced entrepreneurs to adapt capital intensive methods. Britain
could and did adopt the new technology: in particular, she
produced cycles and motor cycles with success. But many of the
new machines, for example in the footwear industry, were
American. In the early 20th century, America went very far, and
France some distance, ahead of Britain in the new car industry.
By 1913 British vehicle output had climbed to 34,000 but this was
three-quarters of the French output and a mere trickle compared
with the flood of America's near half-million cars of 1914. In
contrast, Britain in 1913 was easily the main exporter of cycles,
selling abroad 150,000 as compared with Germany's 89,000 and
small numbers from other countries.

Continuing success – sometimes very marked – was to be found
in the textile machinery, railway locomotive and rolling stock and
shipbuilding industries. It was not surprising that Lancashire's
dominance should have carried along with it a very thriving mill
machinery industry. In 1875, Platts of Oldham employed 7,000
workers. By 1913, some 40,000 found work in the textile
machinery industry which exported three times as much as its
nearest rival, Germany.

Up to 1914, very large sales of locomotives and rolling stock
continued. Swindon workshops, with 14,000 employees, was the
biggest engineering establishment in the country. Great traditions
of excellence were developed at some railway workshops – as at

Derby under Matthew Kirtley. Between 1890 and 1913, 10 large producers sold over 17,000 locomotives to a very wide range of countries.[31]

Ship-building

"There were few industries in the latter half of the nineteenth century in which Britain was more truly the workshop of the world than in shipbuilding". Here is "a success story".[32] As late as 1900–13, Britain was still building a remarkable 60 per cent of the world's ships.

True, there were relative failings. The most serious was the neglect of research and technical training which bequeathed to the 20th century a workforce ill-equipped to compete with more scientifically trained overseas competitors. Chairs in naval architecture, and/or similar fields, were established at Glasgow, Newcastle and Liverpool between 1880 and 1910.[33] There were advanced technical classes at Sunderland and elsewhere. But after toiling from around 6 a.m. to 5 p.m. young workers were in no fit state to absorb mechanics. The basic schooling they received was often quite inadequate. Despite inducements, some firms on the North-east coast found that only about a fifth of their apprentices went to evening classes. In 1913–14 in Sunderland, 38 per cent of engineering, 12 per cent of shipbuilding, apprentices went to such classes.[34] Trade Unions such as the Boilermakers did not warmly encourage technical education. It must be added that though apprentices were not systematically taught and advanced, yet craft apprenticeships were sufficiently efficient to fuel rising productivity and a successful industry.

Industrial relations were not always good. Masters relied on a combination of paternalism and strong action. Craft unions were often engaged in internecine strife. Dermarcation disputes were commonplace. On the Tyne between 1890 and 1893, there was, on average, a major strike each month resulting from demarcation problems.[35] Some firms took on large numbers of apprentices: Unions fought to restrict such numbers. On the Wear, from 1883–85, marine engineering sections of the Engineers Union were on strike for an astonishing 2½ years over this issue.

Local and national strikes were severe in effect. Strikes occurred in North eastern yards in 1871, on Clydeside in 1877, throughout the country in 1897 and 1907–8.

In 1914, the industry was dominated by family firms, sons following fathers normally served apprenticeships in the yards. There was that emphasis on the practical man which dominated so many aspects of British life. For a variety of reasons, yard layouts were often out-of-date and inefficient by latest standards.

Yet, here was an industry embodying much varied technical skill in which Britain remained internationally dominant. Accumulative adaptations, innovation, change were of marked importance. Again, it needs to be emphasised how complex was the whole story of economic development and how incorrect are some easy generalisations concerning Britain's alleged decline.

The general situation was favourable. World commerce increased more than four-fold in value between 1860 and 1913. British foreign trade more than doubled between 1870 and 1910. Before the First World War about half the seaborne trade of the world was still carried in British ships. World output of merchant ships greatly increased in the 19th century, and while the percentage built in Britain fell, it was still 58 in 1913.

Pre-1914 rearmament helped the yards. Spending on Royal Naval shipbuilding and repair, (most, but far from all, undertaken in naval dockyards), rose from under £9 million in 1898–99 to over £19 million in 1913–14.[36]

Statistics show average annual British shipbuilding output rose from 463,509 tons in 1870–74 to 1,037,094 tons by 1910–13,[37] while from 1892 to 1913, outut rose from 1,109,950 to 1,932,153 tons.[38]

In the early 1900s about a fifth of British output was bought by foreign shipowners. As late as 1913, tonnage built was as follows (thousands of gross tons).[39]

	British tonnage for foreign owners	Total German Tonnage	Total American Tonnage
1913	503	465	276

Thus, fluctuations were great. 1886 output was over 60 per cent down on the 1883 figures. But the general trend was markedly upward. Workers benefited: money earnings of all workers at the Leven Yard in Scotland rose from £1.16 a week in 1871 to £1.94 in 1913.[40]

Change, adaptation and improvement were vast. Steam

replaced sail: in the early 1860s a greater tonnage of sailing than steam ships was still being built. By 1910–13 sailing ships were in a tiny minority of ships constructed. Between 1878 and 1900 steel replaced iron. Ships became larger and more powerful. Clydebank's liners developed from the "Servia" of 1881, 530 feet long, 7,392 tons, to the "Aquitania" of 1913, 902 feet long, 47,000 tons. Engines, for example, were radically improved. A main technological triumph of the age was Parsons's steam turbine which made the "Turbinia" of 1897 the fastest vessel in the world. Technical improvements in construction, steering and so on were considerable. Science was applied: W. Froude showed that experiments with models gave information concerning best shapes and proportions.[41]

Ships were built for specialist purposes. Most prestigious were the great liners, reaching towards perfection with ships such as the famous "Mauritania" of 1907, over 30,000 tons and capable of 25 knots. As cargo vessels grew in size a typical ship just before the First War was of over 7000 tons gross. Specialist ships were built to carry meat, fruit, dairy produce from distant lands. In 1872, on the Tyne was built the first specially designed oil tanker.[42]

By the early 20th century – at least in the larger yards – careful designs, planned construction, tested, standardised components had replaced handed-down, empirical, rule-of-thumb methods. Financial and real capital had increased. Value of machinery at the Clydebank yard of John Brown increased from £131,220 in 1899 to £200,691 in 1910.[43]

By 1912, 6 ship-building firms had capital ranging between 1.7 and 5.2 million pounds.[44] There was much integration. Palmer's of Jarrow developed their own coal and iron mines, blast furnaces and rolling-mills, gas works and colliers, in addition to their ship-yard.

It is true that British yards did not install modern equipment and adapt the latest work methods as rapidly and completely as did some foreign yards. Reasons were strong though not necessarily compelling. Machines and permanent constructions might lie in costly idleness in the recurrent periods of slump. In 1908–9, 20 leading shipbuilding firms were working at only about 40 per cent of capacity.[45]

So, an examination of the British shipbuilding industry's record between 1870 and 1914 leads to some modification of easy generalisations concerning the country's economic performance over these years. Here was, considerably, a new product – steel ships with new, powerful, engines, scientifically planned in large yards with much equipment. This was an old, basic, but it was a much-changed industry.

There were faults: too little advanced training and research, failings in industrial relations, some lessening of competition as only a few firms could build, for example, the largest ships and as integrated combines took over not only shipbuilding yards but also armaments, steel, and related undertakings.

The record of the shipbuilding industry between 1870 and 1914 is one of continuing success.

The vast range of small industries

Later, disadvantages resulting from Britain's too great reliance on a narrow range of basic industries will be examined. This record of achievement must also draw attention to the large number and importance of smaller old and new industries which flourished during the period under review.

Thus, when like other activities, the making of hosiery moved from the home to the mill, factories increased in number from 129 to 227 and employees from 9,700 to 19,500 between 1871 and 1885. Over the same period, lace factories (mostly around Nottingham) increased in number from 223 to 431 and employees from 8,300 to 15,000.[46] Hosiery workers' numbers increased by 56 per cent between 1881 and 1911.

The Birmingham and Black Country area was crowded with small industries producing a large range of products, mainly of metal.[47] In 1871–2 they included: iron tubes, tinned hollow-ware, screws, galvanised buckets, chains, nails, brass goods, frying pans, locks, hinges, combs, washers, copper wire, fenders and fireirons, paraffin lamps, gas fittings, coffin furniture, tools, spades and shovels, anvils, jewellery. As some industries declined, others rose, other employment expanded and the area avoided the 20th century fate of regions such as the North-east which concentrated on a few basic industries. Thus, pig-iron output over the Black Country area fell from 726,000 tons (nearly 11 per cent of British production) in 1871 to 293,000 tons (or just under 4 per cent) in 1887. Coal output fell from 10 million tons in 1871 to 8.7 million tons in 1886. The old domestic nail-making industry still employed around 20,000 in 1876 but only a few hundreds in 1914. But other trades grew – numbers employed in jewellery went up from 14–16,000 in 1886 to about 30,000 in 1914, in the brass trade from around 20,000 in 1886 to nearly 32,000 in 1911. Old industries continued to give employment: 8,600 were still making saddles, harness and whips in Warwicks and Staffs in 1911. But new industries – cycles, cars, electricity – had created a large demand by 1914 for fittings which the area could supply – screws, copper tubes for radiators, electrical fittings and a whole host of parts and accessories.

Finally, it would surely be totally inappropriate to leave Birmingham without a mention of George and Richard Cadbury, who inherited an unimportant business in 1861, set out to meet the needs of the new mass market with such success that by 1900 they were processing a third of Britain's cocoa imports and had provided a model factory estate at Bournville.

In the boot and shoe industry another success story may be found. In the 1870s in an area in which reference to shoemakers appeared in records of 1550, it was said that "Northampton stands and has long stood unrivalled for the manufacture of one of the most useful articles – namely boots and shoes".[48] To the closing years of the 19th century domestic, small-scale industry continued with many out-workers in the villages. As late as 1889 in Raunds, with a population of some 3,000, army boots were being made at 260 places.[49] But foreign competition was growing. American machines were introduced and increasingly, they were to be found massed in the factories. Statistics of recovery became impressive, particularly for the period 1903–4. Exports of 462,840 dozen pairs of boots and shoes in 1875 rose to 1,435,134 dozen by 1914. Export values grew from £1.84 million in 1903 to £4.19 million in 1913, by which year the "Economist" – too optimistically – could praise the 'Victory of British Boots'.[50] Not surprisingly, these advances were hailed by free traders as proof of the stimulus offered by competition.

Indeed, there were signs around 1913 that British industry was responding to the challenge of foreign competition. Thus, while in all of the varied glass industry, imports consistently exceeded exports, values of the latter did rise from an annual average of

£875,000 (1878–79) to £1,688,000 (1910–14). Pilkington's output of plate glass leapt from 5.3 million feet in 1904 to 13.4 million in 1914.[51] New machines boosted the output of bottles.

Even in chemicals and electrical goods – industries in which Germans and Americans took commanding leads – British output was by no means negligible. In 1913, though a long way behind the two leaders, Britain was the world's third most important producer of chemicals. Numbers employed in the whole industry rose from 81,000 in 1881 to 201,000 in 1912. Output is estimated to have risen by nearly a half between 1900 and 1913. Output of sulphuric acid, (so important in industrial processes "that its use has come to serve as a rough index of industrial development")[52] increased by over 80 per cent between 1878 and 1913. Value of chemical exports went up from £8 million in 1880 to £24 million in 1913.[53]

In the related field of soap manufacture, in 1889 William Hesketh Lever began production at Port Sunlight. By 1925, his company had become an international giant. He had benefited from rising standards of living and hygiene of the masses.

As will be later emphasised, Britain lagged badly in the new electrical industries. Yet, by 1903, all except two of towns with over 100,000 people had an electricity supply, which drove the tube trains of London and the trams of major towns and gave light and power to homes and institutions, to an increasing number of factories and shipyards. True, firms in Britain were often off-shoots of American and German leaders (Westinghouse, Thomson-Houston, Siemens). Value of total output of the electrical goods industry was over £14 million by 1907, while by 1913 exports were worth £7.6 million.[54]

It is impossible in a brief survey to do justice to all the many branches of Britain's "industry state". Mention may be made of the jute industry which increased output from £3.1 million in 1870 to £6.5 million in 1890,[55] of the well known activities of the Potteries which since the Industrial Revolution had provided the table-ware for millions of people at home and abroad. In 1911, 52,312 were employed in this Staffordshire industry.[56] Typical of much expansion in the food processing industries was an increase in chocolate and cocoa makers from 7,601 in 1901 to 17,876 in 1911.[57] Output of paper rose from about 290,000 tons in 1880 to some 900,000 tons in 1907.

Compared with agriculture and economic services, industry was a main provider of British employment and income in the early 20th century. The censuses of 1881 and 1901, (England and Wales), show that about 35 per cent of all occupied males in 1881 and 36 per cent in 1901 were engaged in manufacturing, which occupied 3,727,000 in 1901, (though a minority of these were actually marketing products).[58] Professional and commercial employment grew rapidly and domestic employment, (which was huge), slowly. Agriculture declined in importance but remained a major provider of work. However, separate sections on agriculture and services follow.

Continuing achievement

What is now emphasised is the important fact that in 1913 the British macroeconomy (or economy as a whole) was still successful. True, it was not without problems which included a failure to grow and adapt as fast and as successfully as vigorous new competitors. But whereas through the period 1945–79 there were continuous and rising inflation, recurrent balance of payments problems, exchange crises leading to devaluations, most of these problems were completely avoided in the period 1870–1914. Prices fell from 1873 to 1896 and rose from 1896 to 1913, but they were still lower in 1913 than in 1870. Britain was normally in overall balance of payments surplus with vast sums invested overseas. The pound sterling was the 1913 equivalent of the 1979 Swiss franc or German mark.

Emphasis is here placed on two main achievements: total employment climbed very considerably, and the general standard of living rose.

That employement grew is very clear. In 1871, 8,220,000 males and 3,650,000 females were occupied in Britain: corresponding figures for 1911 were 12,927,000 and 5,413,000.[59] In contrast to 1970s experience, there were general increases in numbers engaged in manufacturing: in the metal industries from 915,000 in 1871 to 1,923,000 in 1911, in textiles from 1,310,000 to 1,509,000, in chemicals and related products from 66,000 to 201,000. In prosperous years such as 1913 the economy approached a state of full employment: trade unions making returns showed 2.1 per cent of their numbers out of work, though at the bottom of the slumps of 1879 and 1886 over 10 per cent were without jobs.

Undoubtedly, too, economic growth continued, though it must be emphasised that, compared with the period before 1873, growth slowed. Between 1873 and 1913 Gross Domestic Product of the United Kingdom rose by 1.8% a year. Inclusion of income from abroad pushed up growth of Gross National Product to 1.9% a year. Disposable income of the whole population also rose by 1.9% a year.[60] One calculation is that national income per head at 1913–14 prices rose from £26.84 in 1870 to £51.905 in 1913.[61]

Certainly, just before disaster struck there was still in 1914 much certainty that there had been progress and that it would continue. An economist could write in a mood rarely encountered in 1979: "so optimistic are we that we expect to find visible progress even in the infinitesimal lapse of twelve months. To the observer of today, this is a habitual attitude . . . there is practically no difference of opinion as to what constitutes progress. Improvement in the economic condition of the body of the people is in the forefront of our attention".[62]

5.3 Agriculture

Agriculture, horticulture and forestry found work for 1,769,000 Britons in 1871 and 1,553,000 in 1911.[63] Farm workers in England and Wales numbered 1,232,576 in 1851 and 757,552 in 1911: proportions varied from 394 per 1000 in Huntingdon to 26 in Lancashire and 24 in Co. Durham. The decline in numbers was not due to massive mechanisation, but resulted from the fall in cereal prices and in area under the plough. It has been calculated that agriculture, forestry and fishing provided £130.4 million (14.2 per cent) of the national income of 1870 but £104.6 million (or only 6.4 per cent) of the 1901 income.[64]

As already indicated, a widespread but not universal British system of land ownership was one in which the landlord owned an estate on which he maintained buildings, drains and so on; the tenant-farmer rented and farmed a holding on which, (if it were large enough), he employed farm labourers. Overwhelmingly in Britain these workers were males. In 1872, hoping to prove that land-ownership in Britain was more widely dispersed than was often asserted, Lord Derby had a return made. The resulting

New Domesday Survey of 1873, (as it was called), proved the radicals right, for while it found that over one million persons owned some land in the U.K., "even if it was frequently no larger than a cabbage patch, it also showed that four-fifths of the land . . . was owned by less than 7,000 persons".[65] As often, there were failings in the statistical coverage, but the truth of the general picture is amply vouched for by a mass of other evidence. Around the 1870s, 53 per cent of Rutland, 50 per cent of Northumberland, but only 11 per cent of Cambridge and 4 per cent of Middlesex were occupied by estates of over 10,000 acres.[66] In 1892 the Duke of Bedford owned nearly 23,000 acres of Lincolnshire, 25,000 in Devon and Dorset, 25,000 in Bedford-shire and Buckinghamshire – 73,000 in all. The Duke of Sutherland had 1,300,000 acres but they were largely in the less profitable Highlands.[67]

True, in the years just before 1914, angered by Lloyd George's taxes and aware of falling social worth of, and relative economic returns from, their estates, owners were selling off land – perhaps 800,000 acres in the 5 years to 1914. Still in 1914 only some 11 per cent of agricultural land in England and Wales was occupied by its owners and that figure included home farms of the large landowners.[68]

According to figures from 17 counties, the average 1871 farm was of 152 acres. As often, such averages mean little. More important, an 1885 breakdown of farms covering nearly 28 million acres in England and Wales was:[69]

Size in Acres	No of Holdings in each group	Acreage of holdings in each group	Percent of total acreage
5– 50	200,100	3,888,700	14
51– 100	54,900	4,021,000	14.5
101– 300	67,000	11,519,400	41.6
301– 500	11,800	4,472,300	16.1
501–1000	4,200	2,737,600	9.9
above 1000	573	745,500	2.7

So well over half the holdings were small – under 50 acres – but over 40 per cent of the land was farmed on holdings of 100–300 acres. Not surprisingly farms were larger and employed much more labour in the drier, flatter arable South and East than in the wetter, generally hillier, grasslands of West and North. Ratios of farm workers to farmers were 220 to 100 in the latter but 600 to 100 in the former. Wheat growing in particular was considerably concentrated: 10 leading producing counties provided nearly half the wheat acreage. Indeed, as often, large regional variations in the small British island were important.

In 1846, as the major step in the implementation of her free trade policy, Britain repealed the Corn Laws which protected domestic wheat production and exposed her farmers to the winds of foreign competition. Until about 1875 these were very gentle breezes: distances and high freight costs continued to protect the home farmer. Then, from around 1873 to 1896 the blasts struck and for large sections of the industry, they were quite devastating. A series of bad British summers in the late seventies, came at the same time as the ploughing-up of vast stretches of North American prairie, Argentine pampas and Australian wheat-lands, a great fall in transit costs, refrigeration which enabled meats to come to British tables from the ends of the earth.

British consumers gained: many farmers lost heavily. Such were the outline results of a truly major decision of economic policy which surely merits comment.

In the story of modern national economies, it has been, and is, very rare for countries not to protect, support and cosset their domestic agriculture. From 1846 to the 1930s, (with the significant exception of 1914–18), Britain was odd man out. Industry and industrial workers gained for cheap food came to Britain in truly vast quantities and was consumed by the mass of the people. The industrial employer gained since in the absence of free trade, he would have had to pay more to enable his workers to buy the resultant dearer food. Compared with farmers and farm-workers, the new industrial and commercial classes were numerous and powerful. They had the vote and, increasingly, they created the country's wealth. True, after 1884, farm-workers also had the vote but normally they supported free-trade liberals.

However, it is astonishing that classes and institutions as powerful and influential as the landed aristocracy, Oxford and Cambridge colleges and the Church of England, which still had such great interests in the English countryside of 1870, should have tamely stood by and acquiesced in the economic decline of much of agriculture and the consequent fall in rent income. The continuing triumph of free trade does much to vindicate Keynes's statement:[70] "I am sure that the power of vested interests is vastly exaggerated compared with the gradual encroachment of ideas. . ."

The simple, traditional view that British agriculture was ruined in the 1870s and 80s has been challenged and modified by modern scholars. The well-established line was: "some ten years after the Second Reform Bill,[71] corn prices fell and agricultural depression set in. . ."[72] "British agriculture . . . was thrown overboard in a storm like an unwanted cargo". Further in the 1880s "Agriculture was ruined a second time over".[73]

What were the causes, nature, extent of this depression?

In the 1870s a series of unkind summers culminated in the persistently wet, cold spring and summer of 1879.[74] In these bad summers of the 1870s, crop yields were low. On the edge of Salisbury Plain, the Whitaker's farm had a disastrous 1879 yield of only 633 sacks of wheat from 154 acres.[75] Sheep suffered from liver-rot, caused by parasites which throve on the sodden pastures. 1883 saw a severe outbreak of Foot and Mouth disease. Bible reading farmers may well have been reminded of Job.

Bad summers were not new. What was strange to farmers was the fact that prices did not rise as domestic supplies fell, in accordance with the simplest rules of economics. For now the home was but part of a swelling international output. In 1874, less than half, by 1879 just over three-quarters, of wheat for the British market was imported. It was a vast and rapid change.

From North America, Argentina, India, and Russia, the new steamships carried the grain to Liverpool at rapidly falling freight rates.[76] The charge for carrying a quarter of wheat from Chicago to Liverpool fell from 15s 11d, (80p) in the late 1860s to 3s 11d (20p) in the early 20th century. An index of British tramp shipping rates (1869=100), fell to 46 by 1909.

So, North American prairies and Argentine pampas which had exported 15 million cwt of grain to Britain in 1875, sent almost 60 million by 1900. The average wheat price paid to English farmers fell from 56 shillings a quarter in 1867-71 to 27s 3d in 1894-8. The very bottom came in 1894 with an average of 22s 10d a quarter – the lowest for 150 years. Of course, many farmers did not receive the average pay-out. Records of individual farmers confirm the disastrous effects. The Whitakers' low 1879 harvest was sold at 17s 11½d a sack compared with 24s 11d in 1877.[77] Acres under wheat in England and Wales fell from 3,240,000 in 1875 to 1,384,000 in 1885. Between 1879 and 1887, 1½ million British acres were added to permanent pasture. Counties whose yields were relatively low, or where paying alternatives presented themselves, most thoroughly abandoned wheat. Cambridgeshire, which grew about 33 bushels to the acre lost 34 per cent of its 1875 wheat acreage by 1895. Devonshire, with yields around 20 bushels, lost 65 per cent. Leicestershire, where heavy soil made wheat production costly, switched to beef, Kent to market gardening, fruit and dairying.

Nor were beef and lamb producers spared from competition. In the early 1880s, success of new large-scale refrigeration processes enabled cargoes of frozen mutton to be sent from Australia and New Zealand. The first consignment from the latter country came in 1882; 20 years later New Zealand was exporting 4 million carcases a year. After 1867, McCoy, ("the real McCoy"), began the trade in Texas cattle. By the end of the century the Argentine was a major exporter of frozen and corned beef. Later it will be shown however, that, unlike wheat imports, those of meats, (while they were on a vast scale and lowered prices), did not grievously harm home production, which in fact rose.

Certainly, for farmers who specialised in wheat-growing, losses were very heavy. The value of the gross output of English wheat fell from £28.44 million in 1867–71 to £7.64 million in 1894–8.[78] In perhaps the most depressed county, Huntingdon, one farmer in every 150 went bankrupt in the early 1880s. Many rents fell: those received by King's College, Cambridge, which then owned land in 13 counties, fell by practically 39 per cent between 1878–9 and 1893–4.[79] The greatest reductions came in the arable Eastern counties: on one Suffolk estate rent dropped from over £20,000 in 1872–4 to £11,300 in 1890–2.[80] The predictable result was that capital expenditure on buildings, drains, and so on was reduced. With the switch from arable to grassland, something like a third of agricultural labourers left the land over the depression years.

Joseph Arch's Agricultural Workers' Union, which had recruited perhaps 100,000 members at the top of the boom in 1873, could not muster 23,000 by 1879. There were some bitter struggles over wages in East Anglia in particular.

Certainly Parliament was convinced by the still numerous representatives of the agricultural interest that there was depression: two Royal Commissions – in the early 1880s and mid 1890s – were set up and reported, the Department of Agriculture was created in 1889. Modern researchers have admitted that "Britain's persistence in laissez-faire policies at the price of a devastated agriculture is unique in the history of nations".[81]

Yet, the depression was neither complete nor general. General economic and social conditions were in many respects favourable for home farmers. Each year there were more mouths to feed. Standards of living were rising and there was a switch to foods such as meat favoured by the better-off, (economists say that the income-elasticity of demand for such products is high). In 1880, 34.77 million had a supply of 102 lb of meat per head – home produced 68 lb, imported 34 lb: by 1910 44.85 million had 114 lb per head – home produced 63 lb, imported 51 lb. Total home supply had increased by a fifth. Fresh home produced meat sold at a considerable premium compared with frozen imports. In 1895 foreign mutton was being sold in London at 2d a lb, but best English lamb was fetching up to 11d at Salford.[82]

Live-stock and poultry farmers were, of course, helped by the heavy falls in grain prices and by the vast increase in imports of cheap feeding stuffs, particularly of maize and oil-cakes through Liverpool. Because of price differentials, enterprising farmers could sell their own oats and barley and buy cheaper foreign cereals for stock feed. The still very large brewing industry provided a good market for British barley which fell in price by 29 per cent, compared with the almost 49 per cent for wheat, over the depression years.

Perhaps most important of all, there was no foreign competition for something like a fifth (by value) of the output of Britain's farms. Milk was an obvious example. Prices fell steadily (something like a total 15 per cent in London in the last three decades of the century), but quantities and value of output considerably increased. Since increasing volume of goods had to be pulled through the growing towns by horses, there was a lively demand for hay, the price of which does not seem to have fallen. So, in the mainly grassland, dairying, beef and mutton producing counties north and west of the arable belt there was little sign of economic hardship. Lancashire's milk output went up by well over 40 per cent in the period 1870–1900, and Lord Derby's Lancashire rents climbed by a quarter in the period 1884 to 1904.[83]

Particularly near the great London market, producers turned to products other than cereals – to glasshouses, small fruits and orchards. Specialties such as the vegetables and fruit of Wisbech and the bulbs of Spalding, the numerous market gardens of the vale of Evesham, the strawberries of south Hampshire, became well-known features of particular districts.

After 1896 prices steadily rose and the worst was over; indeed, in the dire inter-war era, farmers looked back on the pre-1914 years as being ones of reasonable prosperity. There had been large changes, for British wheat acres which had stood at 3,630,000 in 1874, had fallen to 1,845,000 in 1900 and climbed slightly to 1,926,000 in 1912. By 1907 the price received per quarter had increased to 36s 11d from the 1894 bottom price of 22s 10d. In the period 1907-14 it was, however, still 40 per cent below its 1871 level. Not surprisingly, permanent pasture, which had taken up 42 per cent of farmland in the early 70s took up 55 per cent in 1914. The area of greatest depression was of course the arable East. Scottish farmers seized the opportunities to rent vacant farms in Hertfordshire, Essex and Suffolk, where hard family labour and a switch to oats and/or dairying brought survival.

Many landowners, as has been proved, lost out. Very many labourers left the land, but this was hardly surprising since, particularly for the young and strong, an expanding industrial afforded better opportunities than an often stagnant rural economy. Railways, the police and the Army recruited many village youngsters. Those who remained on the farms became better off, particularly in the industrial counties where farmers had to pay higher wages if they wished to recruit and keep labour. In 1902 agricultural wages varied from 22s 2d in Durham and 20s 7d in Lancashire to 14s 6d in Oxfordshire. Average English farm wages, which had fallen in the early depression years, moved up by about 1s 8d between 1887-8 and 1900-2. Of around 600,000 farm labourers aged 20 and over in England and Wales in 1886 practically all had an allotment and/or a cottage garden: 93,000 had a field potato plot and over 9,000 the right of grazing a cow on the sides of lanes and by-places.[84]

There was some mechanisation and use of fertilisers. Between 1851 and 1914, farm machinery was vastly improved, particularly by the Americans. Mowing, reaping and binding and threshing machines came into widespread use. The late 1870s saw the introduction of the important, successful, reaper plus binder.[85] Increased use of machinery was one obvious reason for falling numbers of agricultural workers.

But conservatism, lack of finance, small fields, hillsides and wet places meant that on many small, family farms, particularly in the West and North, much of the work was performed by hand in the same ways as it had been for centuries. In the 1880s, Tom Mullins, farm worker, was employed on a 75 acre farm near Leek. "There was little farm machinery used in those days. . . Corn was cut with a short 'badging' hook and hay was cut with the scythe".[86] Little artificial manure was used. Probably a similar story could be told of the many family farms in the West and North.

As before and after this period, it is indeed possible to criticise many farmers for their extreme conservatism and lack of enterprise. A sympathetic Rider Haggard spoke of "The appalling obstinacy of the British farmer".[87] It is extremely relevant that Denmark with no obvious natural advantages, but with far better educational and marketing systems, should have been able to export to this island large quantities of the very products – bacon, butter, eggs, cheese – which British farmers could produce. Indeed, just before the 1914 war, Britain was importing some 35 per cent of eggs consumed, 60 per cent of butter, 80 per cent of cheese and 44 per cent of pig meat. Here was clear evidence of a degree of failure.

Yet, it is strongly repeated that modern research has shown that earlier historians exaggerated the effects of late 19th century depression. Cereal production suffered but output of beef, milk, livestock all increased.

In accordance with principles of international trade economics,

Britain exchanged goods which she could produce at a relative advantage for products such as wheat where foreign producers held the advantage. Thus, scarce productive resources – it was argued – were put to most effective use.

Yet there were many who suffered grievously, through no fault of their own. Many farmers lost much of their livelihood and many labourers lost their jobs. There were the very marked social implications of allowing historic communities in Eastern England to sink into depression and the even more important national implications which emerged when the U-boats laid siege to the United Kingdom in two World Wars and survival much depended on raising home food output.

5.4   Growth of service industries

In Stuart times, William Petty formulated what was later called Petty's Law: "There is much more to be gained by Manufacture than Husbandry, and by Merchandise than Manufacture".[88] In 1881, some 12.6 per cent of Britons gained a living from agriculture, forestry, fishing, 43.5 per cent from manufacturing and mining, 21.3 per cent from trade and transport, 15.4 per cent from domestic and personal service, 5.6 per cent from public and professional services. In 1881, therefore, something like 42 per cent were employed in service industries.

Not that all this was necessarily proof of economic advance and of higher standards of living. For, in 1881, more than one in seven of the working population were in domestic service. For very many girls in particular, here was the only sphere in which employment could be obtained. Numbers engaged in domestic service climbed until 1913 – though it will be shown that as a percentage of total population they fell between 1881 and 1913. This was striking proof of the existence of an abundance of labour in a land of growing numbers which, among other effects, lessened that willingness of entrepreneurs to experiment with and invest in labour-saving machinery which was such a dominant aspect of the 19th century American economy.

In Great Britain, total numbers in domestic and personal services climbed from 230,000 males and 1,678,000 females in 1871 to 456,000 males and 2,127,000 females in 1911. In England

and Wales in 1871 the 1,204,477 domestic servants included 780,000 general servants, 140,836 housekeepers, 93,067 cooks, 110,505 house-maids, 75,491 nurse maids. The 105,745 males included 68,369 indoor general servants, 21,202 grooms and 16,174 coachmen.

It is significant that, whereas between 1851 and 1871 the numbers of domestic servants increased much faster than did population, between 1881 and 1901 domestic servants' numbers increased by 0.41 per cent and population by 1.26 per annum. Between 1901–11 corresponding figures were 0.21 and 1.09 per cent.[89] Among many factors at work was the availability of more attractive economic opportunities.

Here in domestic service, was a main 19th century sphere of employment. In 1862 it was asserted that of more than a million domestic servants "nearly two-thirds come out of the rural labourer's cottage".[90] In important aspects, service had changed over the centuries. As late as Stuart times, it was not uncommon for young people of good family to work for a time in the homes of relations or acquaintances. Through the 19th century, the status of domestic servants fell: girls and boys from poor homes sought work in the homes of the better-off. There were exceptions: the governesses who taught upper-class Victorian children might well be the daughters of impecunious clergymen as were the famous Bronte girls. But these were a small minority.

Much of the vast pool of labour draining into domestic work was from an economic stand-point, sadly unproductive and wasted. The households of the aristocracy had long had large staffs of servants: a magnate such as Earl Fitzwilliam employed at least 80 in the early 19th century.[91] The new plutocrats who joined their ranks, copied – and indeed strove to out-do-them. Punch's fictional Sir Georgius Midas, had seven footmen and was upset when only four stayed up to let him in late one night.[92] In the great houses there was a hierarchy of service through which it was possible to climb to the coveted heights of butler and housekeeper. For example, in 1870, William Lanceley started work in the local squire's beautiful home for £8 a year (all of which he took to his poor mother). He rose to become house steward to a great nobleman.[93] But for the great mass of general maids in middle-class homes with one or two domestic servants there could be no promotion. As early as 1883 middle class complaints concerning difficulties in recruiting good servants were being made.[94]

The important fact remains that in 19th century Britain, as in less developed economies in the 20th century, many of a growing population sought employment in domestic service. It was not a highly productive or well-paid occupation. Increasingly, through the 20th century, as more attractive opportunities presented themselves to workers, and as the rising price of labour prevented all but the very rich from hiring servants, the number of domestic servants in middle-class homes dramatically fell. It was a very considerable economic and social change.

But other service industries grew greatly. Of direct significance to production and to real living standards were developments and improvements in means of communication.

Transport and communications

From 1870 to 1913 the main carrier in Britain was the railways – indeed this was the very peak of the 19th century Railway Age, after the stage-coach and the canals, before the motor vehicle. A railway map of 1872[95] shows the whole country crossed, and main – plus very minor – centres connected by lines. There were over 13,000 miles of track open to 1870 and most of the main arteries of the modern railway system were open. Significant later additions included the difficult line from Settle to Carlisle; much extension in Scotland; the line from Sheffield, Chesterfield and Lincoln into London at Marylebone. Around 1900 came important additions to London's tube system, with electric trains to avoid smoke in the tunnels.

Between 1871 and 1913, mileage of track arose from over 13,000 to over 20,000; million passengers carried from 360 to 1425; million tons of freight from 166 to 561. They are impressive figures. Particularly in the early part of the period under review economic effects of the railway system were still widening and deepening: between 1860 and 1885 the weight of goods and minerals carried increased three-fold. Throughout the decades covered, not only were new lines laid but more and more existing lines were served by doubled tracks. Third class travel became common after the Parliamentary penny-a-mile train of 1844. After 1872 all Midland trains carried third class passengers. By

1883 over 400 trains averaged over 40 m.p.h. over their journeys,[96] not so different from most 20th century experience.

The amount of capital and numbers of workers employed by the railways continued to grow, the former was reckoned at £1,000 million by 1896. The growing rentier, or investing classes found railway shares profitable. By 1865 average dividends were around 4.64 per cent.[97] Contemporary fiction portrayed the wisdom and popularity of purchasing railway shares.[98] Numbers employed by the railways increased from 96,000 in 1871 to 373,000 in 1911.

Indeed it would be difficult to exaggerate the importance of the railways over this period. They created the age of mass travel and a mass market; they carried people, goods, milk, letters; they aided the triumph of a national – and indeed international – money economy and (for good or ill) helped defeat the considerably self-sufficient village economy. Railway companies were among the leading, large, modern corporations, financed by shareholders, staffed by growing numbers in many specialist grades.

The advent of the railways had much diminished the importance, (considerable between around 1770 and 1830) of the British canal system. Yet the latter still had a role to play in the conveyance of heavy, durable goods in the major industrial areas. Thus the Aire and Calder Navigation in the West Riding, the Leeds and Liverpool canal, particularly along its stretch through the Wigan coalfield, and some Midland canals around the Black Country were still much used. Reference must be made to the Manchester Ship Canal, opened in 1883. By 1912–13 Manchester was a major port clearing over a million tons of shipping a year.

In general, railway lines could not – as could streets and roads – lead directly to factories, shops and houses. From 1870 to 1913, horse drawn transport conveyed the millions of tons of freight – and many passengers – from and to the depots and stations. The railways recruited many former country boys to care for and drive the hundreds of horses maintained in the great urban centres. In Lancashire towns, teams pulled the drays piled up with cotton bales over the cobbled streets and the resulting urine and dung attracted flies which then visited the open pastry shops with danger to health. Around 1881, there were perhaps 15,000 London "cabbies",[99] largely owner-drivers, carrying passengers in their horse-drawn conveyances.

Bicycles and trams increased the mobility of millions of ordinary people. But already by 1913 a new form of transport – motor vehicles using the roads – had emerged. Until the creation of County and District Councils in 1888 and 1894, roads were the responsibility of a mass of authorities. Turnpike Trusts, which had maintained and charged for the use of many miles of road through the days of the Industrial Revolution finally disappeared in 1895 – though there were still 854 of them in 1871.[100] Over 5,000 large and small parishes maintained, (or did not maintain), roads. In the 1880s it was still possible to journey along a road with very little sign of traffic. "The road might have been made entirely for their convenience. There was no other vehicle upon it. . ."[101] wrote Flora Thompson. Indeed, it was said of Great North Road usage that it was as local as that of an "ordinary parish highway".[102] How different from that roaring four-lane trunk road which was the A1 in 1979!

The new councils achieved much road improvement. By 1914, there were, outside large towns, 28,000 miles of main roads maintained by County, and 112,000 miles of secondary roads controlled by District, Authorities. Britain had "a larger mileage of dustless roads than in any other country".[103] By 1910, 53,000 private cars and 36,000 motor cycles were on the roads.

1840 had seen the introduction of that very beneficial advance – the Penny Post. In 1875 an International Postal Convention was signed in Berne. As H.G. Wells later put it: "A letter now posted in some obscure village can set out on its journey to the heart of Africa, to South America or to China, without more ado than a trifling charge. By affixing a stamp, it is franked to any part of the world".[104]

From 1870 to 1914, British postal services were extraordinarily efficient. Biographies of contemporaries describe their massive correspondence facilitated by frequent collections and deliveries.[105] Employment in the Post Office was secure and much sought after. In "Lark Rise to Candleford", Laura, (like that book's author), joined the service.[106]

By the middle of the 19th century, many of the new railways were served with electric telegraphs. Away from the lines, in 1870 the Post Office bought out the private telegraph business and by 1885 had introduced the 6d telegram. It was widely used, particularly before the telephone brought an improved method of rapid communication. Telephones began to appear in the 1880s. Again, from 1911 the Post Office gained a monopoly. In 1901, the first wireless message was flashed across the Atlantic on which ocean the "Titanic" disaster of 1912 brought home to millions the fact that ships could now send wireless messages.[107] The modern age had truly arrived.

A great trading nation needed not only internal means of transport but also ports and massive port facilities. From 1880 to 1914, roughly a third of Britain's exports went from Northern and Midland mills and factories down the Mersey while roughly a third of imports came up the Thames. Between 1846 and 1881 nearly 250 acres of docks were constructed at Liverpool. Contemporaries marvelled at the construction of "a vast sea wall as solid and enduring as the Pyramids".[108] The 1908 Port of London Act set up one authority, (an early example of many such 20th century public bodies), to control and administer London's docks. These were but two major examples of improvements around the estuaries and ports of the country, which included much investment in facilities for coal export along the Tyne and the South Wales coast and the early use of concrete on a massive scale to build a breakwater at Aberdeen 1870–3.

In the whole very wide field of transport and communications, numbers employed rose from 654,000 males and 16,000 females in 1871 to 1,571,000 males and 38,000 females in 1911: more than a doubling over a period when total employment increased by roughly a half.[109] As with other increases in service industries, this is some proof that specialisation, the extent of the money economy and standards of living were growing.

Retailing

But for some of the most spectacular developments and changes in services – and indeed in the whole economy – we must turn to retail trading.[110]

In 1870, as in previous centuries, British consumers could purchase goods through four main channels of supply. First, there were the producer-retailers who, to a varying extent, combined all the processes of production and selling – the dairy-farmers who sold milk, plus perhaps, butter and cheese; the bakers who took round their own bread; the butchers who

slaughtered beasts, prepared and sold meat; the legion of
craftsmen who made and sold boots and shoes, carts and harness,
clothes and furniture. Craftsmen were still very numerous in
Britain of 1871. Woodnewton with just under 500 people, had a
wheelwright, carpenter, and coachbuilder, a tailor, two bakers, a
blacksmith, two shoemakers, a butcher and a harness maker.[111]
The tiny rural county of Rutland had, (among other craftsmen)
24 cabinet makers, 8 coopers and turners, 69 wheelwrights, 114
blacksmiths, 34 saddlers, 114 tailors and 183 shoemakers.[112] Each
craft often embodied a historic, lengthy, painstaking process like
that involved in the transformation of hide into leather. While
standards must have varied immensely, there was undoubtedly
much pride in work and anyone doing a bad job had often to live
near his dissatisfied customer and to be a likely subject for local
gossip.

Second, there was the multitudinous and varied army of
itinerant tradesmen, selling bread, fish, fruit, clothes-pegs, dress-
lengths, china and so on. From favoured villages, hard-working
gardeners took vegetables and fruit to neighbouring areas.

Third, in 1870, as in centuries past and as in 1979, in scores of
towns, stalls were set out in market halls or squares or along
appointed streets and customers came from the surrounding area.
At Nottingham, and elsewhere, famous Fairs survived. Northampton had a market-square of some 10,000 square yards. Like
other historic towns, Stamford had had markets for hundreds of
years. Around 1890, a farm labourer with a small-holding, once a
week "walked six miles to Leek market with a basket containing
200 eggs on one arm, and another basket with 12 pounds of
butter in it on the other".[113] Here, then in markets of every sort,
was a large source of supply.

Fourth, in every locality, then as now, were the fixed shops,
overwhelmingly kept in 1870 by proprietors working for themselves and controlling one shop. There were 260 shopkeepers
listed in Northampton, (plus sizable numbers of specialists such
as newsagents), not one seems to have been a "big name" of
national significance. From many shopkeepers, considerable skills
and much labour were required. Frequently, they were open
from around 7 or 8 a.m. to 11 p.m. They blended their own teas,
prepared, weighed and packed many products. There were risks
to the customer: adulteration of food was a common 19th century

practice. But sales depended on the reputation of the shopkeeper and the strength of competition, which was rarely absent. Nationally advertised pre-packed products were almost unknown. In many forms of selling, the historic haggling of the market-place was taken for granted and, indeed, expected.

After 1870 changes which were indeed evident between 1850 and 1870 gathered momentum. As often, however, it is wrong to exaggerate their extent. In England and Wales in 1911 there were no less than 607,300 shop properties of which 172,000 were shops not used as dwellings. Many of the other 420,000 must have resembled that kept by Robert Roberts's mother which was clearly of some economic and social importance in an Edwardian Salford neighbourhood.[114] As late as 1954, small scale retailers, who said Marshall, were "losing ground daily" in 1890, still made 60 per cent of retail sales and controlled over 80 per cent of retail outlets.

Main developments between 1870 and 1913 included:

First, a large expansion of middle-class and mass markets consequent on rising numbers and living standards. Between 1860 and 1900 annual consumption of tea per head went up from 2.7 to 6.1 lbs and of sugar from 34.1 to 87.1 lbs; of meat, bacon and ham, from 101.4 lbs (1870) to 130.6 lbs (1896); of tobacco 1.7 lbs (1870) to 2.1 lbs (1900).[115]

Second, to handle increased imports and increased home production, firms of specialist wholesalers arose. More and more, goods were pre-packaged and advertised.

Third, in the retail field, there was marked growth in numbers, size and market share of Co-operatives, department stores and multiple shops. To these developments we now briefly turn. Not the first, but the best-known of Co-ops was opened in 1844, in Toad (T'owd) Lane, Rochdale. The store was run on simple principles of selling essentials of reasonable quality and distributing the profits to members in the form of dividend on purchases. If a customer had spent £10 at the Co-op and the dividend was 2s in the £1, then the customer received a welcome bonus (divi.) of £1. Particularly in Northern industrial area, Co-ops were very successful. Already in 1863 membership of Co-operative retail societies was around 100,000 and sales some £2.5 million. By 1914, membership was 3,053,000 and retail sales some £88 million. Number of separate Societies grew from around 400 in

1862 to 1,455 in 1903.[116] English and Scottish Co-operative Wholesale Societies supplied the retail outlets with goods produced in their own factories, (the first was opened in 1873), such as soap, biscuits, sweets. Degree of penetration of the total retail market by Co-operatives varied greatly across the country. It was highest in working-class, particularly mining, areas. Barnsley in 1911 had a population of 50,614 and a Co-operative Society with over 34,000 members, though some probably came from outside the town. Sales totalled over £1m: an average £31 per member. At Bishop Auckland in Co. Durham sales averaged £37 per member, at Ferndale in S. Wales no less than £79.[117] On the other hand, rural Herefordshire and Rutland each had only one Society. In rural Scotland they were also scarce. Half Co-op sales in 1913 were in the English North and perhaps as much as four-fifths of them were of food. Dividends were still very good though they had fallen slightly from their highest near the end of the 19th century when they averaged a very useful 2s/8½d (13p) in the pound.

Since Co-ops were directed by elected committees, here was a most valuable exercise in practical economic democracy. It may have been a grievous mistake on the part of the Labour movement in the 20th century that it did not attach sufficient importance to co-operative principles and practice.

Important as the Co-ops were, however, their impact was limited. In the whole country, in 1915, they still handled somewhere around 8 per cent of total, about 11 per cent of food and household stores, sales.[118]

In 1850, though there were some medium-sized drapers, there were no department stores in the modern sense of the term. Over the next 25 years a number of famous names (such as Marshall and Snelgrove) emerged and by 1913 they were a well-known feature of city centres. In 1909, Selfridge started building his Oxford Street Store. Advertising attracted customers to large, warm edifices where the main appeal was made not through price but through quality, display, service, amenities and comfort. By 1915, Department stores were selling around 10 per cent of all clothing and footwear.

Multiple shops also date from the 1850s. W.H. Smith's were early expansionists: they had some 200 bookshops by 1914, when Boots had 560 branches. The small retailer continued to exist in growing numbers. Between 1871 and 1891 butchers further increased in number from nearly 76,000 to nearly 99,000, greengrocers and fruiterers from 29,000 to 41,000 and bakers from 59,000 to 84,000.[119] But by 1915, large scale retailers – Co-ops, department stores, multiples – were handling somewhere around 20 per cent of retail sales. This proportion had grown from only 2 or 3 per cent in 1875. Yet, this very significant expansion still left something like four-fifths of a greatly expanded trade in the hands of independent retailers.

In the period 1870–1913 there was a very large drink trade. Writing in 1936 of this century's early years, Ensor emphasised: "the then monstrous evil of intemperance – how monstrous, it is perhaps difficult for the present generation to realise".[120]

In England and Wales in 1891 there were 78,013 innkeepers, publicans and hotel keepers, 17,606 beersellers, 7,883 wine and spirit merchants, 26,312 brewers and 9,088 maltsters.[121] The 1911 Census of England and Wales recorded 137,880 inn and hotel keepers, publicans, beer-sellers and cider dealers. In the second half of the 19th century, there were already signs of the 20th century victory of the large brewery. The number of brewers in England and Wales declined from 2,470 in 1853 to 1,688 in 1901 though there were still 2,638 victuallers with brewing licences.[122]

By the Edwardian period, enlarged affluent classes could enjoy the amenities of growing numbers of hotels, restaurants and clubs. London had luxurious hotels such as the Savoy, famous cafes and no less than 108 "principal clubs" in 1912.[123] Provincial resorts, the Harrogates and Eastbournes, offered much comfortable hotel accommodation. Highly prized chefs and armies of less-esteemed servants found work.

The professions

With the growth of commerce, state intervention, standard of living, education, there came a large expansion of professional and commercial services. Total employment in professional occupations and their subordinate services rose from 204,000 males and 152,000 females in 1871 to 413,000 males and 383,000 females in 1911. In commercial occupations, 212,000 males and 5,000 females were employed in 1871: 739,000 males and 157,000 females in 1911. It is obvious but important that here were fields of much increased employment of women who, in considerable numbers, found work as nurses, teachers and clerks.

19th century developments within the professions were a significant aspect of the evolution of a modern society. Professions such as the Church, Law, Medicine, had a very long history but in the 19th century the most prestigious of them formed their own self-governing societies, regulated and controlled the entry and conduct of their members. Doctors did so after the Medical Registration Act of 1858. Lawyers, pharmacists, veterinary surgeons, engineers, accountants and others formed associations. Economic and social consequences were considerable. Since in the leading professions, entry qualifications[124] were laid down and incompetence or misconduct might well lead to very serious consequences, standards rose. The best professional men and women took a scientific view on evidence, independent of old class or new economic interests. Of course, very many did not attain to such high standards, but advance owed much to Medical Officers of Health who insisted on sanitary provision, to mining engineers who brought more safety to the pits, scientists who analysed watered or germ-carrying milk, journalists who exposed the evils of the slums, and a great host of others.

In 1911, there were in the "higher professions" 184,000 men and women (only 6 per cent were women). Numbers in particular professions were: Church 53,000; Medicine 36,000; Law 26,000; Engineering 25,000; Writing (including editors and journalists) 15,000; officers in the Forces 14,000; Accounting 11,000 and Science including statisticians, and (perhaps unjustifiably!) economists, 5,000.[125]

Also in 1911, there were 560,000 in the "lower" professions. Many were women, nurses and teachers; by 1901 there were 172,000 women teachers.

There were untrained nurses in hospitals before (and after) 1860, but the story of the modern nursing profession may be said to date from that year which saw the foundation of the Nightingale School at St. Thomas's London. By the end of the century most large voluntary hospitals had training-schools and increasing numbers of trained staff were also moving into the Poor Law Hospitals. However, around 1900 of 63,500 female nurses about 25,000 had been trained, using the term in its widest sense.[126] Recruitment of others had been based on varying criteria. Since as late as 1865–72, some 226 doctors and nursing staff at Newcastle's Fever Hospital caught typhus: "Prior to 1873 it was the usual practice to fill up vacancies on the nursing staff from the list of former female patients after their recovery from typhus".[127] However, by 1893, "Nursing has become to be regarded as a recognised calling for which a special apprenticeship must be served and which should only be followed by those who pass certain examinations".[128]

In 1902, the Midwives Act established a Register and reserved the title of Midwife to a trained, certificated woman. The profession was to be controlled by a Central Midwives Board: proved incompetence meant loss of certificate. Though replacement of "handy women" by trained midwives was slow, by 1913 Local Authorities were taking steps to enforce the provision of the 1902 law under which attendance at childbirth, "habitually and for gain" by an untrained woman was illegal.

The Nurses' Registration Act had to wait till 1919. Future nurses were to be trained and certificated: the first state examinations were held in 1925. The inter-war years heard complaints about "absurd" questions and a "far too high" standard in S.R.N. examinations.[129]

Increasingly, then, people could only enter professions such as nursing, if they were trained and had a certificate. There were losses and gains. The young widow who desperately needed work, kept a spotless home, had nursed her children through illnesses, could not enter nursing in the local hospital which was staffed by young certificated spinsters and by probationers, much of whose time was spent on tasks which the widow could probably have performed more efficiently. On the other hand, there were great gains from the presence of trained professionals instead of the hard-drinking, inefficient women of some (perhaps one-sided), Victorian accounts.

Financial services

Between 1870 and 1913, banking, insurance, financial and specialist trading services expanded with the growth of the economy (in particular of the company sector), of specialisation and exchange with the accompanying need of money, of services, investment and trade.

It was indeed fortunate that such services did expand, for it will be noted that over the whole period 1870–1979, they made a striking contribution to national earnings, particularly in the export field.

At the head of the financial system stood the Bank of England. Founded in the 17th century, it controlled the money supply and (in emergency) attempted to safeguard the whole financial structure. Under the Bank Charter Act of 1844, the Bank was obliged to hold reserves sufficient to cover the note issue. The wording on notes then meant what it said. The Bank would pay gold sovereigns for £5 notes. The main coin of the realm was these gold sovereigns each worth £1. Private banks still issued notes, but after 1844 no new banks of issue could be created: existing banks kept these rights until losing them through amalgamation – the last as late as 1921. Increasingly, the Bank of England had a monopoly in England and Wales of note creation.

Through this prestige and power as lender of last resort, the Governor of the Bank might work to avoid major financial collapses threatening the whole credit system. He did so in 1891 when, following speculation in South America the City firm of Barings was faced with heavy losses. By 1913 the Bank controlled the total money supply through the Cash Ratio, Bank Rate and open market operations. Commercial banks had to keep a ratio, or proportion, of their deposits in the form of cash (or deposits with the Bank of England). Bank Rate was the minimum rate at which the Bank would discount bills of exchange. These were just like post-dated cheques and considerable use had been made of them in the Eighteenth Century and later before the issue of cheques became widespread. A trader bought goods on say, 1st Jan 1860 and paid for them with a bill of exchange for £100 payable on 1st April. If the discount rate were 4 per cent per annum, £100 on 1st April was worth £99 on 1st Jan and specialist houses were developed ready to accept the bill of £99.

Bank Rate affected all rates of interest within the economy. If these rose – so the theory said – savings were stimulated, real investment curtailed, foreigners tempted to move funds to London. If they fell the reverse happened. Britain, along with all major countries, was on the gold standard. The currency was tied to gold. Many feel that this made for monetary stability.

Open Market operations simply meant the buying and selling

of bonds (or shares) by the Bank of England. If the Bank bought a bond then Joe Smith sold it and his bank deposit went up. If the Bank sold bonds, the opposite happened. The Bank could therefore exercise some control over the liquidity of the economy.

During the period under review, the Bank began the practice of raising short-term money for Government by selling Treasury Bills. Again this simply meant that the Bank sold a bill or piece of paper on 1st Jan 1910 for £99 and the buyer (if the discount rate were 4 per cent) realised his £100 on 1st April. Treasury Bills were to play a very important role in Government finance after the Second World War.

By 1870, British banks were widely regarded as being among the safest in the world. In general, those bank failures which had afflicted the British middle classes in the early 19th century, and which were to be a dreaded reality in America in the depression years of the 1930s, were a thing of the past. But the City of Glasgow bank failed in 1878 and the Liberator Building Society in 1892.

In 1875, there were still 252 private banks though the 120 joint-stock enterprises were gaining ground. By 1886 the London and County Bank had 165 branches. In Oundle in the 1870s, there were, for example, two banks: the Midland Banking Co., and the Stamford Spalding and Boston Banking Co.

The banking habit was far more developed in Scotland than in England: by 1875, 418,000 Scots had accounts. But in England, too, numbers of bank deposits grew. Around 1860, almost every farmer had an account, said an Ipswich banker.[130] In Scotland just before the Great War there was a bank office for every 3,880 people: in England and Wales one for every 5,150. With this development of the banking habit went a growth in the use of cheques which replaced the inland bill. However, bills remained very important in world overseas trade.

British banks have often been criticised for not sufficiently associating themselves with, and investing in, home industry. German banks became heavily involved in industry putting in funds and placing their representatives on company boards. Traditionally, British banks preferred safe, short-term investment: the type of loan much favoured is said to have been that to a farmer in the Spring which he could repay in the Autumn.

On the other hand, banks did allow trusted businessmen to run overdrafts which helped with the expansion of enterprises.

The foundation and expansion of many companies, plus the great growth of overseas interests in the late Victorian and Edwardian times, led to an upsurge in numbers and activities of financiers, company promoters, stockbrokers and specialists of many kinds. Some made fortunes, some went bankrupt, some managed to do both. One of the most remarkable careers was that of Ernest Terah Hooley. Born in 1859, son of a Nottinghamshire lace-maker, he made millions in the 1890s through his promotion of cycle manufacturing companies, Dunlops and others. Bankrupted in 1898 he still went on to further promotions, dealings, failures and to prison sentences.[131]

Less flamboyant but more successful were a growing number of specialist financial or investing agents. They turned many industrial enterprises into limited companies, charging say, one per cent of the capital floated. They recommended outlets for the money held by rich people. In 1884, the flourishing London Stock Exchange acquired a large new trading floor. Its membership was over 2,000 in 1877, nearly 5,000 in 1914. By 1913 perhaps something like a million Britons held shares.

Large numbers of brokers and middlemen advised and aided importers, exporters, and traders. Some activities were closed to them: for example the new large retail chains bought directly from producers at home and overseas. But as fast as one avenue closed another opened.

The insurance business was vast: here mention is made of its activities within Britain. Increasingly, risks such as that of fire were covered. By 1913, 147 companies were prepared to give fire cover, though a small proportion of these did most of the work. Far greater was the huge "industrial" insurance. British working people had a grim determination to avoid the disgrace of a pauper funeral for any member of the family, so they paid weekly sums to an insurance collector to provide for a decent burial. The typical industrial assurance policy provided only death benefit. No less than 28.5 million policies were in force in 1900 with a face value of nearly £286 millions.[132]

Life assurance – usually acknowledged to be a useful form of saving – was already on a large scale. In 1913 over 3 million policies were in existence with a value of £836 million.

Selling insurance brought £3–£4 a week to many Prudential and other agents. Here was a new career for energetic and ambitious young men.

There was indeed a large and varied range of service employment. In his monumental survey of London life and labour, begun in the late 1880s, Charles Booth described many occupations. Some examples were:[133] reporters and journalists, (some 2,000 periodicals were published in London alone, 500 of these were daily or weekly publications); clerks in solicitors' and barristers' offices; actors, ballet-dancers, music hall performers, artists' models: cricket professionals; undertakers, ("The proverbial jollity of undertakers' men is not so marked now as formerly"), soldiers, postmen, police, civil-servants, municipal officials.

There was an expanding mass of clerical and similar work. By 1913, imported typewriters plus parts were worth over £550,000. At the 1911 Census there were 477,535 commercial or business clerks, including 117,057 females.

By 1913, then, a very major development in 20th century Britain (as in other similar economies), i.e. the relative growth of service industries and of white-collar occupations, was well under way. Growth had been rapid in the period 1870–1913. Between 1881 and 1901, for example, commercial or business clerks increased from 175,000 to 308,000; bank officials and clerks from 16,000 to 30,000; insurance officials, clerks and agents from 15,000 to 55,000.

5.5   Overseas dimension

It is quite impossible to understand British economy and society over the period 1870–1913 without a consideration of the country's great international role. Britain remained a vast provider of manufactures to, and buyer of food and raw materials from, the rest of the world. She was the world's main banker, overseas investor, insurance agent and shipper. She ruled an Empire which was, (in the main), a vast free-trade area.

Indeed an international economy had emerged in which Britain played the leading role. In 1913, the production of well over £500 million worth of visible exports employed a considerable proportion of the working population. Imports of nearly £660 million added greatly to the range of goods available to, and the standard of living of, a great number of citizens. The obvious gap between imports and exports was then more than filled by earnings from services supplied to overseas customers and from investments made abroad. By 1913 these latter totalled some £4,000 million.

Throughout much of the nineteenth century, Britain, the leading manufacturer, could sell the products of its machines to the rest of the world without undue difficulty. From the 1820s to 1914, the annual rate of growth of British overseas trade was 3.3 per cent. True there was a slowing down in the later years of the century. Imports rose by 2.9 per cent from 1870–90, by 2.6 per cent from 1890 to 1900, by 1.5 per cent 1900–13. Exports climbed by 2.1, 0.7 and 3.3 per cent over the same three periods.[134]

Trade figures show large increases. At current prices, the value of U.K. exports jumped from £196 million to 1870 to £291.2 million in 1900 to £525.3 million in 1913. Imports rose from £258.8 million in 1870 to £459.9 million in 1900 to £659.2 million in 1913.[135]

This trade expansion – it is important to note – came in the booms. In severe slumps there was actual contraction, (it could well be that contraction of exports was a main cause of a slump). Thus imports and exports soared in the booms of 1869–73 and of 1909–13 but fell in the slumps of 1874–79 and 1908.

British net imports absorbed a large slice of other countries' exports: nearly 36 per cent in 1840, still 26 per cent in 1873. The extent to which Britain remained a giant warehouse from which overseas products were distributed to other countries is evident from figures relating to re-exports. These averaged £58.2 million from 1871–5, £104.8 million from 1911–13.[136]

Throughout the period 1870–1913, food stuffs and raw materials made up over 75 per cent of total imports – a healthy situation for a predominantly industrial economy. In 1880–4, total raw material imports averaged £141 million – textile raw materials alone were £84 million, timber £16 million, metals and ores £15 million, and hides £4 million. Raw cotton imports rose from £55.9 million in 1871 to £70.6 million in 1913, raw wool from £18.4 million to £35.6 million, timber from £12.3 million to £33.8 million and hides, skins and furs from £6.1 million to £15.1 million.

Main foods imports rose very significantly: grain and flour from £42.7 million in 1871 to £80.9 million in 1913, meats and animals from £10.4 million to £56.7 million, butter and margarine from £6.9 million to £28.0 million and sugar from £18.2 million to £23.1 million.

To pay for growing imports, Britain exported manufactured goods among which textiles remained of vast importance. Of total U.K. annual average exports of £234 million in 1880–4, textiles made up no less than £108 million (cotton goods alone being valued at £76 million). Other main exports (1880–4) were: coal, iron, and steel £38 million; hardware, cutlery and machinery £15 million, clothing £105 million, chemicals and salt £6.2 million.[137]

In 1911–13 just over half the manufactured goods exported were still textiles, one eighth were ironmongery (including bicycles), 8.8 per cent machinery and 3 per cent chemicals. A large range of products made up the total.

While the Empire was of considerable and growing importance to Britain's trade, it is important to note that most of that trade was with non-Empire foreign countries. Just as in the 1970s, foreigners voluntarily came to buy goods in some London stores because these goods were relatively cheap and of good quality so the overwhelming reason why Britain sold goods to the rest of the world in the 19th century was that these goods were cheaper and/or better than those of competitors. Until 1870 competitors were indeed few.

In 1870–1913, as in 1979, much of Britain's trade was with Europe. In 1909–13, 40 per cent of imports came from and 38 per cent of exports went to that continent. America took 24 per cent, Africa 10.1 per cent, Asia 22.3 per cent and Australia 8.8 per cent of exports. America sent 32 per cent, Africa 6.4 per cent, Asia 12.4 per cent and Australia 8.1 per cent of imports.[138]

From 1880–4, Empire countries took just over a third of British exports. In 1904 they bought £112 million and foreign countries £185 million of British goods. In 1907 corresponding figures were £138 million and £288 million.[139]

In the years leading to 1913, as competition stiffened, particularly in Europe and America, the Empire took large and growing proportions of vital exports: by 1913 about half of exported iron and steel, 44 per cent of textiles, 67 per cent of motor vehicles, 58 per cent of railway carriages and the same proportion of hardware and cutlery went to the Empire.[140]

In the century up to 1913, Britain invested heavily in, and British citizens emigrated in large numbers to, overseas countries. Emigration has already received some attention, a note follows on overseas investment.

No country before or since has invested overseas such a high proportion of its national savings as did Britain in the decades before 1914. Total overseas investment reached some £1,300 million by 1885 and over £4.00 million by 1913, D. C. M. Platt considered these figures unreliable and too high, so proposed downward revision. Totals remained very large. e.g. D. C. M. Platt, "British portfolio investment overseas before 1870. Some doubts", *Economic History Review*, Feb. 1980 (equal very roughly to £80-£90,000 million in 1979). Between 1870 and 1914 about a third of total savings went overseas and by 1913 overseas assets made up around a third of the total wealth owned by Britons at home and abroad.[141]

Clearly, here is an economic phenomenon of significance. Britain lost and gained. Under different economic arrangements these vast sums could have been channelled into infrastructure in the many areas such as the North-east and Scotland which badly needed more houses and amenities, or into the newer industries such as vehicles, chemicals, electrical goods to which it was important that Britain should turn. As it was, British money went to build railways, telegraph lines, and so on in India, S. America and other countries.

It went overseas because in general the returns were higher. Over a wide range of shares, the yield on home investment (1870-1914) was 4.60% on overseas 5.72%. Sometimes the gap was wider, U.S. and Latin American railways shares yielded over 8%, U.K. 4.33%.[142]

So investors opted for overseas ventures because, on average, they offered higher returns. Britain as a whole gained since the railways which she financed opened up prairies and pampas which supplied her with food and Indian plains which provided markets for her cotton goods. The inflow of dividends and interest enabled Britain to import more visible goods than she exported and so raise general living standards.

Perhaps more serious than the leakage of savings was that of talent – arguably always the scarcest economic resource. Able young Scots – John Buchan's brother among them – rose through Scotland's educational system and went out to India. So, later, did Humphrey Trevelyan with a Cambridge First and that success in fifteen three-hour examination papers required of applicants for the Indian Civil Service.[143]

For in the 19th century there was a vast outflow of British effort, of emigrants, explorers, geographers, geologists, archeologists, traders, engineers, soldiers, administrators, teachers, missionaries and others. They went for varied reasons, they included the good and the bad, but they left long-lived monuments in many parts of the World.

Economically, the Empire was more important to Britain in 1913 than it had been in 1870. Britain gained from her possession of an Empire. Indian State, and other railways bought British equipment. India did not protect her infant cotton industry against Lancashire as an independent country would have done.

On the other hand, dependent countries gained from stimulation of trade with Britain. In Northern Nigeria, cotton-growing was encouraged to the benefit of both Nigerians and British.[144]

Worthy of note is the verdict of a leading West Indian economist: "The British colonial empire has been exploited less than any other empire in history; for close on a century there were no preferential restrictions on trade, no tribute levied, and very little by way of a caste system in economic life. Peace was established, corruption diminished, justice administered fairly and foreign trade advanced, and public services created and extended. Where this Empire failed, economically, was in its devotion to laissez-faire. . ."[145]

Of course, laissez-faire was the dominant philosophy which was held to have brought success to Britain's own domestic economy, so it is not surprising that it was applied to her Empire. It is merely added here that, with effects, serious efforts were made to bring Western education to dependencies. Among a welter of criticism of the Memsahibs in India it is conceded that some brought education to Indian girls.[146] In the much-altered climate of opinion after 1945, over the few remaining years of Empire, colonial welfare, agriculture, education and economic development were assisted. Often, this worth-while work continued after independence.

5.6 Disconcerting evidence

"Your iron industry is dead, dead as mutton; your coal industries are languishing. Your silk industry is dead, assassinated by the foreigner. Your woollen industry is gasping, struggling. Your cotton industry is seriously sick."[147]

In 1884, in such terms did Randolph Churchill assess his country's economic prospects. Of course he exaggerated, as politicians are known to do, but over the period 1870–1914, major developments did cause difficulties and concern. The mid-Victorian bright day of clear leadership, confidence and success was much clouded over by 1913.

From 1873 to the mid 1890s, there was a downswing in the long Kondratieff cycle with falling prices, difficulties in selling and falling profits. Superimposed on the long downward curve were severe fluctuations in the shorter, Juglar, cycle, with resulting heavy depression and unemployment around the bottom of the slumps. These trends affected the major industrialised countries: in 1876, 210 of Germany's 435 blast furnaces were idle.[148] In all main countries except Britain the strident demands for protection were answered. Tariffs added to the difficulties of exporters. Chauvinistic movements for economic nationalism were sadly strengthened.

Rates of growth of output, income and productivity slowed down over the period 1870–1913. Annual G.D.P. growth, which had been 2.2 per cent from 1856–73 fell to 1.8 per cent between 1873–1913, while, over the same periods, growth of disposable income fell from 2.5 to 1.9 per cent.[149] Real wages per man-year grew by only 1.1 per cent a year during the period 1873–1913 and this improvement was confined to the last quarter of the 19th century. Here was an important economic cause of the marked social tensions of the pre-1914 years.

Total factor productivity (output per unit of input), rose by only 0.6 per cent per year between 1873–1913 (compared for example, with 2.4 per cent between 1951 and 1973).[150]

The many and varied explanations of the late 19th century slow-down, or climacteric, will receive further attention. One persuasive analysis points to the diminution in the rate of growth of that application of steam and steel which transformed the mid-19th century world economy.[151] The conservatism of British workers, and inadequacies of entrepreneurs who succeeded to the positions held by fathers who had pioneered successful ventures, have received much notice. The social structure made it very difficult for bright children of poor parents to rise in those days before late 20th century yielders of corporate powers were much recruited from the meritocracy.

Less stressed have been the facts that income from overseas investment and receipts from coal exports enabled Britain to increase imports without increasing manufacturing exports to the same extent (an interesting parallel here to the situation brought about by North Sea oil sales in the 1970s and 80s).

Not all evidence pointed one way, but some major industries witnessed falls in productivity. Thus, for a variety of reasons, output in tons per man-year in the coal-mines fell from 319 (1879–85) to 257 (1908–13).[152]

Added to deep-seated problems of maturity was the obvious, disturbing fact that recently dominant Britain was meeting increasingly successful competition. Indeed a leading modern authority takes as a major debating point: "Why did industrial leadership pass in the closing decades of the 19th century from Britain to Germany?"[153]

There were symptoms of relative decline. The output of one well-established basic industry – iron and steel – fell sadly behind that of competitors. In 1870 Britain produced half the pig-iron and over 40 per cent of the steel known to have been produced in the world. By 1913, she produced a 6th of the pig-iron, just over a tenth of the steel. The following figures[154] clearly reveal absolute expansion but relative decline:

Steel Production 000 tons

	Britain	*Germany*	*France*	*Belgium*	*U.S.A.*
1870	220	130	80	–	40
1913	7,600	17,320	4,610	2,430	31,300

In large spheres of new scientific and technological breakthrough, in chemicals, electrical goods, vehicles, Britain often lagged far behind the United States and Germany. The German dyestuffs industry was four times the size of the British in the 1880s and 20 to 30 times as large by 1913, when (with serious consequences when war came) Britain was importing nine-tenths of her dyestuffs. Britain's production of sulphuric acid, was a millions tons against Germany's 550,000 in 1900, but 1,100,000 compared with Germany's 1,700,000 in 1913.

In the 1870s Britain was a major producer of alkali or soda, (in large domestic and industrial use for washing and bleaching), by what was known as the Leblanc process. In 1863 a Belgian, Solvay, began to produce soda by an improved process which was soon widely adopted. But here was a clear case of the difficulties arising from being early in the industrial field. Britain had a large investment in existing plants so did not massively switch to the new process. Her Leblanc industry was slowly forced out of production.

As already indicated, Britain lagged in electrical and vehicle industries. By 1900 imports of electrical goods were running at £1,266,000 a year while German and American firms were established in Britain. Britain's 1913 vehicle production was a mere fraction of American, and was less than French, output.

Clearly, Germany was catching up fast as a trader, as the following figures reveal:[155]

	Britain's Foreign Trade		Germany's Foreign Trade £m	
	1890	1913	1890	1913
Imports	356	659	208	537
Exports	264	525	166	505
Re-exports	65	110		

What was particularly disturbing was that by 1913, Germany was considerably outpacing Britain in exports of manufactured goods to other industrialised countries while Britain's lead was to be found in countries which belonged to the formal or "informal" Empire. German goods were cheaper, they were sold with vigour, they were often the product of new industries.

Contemporaries were worried. As early as 1867, French technical superiority in certain blast-furnace processes was accepted "as a reflection of the state of British industry".[156] Around the end of the 19th century alarms concerning growing German and American competition were sounded in books such as Williams's "Made in Germany" and McKenzie's "American Invaders". A very large literature described Germany's advances and successes and Britain's relative failings. It is important to recall that the domestic markets of American and German industrialists were heavily protected.

Again it must be stressed that here is a complex story. In 1913 Britain was still the leading trader, shipbuilder, provider of sea transport, financial services, overseas investment. British influence was still immense in 1913. In Argentina (not, of course, in the Empire), British investment totalled nearly £358 million. Four-fifths of the railways were British owned. In 1913 British exports to Argentina of £21 m easily overtopped German exports of under £12 m. Overwhelmingly, Australia, New Zealand, India bought from Britain. Britain's merchant fleet totalled 12.12 million tons, that of Germany, (largely insured by Lloyds of London) was of 3.15 million tons. (Incredibly, British insurers insisted that they would have to pay if German merchant ships were sunk in war by the British navy.)

Leading industrial states traded much with each other. In 1907, Britain exported to Germany £3,075,000 worth of fully or partly manufactured iron and steel and imported from Germany £4,942,000 worth. Germany was not as efficient at producing fine cotton yarns as was Lancashire. British shipbuilding was still very efficient.

Debate as to whether Britain's entrepreneurs failed over the decades before 1913 has been continued with vigour.[157] Reasonably, it has been pointed out that a developed industrial state such as Britain might be expected to turn from basic industries to services. What went wrong, was not what British businessmen did, but came as a result of the First War. However, decline in the rate of growth of total factor productivity must have been considerably the fault of entrepreneurs who decided how factors of production were to be used.

In short, Britain lost her Victorian leadership. What went wrong? First, while there were clear gains, there were also disadvantages arising from Britain's early industrial start. True, Britain inherited much equipment and many skills. But, for example, a Sheffield steel works might be squeezed in between the river and the gas works and it would be impossible to enlarge it. Compared with American giants, British railway wagons were small. Foundries, gas works, machines, processes, might be relatively inefficient compared with those of competitors installing equipment embracing the latest technology. Vast investment in the gas works meant Britain had far less inducement than had newly industrialised countries to invest in electrical supply.

The second and subsequent generations of industrial leaders often lacked the drive of the first pioneers. Some turned to politics or to other prestigious – or pleasant – pursuits. There was a continuing desire among the successful rich to buy country estates and to join the country aristocracy. Modernising societies should recruit for top posts those best qualified by brains and ability irrespective of class background. Though this is not true of all industries, certainly in steel the vast majority of top men had fathers who were in Social Class I.[158]

Particularly in the period here under discussion, Britain manifestly failed to do this. True, it was possible to rise from humble origins to power and/or wealth, but, overwhelmingly, entrants to Oxbridge, officers of the Armed Forces, members of leading professions, directors of large companies were recruited from top classes. Careful research has revealed that between 1875 and 1925, well over 80 per cent of leaders of the steel industries had fathers who were in Social Class 1. True, a trickle of manual workers continued to reach high positions in steel, and true too in hosiery where production units were generally smaller, successful leaders were not so commonly recruited from the top class.[158]

In state provision of mass elementary schooling and of advanced scientific and technical education, Germany was far, far ahead of Britain. Failings here were more particularly serious since new industries such as chemicals and electrical goods were science based. Again, there is argument. One authority considers that English enterprises in this period were not very seriously hampered by lack of scientific skills;[159] more commonly, writers stress the large German lead, pointing out, for example, that most late-Victorian academic scientists in Britain had studied in Germany or had been much affected by developments in German science. Certainly, by 1913, Germany was still producing far more scientists and technologists than was Britain.

In a society in which conservatism was very strong, much of British management was conservative. There was a natural reluctance to scrap equipment still giving good service in favour of new machines with possible advantages – and problems. There was a marked preference for the practical man who had learned on the shop-floor over the product of an academic or technical institution. Workers who left to improve their knowledge might well find it difficult to get back into their trades. Employers often seemed unwilling to offer improved wages for further output, (true, they might be bound by elaborate, negotiated pay agreements). Too many seemed convinced their workers were born to a certain station in life and an existing standard of living which could not be radically altered.

Workers often strongly opposed innovation. Bessemer developed a type-setting machine which could be worked by women but male workers successfully opposed it. True, as a result of pressure from the union for much reduction of the long working day, gasworks management embarked on a successful programme of modernisation after about 1889.[160] But in other industries developments were not so happy. In boot and shoe production, the industry's "Shoe and Leather Record" considered in 1892 that: "It is no use to mince words. . . The unions are engaged in a gigantic conspiracy to hinder and retard the development of labour-saving appliances". The Webbs confirmed that in the same industry "disputes are endless".[161]

Indeed, criticisms of British workers' conservatism were too general to be ignored. However, though the defenders of management have made out a strong case, it seems difficult to acquit entrepreneurs charged with responsibility for much slower economic growth since the slow-down in the rate of growth of total factor productivity must have been considerably due to their failings.

6. SOCIETY

6.1 The family

With immense strengths and crippling faults, the family was the most important, the basic, institution of Victorian Britain. Before the growth of state social services, family and kin provided for aid-demanding young, sick, unemployed, old. Social cohesion, respectability and decency were much preserved in what could be very hard times. Popular culture, religion and literature – plus Victorian middle-class blindness to some dark realities – strengthened the family. "Honour thy father and thy mother" was the Commandment heard by millions each week in Church and Sunday school. Even the "Edwardian slum child . . . felt an attachment to family life, that a later age may find hard to understand".[1]

Privacy sought, and "keep out" notices erected, by the typical British family remained marked national characteristics well into the 20th century. A survey of working-class wives in the 1930s noted difficulties in bringing community provision to women so determined to keep to themselves. "In England, side by side with the passionate wish to preserve the integrity of the family, there is found the determination to keep it as a whole as *separate* as possible from other families and from outside intrusion".[2]

This led to the well-known preference for a house rather than a flat; to surrounding walls, hedges, railings; to effective curtaining of rooms. Years later a Russian visitor emphasised that: "Britain is definitely the kingdom of private lives. . ."[3]

Certainly the pre-1914 family inculcated respectability and order. "Very many families even in our 'low district' remained awesomely respectable over a lifetime. Despite poverty and appalling surroundings parents brought up their children to be decent, kindly and honourable. . ."[4] Unrelenting morality which emphasised the sinfulness of sex outside marriage, might be enforced. A famous Victorian painting. (The Outcast, 1851),[5] portrayed a father sternly ordering through the open door his "fallen" daughter with her infant. The English illegitimacy rate fell from over 6 per cent of births in the 1840s to around 4 per cent by 1900, (it climbed to above 7 per cent in the swinging 1960s). Though a high proportion of them were conceived before marriage, the overwhelmingly majority of babies were born to married parents. It was well for them that they were, since as late as 1924, 23 per 1000 of illegitimate infants died on their first day and 61 in their first month, contrasted with just under 10 and 33 of legitimate offspring over the same time spans. "These facts seem to presage evil", was an official comment.

As in previous and later periods, the great majority in 1870–1914 married at some stage of their lives. True, Victorians were concerned by the problem of "superfluous" or "redundant" women. Numbers of single women aged 15–45 rose from 2.76 million in 1851 to 3.33 million in 1871, with a rise in the surplus of single women over single men from 72 to 125 thousands.[6] But, of 1,000 girls, unmarried at 15 in 1910–12 the statistical probability was that 818 would marry before they were 50. Early marriage was far less common than it became later in the 20th century. In 1901, 173 per 1000 men and 272 per 1000 women aged 20–24 were married, compared with 334 men and 584 women in 1966. Many men for example in domestic service or in the Services, found it difficult to marry. Women in the Civil Service and teaching normally resigned on marriage. As already noted, emigration, overseas service, higher death rates among boys, added to the surplus of single women. In England and Wales, proportions of unmarried, married, widowed in 1000 females in stated age groups were;[7] (See Table 4)

So most women did marry, though a significant minority remained single while a high proportion (30 per cent) were widowed by the time they were 55–56.

The pressure on women to marry was very great. Commentators were apt to compare unmarried Victorian women with men who had failed in business. In the early 20th century, marriage was still far and away the most important trade open to women.

Table 4 *Marital condition, Females, England and Wales 1871, 1901*

Age	Condition	Number per 1000	
		1871	*1901*
20–25	Unmarried	652	726
	Married	343	272
	Widowed	30	17
55–65	Unmarried	109	117
	Married	589	569
	Widowed	302	314

"Marriage, with its accompaniments and consequences – the ordering of a man's house, the bearing of his children – has by the long consent of ages, been established as practically the only means whereby women with honesty and honour, shall earn her daily bread".[8] In Kilvert's day, a couple "living in concubinage" provided scope for unrestrained rural gossip.[9]

We can never know what proportion of marriages were reasonably happy. Perhaps "men and women do not really like each other very much".[10] When Cicely Hamilton encountered a former friend who had given up professional work on marriage she was told "a story I can only call foul – of insult, brutality and degradation".[11] Some men had a jaundiced view of marriage. "He was, I should say, much happier in his married life than people generally are", wrote Samuel Butler of his hero Ernest.[12]

However, unpleasant or downright horrible marriage might be, people usually endured it. Divorce was still very uncommon. Before 1857, a special Act of Parliament was needed for each divorce. Then the Marriage and Divorce Act allowed a man to divorce his wife for adultery but a petitioning wife had also to prove another wrong such as cruelty. By the 1860s there were some 150 divorces a year and by the 1890s some 600. In Scotland, in the early years of the 20th century only 180 marriages a year ended in divorce or nullity. Normally, women faced great social and economic difficulties if they left their husbands. Very popular novelists, such as Mrs. Henry Wood in "East Lynne", uttered the direst of warnings. Of Lady Isobel she wrote: "Never had she experienced a moment's calm or peace, or happiness, since the fatal night of quitting her home. Oh reader, believe me. . . Whatever trials may be the lot of your married life, resolve to bear them, fall down upon your knees and pray to be enabled to bear them.-. . ."[13]

It must be added that there is considerable evidence of happy homes. Right at the top, the Gladstones were happily married. Other autobiographies echo the feelings of Marjory Allen: "I was singularly fortunate in my parents. Their loving partnership of nearly sixty years with hardly a day apart created for us, their children, a background of deep security and abiding affection."[14]

Certainly there were prostitution, pornography, vice, but one reasonable view is that: "The religion-ruled Englishmen then dominant in the governing, directing, professional, and business classes spent, there can be little doubt, far less of their time and thought on sex interests than either continental contemporaries or their twentieth-century succesors; and to this saving their extraordinary surplus of energy in other spheres must reasonably be in part subscribed".[15] Many men did devote their shortened lives to work and family:

> "Staid Englishman, who toil and slave
> From your first childhood to your grave,
> And seldom spend and always save –
> And do your duty all your life
> By your young family and wife".[16]

Some rebelled against this orthodoxy. Riveting modern research[17] tells the story of Sir Edmund Backhouse, descended from frugal Quaker bankers, bankrupted after accumulating alleged debts of £23,000 at Oxford, who went off to China where he became a scholar and recluse and engaged in very dubious business transactions.

6.2   Children

It is difficult to generalise about the treatment of children in later 19th century and Edwardian families. Certainly, cruelty and violence were not absent. In the midst of his generally happy portrayals, Kilvert tells of shocking alleged incidents: of a man kicking his wife to death, of a widower cruelly beating his neglected children, of the whippings of a girl for lying and stealing.[18] There was no mention then of taking abused children in care! In his very different city slum, Roberts recalled with horror "the regular and often brutal assaults on some children perpetrated in the name of discipline. . ."[19]

Yet, as so often, the evidence is contradictory. From his London experiences, Charles Booth concluded that working class children were "more likely to suffer from spoiling than from harshness".[20] One scholar was convinced that: "The strictness of Edwardian parents did not, however, necessarily imply abundant physical punishment. . . It is not true that families in which children were given a 'good hiding for the least thing' were common. The truth is that they did not need to, because their authority was rarely openly challenged".[21]

Whatever may have been the situation in homes, it is certain that there was very much caning in the preparatory and public schools to which the sons of the wealthy were sent. Highly literate old boys such as Churchill, Orwell, and others described the beatings that occurred. Nor were the children of the poor spared. In one classroom of a Manchester elementary school, we are told that in 1914, 20 to 30 boys were caned each day at 4 p.m.[22] Not all schools were like this. Marjory Allen went to Bedales in 1910, was free and happy with much choice of her own studies and activities.[23]

For the vast majority childhood was indeed short. In 1900 many English children still left their elementary schools at 12. Even before the end of their short school careers, many children, and their parents, were glad of the coppers derived from part-time work which was not always outside school hours.

Of course, there were none of the television sets in front of which children in 1980 sat viewing for an average of over 3 hours a day. So in the former age, children provided their own amusements to a much greater extent. For some, especially if they came from fortunate (not necessarily rich) homes, and lived in or near to rural areas, childhood might be an extremely happy time. Boys in particular could roam or cycle along lanes still free from motor traffic and flanked by masses of wild flowers, climb trees, gather nuts or mushrooms, snowball. Everywhere, a host of games survived, each with its inherited season – conkers, whips and tops, battledore and shuttlecock. Girls had their skipping with traditional chants, their group games and dances. On village greens and in city streets these survived. In "Lark Rise": "beneath the long summer sunsets, the girls would gather on one of the green open spaces . . . and bow and curtsy and sweep to and fro . . . as they went through the game movements and sang the game rhymes as their mothers and grandmothers had done before them".[24] In vastly different Salford: "children came together at some accepted place . . . and quite spontaneously a performance would begin". To songs the girls and boys formed circles and lines and acted out their games which "gave young Edwardians pleasure unalloyed".[25]

There were, (as there still are) many homes where books were practically unknown and where a child might be told to stop reading and get on with something useful. Yet a growing number of children could read and had access to books in schools, fortunate homes, and public libraries, provision of which was another Victorian advance. Like lonely young Philip in "Of Human Bondage", such children "formed the most delightful habit in the world, the habit of reading".[26] They could dip into an increasingly well-stocked treasure house: "Treasure Island" (1883), "Kidnapped", (1886), "King Solomon's Mines", (1885) and a host of other classics.

Before 1914 the famous Greyfriars stories of Frank Richards were already popular. Roberts considered that: "In the final estimate it may be found that Frank Richards during the first quarter of the 20th century had more influence on the mind and influence of young working-class England than any other single person. . ."[27]

In the early years of this 20th century there was much expansion of organised youth movements. One writer[28] links this development firmly with the growth of imperialist and nationalist sentiment in those years, though there were surely other reasons why the churches, for example, should attempt to provide healthy activities for deprived youth in great cities, while the Scouts were an international, not merely national, movement. By 1913, in Birmingham, some 11,000 boys and girls were involved in youth movements and clubs: in Manchester by 1917, some 20,000 boys and nearly 9,000 girls were involved; (there was a

massive increase in boys' involvement over the war years). For
example, the Boy Scout movement spread to Birmingham in 1908
and Scout numbers there rose from 500 in 1909, to nearly 3000 in
1913. Baden-Powell always asserted that he wanted to make good
citizens not soldiers.[29]

Adult activities described on other pages of this work were
shared by children. For many, Sunday worship – one or two
Church services and a Sunday school – remained the norm. Some
looked back with warm memories of "the warmth and enthus-
iasm" of Chapel gatherings and the afternoon addresses with the
boys on the left hand side and the girls on the right.[30] A
Yorkshire boy had to go, dressed up, to Sunday worship and
considered his "greatest privilege was an unself-conscious famil-
iarly with the Bible",[31] with its history and literature.

Playing and/or watching organised games was a leisure activity
which continued to grow in importance between 1870 and 1914.
More children managed to escape with their parents from the
industrial towns and on holidays and day-trips. By 1914, cinemas
were well-established and in Croydon, Malcolm Muggeridge
began going to the cinema around 1914: "On Saturday afternoons
one could get in for threepence"[32] (just over 1p).

In the late 20th century, some old people looked back with
happy nostalgia to their pre-1914 youth. A.A. Thomson remembered the huge meals, the cheap sweets, taking his father's
sovereigns to the bank, watching farmers, shoemakers, blacksmiths at work.[33] From Yorkshire too, J.B. Priestley recalled "a
confused but rich blur of hospitality and conviviality. . ."[34]

Alas, very many were not so fortunate. In Priestley's Bradford,
as in other industrial areas, early school medical examinations
revealed the clearest evidence of massive deprivation, filth and
incidence of ailments. In the inter-war period this was still so and
all authorities agreed that conditions were worse before 1914.

Girls, in particular the eldest girl in a large family, had a hard
time. They were expected to give much help with the never
ending housework, while in some homes there was a tradition
that if food were short, husband and boys had more than wife
and girls. As is made absolutely clear on other pages, there was
much dire poverty and photographs of slum children show
unkempt, under-nourished, ill-clad youngsters.[35]

6.3   Women

In 18th century Britain, as in many ages and lands, women were very important in the economy, working on farms and in domestic industry with husbands and other members of the family. They did not normally enjoy separate payment for such work, hours might be very long and conditions difficult, but families worked together at hours much fixed by themselves and benefited from extra earnings. One authoritive verdict is that: "the Industrial Revolution has on the whole proved beneficial to women", since: "for the majority of workers the factory meant higher wages, better food and clothing and an improved standard of living. This was especially so in the case of women".[36]

Yet, in 1851, of over 2.8 million women in employment, 635,000 were in textiles, 1,135,000 in domestic service and laundry work.[37] Another large source of work for 19th century women was dressmaking, for practically all Victorian girls learned needlework. By 1863, in London alone, some 17,500 girls were employed by dressmakers and milliners. In many dressmaking shops, daughters of tradesmen, farmers, artisans paid a premium and after some years of unpaid apprenticeship became "improvers" and "hands". Conditions varied but were often disgracefully bad with very long hours in cramped, unhealthy work-places followed by rest in crowded, stuffy bedrooms.

After the tragic death of a girl in 1863, the "Times" published a dressmaker's letter describing the incident and "Punch" issued a hard-hitting cartoon showing a rich girl in a flowing dress looking into a mirror in which she sees, not her own reflection but that of the poor dead dressmaker. As late as 1908, girls preparing dresses for Ascot worked from 8 a.m. one day to 4 p.m. the next, while in the 1920s a woman invited to a house for a long day's sewing was given a good lunch and 9d (4p).[37a]

But simpler 20th century fashions, factories and Factory Acts, Trade Boards, abolished the worst of the 19th century sweating of needlewomen.

By 1870–1914 most farm-workers in Britain, (a sharp contrast to the situation in many countries), were male. The dreadful agricultural gang system for women in the Eastern counties was gradually and mainly killed off. Many welcomed what to them seemed improvement. A witness told a Royal Commission in 1867 that "with the spread of education and general improvement the labouring class are beginning to see that the woman's place is by her own hearth".[38]

But the strangulation of cottage industry did mean much diminution of family work and income in areas such as East Anglia. Girls went into domestic work: married women stayed at home, helping on the farms at busy periods such as harvest. To most middle class women, Victorian society denied paid careers. By 1853, a woman diarist, born in 1787, was writing "A lady, to be such, must be a mere lady and nothing else. She must not work for profit, or engage in any occupation that money can command. . ."[39] Indeed, cultured, middle-class Victorians devised a model of the perfect lady. She was brought up to be sexually ignorant, innocent.[40] She did not enjoy sex, but only accepted it as an accompaniment of marriage to please her husband. She stayed at home, engaged in womanly activities such as sewing. She provided a managed, restful home for husband and family.

Tennyson, that poet of his age, summed up in "The Princess".[41]

> "Man for the field and woman for the hearth:
> Man for the sword and for the needle she;
> Man with the head and woman with the heart:
> Man to command and woman to obey;
> All else confusion".

True, like the economic models of academics, this sociological model constructed by Victorian writers could only be accommodated to reality through much adjustment. Women did go out to work, with consequent economic and social gain, though, in 1911, only 10.3% of all urban married women were at work. But in cotton towns such as Blackburn nearly half married women and widows worked. "It'ud give me the bloomin' 'ump", said one woman of staying at home.[42] However, a modern writer notes the long 19th and early 20th century conservative persistence of the view that women should not work outside the home. By contrast, the number of married women in German industry almost doubled between 1895–1907.[43]

Most certainly, many women did not "suffer and be still". Cockney women costermongers, wives in mining and industrial areas who took and managed their husbands' wages and handed him back his "spends", could not be accused of humble submissiveness. 19th century women could achieve learning and fame as the Brontes, George Eliot, Florence Nightingale, Beatrice Webb and others showed. In fields quite approved by male-dominated society they carried through very much endeavour. Thus, of their philanthropic work, a modern scholar wrote: "The energy was awesome; the scale impressive, and the sustained sympathy with the derelict and the down-and-out inspiring".[44] By the 1890s, one calculation had it that half a million women were voluntary workers for, and 20,000 paid officials of, charitable societies.

It is again emphasised that in Victorian Britain views conflicted. Not all men supported the existing system. A famous statement of women's case was in J.S. Mill's "Subjection of Women", 1869. Mill described and denounced existing inequalities and called for equality between the sexes.

For when every exception and qualification has been made, the basic fact remains that women in 19th century Britain suffered from legal, educational, family, civic and employment disadvantages. Partly, but most certainly not entirely, disadvantages were removed by 1914 and much progress was made.

The greatest 18th century legal authority, Blackstone, was very clear: "By marriage the . . . legal existence of woman is suspended . . . incorporated and consolidated into that of her husband", which was popularly rendered as "husband and wife are one and that is he". Important breaches in this male legal domination were the following. In the 1830s, the unfortunate Caroline Norton, separated after an unhappy marriage, was not even allowed to see her own children. An Act of 1839 allowed the Lord Chancellor to arrange for custody of the children of separated parents. Usually, an innocent mother had care until they were seven (though in the 1870s Annie Besant lost custody of her child because of what were then considered her immoral views on birth control).

An Act of 1857 allowed somewhat easier divorce, though not until 1923 could women, like men, obtain divorce for simple adultery. It is repeated that divorce was still very rare.

Important was the Married Women's Property Act of 1870, amended and strengthened in 1882. Now married women could keep separate income and property. Previously, these had legally passed to the husband, (though through trusts rich fathers could settle property on their daughters on marriage).

One controversial field of discriminating action lay in the control of venereal diseases. There were many prostitutes in Victorian England, the police said there were over 24,000 in 1869. Among servicemen in particular, V.D. rates were very high, so the authorities enacted the Contagious Diseases Bill of 1864. In Portsmouth, Aldershot and other naval or army centres, special police could inform on women alleged to be prostitutes. The latter had to submit to medical examination. In 1866 and 1869 further towns were scheduled and women there brought within the Act's operation.

Immense controversy resulted. Over 900 public meetings, more than 17,000 petitions carrying over 2½ million signatures were organised between 1870 and 1885 by opponents of the Acts. Supporters were active too. Mrs. Josephine Butler and James Stansfield, (a cabinet minister who for years threw away hopes of high office to further this unpopular cause),[45] headed the campaign against the Acts which were repealed in 1886. Here was a victory for the women's cause since, as Mrs. Butler put it: "it is injust to punish the sex who are the victims of a vice, and leave unpunished the sex who are the main cause".[46]

Advances in the spheres of family limitation, education, employment and civic participation are described in the relevant sections which follow. They were important but limited. For example, able, middle-class women were admitted to Universities. But at Cambridge those with "certificates of degrees", (they were not admitted to full degrees until well into the 20th century), mainly went into teaching. In the main, other professions and business posts were not open to them.[47] The most publicised failure was that to win the Parliamentary vote before 1918.

Victorian girls were counselled not to go unaccompanied to meet men and certainly for a middle-class girl, a chaperone was considered essential. But modern attitudes were spreading. At a Fabian Summer School in 1908 Beatrice Webb noted, with refreshing trust, that: "The young folk live the most unconventional life . . . stealing out on moor and sand, in stable and under hayricks, without always the requisite chaperone to make it look as wholly innocent as it really is. Then the gym costume which they all affect is startling the Methodist Wales, and the conversation is most surprisingly open. 'Is dancing sexual?' I found three pretty Cambridge girl graduates discussing with half-a-dozen men".[48]

More importantly, women were repeatedly told that marriage was their goal and men were superior. Thus, in "Captain Desmond V.C.", "this great and popular romance", Honor Meredith, General's daughter on India's North-west frontier, falls in love with Captain Desmond. "She knew that, for all her passionate intensity of heart and spirit, this man, whom she had won, surpassed her in both; that in all things he rose above her – and would always rise. And because she was very woman at the core, such knowledge gladdened her beyond telling. . ."[49]

6.4 Births and deaths

For most brides of 1870 pregnancy very soon followed the wedding. An 1874 study of the upper and professional classes revealed that in 42,479 of 51,582 marriages, the first child was born within the first year.[50]

Per 1000 population, the England and Wales birth-rate reached its highest recorded level in 1876 at 36.3. It then fell steadily to an average 27.2 in 1901–10.

Here is one of the most important of all changes in British society after 1870. For the whole family, but particularly for the mother, consequences of a change from around six children per family in 1870 to two children in 1930 were immense. In more detail, legitimate live births per 1000 married women aged 15–44 fell from an annual average of 292.5 over the 3 years 1870–2 to 197.4 in 1910–12. Births were less because married women had fewer children, once their families had reached the desired size they stopped having children.

All classes shared in the fall in fertility. Families of couples marrying in the 1880s were smaller than families of those marrying in the 1850s by the following percentages: professionals and higher administrators down by 33 per cent; skilled, semi-skilled and unskilled workers down by 21, 20, 15 per cent respectively, miners down by 10 per cent.[51] Decline in average family size in upper social groups was particularly marked:

	Completed fertility per 100 wives[52]	
Date of marriage	Class I	Class II
1851–61	625	700
1881–86	422	493

Why the fall in family size? Causation is complex. There was more knowledge of birth-control. In 1826 Richard Carlisle described sponge, sheath, withdrawal. Knowlton in 1832 added to this knowledge,[53] while Dr. Drysdale's 1855 book went through many editions. Prosecution of Bradlaugh and Mrs. Besant in 1877 for re-publishing a birth control pamphlet gave much publicity to the subject. But since as late as the 1930s withdrawal was the main method of birth-control and since this method had been known for centuries, we must seek additional reasons for family limitation after 1870.

All over the world, urban have fewer children than rural dwellers. Particularly to country people, children were economic assets: they worked on the land. Slowly, (and up to the early 20th century some children could start work at 12), working-class parents found they had to keep their offspring at school. Upper class parents had the large expense of sending boys to boarding schools.

So economic considerations were important. It is very relevant that after 1873 the mid-Victorian boom ended with repeated slumps, bankruptcies, unemployment, uncertainty. Many felt the pressures of modern society, of "keeping up with the Jones's". Already by 1875, an article could be published on "Life at High Pressure".[54]

Attitudes changed and as top groups had less children others learned from the always important "demonstration effect"!

By 1888 Beatrice Potter was commenting on Benjamin Jones, manager of the C.W.S. on £400 a year. They had four children and "have taken measures to prevent others from coming, and advise others to do so". Birth control, Beatrice added, "is coming to the fore. I see it practised by men and women who are perfectly pure".[55] There is much evidence that main pioneers of birth control belonged to middle class professional groups to whom modern society offered a structured career and who planned their careers and their families.

Women's lib was not a powerful 19th century movement but it is impossible to ignore the dominating fact that it is women who have children. Childbirth could be an agonising and dangerous experience.[56] Active women with interests were not anxious to spend some 12 years of their lives in pregnancy and breast-feeding. Means to limit births became more readily available: thus by the end of the 19th century, Rendell pessaries were 2s, (10p), a dozen.

Sadly, some used dangerous means of family limitation, eating a plaster containing lead oxide, (which could be openly bought), in order to procure abortion.[57] Back-street abortionists plied a trade dangerous to their clients and to themselves for, if caught, they were liable to lengthy imprisonment.

So, after 1877, the birth-rate began that heavy and – with temporary interruptions – sustained fall over the next century.

Mortality

Families became smaller, but their members lived longer. There is some connection between these two developments, for as more children survived it was no longer necessary to have so many to achieve desired family size.

A high proportion of babies born between 1870 and 1914 never saw their first birthday. The infant mortality rate was 153 in England and Wales in the decade 1891–1900. In the early years of this century, began that dramatic fall which was perhaps the greatest life-saving achievement of the age. The rate was 128 from 1901–10 and 105 by 1914.

The general death rate in England and Wales fell from 22.5 per 1000 in 1861–70 to 13.8 in 1913. Very much hardship and grief was thus avoided. In 1872, Kilvert visited "a young pretty woman dying I fear of consumption".[58] Slowly, over ensuing decades, that dread disease had to loosen its grip.

Health improved and death-rates fell because families were smaller,[59] standards of living rose, education improved as did health and environmental services. More sanitation, water, soap meant less germs, lice, disease. Increasingly those with infectious diseases were isolated. Anaesthetics, antiseptic surgery and other medical improvements saved many lives. Kilvert, aged 38, died of peritonitis in 1879, thirty years later an operation might well have saved his life. In 1871, he had visited a dentist who had shown him "the apparatus for giving people the new anaesthetic laughing gas".[60] In previous ages, the removal of a decayed tooth was a frightening experience.[61]

In modern Britain, as in similar societies, on average women live appreciably longer than men.[62] This does not seem to have been the case in pre-industrial Britain nor was it the case in a less developed country such as India in the 1950s. By 1880 it was clear that women were benefiting slightly more than men from lifesaving trends: life expectancy at birth was 41.35 for males, 44.62 for females. The largest falls in death rates between 1838–54 and 1876–80 were in the female age-group 10–19. In mid-Victorian England about half of the women aged 15–35 who died were slaughtered by tuberculosis. Falls in death-rates from that disease much accounted for improvement. Industrialisation and higher living standards did enable women to find work, pay, better food.

It is a complex story, but death-rates show that the stress and strain of modern societies have killed off men at earlier ages than women.

6.5 Work

In 1911, 93.5 per cent of males aged 15 and over and 35.3 per cent of females of the same age group were at work.[63] Over the period 1871 to 1911 the occupation distribution of the labour force changed as follows.[64]

It is possible to allocate the 18.3 million at work in 1911 to the following occupational groups. (Numbers in thousands),[65]

Higher professional	184	Foremen, inspectors,	
Lower professional	560	supervisors	236
Employers and proprietors	1,232	Skilled manual	5,608
Managers and administrators	629	Semi-skilled manual	7,244
Clerical workers	887	Unskilled manual	1,767

Table 5 *Great Britain Labour Force 1871 and 1911. (000s.)*

	1871		1911	
	Males	*Females*	*Males*	*Females*
Public Administration	106	7	271	50
Armed Forces	124	–	221	1
Professional occupations and their subordinate services	204	152	413	383
Domestic and personal service	230	1,678	456	2,127
Commercial occupations	212	5	739	157
Transport and communications	654	16	1,571	38
of which railways	96	–	370	3
roads	229	3	600	3
sea, canals, docks	191	1	292	1
Agriculture, horticulture, forestry	1,634	135	1,436	117
fishing	47	1	53	–
Mining, quarrying and workers in products of mines and quarries	517	11	1,202	8
Metal manufacture, Machines, implements, vehicles, precious metal	869	46	1,795	128
Building and construction	712	4	1,140	5
Wood, furniture, fittings and decorations	186	26	287	35
Bricks, cement, pottery, glass	97	25	145	42
Chemicals, oil, soap, resin etc.	61	5	155	46
Skins, leather, hair, feathers	68	10	90	32
Paper, printing, books, stationery	94	31	253	144
Textiles	584	726	639	870
Clothing	390	594	432	825
Food, drink, tobacco	448	78	806	308
Gas, water, electricity supply	18	–	86	–
All others occupied	972	106	741	98
Total occupied	8,220	3,650	12,927	5,413

So, omitting all clerical workers and all foremen, practically
80 per cent of the work force were then manual workers who
could be placed in the working classes. Not that contemporaries,
inside or outside the working class regarded that class as being
homogeneous. A favourite division at the time was that between
the "respectable" working class and the rest. Marked economic
distinctions, particularly that between the "labour aristocracy"
and other workers also received attention. There was a minority
of "aristocrats" but many "plebeians".[66] Dudley Baxter had only
830,000 out of 7,800,000 earning 28/s or more a week. However,
in the craft industries, the aristocrats remained a sizeable
minority; nearly 30 per cent in bespoke tailoring and approaching
40 per cent of hatters were getting 40/s or more in 1906. The
great metal industries provided the skilled with relatively high
rates of pay. At the wage census of 1906, proportions of male
workers earning 40/s or more in the skilled industries were:

Iron and steel manufacture	26.8	Various metal industries	20
Engineering, boilermaking	21.2	Shipbuilding	31.6
Shipbuilding	22		

On the other hand, in cotton in the early 20th century, 40 per
cent of workers earned 25/s or less, while in linen and jute over
two-thirds were earning less than 25/s.

By 1870, in large scale inspected and/or unionised industry in
Britain, the worst of the abuses of early industrialisation, often
inherited from centuries of domestic work, had disappeared. A
combination of higher productivity, benevolence; common sense
which recognised that exhausted could not produce as much as
fit, workers; inspection and trade union pressure, had abolished
child labour in textile mills, female and child employment down
coal mines, excessively long hours in a number of industries. In a
small Brattan ironworks in 1871 men worked a week of 56 hours
– 5 days of 10 hours (6 to 5.30 with breaks from 8.30 to 9.15
and 1.15 to 2), plus 6.30 to 1.15 on Saturday.[67] Such hours seem
to have been typical of many engineering works and textile mills
over the final decades of the 19th century. In the 1870s, Disraeli's
Government passed a Factory Act granting a 56½ hour week for
cotton workers. After a North-east strike of 1872, engineers
won a 9 hour day and some builders followed their lead. Iron-

works, gas plants, coal mines very often operated on a shift system and 3 × 8 hours became common. Gas Plants switched from 2 × 12 hours at various dates in the 19th century, particularly in the 1880s. Nationally, coal mines gained an eight hour day in 1909.[68] In Edwardian Middlesborough's iron works: "The working day is now divided into three 'shifts' of eight hours each." But every third week men worked a long 16 hour shift so that a change over might be accomplished.[69]

But very many workers still worked far longer hours. While a summary is made difficult by the immense range of conditions, the following facts emerge from very many. While women had ceased to work underground in coal mines they still laboured on the surface at heavy manual toil. Thus we know of the Wigan Pit brow girls in the 1880s who "with their great rakes guide and sort the coal" amid the "whirling blackness" of the dust.[70] Very many children no longer entered the Northern mills but they were still employed in cottage industries. In lace-making in Buckinghamshire, Bedfordshire, Northants and Devon, (with over 30,000 female workers in 1851), in straw-plaiting in South Bedfordshire (over 20,000 females employed in 1871), in glove making in Somerset and Devon, many young girls were employed. To earn reasonable sums, long hours must have been necessary since in 1864, 3s/6d or 3s/9d (around 18p) was the price paid for 12 pairs of gloves and three workers could make 6 pairs a day.[71]

These were cottage family industries where conditions must have varied enormously. This is equally true of the many rural crafts, which though in decline, still survived in the Britain of 1870–1913. In small Rutland numbers of some male craftsmen were:[72]

	1871	1911
Millers	43	22
Brickmakers	37	15
Sawyers	37	10
Cabinet makers	24	10
Coopers and tanners	8	2
Wheelwrights	69	42
Blacksmiths	114	83
Saddlers	34	24
Tailors	114	63
Shoemakers	183	138

In Northamptonshire, many households and firms were engaged in footwear production: nearly 200 in the town of Northampton alone.[73]

In those very large occupations – agriculture, retailing, domestic service, long hours were very common. Thus, shop-hours were still terribly long. The Roberts' family shop "like its competitors around, opened at 7 a.m. and closed an hour before midnight".[74] In the early years of this century a store even in that well-managed chain – Sainsbury's – would be open till 9.15 on Tuesday, Wednesday, Thursday, 10.45 on Friday, midnight on Saturday. Only on slack Monday afternoons might staff expect some hours off.[75] In 1912 some improvement came with a Shops Act which stipulated a weekly half-holiday for assistants. In the large drink, catering and hotel trades, excessive hours were equally common.

Concerning the vast army of those in service it is impossible to generalise since conditions varied enormously. Some paternalistic employers treated servants well and retained their services over a lifetime. As one example among many, of the Jebb family in Shropshire: "The gardener . . . had worked at the Lyth for sixty years, his son for fifty-two. The coachman and the carpenter both put in forty-two years. Arthur Jebb's nurse Ruth, had refused to retire after thirty-eight years".[76] In large establishments there was a graduated career for life, with food which might be "of the best and no stint".[77] Lady Curzon, (who may have been hard to please), found her considerable staff of English servants tyrannical and inefficient.[78] Servants of a rich bachelor much away from home or cloistered spinster of poor appetite must have had an easy time.

On the other hand, servants could be treated literally worse than animals. Eglantyne Jebb, (who was to found the Save the Children Fund), "never forgot how a neighbouring magnate brought piped water to his dog kennels, yet would not bring the pipes a short distance further for his cottages".[79]

Sole servants working for large lower middle class families might have an awful life. Thus, towards the end of the 19th century, Catherine Cookson's mother went to work with a Tyneside family with four sons, had to do all the housework, very heavy washing and ironing, and was paid half-a-crown (12½p) a week.[80]

A very ugly face of capitalism was to be found in the "sweated" trades and in occupations – particularly in the docks – which still relied on casual labour. In sweated East End tailoring, Beatrice Potter found that some machinists could earn good wages – up to 7s or even 9s/6d a day – but there was a lower end to the trade with poor wages and very long hours – from 8 or 8.30 a.m. to 10 or 11 p.m. Some of the harshest conditions were to be found among piece-workers of the Black Country. Particularly infamous were conditions among chain-makers around Cradley Heath. Women were still engaged in very heavy manual labour including health-damaging use of a great hammer – the "Oliver". Nail-making was a dreadfully sweated manual trade. Much child labour was employed on piece-work – for example – in the making of safety-pins, where a child could earn a penny a day "bending safety pins" i.e. bending the tin clasp around the pins.

Since work on ships in port came in varying temporary bursts, and since main ports such as London and Liverpool attracted a large surplus of unskilled labour, some but by no means all dock workers were recruited on a casual basis.[81] Each morning, hundreds scrambled forward in degrading scenes. Some decades were to pass before casual labour ceased in the docks.

Much industrial work was dangerous. 1900 saw 79,020 accidents with 1045 deaths in factories and workshops. In the pre 1914 decade, over a thousand miners a year were killed. Some workers worked on dangerous processes and/or handled harmful products – lead, paint, grindstones, electricity and so on.

Some of the above-mentioned evils were removed by action taken by employers, trade unions, government, following exposure, in a politically free society, by reformers, journalists, inspectors, workers. Mechanisation meant the disappearance of many bad old trades; the 10,000 women nailers of 1851 were down to only 1700 by the early 20th century, though there were still 2100 hand chain-makers. Improvements resulting from government intervention are examined in a later section. It must be stressed, however, that progress was very varied. Thus, up to 1911, it was the custom of the Post Office to dismiss each year some 5000 boy messengers who had entered that "dead-end job". More enlightened policies were adopted and the boys' services retained.

In 1870–1913, working conditions of very many were far better than they had been in 1800–43 but far harder than they were to become in 1945–80. Very heavy manual work remained. We catch fascinating glimpses of a largely vanished world of Britain's great basic industries, as in the following is a description of a morning on the Tyne in 1913:[82] "There were still three hours of winter darkness when the men of the day shift got up . . . still unshaven, they let themselves out of the little brick terrace houses . . . and hurried downhill guided by the widely spaced gas lamps. . . The pubs were legally permitted to open at six o'clock, five minutes before the works' gates were finally locked shut. The offerings were simple; . . . . Neatly arranged along the length of the bar were thick cups of strong tea and coffee and nips of rum or whisky. At the risk of scalded lips and throats there was just time for both, the debt being chalked up. . . ."

Yet, hard though the work might be in yards, pits or foundries it is possible that the mothers of large families, working at home, had the hardest time of all. The following description is of the day of one who married in the 1880s. She had nine sons and two daughters: the sons – at the age of 12 or 13 – followed their father down the Durham pit.[83]

The day began at 3 a.m. when the eldest son had breakfast before going on shift at 4 a.m. Another son's shift started at 6. No sooner had he gone to work than father would come in from night work. By the time he had eaten and bathed in a tin bath in front of the fire, three children had to be got off to school. Another son returned from work about 11 a.m. Children came in for their mid-day meal from school. Three more sons went on shift at 2 p.m. The son who started work at 4 returned after two. Children came back from school. Father went on shift at 10 p.m., then three sons who had started work at 2 p.m. came home needing food and baths.

On top of all this there was much washing of clothes and baking of bread, (it was then quite customary in Northern mining villages for women to bake their own bread). It was always after midnight when they all got off to bed. The alarm clock rang again at 3 a.m., though it was not always necessary for the mother to get up to see the 4 a.m. shift worker off to work. No wonder it was said of the family that: "In all the struggles of their lives, the hardest burden fell upon their mother. . ."[84]

6.6 Rich and poor

Incredibly, when on leave in 1886 from India, the father of William Beveridge thought: " 'Poverty in Calcutta bears a much less dread aspect than it does in London or Edinburgh. . . There are no gin palaces . . . and not so much terrible squalor' ".[85] While, in fact, the great majority of Britons were far, far better off than the great majority of Indians, there remained much dreadful poverty in late 19th and early 20th century Britain. It seemed all the more inexcusable because it persisted in one of the richest of countries in which a minority enjoyed enormous wealth and incomes making possible lives of ostentatious luxury, enriched by the bounties of technological advance.

Yet Britons did become better off between 1870 and 1914. Statisticians agree on a substantial rise in real living standards in the second half of the 19th century. Real wages of those in full work rose from 100 in 1850 to 183 in 1900. Allowing for unemployment the rise was from 96 in 1850 to 177 in 1900. There was an improvement of not less than 50 and probably nearly 80, per cent in the workers' living standards, between 1850 and 1900.[86]

This improvement did not continue through 1900–14. Prices which had fallen heavily from 1873 to 1896, (down from 122 to 83, with 1850 = 100), rose and wages lagged. By the end of 1912, London real wages were not quite back to 1900 levels. One reason for serious labour troubles is clear.

One determinant of labour's inability to maintain improvement was the falling share of employment income in the national dividend, in spite of a large growth in numbers of salary earners. Percentages of national income going to factors[87] were:

	Wages and salaries	Rent	Profit, interest and mixed income
1880–89	48.2	14.0	37.9
1890–99	49.8	12.0	38.2
1905–14	47.2	10.8	42.0

By 1970s standards these are astonishing figures. In that later period, over 70 per cent of national income went to wages and salaries.

Yet, between 1880 and 1914 improvements were marked. In 1880 12.3 million wage-earners received an average £37.8. In 1913 15.2 million wage earners were paid an average £50.7. Intermediate incomes of those receiving under £160 a year, who were not wage-earners, were paid to 1.85 million in 1880, to 4.31 million in 1913. On average they received £70.3 in the former and £84.7 in the latter year. The well-off, those assessed to income tax, with incomes above £160, numbered 620,000 in 1880, 1,190,000 in 1913. They received an average £854.8 in 1880, £865.5 in 1913.

It is very relevant to add that in 1913, 1,190,000 with incomes over £160 received £1,030 million while 15,200,000 wage earners were paid £770 million.[88]

Authoritative contemporary investigations detail continuing, heavy, inequalities between 1870 and 1914.

Already in 1868, Dudley Baxter had made an apt comparison between the pyramidal peak of Teneriffe rising from the Atlantic and the distribution of income in a wealthy state much as Britain "with its long low base of labouring population, with its uplands of the middle classes, and with the towering peaks and summits of those with princely incomes".[89] He calculated that in England and Wales, income distribution was as follows:

Upper and middle classes	Number of income receivers	Total income £
1. Large incomes (1) £500 plus	7,500	111,104,000
(2) £1000–£5000	42,000	69,440,000
2. Middle incomes £300–£1000	150,000	72,912,000
3. Small incomes (1) £100–£300	850,500	93,744,000
(3) under £100	1,003,000	60,000,000
	2,053,000	£407,200,000
Manual labour class	7,785,000	£254,729,000

In Scotland 272,000 of the upper and middle classes received £42,516,000 while 1,122,000 manual workers took £31,747,000. It is very clear, therefore, that there was great inequality, since in England and Wales, 7,500 at the top received well over 40 per cent of the total amount earned by nearly 8 million at the bottom.

Gross inequality persisted. A 1905 calculation by L.C. Money allotted just over a third of national income to 1¼ million of "the rich", around one seventh to 3¼ million of the comfortable, while 38 million of "the poor" had to make do with little more than half.[90] The distribution of wealth was much more uneven. Money wrote that, in an average year, 27,500 persons died worth £257 million while 686,500 died worth only £29 million. A more modern calculation is that in 1911–13, the top 1 per cent of people aged over 25 owned nearly 70 per cent of national capital.[91] While exact statistics in these fields are notoriously difficult to calculate, the general impression created by the above is correct.

Land, commerce and finance, manufacturing, provided a growing list of the very wealthy, their fortunes scarcely reduced by light taxation. Between 1880 and 1914 there died 282 landowners, 218 commercial men, 161 manufacturers who were millionaires or half millionaires.[92] Land remained of great importance, but a cosmopolitan set of international financiers such as Sir Ernest Cassel, (friend and financial adviser to Edward VII), joined bankers, brewers, newspaper magnates, manufacturers and South African tycoons among the ranks of the immensely rich. Julius Wernher and Alred Beit, died in 1912 and 1906 leaving £14 million and £8 million respectively – fortunes acquired in S. Africa.[93]

True, with economic expansion, numbers in the better off groups were rising, but the gap between the well-off and the poor was very great. Failure to drastically reduce this gap destroyed the 19th century Liberal and opened the way for the Labour Party. Two contemporary views of London graphically illustrate the divide.

On the one hand an able young Scot, on his way to the top, found: "a true city of pleasure, every window box gay with flowers, her streets full of splendid equipages, the Park a show ground for fine horses and handsome men and women."[94]

Yet in the East End of that same city, Jack London in 1902, described dreadful slums, sweated trades, the horrors of fighting, drunken, women. Along the walk of a tiny garden he noted "a mass of miserable and distorted humanity . . . a welter of rags and filth". Among statistics given, of 81,951 Londoners who died in 1884, 9,909 died in workhouses.[95]

Certainly, a minority lived in quite disgusting degradation, while many other decent, hard-working people endured a never-ending struggle to live on low incomes and to make ends meet.

"The bastard of a harlot, born in a brothel, suckled on gin, and familiar from earliest infancy with all the bestialities of debauch, violated before she is twleve and driven out into the streets by her mother a year or two later, what chance is there for such a girl in this world – I say nothing of the next?"[96]

Victorian reformers did not mince their words. In such powerful sentences did General Booth of the Salvation Army call attention to the plight of the "submerged tenth", that is the three million English men, women and children who lived in disgusting poverty.

London's vice, in particular the recruitment for prostitution of young girls, was exposed in a famous 1885 series of articles, entitled "The maiden tribute of Modern Babylon" by W.T. Stead. Parliament enacted that a girl under 16 could not lawfully give consent to sexual relations. (This act was still in force in 1979).

On a vastly greater scale were the important researches of Charles Booth. Perhaps the most significant aspect of his great work lay in the fact that here for the first time, was a careful, scientific social survey of a great city. Booth found that many of the working class lived in comfort and decency. Even in the East End 65 per cent were "in comfort rising to affluence", but this left 35 per cent in "poverty, sinking into want". Many read with incredulous shock that in the rich capital of a vast Empire 30 per cent of the people were living in poverty.

Booth's findings received corroboration when in a 1899–1900 survey of York, where Rowntree showed that nearly 10 per cent of York's people were living in "primary" and nearly 18 per cent in "secondary" poverty. So Rowntree's 28 per cent of poor was nearly equal to Booth's 30 per cent.

Much varied information confirmed the widespread survival of poverty. One of the aims of Toynbee Hall, a University Settlement in London's East End, founded by Canon Barnett of St. Jude's Whitechapel and a group of Oxford men, was "to inquire into the conditions of the poor and to consider and advance plans calculated to promote their welfare." Royal Commissions on Labour, Housing and the Poor Laws dredged deep pools of enquiry. So did reformers such as Mrs. Besant, (who championed the match girls) and the Webbs. Crusading journalists exposed evils: novelists and playwrights challenged institutions and provoked thought. Government appointed Commissions to enquire and make recommendations. So disturbed was official opinion by revelations concerning the nation's health when high proportions of recruits were rejected by medical boards, 1899–1902, that a high powered Committee on Physical Deterioration was set up and reported.

First steps led to others. The appointment of School Medical Officers led to the unearthing of a mass of child filthiness and disease. Year after year, hundreds of Local Authority Health Reports contained damning infant mortality, tuberculosis and other statistics.

That poverty was widespread was clear from researches such as those of Mrs. Pember Reeves in the years before 1914. Investigations were conducted among Lambeth families where breadwinners were mainly unskilled labourers and earning from 18s to 30s (90p to 150p) a week. Their wives were quiet, decent, kept to themselves. Collected family budgets proved that mothers with several children simply did not have enough money to feed their children adequately. For, out of about £1 a week received by the wife, rent took 3s to 9s and other outgoings perhaps 5s. So about 7s to 9s was left to feed perhaps 8 people.[97] For such families a spell of unemployment meant quite desperate hardship. This type of life described by Mrs. Pember Reeves, was very common in Edwardian Britain, i.e. in "the good old days". Some 2½ million adult men, including for example 60 per cent of bricklayers' labourers and over 60 per cent of railwaymen, were getting under 25s a week. Tressell described the struggles of building workers in the early years of the 20th century.[98]

So, there were very harsh class differences and absolute grinding poverty in a very rich land. In what was politically a relatively free country,[99] protest and collective action were to be expected and came.

6.7   Diet, housing, leisure

There is acute controversy concerning the adequacy or otherwise of the national diet around 1900. "It is no exaggeration to say that the opening of the 20th century saw malnutrition more rife in England than it had been since the great dearths of medieval and Tudor times"[100] was one verdict, quite rejected by another researcher: "The statement is almost certainly untrue".[101]

Certainly, there were grounds for concern. There were many poor people who had not enough to spend on food and the cheap foods which many purchased were probably far less nutritious than foods of earlier times. The bread, produced in large modern mills, had lost some of its vitamin content. Margarine, invented in the 1860s replaced butter on many of the tables of the poor; unfortunately, it had not the vitamins found in butter. Factory-made jam which so often accompanied the bread and margarine to make a meal lacked much of the fruit content of home-made jam. In industrial areas such as Lancashire where many went into the mills on leaving school and continued work after marriage, housewives often completely lacked the training, habits, time and energy required to serve up nutritious food. Nor was it simply a matter of women going out to work. Observers pointed to the fact that British women unlike their French sisters did not provide soups from readily available meats and vegetables. In the North-east, where there were very few women who went to work, Lady Bell observed that: "Many of the wives practically do not know how to cook at all, or at any rate do not wish to do so. . . On the other hand there are, happily, many of the women who can cook fairly well". She pointed to the very widespread use of condensed milk: "a threepenny tin . . . will last a fortnight."[102]

Adulteration proved difficult to eradicate though great steps had been taken by 1900. In London around 1895: "The practice of 'washing' or watering the milk though still very prevalent, is less common than it was. At one time certain members of the trade boasted of their ability to make one churn do the work of three. Those 'good old days' are gone".[103] Until 1901 when the practice was banned, dairymen might add formaldehyde to milk to prevent its souring.[104] Unfortunately, this preservative might be injurious to health.

Yet there is strong evidence, difficult to rebut, of improved nutrition over the second half of the 19th century. Lung tuberculosis death rates were practically halved: from 2,772 per million in 1851–60 to 1,418 in 1891–1900. Tuberculosis thrives on malnutrition. There was no effective drug with which to fight the disease so "improvement in diet may have been an important cause of the decline of mortality from tuberculosis during the 19th century."[105]

Over the period 1870–1913, much greater quantities of much cheaper foods were consumed in Britain as imports rose and entrepreneurs such as Lipton made fortunes by catering for the new mass market. Per capita consumption of tea rose from 3.76 lb in 1870 to 6.19 lb in 1913: of sugar from 47.11 lb to 83.22 lb.[106] A Sainsbury employee after 1895 remembered mountains of imported foods ranging from Alaskan salmon to Far East pineapples.[107] Cadbury's of Bournville had 230 workers in 1879, 2,685 20 years later. The homely fish and chip shop – 25,000 of them by 1913[108] – used up at least a quarter of landed fish and provided nourishing meals to very many. Imports of eggs rose from nearly 767 million in 1873 to 2,185 million in 1908 (not including 801 million from Ireland).[109] The important price of the 4 lb London loaf fell from 9.75 pence in 1872 to 5.8 in 1913. In early 20th century Salford, two pounds of New Zealand lamb or 9 lb of flour could be bought for less than a shilling.[110] Foods such as milk, which daily trains brought to the towns in vast quantities, became safer and purer as inspectors tightened their grip.

Housing

The process by which the British became mainly a town-dwelling people continued. From 1841 to 1901, some 3 million migrated from the country to the towns and a further half million moved into colliery districts. In England and Wales, by 1881, 47 towns each had over 50,000 people. Large increases in numbers in mining and heavy industry areas continued to 1913. In the decade 1901–11 the population of Glamorgan increased by 30 per cent. By 1901, over 40 per cent of the English and Welsh lived in 6 great conurbations which between them held over 16½ million people. Greater London alone had 6½ million. The percentage living in conurbations reached its peak in those early 20th century years.

One rapidly growing Northern industrial town was Middles-

brough. "As one owner after another starts ironworks in the
growing place, there is a fresh inrush of workmen and day by day
the little houses spring hurriedly into existence, until at last we
find ourselves in the middle of a town". The following comments
relate to aspects of the environment of millions in the new
industrial areas.

There was "nothing to appeal to a sense of art of beauty". It
was "unhappily for the most part a side issue for the workman
whether he and his family are going to live under healthy
conditions. The main object of life is to be at work; that is the
absolute necessity". Middlesbrough's heavy industrial areas
were thus described: "the black plain with the furnaces, trucks,
sheds and scaffolding: houses in which every room is penetrated
by the noise of machinery, by the irregular clicking together of
trucks coming and going, and by the odours and vapours . . .
from the works and coke-ovens".[111]

There were perennial shortages, for example, in London and in
other areas with heavy inward migration. So, many had to make
do with furnished or unfurnished rooms. There were London
streets in the 1880s where houses were let off in one or more
rooms. Mrs. Pember Reeves found: "The ordinary housing for 8s
a week consists generally of 3 rooms out of a roomed house
where the responsible tenant pays 10s or 11s for the whole, and
sublets one small room for 2s or 3s".[112]

In Scotland, housing provision has long been far less adequate
than in England. Preference for stone, more expensive than
brick, construction, may have been a factor. Many lived in single
rooms. "The single room system, appears . . . co-existent with
urban life among the working classes in Scotland. In Edinburgh
there are said to be 14,000 single-room tenements; in Glasgow
25 per cent of the whole population live in single rooms; and in
Dundee there are 8,221 houses of one room, containing 22,870
inhabitants". In 1911, over 100,000 of Glasgow's 800,000 lived in
one room.[113]

Some housing was disgracefully bad, much was inadequate.
Kilvert told of a visit to Edward Evans "in the dark hole in the
hovel roof which does duty for a bedroom". On another occasion
he found "the stench of the hovel bedroom almost insupport-
able."[114] As late as the 1920s, a writer thus described two-
bedroomed homes in a rural hamlet: "There slept last night in

these five cottages which have two sleeping places apiece. Second cottage, husband and wife, lodger, four children. Third cottage: husband and wife, four girls, two boys and a baby".[115] Probably, conditions were worse around 1900, for families were larger.

At Cradley Heath: "The homes in which these poor people live are generally of the most squalid and deplorable kind. The drains are at the best defective; sometimes there are no drains whatever. In some cases, there is only one privy provided for three homes, and that is in a detestable condition".[116]

Evidence to the Sankey Commission of 1919 "on the abominable housing conditions in mining villages undoubtedly made a very deep impression".[117] Many early 20th century photographs show Durham miners' houses, for example, ranged like troops on parade near the pit-head and, sometimes dwarfed by the slag heap. A 1920 official report, (such houses must have been built before 1914) said of the County's unsatisfactory houses: "Their number is not confined to the congested areas of the towns, but they are to be found in large numbers in . . . practically every colliery centre. . ."[118]

In the North-east, tenement housing was common in towns such as Jarrow. It was thus described in a 1933 Report when very many of the tenement blocks then standing had been built before 1914, ". . . a row of blocks of eight dwellings, each block having a common yard. . . The occupants of all eight dwellings (numbering anything from twelve to forty) share the same yard, use a common water tap . . . and share the two or four sanitary conveniences provided".[119] Since there was very little building during the Great War, the 1913 situation must have been close to that of 1921 and, in the latter year, percentages of dwellings returned as flats, maisonettes and tenements were 62 in Jarrow, 75 in Gateshead, 79 in South Shields.[120] However, in all England and Wales such figures were unusual. In all rural districts for example, in 1911, over 91 per cent of the population lived in ordinary dwelling houses, 0.3 per cent in flats and 8.3 per cent in hotels, institutions, shops and so on.[121]

Yet there were improvements between 1870 and 1914. New houses were built, over-crowding diminished, many moved into suburbs, the environment was increasingly controlled and improved by the Authorities, as is made clear in Section 8.2.

Nearly 86,000 new houses were built in Britain in 1870, 131,000 in 1906, 101,000 in 1908, 86,000 in 1910, 53,000 in 1912. For the fall after 1908, Lloyd George was much blamed for he taxed rising land values in his 1909 budget and therefore caused builders to become less willing to buy land.

Percentages of population living more than 2 to a room in England and Wales fell from 11.2 in 1891 to 8.6 in 1911. They declined in most towns too, for example, in Sheffield from 11.6 to 8.4 but in Sunderland with one of the worst records they actually rose slightly from 32.1 to 32.6. In the following towns the number of persons per inhabited house was:[122]

	1891	1911
Blackburn	4.91	4.39
Bradford	4.72	4.08
Leeds	4.71	4.37
Nottingham	4.65	4.38

Though averages must often be viewed with great caution, it cannot be claimed that, even in 1891, the above numbers were enormous. In Scotland there was improvement: percentages of the total population living more than 3 to a room fell from 25.3 in 1891 to 21.9 in 1911 and more than 4 to a room from 11.3 to 8.6 over the same two decades. The falling birth-rate was a significant factor in accounting for this improvement.

Movement into the suburbs was a most important development in the late 19th and the 20th centuries. Not that suburbs were new, indeed Chaucer before 1400 made reference to one who lived: "In the suburbs of a town".[123] Life in a suburb enabled people to combine nearness to necessary work with access to a countryside which many still loved, plus possession of a house on a plot which gave that privacy and that ability to garden which was so desired by great numbers.

Constantly, people moved from the inner city to the outer suburbs. In 1911 three-quarters of those living in Camberwell were born Londoners. The borough's population rose from nearly 40,000 in 1841 to 260,000 in 1901. Their houses were built by builders intending to sell and (hopefully) make a profit. The adjective speculative applied to a builder then had a ring of truth: it was said that in East Dulwich about 40 per cent of nearly 5,000 houses erected in the previous 10 years stood empty in 1881.

Certainly, there was great competition. In 1878–80 some 416 firms or individuals were building well over 5,000 houses in Camberwell: 220 firms were building from one to six houses each.[124] With so many builders in one part of London alone, it is not surprising that standards of work varied enormously. In 1880 rumour had it that some houses fell down. But Dyos described the activities in Camberwell of a large builder called Edward Yates, who closely supervised work and clearly built to relatively high standards.

An extremely fortunate London borough was Hampstead, where much of the heath was preserved because other residents opposed moves by the leading landowning family to lease land for development – an example of lack of class solidarity! There was much building and Hampstead's population grew from 4,343 in 1801 to 32,281 in 1871 to 85,494 in 1911.[125] Most of the residents were upper and middle class and housing was appropriately spacious and spaced. One building agreement of the late 1860s "envisaged top-class development, making particular provision to preserve all the existing trees in the Avenue and to ensure that houses were set back fifty feet from the centre of the road."[126] Again, private builders built for sale. The Willetts, father and son, built up a high reptutation and large fortune (well over £300,000 by 1906).

The archetypal suburban man was Charles Pooter of "The Laurels", Brickfield Terrace, Holloway, – "nice six-roomed residence, not counting basement, with a front breakfast parlour."[127] The growth of suburbs was particularly rapid in the decades around 1900: in the 10 years before 1911, Ealing's population grew by 85 per cent, Ilford's by 89, Kings Norton and Northfield (Birmingham) by 42, and Wallasey by 46 per cent.[128]

Since 19th century architecture and housing have attracted much criticism, it is particularly interesting to note that a German observer, attached to his country's London embassy, 1896–1903, wrote extremely laudatory accounts of some British domestic architecture: "Everything breathes simplicity, homeliness and rural freshness".[129]

Though it was long before such advanced views gained universal acceptance, already by the 1880s there was a movement away from mid-Victorian furnishings: "I can conceive nothing more terrible than to be doomed to spend one's life in a house furnished after the fashion of twenty years ago . . . a bedroom should be clear of everything that can collect or hold dust in any form; should be bright and cheerful. . ."[130]

Women's magazines and best selling books were a great source of information on home improvements. Technology was aiding the housewife. Gas cookers and gas were cheap. "Fletchers No.4 Gas Cooking Range appears to be the most suitable for family use, being of sufficient capacity to cook for ten persons, the price, complete, being £7". Gas fires in bedrooms could be recommended since: "a good hot gas fire can be obtained for half an hour night and morning at a cost of 6d (2½p) per week or less".[131] The triumph of electricity was postponed by cheap, plentiful, town gas which was easier and cleaner to use than coal.

It must be stressed that most English families lived in a separate dwelling, usually a house, and that the number of dwellings roughly equalled the number of families. Even in Co. Durham, with some of the worst housing conditions in England there were, at the 1911 census, 260,982 structurally separate dwellings occupied and 16,208 dwellings vacant for the 281,445 private families.[132] It is therefore obvious that for almost every family in Durham there was a dwelling. Everything is relative and Britain never had the enormous "shanty-towns" which house millions around the mushrooming cities of less developed countries in the 1980s.

Leisure

To 1914 and beyond, those traditional leisure activities of the countryside – hunting, shooting, fishing, with a very long history, much lore and literature – retained their following. To 1979, angling, for example, occupied leisure hours of thousands.

For most workers, leisure hours were still limited but they were increasing. Pub and church remained main centres of leisure activity, but both were losing their grip.

Drinking did continue on a vast scale. Of early 20th century Norwich it was said that "the public house is the centre of social intercourse among working men".[133] But numbers of on-licences in England and Wales fell from a peak 112,884 in 1871 to 90,586 in 1911,[134] while persons per on-licence rose from 201 to 398.

Excessive drinking was a serious evil in the late 19th century and the large and important temperance movement did much good. Drunken scenes in the towns have been described on many lurid pages. Yet Charles Booth wrote: "Go into . . . the ordinary public house at the corner of any ordinary East End street. . . Behind the bar will be a decent middle-aged woman, something above her customers in class, very neatly dressed, respecting herself and respected by them. The whole scene comfortable quiet, and orderly".[135]

Church and chapel remained centres of much activity. At Pontypridd before 1914 a new curate found: "Besides me, the parish boasted a staff of Vicar, two other curates, a Church Army sister and two Lay Readers."[136] With six clergy, St. Dunstan's, Stepney, offered religion and a very wide range of social activities. In Northern areas: "For a vast number of respectable, intelligent, fairly prosperous families the chapel is the *only* social centre. . ."[137]

But increased leisure hours of many might be spent playing or watching games, walking or bicycling, attending theatres or cinemas, in home entertainment.

The development of organised games – "which on any reckoning may rank among England's leading contributions to world culture"[138] mainly dates from the second half of the 19th century. The laws of Association Football were drawn up in 1863: by 1913 attendances at first class League or Cup Matches were numbered in tens of thousands. 1871 saw the foundation of the English Rugby Union. Cricket was older, but the age of W.G. Grace came in the 1870s and 80s, with the first Australian tour in 1878. Lawn tennis dates from the 1870s. Golf, long played in Scotland, became popular among England's upper classes in the late 19th century.

Towns were still smaller before 20th century sprawls – most of Rochdale's people lived in a compact circle about a mile across[139] – and it was much easier to walk or cycle out of them. Cycling often figures in records of the period. Parties went off to Stonehenge and a girl had to ride up every hill "not to be beaten by the Gotch Boys".[140] In some industrial areas the Clarion Cycling Club, with 8000 members by 1898, was prominent.

Modern television has revived the "good old days" of the pre-1914 music halls.[141] Accompanying radical improvements in suburban transport services, numbers of and attendances at

London theatres increased sharply after the 1860s. There was much popular light entertainment. There were also the light operas of Gilbert and Sullivan, the plays of Ibsen, Shaw, Pinero, Wilde, Galsworthy, Barrie. The 1841 Census recorded 387 actresses, 987 actors in England and Wales: by 1911 there were 9,171 actresses, 9,076 actors.[142]

More schooling and leisure brought more reading. Rochdale's public libraries were issuing around 100,000 books a year by 1900.[143]. Better off homes had pianos. As always, visiting, gossip, and so on, took up much leisure time.

Modern, mass circulation newspapers and weeklies began in the 1880s and 90s – "Titbits" in 1880, "Answers" in 1888 and much more important, the "Daily Mail" in 1896, the "Express" in 1900: "written by office boys and for office boys", was Lord Salisbury's famous gibe, but the newspapers were an enormous success. For good and ill, here was a very major development.

Already, townspeople were getting away to the country and seaside in large numbers, though mainly on day trips. By 1902, Co-op, railway and other excursions took 28,000 out of Rochdale.[144]

Yet, for very many, 19th century Britain lacked the gaiety, the festivals of some other ages and sunnier lands. Sunday in an industrial town, for example, could be a truly depressing day for the young and energetic, with no sport or entertainment.

7. ORDER AND CHANGE

7.1 Great strength of the Victorian established order

In 1885 William Morris said of those who aimed to change society: "They very much underrate the strength of the tremendous organisation under which we live. Nothing but a tremendous force can deal with this force; it will not suffer itself to be dismembered, nor to lose anything which really is its essence without putting forth all its force in resistance. . ."[1]

By the 1870s, the established order was so firmly rooted, so widely accepted and supported, that growing 1880s protest was easily contained. Even in 1910–14, (leaving out Ireland), Britain was not faced with anything approaching revolution or civil war.

Protest there certainly was – it will be later described. Importantly, radicalism survived through the mid-Victorian heyday, though it often found expression in the little-read periodicals such as the "English Republic" of the 1850s, in which abolition of monarchy and House of Lords was advocated.[2]

Nor was meek submissiveness universal. A "Times" letter of 1872 recounts the tribulations of first-class railway passengers whose compartment was invaded at Tottenham, one Sunday evening, by "Extremely offensive and noisy persons who sang obscure and vulgar songs, interspersed with language of the most objectionable description". The ticket-collector took no action: "it was apparent that the third-class could do as they liked".[3]

Police and courts did not always command silent respect. The acquittal of an Inspector in 1876 on a charge of molesting a shop girl in connection with the Contagious Diseases Act roused "a perfect storm of indignation and the Bench was literally hissed and howled at . . . the women seemed ten times more fierce than the men."[4]

Significantly, many working people never mentally entered into the success-seeking materialist world of the Victorian entrepreneurs. An editor of 19th century autobiographies considered that: "the working classes constructed their own exclusive world, remote from the acquisitive, accumulative impulses of the Victorian economy".[5]

Yet, even if it were possible to find space to report each exception to generalisations concerning Victorian stability and success, the fact remains that representative government, the private enterprise or capitalist economy, the existing social structure were so strongly entrenched that they easily withstood even the serious unrest prior to 1914. Complex and interlocking reasons for this state of affairs included the following:

At home and abroad, the British system of government was rightly praised. As already indicated, movements towards full representative democracy were slow but definite. Considerable numbers of the respectable working classes, given the vote in 1867 and 1884, took their duties very seriously. It is indeed interesting to read how thousands of working men in the industrial areas attentively followed the long orations of Gladstone.

A contemporary observer believed that: "England, which had been called the nation of shopkeepers, might with equal truth be described as the empire of working men" for "the working men are in the government of England, our rulers".[6] Escott realised with obvious approval that in his day, working people did not seek Socialism: "The English working man takes, for the most part, a view admirably practical and temperate of the functions of the State".

Realising that: "To coerce the multitude is too often to consolidate sedition", Britain's rulers allowed "free play . . . to every mind and to every tongue".[7] Many could not have agreed, but it is true that the self-confidence of the Victorians permitted a wide political tolerance, perhaps greater in some respects than that of their more uncertain successors. It has been pointed out that even Marx was appraised with much reasonableness and with "an almost universal admission of his stature".[8]

"Englishmen are law-abiding," continued Escott, "because they are persuaded that it is the honest intention of the law to be fair to all alike, and because they believe that in the long run the legislature does not neglect their true interests".[9]

By the 1870s the vast Chartist agitation of the 1830s and 1840s was remembered only by ageing people who had lived on into more prosperous times. There was much evidence of a desire for co-operation and for sharing in success. The boilermakers had a 1872 song:[10]

"Now 'tis true that capital
All the risk must run. . .
So 'tis just and meet
Labour should co-operate
And to help with all their might
Masters to compete".

In the diary of Kilvert, (admittedly a privileged onlooker), or the reminiscences of Flora Thompson, and other records, are described societies of mainly content, hospitable, hardworking people who lived in real communities in which people knew and could respond to each other. Kilvert rejoiced in "these kindly hospitable houses about these hospitable hills. I believe I might wander those hills all my life and never want a kindly welcome, a meal or a seat by the fireside".[11]

Deference to and respect for the upper classes, though not universal, were widespread and influential.[12] The role of Christianity was vastly important but complex. A few clerics were radicals or socialists, supporting Trade Unions and social reform. In the North, Nonconformist preachers often gave support to Radical and to the growing Labour movements. In the lives of many reformers, including that of perhaps the greatest – Lord Shaftesbury – religion was the dominant concern. Christian bodies, (particularly, but not only, the Nonconformists), supplied many of the workers for temperance. In the most hopeless slums, the work of the Salvation Army to bring some light and decency is well known.

Yet the Churches, particularly the Established Church, were a conservative and stabilising force. In thousands of Anglican parishes, year after year, boys and girls preparing for confirmation were instructed in the Catechism.

"*Question* – What is thy duty towards thy neighbour?
Answer – My duty towards my neighbour is to love him as myself, and to do to all men as I would they should do unto

me. . . To honour and obey the King, and all that are put in
authority under him. . . Not to covet nor desire other men's
goods; but to learn and labour truly to get mine own living,
and to do my duty in that state of life, unto which it shall
please God to call me".[13]

Of course, it is difficult to say how much, (if any) effect had the
Sunday sermons of such as Flora Thompson's parish priest with
his constant exhortations to remember duties to social
superiors.[14]

Yet, "Evangelical discipline, secularized as respectability, was
the strongest binding force in a nation which without it might
have broken up".[15] A frequently cited dividing line within the
working classes was that between those who remained respectable and those who did not. "We were called the respectable
working class", said the son of a Bolton iron moulder who was
brought up to touch the cap 'as a mark of respect' to such people
as doctors, solicitors and schoolmasters.[16] Even in the harsh
slums of the industrial North many housewives slaved away,
polishing kitchen ranges, whitening doorsteps and keeping their
children's hair free of ticks.

The efforts of family, Church, or Chapel, were powerfully and
increasingly re-inforced by the schools. "They need a great deal
of encouragement but some of them are beginning to make a
start. They come cleaner than they did; and that is a great step
towards civilisation!", reported a classteacher in a London Board
School.[17] "The glorious reign of Queen Victoria, the Year of the
Jubilee, the 21st of June 1897, was celebrated" – thus it was
reported in the log book of Akenfield village school.[18] There is
no doubt that the typical school attempted to instill patriotism.
However, one may be cynical about the results of such efforts
and remember that schooling with resultant literacy brought
widening access to printed pages which did not all bring succour
to the established order.

The Victorian capitalist economic system continued to receive
vast intellectual and general support. Malthus had stated the
prevailing middle class conviction: "If no man could hope to rise
or fall in society; if industry did not bring its own reward, and
indolence its punishment; we cannot hope to see that animated
activity in bettering our own condition which now forms the

masterspring of public prosperity".[19] Very many agreed with the
theories expressed in the popular works of Smiles (e.g. "Self-
help"). "What some men are, all without difficulty might be". At
the end of the 19th century, the Chief Registrar of Friendly
Societies wrote: "it remains as one of the great glories of the
Victorian era that . . . welfare has been established in a very
large degree by the labours and the sacrifices of working-men
themselves. . . ."[20] People put small savings in Friendly, Co-
operative, Building and Insurance Societies and in Savings
Banks. By 1904, registered friendly societies had well over 5
million members and funds of over £40 million. Approaching 6
million savers in Post Office Savings Banks had deposits of £83
million in the early 1890s. Trustee Savings Banks had 1.7 million
members in 1905 and funds of over £60 million.[21] The
considerable membership of the Co-ops and role of the Insurance
companies have already been noted.

Free trade remained the accepted dogma of many leading
economists[22] and (judging from the 1906 election results when
the Liberals swept to power largely on an anti-Protection
programme), of the electorate at large.

But the central pillar of the existing economic system was
private property, and that pillar was increasingly buttressed and
strengthened by the institutions and vested interests of a highly
developed, advanced society.[23]

People seek security and esteem. Many believe these are best
achieved through possession of property. In 19th century Britain,
the most prestigious form of property – land – was largely held by
the few. Around 1900, 320,000 farm tenants rented from only
10–15,000 landlords. But ownership of other forms of property
was much more widely diffused. Over a million were proprietors
of one kind or another – house owner-occupiers or landlords,
shopkeepers or publicans, traders or manufacturers or artisans
with a workshop etc.

Important professions and business groups made their money
from property. In England and Wales in 1910, there were nearly
17,000 solicitors, (with roughly 2½ clerks to each solicitor), and
over 11,000 auctioneers and estate agents.[24] Immensely complicated land law helped to ensure that the family solicitor became
"a regular annuitant" on an estate.[25] Solicitors enjoyed that
monopoly of conveyancing which they were to retain into the

20th century. Property was still a favoured recipient of many local funds channelled through solicitors' hands.[26]

In closing years of the 19th century, Lord Salisbury had no difficulty in rallying the thousands of small property-owners – fearful of the new Socialism and anxious about rising rates – behind the Tory banner. As usual in Britain, it was not simply a reactionary triumph. As a National Unionist Association publication put it in 1913: "The maintenance of the principle of property and of that stability of the body politic . . . depends in the ultimate resort, on the existence within these Islands, of the vast majority of its inhabitants living under social conditions which . . . . permit them to believe in and practise the ordinary civic virtues."[27]

So, now unknown but then very influential professionals and politicians such as Sir Albert Kaye Rollitt, President of the Association of Municipal Corporations after 1890 advocated municipal progress as "a necessary complement of Individualism . . . for political and social stability. . ."[28] Municipal provision of services strengthened the middle classes, providing jobs for engineers on roads, sewers and tram-ways, for doctors in hospitals, and contracts for businessmen and builders.

It is very, very important to note that while with self-sacrificing endeavour, missionaries were preaching socialism in Bradford, Lord Salisbury, appealing to the realities of tenure, was more successfully rallying support for existing institutions.

7.2   Protest and collective action

From 1870 to 1913 – as in 1979 – the most important economic associations of working people were the Trade Unions. By 1870, the ambitious, grandiose schemes of earlier 19th century decades had been abandoned. In 1871, Gladstone's administration enacted a Trade Union Act and a Criminal Law Amendment Act. The first gave unions legal status. They were not criminal bodies in restraint of trade, they could be registered and have their funds protected. The second was far less pleasing to the unions for picketing was not legalised while anything approaching intimidation was illegal. The worst of these great handicaps to striking were removed by the Conservative legislation of 1875 which legalised peaceful picketing. Important too, was the Employers and Workmen Act of 1875 which in general made breach of contract a matter of civil, not criminal law. Previously magistrates had been able to threaten strikers with imprisonment for breach of contract.

In the mid-century decades of prosperity, skilled workers formed craft unions which were an expansion of the Clubs of the 18th century. Realising that "scarcity enhances value" they sought to push up wages by limiting entry to their crafts and insisted on long spells of apprenticeship. These associations of the skilled were often called amalgamated societies, such as the Amalgamated Society of Engineers (1851) and the Amalgamated Society of Carpenters and Joiners. Their secretaries (for example – William Allan of the Engineers and Robert Applegarth of the Carpenters), were moderates who worked together in what the Webbs later called "The Junta". They charged relatively high subscriptions, proceeds from which went to pay social security payments in sickness, injury, old age, unemployment, death. A gainful symbiosis with capital was furthered: class conflict and strikes (in the main) were eschewed.

One authority on trade union history argued[29] that too much emphasis has been given to the amalgamated, skilled unions in the period 1850–75, since, in important respects, their principles and policies were not characteristic of the trade union movement as a whole, for example, of mining, iron and steel, textile, and a host of small unions. In very important cotton, local unions remained the rule. Further, Cole maintained against claims to the contrary, that in the late 1860s and early 1870s there was considerable trade union militancy, manifested even among farmworkers. It was the onset of depression which put unions on the defensive and led, for a time, to less militant attitudes.[30]

Certainly, after 1873, the long drawn out fall in prices and profits caused great difficulties for unions. 1875–80 was a time of "defeat, disaster and dissension",[31] but not of utter ruin. Most unions, while losing members, managed to survive.

The 1880s saw a major build-up of socialist teaching and of trade union militancy leading to the growth of unions, particularly, but not only, of the unskilled. Among varied reasons for such developments were the following: glaring differences between rich and poor; distress in the slumps of the period; a national system of transport which enabled speakers and ideas to quickly traverse the length and breadth of the island; the rise of a school-taught population which could read papers, pamphlets, books.

Henry George's "Progress and Poverty" is said to have sold some 100,000 copies in three years after its 1879 publication. The Social Democratic Federation, Independent Labour Party, and Fabian Society, founded in the 1880s or early 1890s, attracted the support of some of the most brilliant and dedicated of the age. In London, in provincial centres such as Bradford, in Scotland, there was great endeavour to convert people to socialism, expose evils, proposed remedies. Working men sent members of their own class to represent them in a House of Commons which was still very largely a preserve of the rich – partly for the very obvious reason that Members were not paid until 1911. Not the first, but one of the most dynamic was James Keir Hardie, who was organising miners in Ayrshire after 1880, secretary of the Scottish Miners' Federation in 1888, and an abrasive Member of Parliament 1892–5. "The Leaders of the New Unionists (1884–89)" wrote the Webbs, "sought to bring into the ranks of existing organisations – trade unions, the Municipality, or the State – such masses of unorganised workers who had hitherto been entirely outside the pale, or inert elements within it".[32]

So in the late 1880s the unskilled joined unions which turned to militancy to achieve much-needed gains. Combinations were widespread.[33] In London famous strikes occurred: in 1888 that of Bryant & May's women match workers, in 1889 that of dockers who won their sixpence ("tanner") an hour. Organised by Will Thorne, workers at the gas plants secured the 8-hour (instead of 12 hour) day. In 1889 local miners' unions (with the exception of those of Northumberland and Durham and of South Wales), formed the Miners' Federation of Great Britain. Existing skilled unions were stimulated to expand: membership of the Amalgamated Engineers leapt from under 54,000 to 1888 to 71,000 in 1891.

In the 1880s too, there occurred the most serious riot in London in the second half of the 19th century. On "Bloody Sunday", 13th November, 1887, police had to be aided by the Guards to clear Trafalgar Square. While there was no shooting, fighting was so severe that over 100 were injured, of whom two later died. As usual after such disturbances, bitterness and denunciations long survived.

The 1890s, a period of much imperialist euphoria and Conservative rule, formed an unfavourable seed-bed for union growth. The employers, having also discovered strength from combination, counter attacked and gained a significant victory in the engineering industry in 1897–8 when a long lock-out ended in union defeat. Legal judgments went ominously against the unions. In Lyons v Wilkins 1896, an injunction was issued, and upheld in the courts, to prevent the picketing of a manufacturer's premises. Far more serious and famous was the Taff Vale case of 1901. In 1900 following a strike in the Taff Vale Railway, the company sued the Amalgamated Society of Railway Servants and was awarded £23,000 by a court. If such a precedent were always to be followed, then strikes would become impossibly expensive. But in 1906, Liberal, plus Labour, victory at the polls was followed by an Act restoring the pre-1900 legal status. Further, in the 1909 Osborne case it was ruled that a union had not the legal right to make a levy to aid the funds of a political party, but a 1913 Act gave unions that power – subject to considerable qualifications.

7.3   Unrest 1910–14

In the opening decades of this 20th century, added to the clamour for more battleships and the dangers of international rivalries which produced catastrophe; to the perennial Irish problem which surely would have produced civil war but for overriding claims of 1914; to the bitter constitutional conflict of "Peers v People" which brought great reduction in the powers of the Lords in 1911; the nation was afflicted by widespread, nasty and sometimes destructive labour unrest and by considerable, unprecedented, violence from women.[34]

Each major confrontation produced bitterness and nastiness which spilled over and made worse the other conflicts. After 1906, the Peers clearly used their blocking power to frustrate the enactment of measures for which a moderate Liberal government had an electoral mandate. Lloyd George engaged them with the full employ of his considerable demagogic talents. After very bitter Parliamentary and public struggles powers of the Lords were reduced in 1911.

Clearly most serious was the refusal of a group of Army Officers to force Ulster into a united, self-governing Ireland. Conservative politicians, and others enthusiastically embraced the cause of the Ulstermen, Kipling, for example, gave the then enormous sum of £30,000.[35] Schemes of social amelioration, which now seem very moderate, (for example the National Insurance Act of 1911), provoked extravagant opposition, with strident public pronouncements of refusal to lick insurance stamps.

In this work attention is limited to labour unrest and the suffragette campaign. It is not difficult to account for the former. Prices were rising: the cost of living went up around 14 per cent between 1902–13. High hopes following the sweeping Liberal-Labour Parliamentary victory of 1906 evaporated as the difficulties of daily life did not disappear. The adoption of intransigent attitudes by example-setting groups led many workers to do the same. Their opinions were somewhat strengthened by the spread of syndicalist[36] ideas, though these were not greatly influential in Britain.

In 1907, the likelihood of a national railway strike was only averted by Lloyd George's intervention. On the railways industrial relations were turning sour for management, believing that necessary discipline – as in the Armed Forces – implied the non-existence of unions, refused (except in the case of the North-Eastern Railway) to recognise them. Troublesome railwaymen might well find themselves posted to isolated country stations.

The years of serious dislocation began in 1910 which saw pit strikes in the North-East and South Wales. In Tonypandy there was rioting and one fatal casualty, responsibility for which was still the subject of argument in the late 1970s. In 1911 an unusual Tropic summer added to the tensions in the crowded, baking, cobbled town streets. Dockers, carters, seamen and all railway men came out. 1912 was even worse. The miners struck for day rates of 5 shillings for men and 2 for boys. They won, but London dockers, faced with the strong Lord Devonport, Chairman of the Port of London Authority, lost. "Oh, God, strike Lord Devonport dead" said Ben Tillett to the crowd.

1913 saw over 1,400 individual strikes and the ominous

formation of a Triple Alliance of miners, railwaymen and transport workers. Before they were called upon to put unity to the test, many members were going into another kind of action.

A few statistics reveal the growth of trade union membership and militancy over those troubled years. In 1904, trade unions had just under 2 million members: by 1913 they had over 4,100,000. In 1904, there were 346 industrial stoppages causing the loss of 1,460,000 days. In 1912 there were 834 stoppages and working days lost totalled nearly 41 million.

A boy in a Salford slum witnessed the local clash of 1911.[37] "Then . . . . in the heat of the finest summer for a century, came the explosion. The local seamen struck first, to be followed . . . . . by the dockers, carters and miners.

"Beyond the end of our narrow lane we saw huge crowds go milling past in the stifling heat, then, a few minutes later, the rout. . . ! A score ran towards us, their clogs clattering over the setts, pursued by mounted police."

A local priest "spoke to the press of conditions: 'These men are not hooligans. I live among them and know their poverty' ".

The strike had been on a large scale, serious and unpleasant. Troops were sent to the worst affected industrial and seaport towns. In Liverpool, two men were killed in a 1911 clash between troops and rioters.

Votes for Women

Between 1905 and 1914, serious and nasty violence accompanied women's struggle to gain the Parliamentary vote.[38] Argument and peaceful demand for the vote had continued since the 1850s. In 1867, women's suffrage societies were formed in Manchester and London. The 1870s saw large petitions in the country and repeated private members' bills at Westminster.

Following heavy defeat in 1884 of a Parliamentary move to give women the vote, the movement went into decline from 1884 to around 1897, but, at the beginning of the 20th century, there were 16 societies affiliated with the National Union of Women's Suffrage Societies, which was led by Millicent Fawcett.

Between 1869 and 1907, some women gained the right to vote for and sit on School Boards, on county borough, district, councils, and to be Poor Law Guardians. In Australia and New Zealand, British colonies, women had the Parliamentary vote.

Thunderstorms began to gather over the peaceful landscape after Mrs. Emmeline Pankhurst founded the Women's Social and Political Union in 1903. Determined and able women joined – her daughters Christabel and Sylvia, Teresa Billington, Annie Kenney, Emily Davison, Mrs Pethick Lawrence, Mrs. Charlotte Despard.

In 1905, Christabel Pankhurst and Annie Kenney provoked trouble at a major Liberal meeting in Manchester. Arrested, they went to prison rather than pay fines. Resulting publicity delighted them: militancy was news. So meetings were disrupted, women marched, scuffles with police resulted in arrests and imprisonment. The Women's Union gained publicity, support, funds, and a monthly (later weekly) paper, "Votes for Women".

From 1908 onwards, following refusals by the Liberal Government to grant women's suffrage, violence became progressively nastier. Windows were smashed, large demonstrations clashed with large police detachments. Women chained themselves to railings, protested in court, went to prison. By 1913 there was serious arson, (in June 1913 alone, over £54,000 worth of property was burnt) plus cutting of telephone lines, ruining of mail in letter boxes, spoiling of golf greens and so on.

British police had neither cars nor motor-cycles to pursue the fast vehicles used by young suffragettes. Only 8 arrests followed 42 cases of major arson between April and November 1913.[39]

Yet, over the campaign, over a thousand were arrested and some suffered horribly. They refused food and were forcibly fed – tubes were forced down the throats of struggling women. In 1913, such victims, health sometimes grievously impaired, were temporarily released under the Prisoners (Temporary Discharge for ill-health) Act, aptly called the "Cat and Mouse" Act.

On June 4th 1913, Emily Davison was killed when she ran in front of the King's horse in the Derby. Thousands of women, some in white with laurel wreaths, followed her coffin.

"The argument of the broken pane", Mrs. Pankhurst later declared, "is the most valuable argument in modern politics".[40] Even in the context of her own struggle, she may have been sadly wrong. True, violence gained much publicity for the women's cause, but it so alienated members of Cabinet and Parliament and great sections of the public that a successful, compromise franchise bill, which might have been pushed through if backed by massive support and argument, had to wait until 1918, when women had clearly played a vast role in the total war effort.

There were powerful reasons for the suffragettes' lack of success before 1914. Prime Minister Asquith was long unsympathetic. Suffragettes were considerably recruited from the middle classes and lacked a mass following, though Sylvia Pankhurst, George Lansbury and others did try to organise working class support.

Mrs. Pankhurst and Christabel became extremely autocratic leaders, driving out colleagues such as the Pethwick-Lawrences and Mrs. Despard.

Christabel, in particular, put out some quite ludicrous propaganda, claiming that 75 to 80 per cent of men had been infected with venereal diseases before marriage. Autocracy, escalating violence, extreme propaganda alienated many: between 1910 and 1913 there were marked falls in numbers of new members joining the W.S.P.U.

Like any organised game, Parliamentary democracy collapses if too many break the rules. In 1910–14, Lords and strikers, Ulster and Irish volunteers, suffragettes, some Army officers, in varied ways acted outside the democratic process. They were very trying years in which "the fabric of democracy came into real danger".[41]

Yet, in 1914-16, nearly $2\frac{1}{2}$ million men volunteered to serve in Kitchener's Army conclusive proof, surely, that a large amount of social cohesion existed in Britain.

8. GOVERNMENT

8.1 Growing role of the Authorities

As indicated in Chapter 3, the growth of the Public Sector has been a truly major feature of 20th century development.

The economic role of the Public Sector in a modern economy may be thus summarised: provision of public goods, (e.g. maintenance of law and order, sanitary provision and so on), overall management of the economy; reduction of inequalities by taxing the rich and aiding the poor. In 1913, Government did not manage the economy but it had long provided some public goods; it regulated certain conditions of work and life; through taxation and provision of social services it lessened the very worst inequalities. For long it had cared for the very poor – the paupers.

While 19th century laissez-faire philosophies were never completely obeyed, certainly observance could go to amazing lengths, as during the Crimean War, when, at war with the Russians, the British Government allowed the latter to raise a loan on the London money makret, this being in "the ordinary way of business" observed the Foreign Secretary.[1]

However, in 1870 Gladstone presided over a government exercising the following functions: provision of armed forces, diplomatic services and imperial administration; maintenance of law and order with resulting courts and prisons; payment of a grant for popular education; regulation of hours and safety conditions in workplaces covered by Factories and Mines Act; payment of interest on the National Debt; provision of indoor (workhouse) or outdoor relief for paupers; regulation and control of sanitary and public health conditions.

British practice much emphasised the role of local authorities. For example, local Medical Officers of Health were appointed to supervise sanitary conditions under the general control of Local Government Board, set up in 1871.

Between 1870 and 1913 there was a large increase in expenditure on the Armed Forces. There were also considerable developments in regulation, education and social services. Of course, all this meant the transfer to public use of financial, human and material resources.

U.K. annual tax revenue rose from an average of £65.3 million in 1871–6 to £72.9 million in 1881–6, yet in 1890 government spending was a mere 8 per cent of national product. In 1885–6, the standard rate of income tax was 8d in the pound – scarcely confiscatory. Allowances meant that even in 1905–6, after the standard rate had been raised to 1s to pay for the South African War, a man on a salary of £600 a year – truly a middle-class income in those days – paid less than 10d (about 4p) in the pound.

Lloyd George's 1909 budget raised income tax to 1s 2d, with a super tax on incomes above £5000. The pound in 1909 bought more than 20 times as much as the pound in 1979 so it is obvious how light direct taxation still was.

In 1894, Harcourt reformed and extended death duties. Again, they were not onerous – 8 per cent on estates over £1 million – but they were bringing in £25 million by 1913.

Indeed, Government income and expenditure did rise appreciably over the period 1870 to 1913. Central government revenue averaged £75 million in the 1870s and £150.6 million in the first decade of this century. Figures for expenditure were £66.1 million in the 1870s and £143.6 million from 1900–09.[2] Total receipts of local authorities in England and Wales rose from £30.4 million in 1868 of which £0.8 million came from Government grants to £160.8 million in 1913 of which £21.0 million was from grants. Expenditure (other than out of loans) of local authorities rose from £40.7 million in 1875 to £140.33 million in 1913.[3]

Excluding the police, in 1911 there were twice as many servants of central government and considerably more than twice as many local government servants than there had been in 1891.[4] Central and local government employed 104,000 in 1891, 226,000 in 1911. Indeed, another reckoning, which excluded "industrial" categories in dockyards, post office, gas and water, but included teachers, gave central and local government 632,000 employees by 1914.[5]

Increase in state activity was definite but modest. It could be seen in more regulation, better education and social services.

8.2 Regulation

In 1870, Britain was protected from external aggression by her Navy. Within the country, the police forces, with the Army in reserve for rare appearances on the streets, maintained law and order.

Expenditure on the police by local authorities more than doubled between 1884 and 1913 – from £3.4 to £7.5 million.[6] For many strong young men, particularly from the countryside, the police service offered an excellent career compared with existing alternatives – around £2 a week for sergeants after 1912, with a two-thirds pension.

Those who broke the law were liable to receive severe punishment – flogging plus a long term of imprisonment for robbing with violence, for example. In 1870 the aim of prison was punishment. In Northampton County Goal the tread-wheel was still in use and silence was strictly enforced throughout the prison. For 94 male and 16 female cells there was a very small staff – Governor, chaplain (half-time), trades instructor, schoolmaster, 4 wardens and a night watchman – surely a remarkable example of Victorian economy![7]

By 1914, there had been much prison reform. In 1877, the Home Office assumed control of local prisons and established the Prison Commission. The Chairman of the latter in the early years of this century, Sir Evelyn Ruggles-Brise, was the driving force behind much change.[8]

By the end of the 19th century, it was officially stated that the aim of a prison sentence was to strengthen and improve character. The Prison Act, 1898, repealed the rigid prison rules then in force and allowed the Home Secretary to introduce changes. The probation system dates from 1907. The Children Act 1908 prohibited imprisonment of offenders under 14. The same year saw the incorporation into the penal system of Borstal training, experimentally launched in 1902. In 1914 came the Criminal Justice Administration Act, specifically intended "to reduce the number of cases admitted to prison". Courts could no longer immediately commit to goal a person who could not pay a fine. Just over half of no less than 170,000 persons sent to prison in 1902, went in for non-payment of fines. Indeed, most sentences were very short. In 1911–12 of a total of 175,749 prisoners received, only 39 were sentenced to over 7 years, while 54,403 were in for one week or less, and 74,000 for between one week and one month.

Very much contemporary evidence testifies to a widespread safety of life and property in late 19th and early 20th century Britain compared with the state of affairs in many ages and lands. Edith Holden was surely typical of many when she took it for granted that she could roam alone through the Warwickshire woods and fields in her studies of wildlife.[9]

Acting on produced evidence, the Authorities took steps to remedy some of the most glaring evils of early industrialisation. First, necessary statistical and other material had to be collected. There was a census each decade after 1801. Registration of births and deaths began in 1836: gradually the need to obtain a death certificate meant that people could not simply die unnoticed. Nor was statistical enquiry limited to the Registrar-General's Office and the Board of Trade: Manchester, London, and other major centres had statistical societies after the 1830s.

Perhaps the best known example of state regulation came with the Factories and Mines Acts. The first effective Factory Act of 1833 appointed inspectors to enforce regulations. True, factory inspectors were always quite insufficient in numbers for their vast duties, but by 1913, 222 inspectors made a total of 406,445 visits. An official view of the pioneer inspectors after 1833 was that: "Wisely enough, they evidently relied for the successful discharge of their functions on education and persuasion of the employers of that day rather than on the full exercise of the autocratic powers conferred on them."[10] Others have noted the very small fines imposed when inspectors did prosecute: an average £2 as late as 1924.

The regulation and inspection which began in the textile mills had spread by 1871 to most industrial processes. In that year the inspectors had access to over 100,000 work places. Pollution was reduced, health and safety improved. Manufacturers who each year had poured thousands of tons of harmful and very unpleasant hydrochloric acid into the atmosphere were persuaded to turn it into saleable products. Dangerous trades and practices were brought under scrutiny. "The attention of the Chief Inspector of Factories was drawn by Miss Anderson, Her Majesty's Principal Lady Inspector, to the practice of licking labels in thread mills in 1895".[11]

Ill health resulting from appalling housing and environmental conditions was a danger to all lives and a cost to the whole community. Epidemics spared none: a dreadful visitation of cholera in 1848–9 killed 54,000. Ill health meant poverty and higher poor rates. In 1848, the Public Health Act set up a central Health Authority, the General Board of Health. Local authorities could – but were not obliged to – take powers to construct sewers and water installations, control filth and refuse, pave streets and so on. In 1871 central control of local authorities passed to the Local Government Board; 1875 saw the passage of Disraeli's great Public Health Act, the foundation of sanitary legislation over many decades.

Gradually, over the central and later decades of the 19th century, urban areas appointed Medical Officers of Health: one official wrote in 1865: "I venture to submit that . . . it ought not any longer to be discretional in a place whether that place shall be kept filthy or not", while another, between 1858 and 1871 approved over 1,680 local schemes mainly for drainage and water supply, and in nine cases superseded the local Board.[12] On the other hand, it has been maintained that following the establishment of the Local Government Board, officials trained in penny-pinching Poor Law administration dominated the office. This meant that the medical department was poorly staffed and overworked. A Departmental Committee of Inquiry set up in 1898, found "that morale within the Department had almost completely collapsed" and that "central administration of state medicine had been reduced to a living shadow".[13] Between 1872 and 1898 Medical Inspectors had accomplished only 1,326 sanitary inspections, an average of under one inspection per sanitary authority in 26 years.

The Department Committee recommended the appointment of

more medical staff and after 1900 the Medical Department improved.

Certainly, in the industrial areas, the period 1870–1913 yielded unmistakable evidence of a tightening official grip on public health. In Newcastle-upon-Tyne, in 1884, 12,565 notices (formal and informal) were issued concerning various insanitary conditions. In 1886 an outbreak of enteric fever in the city led to an enquiry which found that "the probable cause of the spread of the disease was the open privy system".[14] In the affected district were 196 open middens, plus 33 slaughter houses, 12 cow-houses, 79 stables and a tripery – clear evidence of the survival of rural aspects even in a large city. In Newcastle and Sunderland there was a massive switch to water closets in the two decades around 1900. Newcastle had nearly 22,000 water closets in 1891 – approaching 49,000 in 1912. Three quarters of Sunderland's houses had water closets by 1910.

South Shields's Medical Officer took up his "no easy task" in 1875. When he established "a new order of things – much surprise was excited in the minds of the inhabitants".[15] In 1875, 2,834 notices were served: cellar dwellings were banned though 78 remained at the end of the year.

A watch on foods was mounted: in 1910 the Sunderland Public Analyst inspected milk, butter, preserved peas, sweets, among other foods. Slaughter-houses were reported upon: "disgraceful" was the verdict.[16]

Before the end of the 19th century listed infectious diseases had to be notified. Increasingly, victims were removed to isolation hospitals. Of Darlington's scarlet fever cases, 31 per cent were removed to hospital in 1885, 71 per cent by 1900, 95 per cent in 1912.

Scientific and technological advances aided the health officers. No longer did they write, as one had done in 1852, that a ship on which thirteen had died from cholera, "had passed through a stratum of atmosphere charged with the cholera poison".[17] They looked for germs in water, milk, foods. In Co. Durham, 271 bacteriological tests were conducted in 1902. Newcastle was ahead of many Authorities when in 1912, 106 samples of milk were examined for presence of the tubercle bacillus. Improvements in engineering enabled the considerable sewerage and water undertakings to be constructed.

Indisputably, the British towns of 1913 were far cleaner and healthier places than the towns of 1840 on which Chadwick had written his damning Report.[18]

8.3 Education and social services: the foundations of the Welfare State

To remedy evil, to produce succour for the needy, to educate the young, Victorians greatly relied on voluntary effort of which they contributed an immense volume. Thus, drink was combated by a large temperance movement; insurance against some catastrophes of life was provided by the great friendly societies; the known membership of societies making a return in 1872 was 1,857,896; total membership was perhaps twice that number. The Oddfellows alone had 434,000 members in 1870 and the Foresters 361,735. They were particularly strong in the industrial North: by 1875 the Oddfellows had 111 lodges and the Foresters 136 courts in Co. Durham.[19] Main benefits offered by friendly societies were sickness and funeral payments, but many entered into contracts with club doctors to provide services in return for a fixed payment per member. It was a nasty business to be in. "It was no secret that many of these appointments were obtained by bribery and corruption".[20]

Societies offered good fellowship, plus some insurance, plus (sometimes)· moral uplift. The Rechabites – some 140,000 members by 1900 – insisted on total abstinence.

National and local charities aided the needy and sick. The Charity Organisation Society, 1869, insisted that the main aim of charity was to set the recipient on his feet again. It gained a reputation for severity but is credited with the invention of case-work.[21] There were vast numbers of local charities – often the result of some bygone bequest. The churches carried out much social work. One might single out the large provision for down-and-outs by the Salvation Army, care of unmarried mothers by the Church of England Society, work in poor northern areas by Catholic nuns, charitable endeavour by the Quakers in towns such as Darlington.

Voluntary Dispensaries were numerous and operated on a very large scale. The 1909 Poor Law Commission Report recorded that: "One striking feature brought out as the result of our inquiries . . . is the existence, in certain large urban centres, of extensive free dispensaries".[22] Newcastle Dispensary employed seven doctors, treated over 20,000 patients a year, and was responsible for most of the outdoor medical work among the city's poor. Northampton's Dispensary staff attended 59,205 cases in 1872 – 14,600 at patients' homes. Well over 60,000 prescriptions were issued.[23] Nor were dispensaries limited to big towns as the Royal Commission suggested: certainly they were to be found in the 19th century in Hexham and Barnard Castle, for example.

Perhaps the finest monuments to voluntary endeavour and civilised concern were the voluntary hospitals. Some of these – such as the famous London Teaching Hospitals – had long histories. They grew over the period under review. The number of beds in voluntary hospital in England and Wales rose from 29,520 in 1891 to 43,221 in 1911. Per 1000 population, the rise was from 1.02 to 1.20.[24] While the average voluntary hospital was small, (62 beds as late as 1921), and many were indeed rural cottage hospitals, the institutions which were responsible for much patient care and on which most attention was focused, were the major hospitals of the large cities. Fairly typical were the Royal Victoria Infirmary in Newcastle and the Royal Infirmary in Sunderland. Such hospitals were often situated in the middle of great industrial and working class centres so that the poor were favourably situated to make large use – as they did – of in and out-patient facilities. Very much of the necessary finance came from voluntary gifts and subscriptions. While this meant that hospitals were often scraping along on incomes insufficient for optimum development, it also implied much local involvement. In industrial areas, for example, mines, works, associations, supported the local hospital and, in return, sent Governors to the controlling body of that Institution.

Until 1870, education, too, in England and Wales mainly depended on voluntary endeavour. Two great societies, the National Society for promoting the Education of the Poor in the Principles of the Established Church and the Nonconformist British and Foreign School Society, both founded in the early 19th century, provided schools. Achievements were considerable: adult male literacy in England in 1850 has been given as 69 per

cent,[25] and most of the children in villages and other stable
communities went to school. Difficulties arose in rapidly
developing mining and industrial areas such as S. Wales or West
Midlands when the proportions of those who were literate
sometimes fell drastically.

Scotland had a happer educational history: there was a
tradition of the parish school financed out of public funds and the
Universities were far livelier and democratic than their English
counterparts.

Tragically, strong sectarian bigotries forbade much government
intervention in education for most of the 19th century. In 1833, a
grant was made – and a Privy Council Committee, plus inevitable
Inspectors, appointed to administer it. Very late, direct state
involvement came in 1870, when W.E. Forster of Gladstone's
Government, managed to pass an Education Act. School Boards
were to be elected in the local areas and these were to provide
Board Schools. In 1880, school attendance was made compulsory. Schooling became free in Board Schools in 1891. By 1900,
over 2 million children were attending nearly 6,000 Board
Schools while 2½ million went to 14,000 voluntary schools.

To educate the children whose parents could pay fees there
were large numbers of schools of all sorts and sizes –
"Grammar", private and "public". Thus, the list of Trades and
Professions in Northampton of the early 1870s included 42
"Academies" many being private schools kept in houses by
ladies.[26] Like many others, the town had a long established
Grammar School. Often these were named after the monarch in
whose reign they were founded. They survived but until the
decades following 1902, numbers attending them were often small.

One reason for this was that it became the custom for the
upper classes to send their sons to public schools. Here we have a
national phenomenon of importance. Throughout the century
covered by this work, most British cabinet ministers, judges, and
top professionals had been educated outside the state educational
system at public schools. Essentially, the latter were a creation of
the 19th century, for though some – like Eton and Winchester –
had long histories, many new ones – Marlborough, Wellington,
and others – were founded in the last century while old
foundations greatly expanded. Oundle had a mere 91 boys in
1892 but over 500 thirty years later.

Sanderson, outstanding Head from 1892 to 1922, vastly expanded science and engineering, (with much else) at Oundle. But at Rugby before 1914, "science was despised as a subject, the Science Masters, even at Rugby, were of very poor calibre".[27] J.B.S. Haldane, who became a Communist Professor, wrote: "From an intellectual point of view the education available at Eton in 1905–11 was good". He left able to read 4 languages, (other than English), and do research in chemistry and biology.[28]

Kipling lambasted the: "Flannelled fools at the wicket or the muddied oafs at the goals", and certainly there was great emphasis on organised games. Beveridge's "chief recollection of Charterhouse was of having felt inferior . . . because he was not good at games", while a Northumbrian squire remembered that at his preparatory school: "Athletics were of much more consequence than mere scholastic attainment".[29]

While the best of the pubic schools gave a good (mainly Arts) education, the public school system was open to the grave criticisms that it was clearly divisive and there was too much emphasis on classics long after national interest required shifts to science and modern subjects. Perhaps public school boys were trained to become "leaders" – officers in the Services[30] or colonies – rather than makers and sellers of steel or electric fittings. Certainly, England suffered greatly for failing to develop in the 19th century an effective national system of large-scale secondary education. Before the end of the century a few school boards gave scholarships to famous local Grammar Schools and/or developed "higher" elementary or higher grade schools. There was considerable expansion of technical education, particularly after the Technical Instruction Act 1889. The Technical Instruction Committee of the L.C.C. (Chairman Mr. S. Webb), was especially active. But all this was unco-ordinated and unsatisfactory.

Reform came with the 1902 Education Act. School boards were abolished and all state schooling – elementary, secondary, technical – placed under local authority, i.e. mainly county or county borough, control.

As usual, local authorities varied considerably in resources and vigour but there were major improvements in state schooling between 1902 and 1914, though it remained possible for pupils over 12 to obtain exemption from full-time education while a considerable number of children, who had attained certain proficiencies, left at 13. More children did remain at school as a proportion of the total age group, 41.5 per cent of children aged 12–14 were at school in 1901, 57.5 per cent in 1911. The numbers of children under 14 working half-time in cotton factories fell from 62,000 in 1878 to 19,000 in 1907. In England and Wales, numbers of teachers, (aged 20 and over), increased by nearly a third between 1901 and 1911, (males by 30.4 per cent, females by 33.6 per cent).[31] The total (all grades) was 251,968 in 1911. In L.E.A. schools these were 127,718 females and 48,138 males. Most of the women were unmarried, there being 115,618 single but only 9,556 married and 2,544 widowed teachers. Numbers of certificated teachers rose appreciably though it is very obvious that many were still uncertificated.

Certificated teachers (England and Wales)

1901	*Male*	25,122	*Female*	40,979
1911	*Male*	34,013	*Female*	66,983

Better late than never, England expanded her secondary schools and made some provision for able working class children.[31a] After 1902, grammar schools received grants of public funds while additional new secondary schools were built. In 1907 grants to secondary schools became conditional upon a quarter of the places being given free to pupils from public elementary schools. In 1907, only 7.5 per cent of 12 to 14 year olds attended secondary schools but opportunities were slowly increasing. By 1914, the 1,123 secondary schools in England and Wales were attended by nearly 200,000 children, a third of whom had been awarded free places on transfer from elementary schools. Almost another third also began their schooling in elementary schools but their parents paid the modest fees.

For many of the ablest working class boys and girls, teaching offered an avenue of promotion up the social scale. Training was paid for. It was virtually impossible in England for a working class child to become a doctor or to enter a similar profession – to the overwhelming majority the medical school fees were a barrier as high as Everest. Just before 1914, a male certificated teacher earned an average £147 and a woman £101, (higher in London).

They were modest salaries, but attractive to families dependent on average industrial wages of around 30s (£1.50) for men and far less for women. Particularly with the large classes of the industrial areas, (and pupil to teacher ratio in elementary schools in 1901 was 48.5), teachers made a very significant contribution to social advance. Many thousands of women gave their whole lives to the work, for marriage then usually meant resignation.

University education was also considerably expanded before 1913, though advances were late and insufficient. The ancient foundations of Oxford and Cambridge which had sunk very low in the 18th, were reformed in the middle decades of the 19th century. It was however, difficult for any but the rich to gain admission. As already indicated, Scottish Universities remained more active through the days of Adam Smith and later. Scotland had 5 Universities in 1800: Edinburgh, for example, had a famous medical school.

London University received its charter in 1836. Among its constituent colleges of early Victorian days were University and King's. Before 1914 the London School of Economics and Imperial College brought much needed re-inforcement to social science and technological education. Much of London's work was concerned with examining and granting degrees to external students, largely at provincial colleges. Durham University was created in 1832; Manchester in 1884; while a considerable group of civic, red-brick Universities, (Liverpool, Leeds, Sheffield, Birmingham, Bristol) achieved independence between 1900 and 1909.

Women gained from these advances. While a few such as George Eliot received a good schooling early in the century, there was very much need for improvement and enlargement of opportunities. For the fortunate, these came with schools such as Cheltenham and North London under the famous Misses Beale and Buss, with permission to sit Cambridge Local Examinations in 1866, with the foundation of Cambridge and Oxford women's colleges after around 1870. At London and provincial Universities women had the same status as men.

The overwhelming majority of nurses and a considerable majority of teachers were women. Their numbers prove that their schooling and training were on a large and growing scale. Similarly, very large numbers of girls were now sufficiently schooled to become clerks and typists in industry. A very few (there were only 11,000 women or 6 per cent of the total in the higher professions in 1911), managed to become doctors, authors, editors, journalists and so on.

England paid a high price for her considerable neglect of state education in the 19th century. German primary and technical education were superior to their English counterparts. In Prussia and Saxony in the 1860s, practically all children attended school. At a higher level, scientific and technical education were vastly more developed in Germany. Journals of scientific societies present abstracts of papers and books in their relevant field. In 1872, the British Chemical Society's journal contained 151 British, 809 German abstracts. Ten years later, 232 were British, 1442 German.[32] In 1908 there were in Germany, in universities and technical institutions of university rank, over 60,000 students. England and Wales had 12,000 students in universities or university colleges, plus a mere 2,768 students in 31 technical institutions not of university rank.[33] The 1908–9 Report of H.M. Inspectors of Education contains the doom-laden comment: "The slow growth of these technical institutions is . . . in the main to be ascribed to the small demand in this country for the services of young men well-trained in the theoretical side of industrial operations."[34]

As usual however, many points of view deserve consideration. Britain had highly developed industries and taught her future workers in apprenticeships at work and at night school. As a newer industrial state Germany had to concentrate more on theoretical training in teaching institutions. Britain contributed to the world more than her fair share of scientists and of scientific advances. She did survive two world wars which made huge demands on scientific manpower and production. Among the contemporaries of the young H.G. Wells there was an upsurge of interest in science and literature. That tragic generation which went to war in 1914 included an astonishingly well read minority. Waiting to attack on the Somme: "They talked of ordinary things . . . of if you'd ever read the books of Mr. Wells. Of the poetry of Rupert Brooke. Of how you really couldn't very well carry more than one book at a time in your pack."[35] Poems, prose, letters, of combatants and nurses provide a harvest of war literature unmatched, surely, in the Second World War when the general standard of education was higher.

The Poor Law

Since Tudor times, the State had assumed responsibility for the care of the very poor. The Poor Law Amendment Act, 1834, divided the country into Poor Law Unions each under a Board of Guardians and all under central administration and inspection. The Guardians offered two forms of relief: indoor (meaning the workhouse) and outdoor (meaning an allowance or relief).

Dickens's genius, some scandals, undeniable penny-pinching, have given the Victorian Poor Law a very bad name. Yet, even in closing decades of this 20th century, the great majority in this poor world lack a state social security system as comprehensive as that provided by 19th century Britain.

First, the majority of paupers were not in the workhouses. In 1906, in Durham, 6,857 paupers were in institutions, of whom 3,824 were in workhouses (excluding infirm ward), 2,256 were in infirmaries or infirm wards, smaller numbers were on training ships, in cottage homes and so on. 21,887 were on relief. This proportion on outdoor relief was high. In 1907, in England and Wales, 128 Unions were relieving 111,213 paupers in institutions, 138,688 were on outdoor relief.[36]

Many paupers were sick in body and/or mind. Increasing provision was made for them so that one writer considered that "The National Health Service has its direct roots in the medical services of the Poor Law.[37] Researches such as these carried out locally by higher degree students at Newcastle University[38] have shown that while workhouses were indeed cold, hard, unsatisfactory places, there were improvements brought about by professional staff and concerned citizens. By the early 20th century Sunderland Union had a new infirmary.

True, conditions could still be very bad indeed. That great authority, Burdett, wrote of many hospitals in 1893, "in those sick wards . . . the condition of the patients . . . is a disgrace to our modern civilisation." He looked forward "to the time when the County Council will take over the administration of the entire poor law system".[39] He did not live to see the change in 1930.

But there were improvements in the hospitals. After about 1871, Unions began to provide separate infirmaries, or infirm wards. Workhouse infirmaries began to be called state hositals. In London they were placed under separate managment in 1867.

There were large increases in staff as the following figures show:

Workhouses and Infirmaries (England and Wales)[40]

	1875	1907
M.Os. (including assistants)	747	1016
Dispensers and assistants	23	71
Nurses	1686	6537

When the 1834 Act denied relief to the able-bodied it expressly exempted from that denial the sick and the mentally defective. Each Poor Law Union was divided into medical districts. Doctors were recruited and required to visit the aged, infirm, sick and disabled. The first free health service to be supplied to vast numbers on a national scale was vaccination, administered by the Poor Law authorities. In spite of much local incompetence, some ten thirteenths of babies born were vaccinated by 1845.

Poor Law doctors were badly paid and overworked. As late as 1910, Beatrice Webb wrote: "Of all branches of the public service, that of the Poor Law Medical Officer seems the most hardly treated, the least appreciated, the most depressed".[41] Yet Hexham workhouse had only three medical officers over the whole period 1843–1930[42] and a historian of the service considered that: "The Poor Law Medical Officers, who gradually became an organised body, stand out particularly as good public servants, fighting not only for recognition and improvement on their own behalf but also for positive health measures".[43]

Outdoor medical relief of the sick poor continued to be provided by Poor Law authorities until 1930 when the Local Authorities assumed responsibilities and provided services until the advent of the National Health Service.

The years before 1914 saw the foundation of Britain's Welfare State – an important 20th century construction which has been given some, and must here be given further description. The State stepped in to help some of the injured, old, sick, poor, unemployed or badly paid. Why?

First, there was irrefutable evidence produced of large-scale poverty, ill health and gross inequality;

Second, patriots were concerned at the threat to national greatness posed by alleged physical deterioration;

Third, in a politically free society, exposure of wrong was accompanied by suggested remedies. For example, as early as 1878, the Rev. W.L. Blackley wrote articles on "National Insurance";[44]

Fourth, Germany provided a quoted example of state insurance. Already in the 1880s to "dish" the socialists, Bismarck introduced insurances against sickness, accidents, old age. Indeed, there was little that was unique about Britain's welfare provisions. A number of advanced states made similar advances;

Fifth, a group of extremely able state servants – Morant, Beveridge and others – had the commitment, competence, and stamina necessary to devise and operate the requisite legal framework and administrative machinery. Beveridge, for example, believed that reform might heal obvious rifts in society and lead to a united, organic State;[45]

Sixth, ambitious Liberal ministers, in particular Lloyd George, naturally anxious to further their careers and to gain public approval and votes, as well as to improve social conditions, pushed through reforms;

Seventh, the Welfare State has always been a compromise between laissez faire capitalism on the one hand and socialism on the other. Private ownership remained but an increasing slice of the proceeds of the productive system were channelled by the State into the amelioration of the living conditions of the poorest sections of society.

The main girders laid in the foundations of the Welfare State were:

The Workmen's Compensation Act, 1898, enabled those injured in industrial accidents to claim compensation. On the Durham coalfield, owners and men established a joint compensation committee and the system is said to have worked well.[46] Certainly, in subsequent years very large numbers benefited from compensation though awards were often denounced as inadequate.

After the Relief (School Children) Order of 1905, and the Education (Provision of Meals) Act of 1906, necessitous children could be fed at public expense. Here was an important move: the state was stepping into "the most elemental of all fields of parental responsibility, the provision of meals for children".[47] Progress was slow and uneven. Bradford, for example, had a good record in the feeding of children, but by 1911–12, 131 out of 322 education authorities in England and Wales were providing meals and by 1912–13 some 350,000 children were benefiting. The Education (Provision of Meals) Act 1914, gave the Board of Education power to compel Local Authorities to undertake the service.

After 1907, Local Education Authorities were required to provide medical examination of school children in state schools. There were at least three examinations – after entry, at about 8, before leaving. Additional inspections (for example to detect hair infestation) and re-inspections were common. Inspection threw up a vast mass of filth, deprivation, disease which called out for treatment. This was often made available in eyes, nose and throat, dental and other clinics. Very large numbers of children suffered from medical complaints and/or were filthy, under-nourished, infested with nits. An indication of the vast scale of the work may be gained by reference to one Authority's work in 1921 – when conditions were better than in 1908. Newcastle then examined over 17,000 of its 48,000 elementary schools pupils: 12 per cent had dirty heads, nearly 14 per cent enlarged tonsils, 17 per cent or more decayed teeth, 1.4 per cent impetigo.[48]

Feeding necessitious, and medical inspection of school children "marked the beginning of the construction of the welfare state".[49]

In 1909 Government began to pay Old Age Pensions. It was a modest and thrifty start, 5s (25p) a week at age 70, with a reduction to 7s 6d for a married couple. An income of under 10s a week meant reduction, 12s a week denial, of pension. But the pensions were immensely popular among the grateful old and their families – they conferred some independence and removed fears of the workhouse. They were paid for by taxes.

The most comprehensive measure of these years was Lloyd George's 1911 National Insurance Act. In return for weekly contributions paid by employers and workers, most manual workers were covered by health insurance and a limited number of workers in certain trades were covered by unemployment insurance.

Pre-1914, an insured worker could go to a doctor whose name was on a list or "panel" of practitioners willing to offer such service and (provided the doctor accepted him which he normally did), receive free primary medical care and treatment. He (or she) was also entitled to a modest payment while off sick or disabled. Wives of insured men and women who were themselves insured received a benefit on confinement. Usefully, sufferers from tuberculosis were entitled to free sanitorium treatment.

Here, then was a system of importance under which millions lived for the next three decades until the National Health Service was introduced. Before 1914 nearly 14 million were insured by Health Insurance; by 1938 numbers had grown to 18 million – 12 million men, 6 million women.

True, the system had grave defects. It did not give comprehensive national coverage. The middle classes and the vast numbers who were not at work – mainly wives and children – were not insured. Family doctor but not specialist care was provided. Care of eyes and teeth was not generally provided – though some Friendly Societies had relevant schemes to provide such insurance. To gain acceptance for his scheme, Lloyd George compromised hugely. Payment of benefits was left in the hands of insurance companies and Friendly Societies though the resulting expenses and divergencies of administration were vast. National and local administration were placed in the hands of Insurance Commissions and Committees, not of existing local authorities which controlled growing Public Health Services.

Yet, gains from the health insurance system were very great and beneficial. Lady Bell had pointed out the grim truths that: "The question of health, so important a factor in the existence of all of us, assumes still greater importance in the lives of the workmen". For the worker "goes out . . . as usual, no matter what the weather or how he is feeling, in order to not lose a day's work . . . then follows an illness in which mental suffering is bound to be added to all the rest."[50]

After 1912 free medical attention plus sickness benefit, (a meagre 17s a week was a common Friendly Society payment in the 1920s), removed the worst of such fears. In addition, the early, skilled, attention to sickness diminished the ravages of epidemics. Tuberculosis was more frequently treated. Medical research received an injection of funds.

Unemployment was not a serious national problem between 1912 and 1921. From the latter date until 1940 unemployment and insurance against it did become very great national concerns.

In addition to the welfare measures outlined above; the

1905–14 Liberal administration passed in 1909 the Trade Board Act. In four "sweated" industries – tailoring, paper-box making, lace and chain-making – Boards were set up to fix minimum rates of pay which were then enforced by law. The procedure was later much extended to other occupations.

In 1910 Labour Exchanges were opened. Here was a sensible state addition to the free market mechanisms. Employers could notify vacancies and workers could apply for them.

With reason, Beveridge said of these pre-1914 days: "It seemed a time full of event and high endeavour, working with great allies and leaders to make a better World".[51]

PART III: 1914–45

9. OUTLINE OF THE PERIOD: DEEP TRAGEDY BUT ALSO PROGRESS

If modern Britons could have chosen when to live, they would have been wise to have avoided the years 1914–45. A man born in 1896 very probably served in the 1914–18 War. If he survived, he could have been among the three million out of work in 1933 – an army of unemployed made up of constantly changing ranks of unfortunates. Six more years of total war began in 1939.

From 1914–18 and again from 1939–45, Britain was at war. She was actively engaged for a longer period than any other combatant. Between the two great struggles, the country experienced a marked decline of her basic industries – agriculture, coal, textiles, iron and steel, shipbuilding. In addition, the great international slump of 1929–33 produced an avalanche of unemployment. Yet there was much economic and social advance.

Experiences varied enormously. Some prospered in the wars – women who could move from domestic service to munitions or air-craft plants, landlords of pubs near airfields and military bases, farmers, young men of modest backgrounds promoted to Major or its equivalent, administrators brought into swollen Ministries. As often, there was every sort of contradiction in the human condition: in 1940, servicemen might be living in complete safety in Devon while their families were heavily bombed in London. In 1933, while millions were out of work, the standard of living of the four-fifths in work rose as prices slumped.

Yet it is impossible to adequately portray the hideous sufferings[1] brought by the two wars. True, Britain escaped invasion, occupation, defeat, the recalled memories of collaboration, resistance, extermination which still plague many Continental countries. But the struggles had most profound effects on

British people and society: after 1918 and 1945 there were deep gulfs between those who had experienced, and those born too late to know of, the horrors of war.

Britain played a leading role in the World Wars – a role which a more demonstratively patriotic or military people might well glorify. In 1918, British and Empire armies shouldered the major burden of the final offensive against the German army on the Western Front. Better known is Britain's decision to continue the struggle, alone, in 1940, a sacrifice which surely still deserves praise and gratitude, for Hitler's Nazism was very evil. But major sacrifices of the Second War, such as the long terrible slog up Italy of the "poor bloody infantry", have received relatively little publicity.[2]

Many Britons, alive in 1930 or in 1980, could have told stories of great suffering and strain resulting from war. Apart from the obvious cases of the blind, disabled, bereaved, many hundreds of thousands had endured the cold, flooded, dangerous trenches of Flanders in the First War, or months in baking tanks in Libya, or appalling treatment of prisoners of war in the Far East, or convoy duty in the North Atlantic, or thirty flights over Germany in the Second. The wars altered – and in many cases wrecked – the lives of those unfortunate enough to be caught up in them.

Their wider profound political, economic, social and psychological effects will be noted later. Here it is merely mentioned that Britain in 1945 was a vastly less important World power and economy than she had been in 1914; she was dwarfed by the new super-power the U.S.A. and U.S.S.R. She emerged victorious from two wars which left her weaker and poorer.

10. THE GREAT WAR

10.1 Tragedy

In July, 1914, Vera Brittain visited Uppingham School, where her brother Edward, his friends Roland and Victor were in their last term. Four years later, these three fine young men (one with marked talent as a poet another as a musician), were dead, along with around three-quarters of a million other men from the United Kingdom and 200,000 from the Empire, making nearly a million in all. Over two million were wounded – many shattered for life in mind and/or body.

Until 1916, those who joined up were volunteers – often the fittest, most idealistic, best educated of their generation. Of 14,561 Oxford University men who went to war, 2,680 were killed.[1]

On the other hand, there were those like William Beveridge: "Not only was he never personally involved in fighting but, untypically in that era of death and telegrams, he lost no one dear to him".[2] A few pitched into the thick of the fighting, clearly enjoyed it.[3]

How can anyone portray such a vast sea of tragedy as that resulting from 20th century war? "Perhaps historians ought not to attempt to describe the effects of the First World War upon the people of Great Britain. The magnitude of the struggle, the appalling cost in lives and wealth, and, most important, its incalculable disruption of the careers and aspirations of 40 million individuals, the British Nation, confound both language and scholarship".[4] However, it is clearly quite impossible to understand British life and attitudes after 1918 without reference to the effects of the war.

There was the sheer horror and pity of the slaughter. In practically every town and village appeared a War Memorial of some form. Each November, round such monuments gathered those who remembered the dead. Through the 1920s, in particular, gatherings were very large and poignant. They continued and the Second War added further, (but happily fewer than before), names to the rolls. For years there appeared in the "Times" and other papers, on days such as July 1st, columns of "In Memoriam" notices. On July 1st 1916, 57,470 soldiers – mainly from North country "Pals" battalions were killed, wounded or missing on the Somme.

Many who fought and survived were haunted by their experiences through the rest of their lives. Later generations can only marvel at 1914 attitudes when tens of thousands rushed to volunteer and think with pity and admiration on the sufferings and endurance of the men.

Thus, Frederic Manning, an "intellectual of intellectuals",[5] joined up in the King's Shropshire Light Infantry, and with quotations from Shakespeare at the head of each chapter, set down the experiences on the Somme of his Private Bourne.

True, many factors other than patriotism could have caused men to volunteer in 1914. True, too, bitter disillusionment, and horror sometimes followed early idealism, as readers of Sassoon well know. Nasty aspects of the war, not well publicised, included the following, There was much stealing, as in the Second War. With commendable caution, F.E. Smith asked that cigars sent to him be labelled "Army Temperance Society, Publications Series 9."[6]

On a far more tragic level, over 300 unfortunates were sent before firing squads after sentences for offences such as desertion and cowardice, sometimes committed by men shattered by intolerable strain.

10.2 Effects on society

In the first war civilian casualties from air raids, (under 1500), were but a small fraction of those of 1939–45, but worsening diet and environmental conditions brought a steep rise in tuberculosis deaths and may well have multiplied the ravages of a dreadful influenza epidemic in 1918. Following figures clearly reveal the sad reversal of progress in reducing tuberculosis mortality among the young, (particularly girls and women).

Table 6   *England and Wales: Tuberculosis mortality per million*[7]

Ages		1891	1912	1918
10–15	Males	643	431	623
	Females	946	662	943
15–20	Males	1,412	938	1,384
	Females	1,882	1,251	1,812
20–25	Males	2,386	1,511	1,832
	Females	2,106	1,400	1,941

These girls of 15–20, whose tuberculosis death-rate rose by nearly a half between 1912 and 1918, had no memorial erected to their memory, as often had their brothers, but surely they were equally the victims of war.

However, it is true that the War gave vast experience, and led to improvements in surgery, blood transfusion, anaesthetics, immunisation and other aspects of medicine.

There already were more women than men in 1914. The slaughter of young men made worse this imbalance. In 1911, in England and Wales, there were 155 males aged 20–40 per 1000 population: in 1921 there were 141. Again per thousand population, the number of widows had risen from 38 to 43.[8] On the other hand, the very heavy emigration of the pre-war years ceased during the war so there was no longer this drain on the home population.

Undoubtedly, with much resulting unhappiness, thousands of women were widowed, or remained spinsters, for life. Thus the birth-rate was reduced. However, the main cause of the reduced birth rate was – as already indicated – the determination of parents to have smaller families. This long term trend from 1870 to 1940 was perhaps made more definite by the First War since thousands of young men learned about male contraceptives, the use of which was encouraged by authorities worried by the incidence among the troops of venereal diseases which reduced numbers of effective fighters.

The War much affected many attitudes – to Victorian certainties concerning the march of civilisation and progress, religion, authority, class, sex, the press.

Hopeless attacks in conditions so bad as to defy description,[9] clearly lying propaganda, blunders and failings of nation and armies committed to a new kind of total war, all nursed deep anger and lasting cynicism. "From that moment all my religion died,"[10] wrote a survivor of the Somme massacre. Scepticism grew: that it lasted and proved to be dangerous was confirmed by Second World War disbelief concerning the truth of Hitler's death camps.

In a famous poem Wilfred Owen wrote that anyone seeing the terrible death of a gas victim would not think it sweet and seemly to die for one's country.

War hurried along the assault on Victorian prudery. There was the much-publicised advent of war babies. Local Authority clinics treated V.D. Divorces rose from 596 in 1910 to 1,629 in 1920. Much shorter skirts, public smoking of cigarettes, use of cosmetics by working girls with much more spending money, were symbols of some women's greater liberation.

Changes should not be exaggerated. D.H. Lawrence's "Rainbow" was banned. Much later, writing a war book in 1937, David Jones could not use the "impious and impolite"[11] words of soldiers. A woman who grew up in a Surrey suburb in the interwar period recalled that: "our sex life was expected to be (and generally was) almost non existent before marriage and certainly abortions or illegitimate babies were never heard of in our circle. . ."[12]

Not surprisingly, attitudes much changed by the carnage included those to "King and Country", Empire, War. There was scarcely any lasting exultation over quite remarkable victories. A deep longing for peace swept over the nation and was an important factor inhibiting rearmament in face of Hitler's obvious threats.

The imperial ideal received blows. Young men who might have gone to rule the colonies died in France. Nationalist movements grew in Ireland, Egypt, India. Indian domestic industry expanded since British goods were not available. Over the inter-war period anti-imperialist propaganda was powerful in Britain itself.

Effects of the war on the class system were complex. There was cheerful comradeship between officers and men in the fighting zones,[13] but the privileges of staff officers were resented, as were the successful business men and others who stayed at home and did well.

The landed aristocracy, which had been steadily losing political, social and economic power since the mid-19th century, was finally very largely eclipsed. Losses among sons who became junior officers were great. As will be shown, taxation rose steeply and inequalities in wealth-holding were slightly reduced. Just after the War a very large change occurred in land-owning. A leading authority concluded that between 1918 and 1921 perhaps 6 to 8 million acres of English land changed hands. Some went to other landowners but much was bought by farmers. In 1914 owners occupied 11 per cent of English and Welsh land – by 1927 this figure was 36 per cent. So a quarter of the land in England and Wales passed into owner occupation. It was a very important development which has not received the emphasis it deserves. Transfer of land on this scale over such a brief period of time had probably not occurred since the Norman Conquest. Higher death duties, declining political and social significance of land-owning, failure during the war of rent rises to match increases in land values – these were among factors influencing landlords to sell. In May 1920, the "Times" reported: "we all know it now, England is changing hands". The exaggeration contained some truth.[14]

It must be emphasised, however, that in 1919 there were many in Britain who wished to return to the conditions of 1913. It was impossible to go back in time or attitudes but it is a mistake to exaggerate the scale of the changes. The typical English village, in particular, in 1920, was not so vastly different from the village of 1913.

10.3 Effects on the economy

To the British economy the Great War was a major disaster, though there were some stimuli and benefits.

Costs were enormous. Thousands of young men died and were a permanent loss to the labour force. For over four years, resources were devoted to destructive war production. Capital was diminished. Total gross reproducible assets, which had risen by 2.4 per cent a year from 1873–1913, actually fell by 0.4 per cent a year over the period 1913–24.[15] Particularly serious was the fall in overseas assets in the two World Wars. Much emphasis should be given to the fact that: "over a period of nearly 40 years from the beginning of World War I the total real wealth of the United Kingdom scarcely increased at all – a phenomenon that must have few parallels in the history of an advanced economy."[16]

Normal trade was disrupted. Non-industrialised countries could not obtain manufactured goods from Britain so turned to other suppliers or made their own. The pre-war world economy of relatively stable exchange rates was shattered and economic nationalism throve. The new economic leader – the United States – unlike Britain in its hey-day – protected its home market. Sluggish growth before 1913 and slow adaptation to a world of new industries such as electrical goods, vehicles, chemicals, meant that for some years after 1919 Britain was not well placed to take advantage of changed situations. Income and standard of living suffered. Britain's gross national product fell by 0.2 per cent per year over the period 1913–24.[17] True, real wages increased by 1.3 per cent a year but there were serious falls in other forms of income.

Some financial costs were immediately obvious. The War cost the British Government around £9,000 million, over two thirds of which were borrowed. So the National Debt soared from under £700 million in 1914 to nearly £7,500 million in 1918. Payment of interest became a very significant charge on inter-war governments and curtailed social service spending. Britain had lent about £2,000 million to other European countries. Russia – the main borrower – repudiated the debts. In contrast, Britain agreed to pay back in full, plus interest, borrowings of some £900 million, to the U.S. (It appears that over the post-war years Britain received in payments from debtors nearly as much as she paid to the U.S.)

However, a very decisive switch of predominant economic and financial power from Britain to the U.S. had occurred. By 1916[18] Britain was largely dependant on the U.S. for vital raw materials, to pay for which £305 million worth of gold was shipped westward between 1914 and 1917, while the British treasury alone sold 750 million dollars worth of British-owned American securities and loans were raised.

Trade depends on ships. So many were sunk or requisitioned that by 1917 it was either enormously expensive or downright impossible to find a ship in which to send goods overseas.[19] India, (Lancashire's best overseas market) imported 3,000 million linear yards of cotton piece-goods in 1913–14, 853 million in 1918–19. So Lancashire cotton was badly hit and except in a brief post-war boom, never recovered its 19th century position.

True, some other branches of the economy flourished in the War. An obvious example of output expansion and income enhancement directly due to the exigencies of war was that provided by the farms. Over the period 1909–13, the yearly average food supply of the United Kingdom was 22 million metric tons of which 9 millions were imports including over four-fifths of cereals and all sugar, cocoa and chocolate.[20] The U-boat campaign starkly revealed the dangers of such a policy. In April 1917 there were stocks of food left for six weeks only. The main inducement was that most potent of all – a rise in producer prices and therefore of income. Wheat, which had sold for around 20s a quarter in the pre-war years, touched 86/4d in 1920. There were also state prodding and guarantees. County Committees were set up to control farming. They were largely composed of local landowners and attempted very little coercion. The 1917 Corn Production Act guaranteed prices and wages. Certainly, the growth of output was spectacular. From 1918, some 3 million more acres went under the plough. Women Land Army workers plus some German prisoners-of-war helped the farmers. Compared with average 1904–13 harvests, those of 1918 were up as follows (in million tons): wheat up from 1.56 to 2.58, oats 3.04 to 4.46, barley 1.52 to 1.56 and potatoes 6.59 to 9.22.[21] Farmers enjoyed a brief period of relatively great prosperity before disastrous depression struck them in the inter-war years. To add to the difficulties of many, they bought their farms from landlords at the very peak of the market around 1920 when land prices were still high.

Modern wars are fought with immense quantities of steel, guns, shells, ships, aeroplanes, tanks, vehicles. After early failings – there were serious shortages of shells on the Western Front in early 1915 – the wide range of steel, engineering and munitions industries vastly increased their output.[22] Steel-making capacity was increased by half. Numbers employed in iron and steel went up from 311,000 just before the War to 403,000 in 1920. The War brought a great boom to Britain's shipyards. Those on Tyne, Wear and Tees alone built 1130 ships of 3,324,912 tons and carried out repair work on nearly 8,000 merchant and navy vessels which were dry docked.[23]

There was much rapid technical innovation with later valuable applications to peace-time industry. Aircraft performance was improved. In 1914, military aeroplanes had a maximum speed of 80 mph: by 1918 this was 140 mph. There was a great expansion of the wireless, chemical, electrical and vehicle industries, largely to meet the needs of war, partly because Britain had imported large quantities of chemicals from Germany in the years before the War and could no longer do so. Though, perhaps sensibly in view of the Flanders mud, the Army still greatly relied on horse transport – by November 1918 Army vehicles totalled 56,000 lorries, 23,000 motor cars and 34,000 motor cycles.[24] New alloys were employed in aeroplanes and tanks: new methods allowed home-produced iron ore to be used in place of imported ore in the making of high-grade Sheffield steel.

Not surprisingly in view of the fact that nearly 5 million industrial workers joined the forces, industrial production did decline. One index[25] (1924–100) shows a fall from 90.5 in 1913 to 73.8 in 1918. But large sectors of industry and numbers of people benefited economically from the War.

For after 1914, when initial dislocation produced some unemployment, there was a rising demand for labour with resulting full and regular employment, long hours, much over-time. As in some other periods of inflation and labour shortage, the unskilled did relatively well in the War, as did women and juveniles. Many families, receiving allowances because men were away in the Forces and pay packets from working wives and youngsters, felt much better off. In Salford: "By late 1916 abject poverty began to disappear from the neighbourhood. Children looked better fed".[26] Glasgow statistics tell the same story: school children designated underfed and ill-clad fell from 264 in the war's first year to 68 in 1916–17.[27]

To women the War brought greater economic opportunities. Once again, a stimulus was given to an existing development, for women had increasingly moved into services and manufacturing industry before 1914. Now they could move out of their homes or ill-paid work such as domestic service. Numbers of female indoor servants fell by over 300,000: from 1,403,000 in 1911 to 1,072,00 in 1921. It will be noted that the post-war figure was still large. Over the war years, numbers of women and girls in industry rose from 2,179,000 to 2,971,000. In transport, the increase was 18,000 to 117,000; in banking and finance from 9,500 to 63,700 (by 1917); in commerce from 505,000 to 934,000; in national and local government, (including education) from 262,000 to 462,000.

Nearly 100,000 women (including Winifred Holtby) joined the auxiliary services, (the Women's Army Auxiliary Corps and similar branches for the Navy and Air Force). Over 100,000 became nurses and around a quarter of a million went to work on the land. For the first time, women police officers were appointed.

Economic uplift and independence brought confidence, higher standards and change. "Slowly clogs and shawls generally began to give way to coats and hats".[28]

Juveniles gained and lost from the War. On the one hand: "It was among boys and girls under eighteen that the wartime rise in wages was most marked."[29] On the other hand many children left school early to go into employment, or while still on the school rolls missed many lessons. At Akenfield in 1915: "The farmers are taking the boys from the school for the threshing. . .", and still in 1917: "The boys are being kept away from school by the farmers".[30] Nationally, there was a serious rise in juvenile delinquency.

The entry into industry of large numbers of women brought a marked improvement in welfare facilities. Particularly in large munitions plants, women welfare officers, canteens, rest-rooms and medical facilities were provided. Provision of such facilities in industry survived the War. Again, they were not all entirely new, but the War gave a great stimulus to their growth. Here was an example of a gain from the tragedy.

As a reward for great contribution to the war effort, (and surely because few must have desired a resumption of the very nasty pre-1914 struggle), women over 30 gained the vote in 1918.

10.4 Effects on Government

In the very dangerous days of April 1917, Government pushed

not important

through the Corn Production Act. It guaranteed prices of wheat, oats, potatoes; fixed a minimum agricultural wage and set up local wages boards; controlled farm rents; made possible compulsory cultivation of parks and ornamental gardens; allowed tenant farmers to shoot pheasants devouring crops. Watching the clock as the War Cabinet discussed the measures, ex-Conservative Prime Minister Balfour said: "As nearly as I can reckon, we have had one revolution every half-hour."[31]

For, as a result of War, Government interfered, controlled, taxed, spent far, far, more. Individual freedom, citizen's rights, laissez-faire, free trade were considerably curtailed. True, after 1918, the intervention, the spending, were very much reduced, but to nothing like their 1913 levels. To this day, some of the changes introduced in 1914–18 remain and are of much relevance to millions. For example, British Summer Time was introduced; pub opening hours were reduced because it was held too much drinking was harming the war effort – in particular pubs were closed in the afternoons; passports were required for journeys abroad, (before 1914, of European countries, only Russia and Turkey had required passports for entry); paper notes replaced gold sovereigns.

Not surprisingly in such a titanic struggle, Government assumed very great powers. The Defence of the Realm Acts, (D.O.R.A.), of August 1914, and later, gave the Authorities power to issue Regulations on a very wide range of matters. In the main, in Britain, the right of trial by jury was retained, though in the prevailing atmosphere this did not save all accused. A Derbyshire woman school teacher was sentenced to ten years imprisonment in 1917 for allegedly plotting to murder Lloyd George by pricking him with a poisoned needle. Evidence was largely supplied by a Government agent,[32] in the tradition of a century before the trial.

There was much control of labour and some attempts to control militant trade unionists. In 1915, a system of "Leaving Certificates" was instituted; a worker could not leave one war production factory to take up work in another without a certificate from the employer, that he left with consent. There were constant struggles over "dilution": much work previously done by skilled men was now performed by the unskilled – often women. There were strikes – though the strike record over the

War years was very good compared with periods before and after the War, the yearly averages (in million days) of lost time due to strikes being: 1910–14, 17.9; 1915–18, 4.2; 1919–21, 49.1.[33] On "Red Clydeside" two socialist papers were suppressed; a number of militants were sent from the area to other places where it was considered their influence would be less; some strikers were fined.

On the other hand, there were always to be found defenders of individual rights and supporters of those in trouble with the Authorities. Thus Lord Hugh Cecil, a High Tory, opposed a clause in the 1918 Representation of the People Act which denied for 5 years conscientious objectors' right to vote. Robert Graves helped Siegfried Sassoon when the latter, a serving officer, could have been in very serious trouble for anti-war writing. There were questions and protests in Parliament concerning bad treatment of conscientious objectors. Lloyd George took great pains to conciliate, and keep on good terms with, working people. William Beveridge – surely no reactionary – considered that the War, by creating a scarcity of labour, had put the workers in a very strong position. When Lloyd George became Prime Minister and a Ministry of Labour was set up: 'For political reasons many senior posts in the new Ministry were given to trade unionists.'[34]

The 1914 slogan was "business as usual" and until 1915 Government mainly relied on uncontrolled private enterprise to provide war material. Difficulties arose, for example: firms contracted to deliver large quantities of shells on the assumption that they would be able to sub-contract a part of their orders to other works, and then discovered that these works were also being sought after for a like purpose by rival firms; with the result, incidentally, that the aggregate of shells actually delivered fell enormously below the aggregate for which contracts had been made."[35]

So, in 1915, a Ministry of Munitions was established under the dynamic Lloyd George. By the end of the War it was directly managing some 250 Government factories, (such as shell-filling works), quarries, mines, and supervising the production of 20,000 controlled establishments, left in private hands but working on Government orders. From 1915–18 the Ministry spent £2,000 million.

Government took control of transport – ships, railways, canals – and the coal mines. Very considerable rationing of food had to be introduced though, apart from sugar, it never applied nationally to most basic foodstuffs – as in the Second War. Some prices were controlled and subsidised. Of much future significance was the control of house rents which began in Glasgow in 1915 and became general.

Massive government intervention brought benefits. New machines were installed in war factories, improved management was encouraged. As already indicated, industrial welfare was improved.

A very important, but more controversial, development was the marked growth of government co-operation and working together with employers' organisations and trade unions. Trade Associations, which had grown in numbers and influence in the decades before 1914, gained strength and experience. Trade Unionists grew in numbers and power: membership increased from just under 4 million in 1913 to 8 million in 1919. A modern historian[36] has attached great significance to this growth of corporatism in Britain in the 20th century – this virtual alliance between the State, employers' and workers' organisations.

The Great War did not revolutionise or fundamentally change the nature of British society. After all, the typical British village, factory, mine, church, school, was much the same in 1920 as it had been in 1913.

Yet changes had been important and they had been rushed on by the War. A number have been sketched on preceeding pages. In a thousand ways, great and small, the Great War influenced the future course of European and British history. An example of how the effects of the catastrophe penetrated the most patriarchal agrarian areas of the country came from what was then the East Riding of Yorkshire. Winifred Holtby's father, owner of a large farm, faced by a strike of agricultural workers "disconcerted to employers who had been masters for generations and understood no other relationship", sold up and moved.[37]

11. THE ECONOMY BETWEEN THE WARS

11.1 Decline of basic industries and World slump

In the 1980s, studies of Britain's inter-war economy acquired contemporary relevance. In both periods unemployment became a seemingly intractable problem.

The period 1919–39 saw very serious contraction of Britain's staple industries, the worst depression and the highest unemployment figures till then recorded, the prolonged misery of heavily depressed areas with massive under-employment.

Total effective demand was insufficient to call forward an output sufficient to give employment to all seeking work. The main cause of insufficient demand was contraction of overseas markets.

In the 1920s, export industries were depressed in comparison with 1913 levels and quite heavy unemployment resulted. This ill was made vastly worse when the Great Slump, which had begun in America in 1929, smote Europe in 1930. Recovery began in late 1932. By 1937 there was something approaching full employment in Britain's South-east but in the old industrial areas of North and West, heavy under-employment persisted until war again found work for all.

Over the period 1921 to 1938, the unemployment rate among persons covered by the unemployment insurance scheme averaged 14.2 per cent, varying from a minimum of just under 10, to a maximum of just over 22. At the very bottom of the slump, before the turn-up which had begun had had time to show itself in the unemployment figures, there were nearly 3 million (2.95 million) out of work. It must be emphasised that these were insured workers and that the health and unemployment insurance schemes applied in the main only to manual workers. After 1923 about 60 per cent of all at work were covered by insurance. White collar workers earning over £5 a week, railway workers, civil servants, teachers, police, domestic servants, farm workers, those under 16, and the self-employed were not covered. (Farm workers were brought into the scheme in 1936: those under 16 in 1935, domestic workers in 1938). Uninsured were less likely than insured workers to be out of work. It follows that the percentage of unemployment in the whole work-force was lower than that among insured workers, though the total number out of work was of course increased by inclusion of the uninsured.

Insurance scheme returns show an average 14.2 per cent unemployment between 1921 and 1938: around 11 per cent of the whole workforce were out of work.[1]

Structural unemployment

The Great War was followed by a short-lived boom as firms produced to full capacity to meet unsatisfied demand. With what proved to be rash confidence, equipment (for example in cotton and shipbuilding), was much expanded. In 1920 as a whole only 3.9 per cent of insured workers were unemployed.

But before the end of 1920 a slump began. From 1921 onwards, Britain's basic industries – cotton, coal, iron and steel, shipbuilding – were in very serious trouble. By May 1921, 23.4 per cent of insured workers were out of work and the percentage for the whole year was 16.9. There was some recovery in 1924 and again in 1927 when the percentage out of work fell just below 10 per cent but between 1921 and 1929 this was the only year when less than one in ten insured workers were unemployed.

As already emphasised, the Great War shattered that inter-national economic order over which Britain had presided and which had brought rapidly rising world trade and development. Growth in volume of world trade had been running at well over 40 per cent per decade in the early 20th century. But now came a disastrous slow-down. The rate of expansion fell to around 8.5 per cent per decade just after the World War and to a mere one per cent in the Thirties, even after the recovery up to the boom of 1937. The slump years witnessed a sad fall.

Of the stagnant volume of trade, Britain's share declined from

14 per cent in 1913 to 11 in 1929 and 10 in 1937. Between 1913 and 1929, while British imports rose by 1.1 per cent per year, exports fell by 0.5 and re-exports by 0.4 per cent. It was a serious reversal of the trend of 1900 to 1913 when exports had grown by 3.3 per cent per annum.[2] During the inter-war period, overseas trade became relatively less important to Britain, as industries increasingly turned to satisfying domestic demand. As a percentage of national product, exports fell from 33 in 1907 to 27 in 1924 to 15 in 1938.[3]

Primary producers were earning less money to spend on industrial products from countries like Britain. Because of loss of life and economic dislocation resulting from the War, demand for primary products had not risen as high as had production stimulated by the high prices of 1915–20. Stocks accumulated: prices fell. Already in 1927–28, before the Great Slump, nearly 12 million bags of coffee were piled up in Brazil. Rubber fell from 70 cents a pound in 1925 to around 20 cents in 1929; wheat from 2.10 dollars a bushel in 1914–25 to about 1.15 in 1929. The season's average Liverpool price in pence per lb for American middling raw cotton fell from 25.31 in 1919–20 to 11.89 in 1920–21 before fluctuating between 8.15 and 17.61 in the Twenties and plummeting to 4.82 in 1931–32.

Britain's domestic firms and consumers clearly gained from these falls in raw material prices. Indeed the inter-war movement of the Terms of Trade in Britain's favour must receive much emphasis. If 1913 export prices divided by import prices are represented by 100, then average figures for 1921–29 and 1930–37 are 127 and 138. This is a major reason for the improved standard of living of the majority who could buy cheaper bread, chocolate, cotton goods, tyres.

On the other hand, with diminished incomes, primary producers could buy less manufactures from Britain.

Winston Churchill, Chancellor of the Exchequer, added to industry's difficulties when in 1925, acting on the advice of the Treasury and Bank of England, he restored in a modified form the Gold Standard. The pound was again linked to gold and, most important, the dollar exchange rate of 4.86 dollars to the pound, was restored. Keynes was convinced that the pound was over valued, that the rate should have been about 4.40 dollars to the pound. Others did not agree.[4] But Keynes rightly pointed out that to make the higher rate stick, domestic deflation and wage-cutting would be necessary.[5] Until 1931, British exports were harmed and imports cheapened by an artificially high exchange rate.

So, for a variety of reasons, in the 1920s while other countries, such as the United States, were experiencing considerable booms, Britain's old, basic, largely export industries were in difficulties. There was heavy structural unemployment among the trades engaged in, and in areas dependent on coal, cotton, shipbuilding, iron and steel, heavy engineering. Areas such as the North-east, Clydeside, South Wales were particularly badly hit. Changed fortunes after 1920 of some major basic industries are now briefly examined.

The basic industries

Cotton encountered increasing competition from overseas countries equipped with the necessary machinery, (often purchased from Britain). We have seen how the Great War reduced Lancashire's and stimulated overseas output. After a brief 1919–20 boom, these trends continued, as the following depressing statistics reveal.[6]

	Cotton Yarn (million lb)		Piece goods (million sq. yds.)	
	Production	Exports	Production	Exports
1912	1,982	244	8,050	6,913
1930	1,047	137	3,500	2,472
1938	1,070	123	3,126	1,494

Raw cotton consumption (thousand tons) was down from nearly 900,000 (1909–13) to 569,000 (1938).

Numbers of looms (thousands) fell from 786 in 1912 to 495 in 1938. Workers in cotton numbered 575,000 in 1926, 378,000 in 1939. As a proportion of British exports by value cotton goods fell from a quarter in 1910–13 to 12 per cent in 1937–39. A major reason for declining exports was the growth of domestic output in what had been the largest pre-war market – India. A lesser factor was the continuing rise of Japanese competition.[7]

The Indian Market, Cotton piece goods – million linear yards

	Average 1909–13	1938	Change
Indian home production	1,141	4,250	+ 3,109
Total imports into India	2,741	724	− 2,017
of which from U.K.	2,669	258	− 2,411
from Japan	4	441	+ 437

Here then was one obvious cause of Lancashire's problems.

Shipbuilding and shipping industries were also badly hit. Annual tonnage of steam ships (in thousand tons) built and first registered in Britain fell from 724.5 (1910–19) to 615.5 (1920–29), to 290.7 (1930–38),[8] (average per annum per decade). Total launchings of merchant ships in the U.K. fluctuated very considerably in the 1920s – falling from over 2 million to 646,000 from 1920–23, rising to over 1,400,000 in 1924 and 1930 before plummeting to a disastrous 133,000 in 1933.

An index of tramp shipping freight rates (1869=100) which had risen from 45 in 1908 to 751 in 1918 was down to 85 at the bottom of the Slump.

The following figures[9] reveal the decline of the iron and steel industry prior to recovery in the Thirties.

Annual averages for each 5 years, (all in thousand tons)

Year	Iron ore production	Iron ore Imports	Pig iron Output	Iron & Steel Exports	Steel Output
1915–19	13,889	6,220	8,701	2,540	8,938
1920–24	8.996	4,730	6,060	3,303	7,067
1925–29	9,984	4,353	6,042	3,911	7,647
1930–34	8,926	3,424	4,729	2,240	6,733

Before and after the Great War over a million men worked in the coal industry. Exports were badly hit by the War and in 1920 were only a third of those of 1913. There was a brief upsurge in 1923, when following the French occupation of the Ruhr, Germany's main industrial area came to a standstill and British coal exports reached an all time record of 79,459,000 tons. Throughout normal years in the Twenties, exports were around 50–60 million tons before dropping heavily to under 39 million in 1938.

For coal, market conditions were unfavourable. Demand fell as ships and some large scale consumers switched to oil, as hydro-electric schemes were completed on the Continent, as Polish mines – paying lower wages than British competitors – took European markets. The Royal Navy used about 1.7 million tons of coal in 1913–14 but only about 110,000 tons in 1932. By 1930 some 40 per cent of the world's merchant ships were oil-burning. Some London hospitals and glass manufacturers had turned to oil. Polish exports took an appreciable part of the Scandinavian market in the late 20s. In the first 6 months of 1928, 24.57 million tons of British coal were exported compared to 35.5 million in the first 6 months of 1913.

That domestic consumption also fell is clear from the following figures:[10]

Table 7 *Coal consumption, Great Britain, 1913, 1925, 1932 (million tons)*

Purpose for which used	1913	1925	1932
Gas works	16.7	16.45	16.37
Electricity works	4.9	8.08	9.81
Railway locomotives	13.2	13.36	11.70
Coasting steamers	1.9	1.16	1.19
Coal mines	18.0	15.42	12.04
Pig iron manufacture	21.2	12.03	6.56
Iron and steel works	10.2	9.26	5.37
Domestic	40.0	40.00	40.00
General manufacture and all other purposes	57.7	53.81	46.46
TOTAL:	183.8	169.57	149.50

The increased consumption of electricity works, continuing large use of coal on the railways and heavy domestic purchases will be noted.

In a free market with hundreds of competing suppliers and very many buyers, there were violent fluctuations in price. Average selling values per ton raised at the pit were 34s 7d in 1920, 17s 8d in 1922, 18s 10d in 1924, 16s 4d in 1924, 13s 3d in 1932. In the face of intense competition, export prices fluctuated even more than home prices. Average values per ton (f.o.b.) of large steam coal exported were 89s 6d in 1920, 24s 9d in 1922.

Pits which had made large profits in 1920, often sold at a loss in years such as 1921, 1925, 1928, 1932. In 1921 Government handed back the mines to their owners. They could hardly have chosen a worse time for the latter. In Durham, in the first quarter of 1921 each ton of coal was being sold at a loss of 4s 2d. In the second quarter of 1925 the loss per ton was 1s 5d.[11] Pease and Partners and the Consett Iron Co., (both considerable mine owners in the North-east) which made good profits and paid dividends before 1913, paid no dividends at all 1925–35.

Owners determined to cut costs by reducing wages. The most serious labour troubles in Britain's modern history resulted, culminating in the 1926 General Strike. There were prolonged coal stoppages in 1921 (March to July) and 1926 (May to November). In each struggle, the miners were defeated and those who had work to go back to did so on far worse conditions. In County Durham, the index of average real earnings per shift, (1914=100), fell from 109.7 in 1921 to 79.9 in 1922 and from 93.1 in early 1926 to 78.2 in 1929.[12] Also in County Durham, nearly 60,000 miners were out of work by August 1921, and the number of wage earners on Durham colliery books fell from 170,181 in 1823 to 128,283 in 1927, to 101,129 in 1933.[13] True, Durham – a major exporting area – was particularly badly hit, but the decline of South Wales production was even more dramatic (from 56.8 million tons in 1913 to 34.4 in 1933). Scotland and Lancashire also suffered badly but falls in Yorkshire and the Midlands were far less – the figures being:[14]

Coal: Millions of tons produced

Year	North East	Yorks	Midlands Derby, Notts Leics, Warwicks	Lancs	Staffs	S.Wales	Scot.	U.K.
1913	56.4	43.7	38.8	28.1	14.9	56.8	42.5	287.4
1933	40.1	37.3	32.5	13.2	11.7	34.4	29.2	207.1

Numbers employed in the mines fell from 1,127,900 in 1913 to 790,000 in 1938. In 1928, 14.37 per cent of insured workers in the coal industry were wholly unemployed while 7.54 per cent were temporarily stopped. In 1933 these sad figures were 21.92 and 10.73.

Therefore, even before the shattering hurricane of world economic depression hit British industry, there was clear evidence of marked decline of basic industries, with heavy unemployment in the old industrial areas. The very serious social consequences of these developments will be detailed later.

The Great Slump – 1929–33

In Britain, as in the rest of the World, the Great Slump ranks with the World Wars among that small group of great catastrophes which have most shaped subsequent events, attitudes and careers.

Once a serious recession starts in a largely uncontrolled free enterprise economy, a vicious circle of causation is almost certain to make it worse. Whatever may be the actual firing mechanism, a stock market crash leads to diminished financial holdings by the wealthy, less investment, lay-offs, falling demand, prices, output, employment. A man thrown out of work in Newcastle cannot afford a new suit and a Yorkshire woman becomes unemployed. So it goes on.

The famous Wall Street collapse of 1929 signalled the beginning of the Slump. The story has been told in gripping detail. The market slump: "reflected in the main the change which was already apparent in the industrial situation".[15] American production had turned down.

Prices, output, employment collapsed very dramatically. From 1929–32 export prices fell by the following percentages: rubber (British Malaya) 84, wool (Argentina) 72, coffee (Brazil) 65, bacon (Denmark) 64, petrol (U.S.A.) 47, coal (U.K.) 28. These are merely examples of world trends. Practically all economies, (except the siege economy of the Soviet Union which was suffering its own great hardships following forced collectivisation and the deaths of many thousand of peasants), were vitally affected by these world events. Thus, the value of Spanish exports fell from 2,300 million pesetas in 1930 to 740 million in 1932.

Some important export prices fell dramatically: thus U.K. white cotton piece goods prices fell by 48 per cent from 1929 to 1932.

The value of world trade, reckoned at over 68 billion dollars in 1929 was down to under 27 billion by 1932. Of course, the fall in prices accounted for much of this, but even volume of trade dropped by over a quarter. Overseas primary producers could not afford to buy British shirts or bicycles. The whole world economy suffered.

Yet Britain suffered less from the Slump than some other leading manufacturing countries. Thus, between 1929 and 1932, manufacturing output (1913=100) fell in the US.A. from 112.7 to 58.4, in Germany from 108 to 64.6, in Britain from 109.9 to 90.[16] Unemployment rates were much higher in the U.S., Canada and Germany. Percentage falls in prices of industrial shares between 1927 and 1931 were 61.7 in Germany, 59.7 in the U.S.A., 55.7 in France, 45.0 in the U.K.

The most dramatic evidence of slump in Britain came with the avalanche of unemployment. In early 1929 the insured unemployed numbered around 1,250,000. In early 1930 this total was 1,750,000 and by early 1931 about 2,600,000. 1932 was the worst year with 2,850,000 out of work in January and a yearly average of nearly 22 per cent of the insured work-force unemployed. Unemployment peaked in January 1933 with 2,950,000 in the dole queues. By summer 1935 the total was again under 2 million. Percentages of insured workers unemployed rose from 10.4 in 1929 to 22.1 in 1932 before falling steadily to 10.8 in 1937. To very many who lived through these years, the outstanding feature of the performance of the British economy was its inability to provide work for all those seeking it.

About 1934, a Ministry of Labour investigation revealed that in an extremely depressed economy, 52.1 per cent of the insured males and 64.3 per cent of the insured females made no claim for unemployment over the year. Of the males unemployed in the twelve months over one-seventh were unemployed for four weeks or less, and over one-third for twelve weeks or less.[17]

But while statistical evidence may confirm that "the major problem is that of intermittent rather than chronic unemployment", yet through the Thirties as one year of underemployment succeeded another, in certain age-groups, occupations, regions, chronic long-term unemployment constituted a great and growing economic and social tragedy.

In 1931, nearly one in five of the unemployed had been

continuously out of work for more than six months. In 1935 the
Unemployment Assistance Board completed a sample survey of
over 220,000 unemployed. About 30 per cent had been out of
work for more than two years, and, of those, 10 per cent had
been unemployed for more than five years. The result of the
Slump and the rise in unemployment figures meant that whereas
in 1927 a figure of some 1,100,000 unemployed meant about 4
million claims for benefit, nearly 3 million unemployed in 1932–4
meant about 6 million claims. Roughly speaking, an average
unemployed man claimed for 3 months in 1927, for 6 months in
1934.

National averages disguised large differences between men and
women, between particular age groups, occupations, regions.
The Ministry of Labour investigation referred to above revealed
that 3.7 per cent of insured males but only 0.5 per cent of females
had been out of work for the whole 52 weeks covered.[18] (Of
course very depressed industries such as mining, shipbuilding,
docks employed no women). With exaggeration, it has been
claimed that over the years 1920–38: "One group of workers,
those under 18 years of age, were conspicuously free of the blight
of unemployment. In contrast to the nationwide average of
14 per cent, unemployment among juveniles averaged only 5 per
cent".[19] Accurate figures of juvenile unemployment over the
period are not available, but it most certainly was a problem in
depressed areas. In the North-east, for example Juvenile
Instruction Centres were established. However, as often, older
people, thrown out of work, found it hard to get back. Of 98,000
men who had been unemployed for two years, nearly a third
were over 55 years of age, while men aged 25 to 34 only, "a
small fraction" were out for the whole period.[20]

That the unskilled were more likely than the skilled to be out
of work is clear from the following figures which reveal the much
differing experiences of various occupations.

In 1931, percentages of the total male labour force out of work
in England and Wales were:[21]

Unskilled manual workers   30.5
Skilled and semi-skilled manual workers 14.4
Salesmen and shop assistants   7.9
Clerks and typists   5.5

Higher office workers	5.1
Professions	5.5
Retail traders	2.3
Farmers	0.5
Other proprietors and managers	1.3

In 1932, while unemployment among those engaged in commerce, banking, insurance and finance was 5.6 per cent, it was 60 per cent in shipbuilding and ship repairing. Over the period 1924–38, mean levels of unemployment in some of the worst affected industries were:

Docks and harbour service	30.6
Shipbuilding	37.1
Steel melting etc.	27.4
Pig iron	23.8
Coal mining	20.9
Shipping	24.4

It followed that areas dependent on the old, basic, declining industries suffered very badly indeed. In 1930, when the national average percentage of unemployment among the insured was 16.1, figures for least and worst affected Regions were:

London	8.1
South-east	8.0
South-west	10.4
North-east	20.2
North-west	23.8
Scotland	18.5
Wales	25.9

Counties heavily engaged in coal-mining, such as Durham or Glamorgan, towns dependent on shipyards, such as Jarrow, registered quite appalling unemployment figures. In January 1933, 77 per cent of workers were out of work in Jarrow, 68 per cent in Merthyr, 54 per cent at Clydebank,[22] 40 per cent in County Durham.

In the 1930s, Britain was a land of two nations. One was the relatively prosperous area south and east of a line roughly drawn from the Humber to the Dee to the Severn. A woman who grew up in Surrey wrote: "No record of the legendary Thirties would be complete without some reference to the Great Depression and the tragic unemployment that resulted – but, to be honest, I cannot recall that it affected any of my immediate circle of family and friends". "Most of one's friends' fathers worked in the Civil Service in London, or the Bank, or in some City firm, and there would be a daily stream of them walking to and from the station. . ."[23]

It was very different in the North of England, in Wales, Scotland. Here still lived half of Britain's workers and here were two-thirds of the unemployed.

But even in the North were considerable pockets of middle class and skilled working-class comfort. In growing suburbs of Sheffield or Newcastle, in plush seaside resorts such as Southport or Whitley Bay, lived increasing numbers of middle-class owner-occupiers. Sheffield steel and I.C.I. chemical workers were not poor. George Orwell quite failed to portray large sections of Northerners.

In Blackpool, Roy Fuller, born 1912, after private schooling went into a solicitor's office where the "articled clerks were idle beyond belief". Rising early to attend law classes in Manchester he found that his mother had "even put the water in the egg-pan the night before". In his office was an engrossing clerk from a poor family who rose to become a solicitor and fulfilled the provincial dream of material success.[24]

This having been said, the grim reality remains that Britain's old basic industrial areas were very depressed indeed in the inter-war period. For example, the North-east region in 1923 was still very heavily dependent on five basic industries, (mining, engineering, ship-building, iron and steel, chemicals), in which were employed nearly two-thirds of the region's insured workers.[25]

Depression struck like a cyclone. North-east shipyards, which had built nearly 950,000 tons of shipping in the boom year 1920, could only launch a pitiful 37,000 tons in 1933. The shipbuilding labour force of 104,631 of 1921 was down to 78,212 by 1931 and of these a dreadful total of 48,000 were on the dole. In Jarrow, Palmers' closed in 1936. 200 marched to London to call attention to "the town that was murdered".[26]

30 per cent of Durham miners were out of work in 1932. The town of Crook which "may be reckoned as lucky, only about 40 per cent of its workers being unemployed",[27] was one of the stricken towns selected for a scientific study of long unemployment,[28] to which further reference must later be made. The economic waste of unemployment is made clear by such statements as "17 per cent of the men interviewed in Crook were classified as decidedly intelligent and 64 per cent as of good average intelligence". Yet, a horrendous 71 per cent of these Crook unemployed had been out of work for 5 years or more as compared with only 3 per cent of sample in a London borough.[29]

Counting Britain's unemployed as 100, Durham's was over 170 between 1927 and 1936. Still, in May 1936, 27.7 of Co. Durham's insured workers were unemployed, compared with Greater London's 6.8 per cent. The effects in the area of the Great Depression are clear from the following grim figures.

Table 8 *Percentages of insured workers unemployed: monthly averages*[30]

	1929	1932	1937
Durham	17.9	40.5	19.5
Northumberland	16.1	31.2	15.4
The Hartlepools	23.1	48.5	22.5
Sunderland	20.8	46.7	25.6

Around 1932, at the bottom of the World Slump, unemployment was a serious problem in all areas. But before and after the worst years, heavy unemployment was concentrated in the West and North. Table 9[31] makes this clear:

In service industries, where many workers were not covered by national insurance, levels of unemployment were generally much lower than in manufacturing industry. Unfortunately such industries were not nearly as important in the heavy industry areas as they were in London. In all Co. Durham, only 13 per 1000 males in 1921 belonged to the professions and only 23 per 1000 were clerks (as compared with 64 in London).[32] Further, there was very much disguised unemployment for in mining, steel and shipbuilding towns, very few girls and women could find work. In 1921, only 11.4 per cent of females in Easington were at work. Throughout the country, it was very usual for women in teaching, nursing, the Civil Service, to resign from their posts on marriage. They might be unpopular if they did not. In Sunderland, in 1933, the complaint was made that "A young married woman has been appointed to the school at Ryhope . . . when there are so many young teachers who are unable to obtain positions, surely it is unfair". In 1937 Sunderland authorities decided to dismiss 17 teachers and a married nurse.[33] Clearly, published unemployment figures did not take account of much hidden underemployment. Depth of the pool of resulting unhappiness among bright, active, women can only be guessed at.

Table 9 *Regional Distribution of Unemployment 1929–37*

Region	Percentage of insured workers (aged 16–64) who were unemployed		
	July 1929	*July 1932*	*July 1937*
London	4.7	13.1	5.5
South-east	3.8	13.1	5.0
South-west	6.8	16.4	6.2
Midlands	9.5	21.6	7.0
North-east	12.6	30.6	11.3
North-west	12.7	26.3	12.9
Scotland	11.2	29.0	16.1
Wales	18.8	38.1	19.9
Gt. Britain	9.7	22.9	9.9

11.2 Adjustment, recovery, advance

The inter-war period has such a bad reputation that any mention of progress is liable to be greeted with scorn by the many who suffered and by those who learned from them. Yet millions must be aware of great technical progress over those years, for they have seen films of the planes which flew against Richtofen in 1918 and of the greatly superior Hurricanes and Spitfires which – warned by radar and guided by wireless – defended Britain in

1940. No British homes in 1919 – but most in 1939 – possessed a wireless set; by the latter date, very many had electric light, cookers, and hoover cleaners; millions saw the new "talkie" films in plush cinemas; roads in, say, the Peak District, were already thronged with lines of cars on sunny summer weekends. In advanced, industrial societies, technological advance is so built into the system through organised research, innovation, investment, that it continues even in the most adverse of periods. The international discoveries, inventions, progress associated with the provision of wireless provide a fascinating story.[34]

Structural change

There were major switches in employment from the old basic to new industries, to services, to public untilities. Even in Northumberland and Durham, certainly as depressed an area as any in England, there was considerable diversification between 1923 and 1937.[35] Coal mining lost 62,000, shipbuilding 20,770, engineering 9,080. But distributive trades gained 32,280, building and contracting 37,430, hotel and boarding-house services 6,770, chemicals 9,120, electrical industries 4,770 and so on. Even in that very hard hit area, total employment rose between 1923 and 1937 by 29,350. Employment in Sunderland rose by 8,000, in Newcastle by 23 per cent.[36] Still in 1938, Co. Durham had 20.7 per cent of insured workers on the dole, Sunderland 26.8 per cent.

In 1921, the total British labour force was 19.36 million, of whom an average of 17.62 million were at work during that year; in 1931 the labour force was 21.86 million, of whom an average 20.07 million were in work. Between 1923 and 1937, numbers in the distributive trades increased by over 800,000, in public and private services by 560,000, in building and public works construction by 485,000, in transport by 119,000.[37] Decline in old heavy industry mainly located in the North and West and rise of new consumer, service industries mainly in the Midlands and South-east involved a considerable migration to these latter areas. In England and Wales, the South-east gained more than 600,000 people in the Twenties and a further million in the Thirties: numbers in the North and Wales fell by nearly a million.[38] Heavily afflicted towns lost population: that of Jarrow fell from 35,576 in the 1920s to 30,700 in 1939. The following table clearly reveals the relative decline of old established industries and the emergence of that economic structure to which Britons were to become accustomed over some decades following World War II, a structure in which the engineering industries, public utilities and services were to provide increased slices of employment.

Table 10   *U.K. Employment: 1923 and 1938*[39]

Industry	Insured persons working June 1938	Percentage increase (+) or decrease − since 1923
Distributive trades	1,911,218	+ 64.5
Building and contracting	1,141,203	+ 63.2
General engineering	591,430	+ 16.8
Hotel, restaurant, etc. services	394,877	+ 71.7
Road transport	385,312	+ 73.1
Motor and aircraft engineering	360,836	+109.4
Local Government service	317,323	+ 49.8
Electrical manufacturing	275,120	+128.7
Printing, publishing, book-binding	268,564	+ 27.6
Gas, water, electricity supply	205,177	+ 34.2
Tailoring	190,776	+ 8.5
Laundries, dyeing, etc.	168,629	+ 69.5
Professional services	165,608	+ 61.7
Bread, biscuit, cake-making	163,446	+ 15.7
Furniture making	132,422	+ 57.3
Entertainments, sport etc.	127,731	+150.5
Coal mining	701,713	− 41.5
Cotton manufacturing	251,184	− 33.2
Woollen and worsted manu-facturing	164,731	− 32.3
Iron and steel	152,965	− 17.7
Railway service (non-permanent workers)	149,508	− 14.0
Shipbuilding	139,968	− 4.8
Dock, Harbour etc. service	118,270	− 14.6
Boot and shoe manufacturing	111,792	− 11.9
TOTAL: All industries	12,075,268	+ 21.5

A study of the above figures reveals not only the decline of basic, but also the rapid growth of new, industries – motor, aircraft, electric engineering, and so on. That the general standard of living was rising is clearly demonstrated by the mammoth growth of numbers engaged in entertainment and sports, hotel, restaurant and similar services.

Electricity

Perhaps in no other field were advances over the inter-war period so obvious and important as in electrical engineering and supply. At the end of the 19th century, inventors such as Sir Joseph Swan were among leaders, but the presence of existing supplies of ample cheap energy – coal, and gas, plus failure to co-ordinate the many new producers of electrical power meant that Britain lagged badly in this field. Now this situation was much changed.

In electrical engineering, numbers of insured workers grew from 174,000 in 1924 to 367,000 in 1937. Britain roughly drew level with foreign rivals in engineering and went ahead in national electricity supply. For in 1926 was established the Central Electricity Board.[40] Before that date, over 400 stations many of which were very small, had generated local supplies of electricity. Now the whole system was connected up by a national "grid" over high-tension wires. By 1935, generation of power had been concentrated in about 144 stations increasingly producing a standardised voltage: by 1929 half the domestic current was at 230v. Output rose from 12.7 million KWH in 1926 to 35.8 in 1939. In pence per KWH, prices for household consumers fell from 3.815 in 1925 to 1.598 in 1938. The number of consumers rose from 730,000 in 1920 to 8,920,000 in 1939. In industry there was a very considerable switch to electrical in place of steam power. Domestic users too, benefited from the spread of electric power. Production of vacuum cleaners grew from 37,550 in 1930, to 409,345 in 1935: ex-works price fell from an average £14 in 1930 to £8 in 1934. Between 1930 and 1935, output of electric cookers more than trebled.

Motors

The annual output of motor vehicles (excluding motor cycles) rose from 95,000 in 1923, to 511,000 in 1937. Employment rose from 220,000 in 1924 to 380,000 (including workers in the aircraft industry) in 1938. In thousands, registered motor vehicles increased from 208 in 1913 to 2,422 in 1938. Whereas in 1913 there were over 100 manufacturers, by 1938 the "Big Six", Nuffield, Ford, Austin, Vauxhall, Rootes and Standard were producing nine out of ten passenger cars and just over eight out of ten commercial vehicles. American-type assembly line plants had been established. There were increases in productivity and reductions in prices, (a new small car could be bought for just over £100 in 1938), but a 1935 estimate was the Americans produced three times as many cars per worker as British makers. As often, however, the evidence is mixed: Britain exported far more motor vehicles than she imported, so products must have been competitive.

Figures were:[41]

	Imports (annual average)		Exports (annual average)	
Motor vehicles	Volume (Nos)	Value £	Volume (Nos)	Value £
1930–38	10,950	1,666,000	59,400	8,171,000

The car industry, like the electrical and wireless, provided openings for large numbers of retailers and service workers. This rise in the number of small entrepreneurs in garages and service establishments was a counterflow to the much quoted trend towards concentration in industrial production. Similarly, the advent of electric power greatly helped small producers who did not now have to install steam engines and driving. The growth of the car industry was also important since it stimulated output in other new, and some old, industries, as the followng list of quantities of materials used in the manufacture and repair of motor vehicles in 1936, makes clear.[42]

Iron and steel	900,000 tons	Glass	8,830,000 sq. feet
Brass and Copper	13,000 "	Paints	2,350,000 galls.
Lead and lead oxide	8,100 "	Rubber	63,000 tons
Aluminium and bronze	450 "	Timber	111,000,000 board feet

Clearly, the rubber industry was a beneficiary of the growth of car output. Exports of pneumatic tyres averaged £2,712,000 between 1930–38. Rubber was increasingly used for footwear, clothing, belting, among other products.

Other growing industries

Other growing industries were rayon, chemicals, wireless. Between 1920 and 1929 production of rayon increased from 6 million to nearly 53 million lbs, while between 1921 and 1929 the price of viscose yarn fell from 150 to 63 pence per lb.

In 1926, I.C.I. was formed from the merger of four leading chemical companies, including Brunner Mond which already had a factory producing synthetic ammonia on Tees-side. In 1935, before much expansion in the late 1930s, 9,000 were employed at Billingham.

At the end of 1922, only 36,000 Britons held wireless licences: by the end of the decade the number was nearly 3 million, and when War again came it was up to nearly 9 million. Output of new sets reached a peak of 1,918,000 in 1937. Annual turnover of the wireless manufacturing and service industry increased from £1,800,000 in 1926 to nearly £30 million in 1931. In hard-hit years and regions, these new industries continued to thrive. Readers of the "Northern Echo" in 1927 were advised "How to choose your wireless set".[43] By 1937 the Sunderland Branch of the Electrical Association for women "had provided training for women in the technicalities of electricity."[44]

Over the years of slump, Britain's output fell less severely than did output in a number of Western countries, while recovery to above 1929 levels was more convincing in Britain than in some other states.

The following figures show, in percentages, falls in industrial output from 1929–32 and rises (if any) from 1929–37.[45]

	1929–32	1929–37
U.K.	−17	24
Germany	−42	16
Canada	−42	0
Belgium	−31	−6
U.S.	−46	−8
France	−31	−28

The "Economist" index of business activity, (1924=100), based on 20 indices of employment, bank clearings and so on – fell from over 100 in 1929 to under 95 in late 1931, hovered around the mid 90s through 1932 and early 1933, then climbed quite rapidly to reach 110 again in 1934. By 1935, business activity was back to its 1929 level and there was a further considerable rise of activity up to 1937. The most obvious evidence of recovery was the fall in numbers of registered unemployed from 2,756,00 in 1932, 1,709,000 in 1936, under 1,500,000 in the summer of 1937.

Apart from the obvious fact that Britain's was part of world recovery, factors peculiar to Britain aided employment and growth. They included the role of the Authorities, the large house-building programmes, the growth of new industries (to which reference has already been made).

The Authorities' role

In accordance with long-standing economic orthodoxy, the National Government after 1931 determined to, and did, balance the Budget. By 1933–34 there was a surplus of over £34 million. To achieve this, taxes had been increased and public spending cut. Public servants (including teachers) had their salaries cut by ten per cent. In some cases, (teachers were threatened with a 15 per cent cut), reductions would have been higher but the sailors of the Atlantic fleet, based at Invergordon, refused to carry out orders on 15 September 1931 and such was the alarm caused by this "mutiny" in a famous service that there was some revision of the pay reductions.

It must be pointed out that so large were falls in prices over the Slump years that even with the above-mentioned reductions, civil servants and others became better off in real terms. Between 1929 and 1933, the cost of living fell by 14½ per cent. Since average money wages fell by only 4½ per cent, those in regular employment could buy more, and undoubtedly this was a factor making for recovery.

It can be argued that since London was still a very important international financial centre, a reputation for fiscal rectitude was important in restoring and maintaining confidence. Further massive Government spending would have raised prices and added to the difficulties of competing export industries.

In other respects, action by the Authorities did further the up-turn from the Slump. In the Autumn of 1931, Britain went off the Gold Standard. Relative to the dollar the pound fell in value – from 4.86 to around 3.30 by December 1931. This helped exports and made imports more expensive. The gain was temporary since, in 1933, President Roosevelt deliberately reduced the exchange value of the dollar, which fell to around 5 dollars to the pound.

More dramatic was the ending of Free Trade, one of the great pillars of 19th century Liberalism. It had not survived intact to 1931: there had been the McKenna duties imposed during the Great War on imported luxuries, while in the 1920s commercial vehicles, dyestuffs, and a small group of other industries were protected. Still in 1930, the great majority of imports into Britain were not subject to duties.

Since protection was clearly coming and since foreigners would be very likely to rush goods to Britain before duties were imposed, in late 1931 Government introduced the Abnormal Importations Act as a "temporary means of preventing excessive imports". In 1932 a general 10 per cent duty was clapped on imports but Empire goods and some foodstuffs were among items excluded. After nearly a century of Free Trade, Britain again protected home industries. Here was an important change.

For the rest of the Thirties, British industry was considerably protected from foreign competition. Duties on foreign steel were raised to $33\frac{1}{3}$ per cent. A half of imports paid from 10 to 20 per cent. It is not easy to be certain about economic effects. There was much revival in the steel industry, but general recovery and re-armament were powerful causes. On the other hand, makers of motor cars, for example, grumbled much about alleged deficiencies and high prices in the steel industry. The cost of living was pushed up somewhat. But to very many people in the Thirties, the overriding factor was that of obtaining work, so any change which increased employment was generally welcome.

An important development resulting from protection was that – some decades after the peak of Victorian imperial power – the Empire became more important than ever in Britain's trade. In the 1920s, Imperial Conferences attended by representatives of the self-governing Dominions agreed on measures of imperial preference in trade. Britain's adoption of protection enabled her to give far greater exemptions to Empire countries and following the Ottawa Conference of 1932, these countries increasingly favoured Empire goods in their schedules. U.K. trade with the Empire increased as follows:[46]

	Per cent of U.K. imports from Empire	Per cent of U.K. exports to Empire
1913	25.0	32.9
1937	37.3	39.7

In 1937, Bank Rate, (later called Minimum Lending Rate), was reduced to a very low 2 per cent, at which figure it remained, (except for a brief interval in 1939), until 1951. It is difficult to describe the economic effects of cheap money. One can lead a horse to the water but one cannot make it drink. The Authorities can offer money at low interest rates but businessmen may not wish to borrow. This is very likely to be the case when profits are low or non-existent as in 1932. On the other hand, advantages of being able to borrow cheaply are very great. Local Authorities completed large housing and other public works schemes in the Thirties and it was a vast advantage to them that they could obtain finance at low rates. Even more obvious, perhaps, were the gains reaped by builders and home buyers.

Housing

Provision of new houses from 1934 to 1939 was on a vast scale. Builders are notoriously dependent on borrowed capital before they can sell their completed houses. Then, as now, home buyers often relied on Building Societies. In 1932 the mortgage rate fell to 5½ per cent. Though there were other factors at work such as the fall in building costs and the rise in real incomes, it is very reasonable to conclude that cheap money was a major factor accounting for the large house-building programmes of the 1930s.

Over the six years 1934-39, housing completions averaged considerably over 300,000 a year. Very many products go into a modern house, (cement production went up from 4.39 million tons in 1932 to 8.34 million tons in 1939). Further, new occupants of a house often spend heavily on furniture and fittings. The housing boom stimulated a host of industries making bricks, tiles, glass, electrical and sanitary fittings, curtains, carpets and so on.

Farming

As already indicated, over most of the inter-war period, agriculture was a depressed, declining industry. As late as 1936, the writer Henry Williamson bought a run-down arable farm in North Norfolk, plus cottage, for £2,250. He was warned by a local expert: "It is a very bad time to begin farming, even with experience, just now. Indeed, many farmers with experience are wishing they could get out of it before losing all their capital".[47]

Yet, Government did much for farming. In 1925, sugar beet producers were given a subsidy and through most of the 30s over 350,000 acres were devoted to this new crop. In 1928 agricultural land and buildings were freed from rates.

The 30s saw important measures of organisation, control, subsidy and protection. Marketing Boards were set up to control the sales of milk, hops, potatoes, bacon and pigs. Typical was the Milk Marketing Board, 1933: prior to its establishment firms had bought milk from farmers in a free competitive market in which thousands of often small-scale producers were at a disadvantage in years of slump. After 1933, prices were laid down in advance by the Milk Board. Producers gained, but as often with guaranteed prices, surpluses grew, though the Board did make worth-while efforts to increase consumption.

Marketing Boards were exported to their colonies by the British and became very significant in, for example, Africa. They have been much praised – and criticised.[48]

After 1932, Government guaranteed wheat prices, paid subsidies to meat producers, levied import duties on oats, barley, horticultural produce.

From 1924, statutory minimum agricultural wages were laid down for each County by Wages Boards. Wages were low, averaging around 32s (1.60p)[49] in the mid 30s, though most workers also had "perks" such as free house, garden, milk. But in money terms a family man was roughly as well off on the dole – after 1935, with a wife and two children, he received 32s a week.

Not surprisingly many – particularly the young – deserted farming. Some 10,000 workers a year moved into other jobs over the inter-war period, further evidence that the economy was not entirely stagnant.

Intervention

Government also intervened in transport and industry. Capitalism survived the slump but increasingly it was regulated, large-scale capitalism. Public corporations were established: the B.B.C. (1926), Central Electricity Board (1926), London Passenger Transport Board (1933). The Coal Mines Act (1930), gave owners power to fix minimum prices and set quotas of production and reduced the miners' day to 7½ hours.

Road and Rail Transport Acts of 1930 and 1933 divided the country into areas, each under a Traffic Commissioner with powers to license public vehicles and (after 1933) to suspend or revoke licences of those not complying with regulations. Unfortunately, in rural areas many small operators were squeezed out by large companies: often fares rose, services were cut.

With much active encouragement from Government and the Banks, industries such as steel, cotton, shipbuilding, underwent major amalgamations and closures with scrapping of unused machinery, plants, yards. In a new industry, sugar beet processing, Government in 1936 organised the amalgamation of existing factories under the British Sugar Corporation Ltd.

Economic growth

In the vital sphere of growth of the economy and of productivity, the British economy performed quite well in the inter-war period, better than it had before 1914. K.S. Lomax's index of industrial production shows a growth from 92.6 in 1913 to 100 in 1924 to 147.7 in 1937.[50] Britain's rate of productivity growth compared well with that of European competitors.

Between 1924 and 1937, Gross Domestic Product increased by 2.2 per cent a year while disposable income grew by 2.4 per cent a year, (the terms of trade were favourable and imports cheap). Total factor productivity in manufacturing, which had crept up by only 0.6 per cent a year between 1873–1913, rose by a more reputable 1.9 per cent between 1924 and 1937.[51]

Among reasons for rising output[52] were the following. The lash of economic necessity was laid heavily on many backs and much strain resulted. Faced with a large number of unemployed, plus weakened unions, with profits falling badly in the slump years and survival much at risk, firms could retain or recruit the ablest, strongest, most adaptable and sack or ignore the slow, the handicapped, the "trouble-makers". Employers could and did introduce assembly lines, new machines, working arrangements based on scientific work-study, new sources of power. Services were efficient, for posts in the Civil Service, Local Government, teaching, banking, police, were very much sought after. Vast quantities of work went, for example, into new publishing ventures such as "Picture Post" or Penguin Books. Great endeavours were made to increase circulations of popular newspapers.

Apart from keen human endeavour, there were other reasons why production rose. Investment was switched from overseas to home, from declining to growing industries. Investment statistics were:[53]

	Net domestic capital formation		Net foreign lending		Total investment as per cent of G.N.P.
	£ million	per cent of G.N.P.	£ M	per cent of G.N.P.	
1910–23	65	3.0	180	8.2	11.2
1924–28	280	6.6	62	1.5	8.1
1929–33	186	4.6	−5	−0.1	4.5
1934–38	347	7.7	−22	−0.5	7.7

So after 1929, though investment as a percentage of G.N.P. was low, it was at home. The vast foreign lending of pre-1914 days ceased, indeed there was some return of funds. Here was a major change and, further, a cause of depression in the primary producing areas. Cessation of overseas investment was accompanied by cessation of emigration – indeed again there was some flow from countries at least as depressed as Britain. As already indicated a considerable slice of home investment went into new industries. Between 1920 and 1930, five growing industries, motor vehicles, chemicals, paper and printing, rayon, electrical engineering, absorbed a third (£251 out of £750 million) of gross capital formation. But new machines went into the coal mines too. In 1913, 8½ per cent of coal was cut by machines; by 1931, 31 per cent, and 17 per cent conveyed mechanically.[54]

There was rapid technical progress over the inter-war years. Aeroplanes, radar, wireless have been mentioned. Chemical firms, I.C.I. and others, developed new products such as plastics.[55] Obvious to millions were the great improvements in radio sets, in film-making techniques. By the end of the 1930s, Britain had the first television service in the world. There were continuous improvements in motor vehicles.

In short, the inter-war period was one of very marked contrasts: declining and decaying industries and stagnant areas on the one hand, new expanding industries and much technical progress on the other.

Regional aid

In the 1930s, the first serious official efforts were made to lessen acute regional imbalance. In accord with a well-known modern tendency to improve nomenclature deemed unpleasant or offensive, "Depressed" became known as "Special" Areas, though a current journal reasonably submitted "that the proper label is 'diseased'."[56]

Modest public funds, plus a gift of £2 million from Lord Nuffield, were allotted to these areas, narrowly drawn in 1934 in South Wales, Durham and Tyneside, West Cumberland, Clydeside and North Lanarkshire. Most money went on basic infrastructures: valuable, if unromantic, schemes of sewerage, sewage disposal and drainage absorbed over £2,700,000 up to 1938. Hospitals, site clearance, amenity schemes all attracted useful grants. In Durham and Tyneside, grants of more than £1 million went to such public utility schemes.[57] Many did benefit: Sunderland was helped to lay out 449 allotments with small glasshouses and toolsheds.

Industrial estates, as at Team Valley near Gateshead, were laid out ready for occupation by firms. By September 1937, 76 factories had been built at Team Valley and 19 more were being built.[58] True, they must have been small workshops since total contribution to employment was not large, but an expert on the regional problem considers that the establishment of trading estates "was one of the few really important policy measures which the Commissioners were able to institute".[59] In 1937, firms in Special Areas were given some tax concessions.

The 1930s, then, saw deliberate injections of aid into the less fortunate areas of the United Kingdom – a policy which was to be much developed in the decades following World War II.

12. SOCIETY BETWEEN THE WARS

12.1 Survival of much of the old order

In 1918, the Director of Intelligence in the Home Office wrote: "Among the advanced people, there appears to be a quiet certainty that revolution is coming".[1] We now know that it was not.

Aftermath of the Great War, Russian Revolution and its consequences, Fascism in Italy and Germany, Civil War in Ireland and Spain, aggression in Ethiopia, China and Europe, nationalism in the Empire, unemployment and strikes at home, all made the inter-war period a much troubled time. Yet Britain's established order of parliamentary government, capitalist economic system, class hierarchy and the rest, survived intact – changing and modified, it is true, but basically much the same.

True, modern Britons are not a fiery revolutionary people. Looking at a 1935 Hyde Park May Day Labour rally, Vera Brittain (not a parochial nationalist), noted: "the usual British crowd whose psychology is the despair of continental countries: tolerant, humorous, long-suffering: nobody out at elbows, yet nobody really well-dressed. Nothing could have been further from revolution than its air of patient respectability and its unrivalled faculty for turning everything into a picnic".[2]

But perhaps the main reason why nothing approaching a revolution occurred in Britain was that over the inter-war years standards of living of the majority rose, as proved in the previous chapter.

There was in Britain practically unchallenged support for the existing system of Government. While in Europe long-established monarchies toppled, that of Britain remained. There was happy mass participation in the Jubilee celebrations of 25 years of George V's rule in 1935. After a crisis which gripped public attention to an extent which few others did, George's son Edward VIII abdicated in 1936 so that he could marry Mrs. Simpson. Much helped by his wife, Edward's brother, George VI became a hardworking constitutional monarch who worried himself into an early grave.

Though Parliamentary government had serious faults, it did provide that most essential element in representative democracy – government by consent of the governed. True, Lords filled many influential posts in Government and in that era of mainly Conservative administrations most M.P.s were drawn from the wealthy classes.[3]

Yet M.P.s were elected by the people and they were not all hard-faced businessmen. Harold Macmillan, early disciple of Keynes, sat for depressed Stockton-on-Tees. Many Members were genuinely concerned to protect traditional British liberties in face of State interference.

True, some individual liberty was diminished by the Public Order and Incitement to Disaffection Acts of 1937, though street thuggery had made necessary measures banning, for example, the wearing of political uniforms.

Ministers were sensitive to opinion and acted to investigate serious complaints raised in a free press. Thus in 1935, the Unemployment Assistance Board, set up to take payments to the unemployed out of politics, tried to apply uniform, national scales, in place of considerably varying local allowances. There was such an outcry, particularly in Wales and the North, that Government (though it had a large majority in the Commons), ignominiously abandoned its attempt and conceded that where existing scales were more favourable they could continue.

Late in 1934, the "Times" published a letter from a Sunderland consultant, Dr. C.F. Walker, calling attention to serious health deterioration in the North-east. Government sent a medical team which published a report.[4] Exposure and discussion of a harsh situation were not without value.

Paternalist Stanley Baldwin, urged on by his King, seriously and not unsuccessfully tried to reduce class bitterness after the trauma of 1926.

Labour, which provided the main Opposition after 1918, was a moderate, democratic party. Through the slump years it retained much working-class support in the old industrial areas. Communists and Fascists never received in Britain that mass support resulting in large blocks of elected members which they gained on the Continent. True in some smitten areas such as South Wales, Communists gained local union and political influence, while Fascist marches through Jewish East End areas provoked trouble, but in the country as a whole, Fascists and Communists were tiny minorities.[5]

Much of pre-1914 class hierarchy remained. Class was still a strong reality: the upper and middle classes retained their servants. Naomi Mitchison, 21 in 1918, wrote: "Middle or professional class housing depended on having servants to cook, clean and generally take charge. Now this pattern of having servants is probably the strangest pattern of our lives for those two generations on who may well find the idea not only embarrassing but definitely shocking".[6]

Another young married writer had "a resident maid, a 'cook-general', who considered herself well paid with thirty shilings a week and 'all-found' . . ." for which, she "did all the housework, the cooking . . . and took the baby out in the afternoons".[7]

Indeed it is often forgotten how widespread was the practice of keeping servants well into this 20th century. In 1931, there were still over 1.3 million domestic servants and 23 per cent of occupied women were servants.[8]

In a complex story it is clear that upper and middle class Britons could be snobbish and autocratic. Thus, Vita Sackville-West was a snob: "she attached exaggerated importance to birth and wealth and believed that while the aristocracy had much in common with working people, particularly those who worked on the land, the middle class (or 'bedints' in Sackville language) were to be pitied and shunned. . ." Her husband, the immensely cultured Harold Nicolson, shared such prejudices.[9]

A gardener who started work in 1942 on a Suffolk estate found: "There were seven gardeners and goodness knows how many servants in the house. It was a frightening experience for a boy, Lord and Ladyship were very very Victorian and very domineering. It was 'swing your arms' every time they saw us".[10]

In Scotland, in 1924, 18 year old Jean Rennie, with a Higher Leaving Certificate, but no money for University, had to go into

Service.[11] To test a servant's honesty, half-a-crown had been left under a rug. She glued it to the floor!

Knowledgeable and discerning observers of the country scene did criticise. "This local gentry of ours is the flotsam of feudalism . . . an assumption of rank, a requirement of consideration which is without a just basis of knowledge, intelligence and duty. . ."[12]

Workers, too, could be conservative. Williamson on his Norfolk farm spent £15 on clearing rats. "£15 was a lot of money, etc. etc. Why, other farmers never bothered about the rats . . . confronted again and again with this sort of slowly uttered serious criticism I found that my patience was gone. . . There was no creative feeling behind the obstructive mentality".[13]

Of course, there are other sides to the story, but in the light of Britain's continuing difficulties in the labour relations fields, it is important to note the inheritance from a past which was not always pleasant. Class attitudes might be seen at their worst overseas. In 1941, a young Australian, posted to Singapore, found practically every hotel shut to "other ranks" and was treated with disgusting rudeness by British women he was defending.[14]

Morality

1920s London society's "bright young things" were sure they were blazing new trails of personal freedom. Millions of staid, ordinary British citizens did not follow their examples. Much of Victorian censorship and reticence in published matter remained. Books such as "Lady Chatterley's Lover" were banned. Plays and films portrayed nothing approaching explicit sexual scenes. That increasingly important organisation, the B.B.C. under John Reith's calvinistic domination was a model of Christian rectitude, giving listeners not what they wanted, but what was considered good for them. Most certainly, excellent programmes of music, drama and for children were relayed. But by 1970s standards, control was harsh. An employee involved in divorce thought it wise to resign before being pushed out.[15] Later a top comedian, uninhibited Max Miller, was banned for 5 years from the B.B.C. More seriously, the B.B.C in the late thirties did not give a lead in fearlessly analysing the increasingly desperate European situation and its likely consequences.[16]

Before mechanisation

Ordinary life in the inter-war period could be very different from that of 50 years later. Just after the Great War, a young Londoner went as a pupil to a Suffolk farm. He has left a fascinating account[17] of a vanished world, of ploughing with horses, threshing, harvesting, of the hard manual labour and the many real skills involved.

In the home, there was still very much work to be done, for it was: "a period with few disposables; babies nappies were only just coming in late in the Thirties, though disposable sanitary towels were by then not universal but usual. No fridge, no dishwasher, no electric liquidiser or whisk . . . , no detergents and no drip-dry, for that matter no washing machines or spin-dryers, instead scrubbing with bars of yellow soap and the irons heating on the stove. Sheets and towels went to the laundry, but other things were washed at home: Lux Flakes started in the Thirties, and by then we had an electric iron."[18] Of course, most households did not send sheets to the laundry nor did they have servants to do the rest of the work.

As the above examples reveal, many old institutions, systems, ways of life, (changed, it is true but still there), survived in inter-war Britain. There was the old England of the guide books seen by Priestley in 1933.[19] But there was also the Britain of the depressed areas and the dole queues to which we now turn.

12.2   Unemployment, poverty

As already indicated in Chapter 11, decline of basic industries (plus effects of serious industrial disputes) caused heavy unemployment and much suffering in old industrial areas. Thus, in April 1928, so obvious was the hardship that London's Lord Mayor launched a Fund to help the distressed in South Wales and the North-east. Records of local Committees set up to administer the Fund convey the clearest evidence of heartbreaking poverty.[20] In Co. Durham a South Hetton wife told how her husband "met with an accident at the colliery and was off work for nine weeks . . . we had 19s 3d a week compensation from which we paid 10s 6d rent and 6d for water and light and there are three of us to keep. I was in the infirmary for one month . . . with sugar diabetes and got a diet sheet. . ."

Emily, aged twenty-five, daughter of an unemployed miner on 17s a week, was herself out of work with no income: "The Local Committee considered that this is a special case and Emily should be granted boots, clothing and a quilt".

Some did not even receive the dole: "I am not a miner but have been unemployed since August. . . I am not in receipt of unemployment benefit. . . (I am) the sole support of my mother . . . a widow". A young man who had passed his examinations but could not get into Training College asked for help to go to Australia. Alas, there were no funds for that.

Offers of help were received: a Norfolk farmer sent five tons of best potatoes and to the Durham Medical Officer of Health came an offer to collect childrens' boots from someone "impressed by your statement that you had 1,200 children attending school without shoes and stockings".

In the industrial North-east, bare-footed children were a problem to the Health Authorities. There is simply no doubt about this. Anyone disputing it should consult the Reports of local School Medical Officers.[21]

The extent of unemployment and poverty grew vastly as a result of the Thirties slump.

"No one who had any close contact with the unemployed during the great depression, can think of that period and of their plight as being other than a catastrophe of the first magnitude. Those years of acute unemployment were years of deep tragedy, of unspeakable suffering, of much wreckage of human lives. Nothing can undo the mischief which was done."[22] So wrote Henry Mess who had been Director of the Tyneside Council of Social Service in the years of Slump.

The unemployed were paid an allowance which in early 1931 amounted to 17s (85p) a week for an adult man, 15s for a woman; a married man received an extra 9s for his wife and 2s for each child. In the Autumn of 1931, as already mentioned, these payments were cut, for example, the rate for man and wife went down from 26s to 23/6d. Tighter regulations excluded many married women from benefit. Most unpopular of all was the "Means Test". After an allotted period on full insurance benefit, an applicant was handed over to the local Public Assistance Committee, which conducted a test of means before deciding on how much to pay in "Transitional Benefit". For example, savings and earnings of an unemployed father's children could be taken into account.

In practice, Local Authorities varied greatly in generosity in their administration of the regulations. In Rotherham, Merthyr Tydfil, Co. Durham, the overwhelming majority of the applicants continued to receive maximum payments. In November 1932, Durham County Public Assistance Committee was unseated and replaced by three Commissioners. But much local variation remained for some years though in 1935 the Unemployment Assistance Board assumed responsibility for scales of payments. With economic recovery and rising prices, rates became more generous. The 1931 cuts had been restored in 1934; in 1935 the child's allowance was raised from 2s to 3s; on the outbreak of the 1939 war, standard benefits were 17s for a man, plus 10s for his wife and 3s for each child.

In the 1930s, as in the 1980s, there was much concern expressed among the fortunate about the amounts paid in unemployment benefit. Those genuinely out of work were caused distress. No doubt some did cheat. Orwell found that a keeper of a tripe shop and boarding house "was dodging the Means Test and drawing an allowance from the P.A.C."[23]

Many of the unemployed were family men with dependents.[24] In June 1934, of 165,873 unemployed in Co. Durham and Tyneside, 52,506 were married men over the age of 35.[25] In 1936, with economic recovery well on the way, Sunderland's Health Department conducted a survey of 445 families who had moved from the slums to new council housing. No less than 197 families were solely, and 146 families partially dependent on unemployment benefit.[26]

"Memoirs of the Unemployed"[27] first broadcast by the B.B.C. (a social gain from the new radio), and published in the "Listener" in 1933, recount the saddening experiences of 25 unemployed persons. Psychological pressures were among the worst but references to the obvious inability to afford adequate diets were also common. Examples included: "I am given to understand that certain health authorities state that there is no deterioration in the health of the unemployed. I should imagine those gentlemen in question (salaried at, say £500 to £1,000 a year) had just finished an excellent dinner and partaken of wines, and whilst in that state of well-being had passed such a statement. There *is* a growing weakness in the unemployed through undernourishment".

"I hardly know yet how I managed to dress and drag myself along to my panel doctor. The good man told me . . . I was very much run down, anaemic in fact, and he advised me to change my diet and take chicken soup, fresh eggs and milk puddings – oh, and a small bottle of stout daily. The irony of it!"

A careful analysis of household budgets of several unemployed families in 1933 raised doubt as to whether "any of these budgets provide an adequate diet for either the adults or the children".

Hardship and want did not merely afflict the unemployed. Indeed the latter were spared the sweat and dangers of work. Coal mining still involved much heavy and dangerous work which brought much risk to health.[28] 1,101 miners were killed and 4,739 seriously injured in 1922 in Britain: in Co. Durham alone, 101 were killed in 1936. As one tragic example among very many, in 1927 a Sunderland miner's widow, with a boy of five and girl of three was paid £500 compensation, without prejudice to a further payment. Pages and pages of similar cases in records at Miners' Union Headquarters in Durham make sad reading. Dangers to health were many and varied: "as a result of the pitman lying on his side at the dimly-lit 'face' hewing coal, there develops a peculiar lateral oscillation of the eyeballs, which creates a sense of insecurity in walking, also a derangement of his sight".[29] This was miners' nystagmus.

In 1969, Durham researchers revealed what had happened to a significant group of boys who started work in local pits in the 1920s and 30s. In 10 pits employing over 13,000 men, 1,303 (nearly 10 per cent) were medically disabled in some way. Nearly 30 per cent of the disabled suffered from pneumoconiosis, 16.7 per cent from back injuries, and nearly 19 per cent from injuries to limbs. 16 men had had a leg amputated.[30]

For all the sweat and dangers, pay of miners in the inter-war period was not good. Durham miners, working in a hard-hit area much depended on exports, were paid on average 8s 0¾d (40p) a shift in 1930, compared with a national 9s 3¼d (46p). In 1935, Durham pitmen campaigned for a wage large enough to maintain their families as "human beings should be maintained in a civilised community".[31]

True, there were valuable additions to money earnings, though there were also expenses. True, too, individual earnings varied greatly. In 1927, a judge at Newcastle held that a miner who had an income coming into the house of £10.3s.5d. a week, plus free house and coal, was not dependent on a son who had been killed. The son, a coal-cutter, had been earning well over £5 a week so total family weekly income had been over £15.[32]

One of very few good results of the Great Depression was that numbers of factory accidents fell very considerably. With increased mechanisation they had risen in the early decades of the century. Numbers of accidents (with totals of killed in parentheses were:

1900	1920	1925	1931
79,020 (1045)	138,702 (1404)	159,693 (944)	113,249 (755)

Accidents in shipbuilding fell dramatically from over 14,000 in 1924 to about 4,000 in 1932.[33] But again, obvious accidents were not the only dangers to health. In the shipyards; "Holders-up of iron plates . . . as a consequence of the excessive hammering of the rivets, have even at a comparatively early part of their career the sense of hearing blunted, so that there are few boiler makers after fifteen or twenty years service who had not lost the greater part of their hearing".[34]

In occupations employing large numbers, wages remained low and/or hours of work very long. In October 1938, average weekly earnings of women over 18 in the cotton industry were 31s 6d.

Experiences of many in the depressed areas were summed up in a letter published by a Northern newspaper in 1975:[35] "I am sixty-four and lived in Seaham Harbour from 1921–1935. I worked on leaving school in 1924, as errand boy in Hunter's tea stores from 9 a.m. to 7 p.m. Monday and Tuesday, 9 a.m. to 1 p.m. Wednesday, 9 a.m. to 7 p.m. Thursday, 9 a.m. to 8 p.m. Fridays and 9 a.m. to 9 p.m. Saturday, all for six shillings a week old money".

(Various short-lived jobs followed: in 1926 a medical discharge from the Army).

"Then followed years of unemployment, 14 shillings a week old money. After thirteen weeks, the Public Assistance Committee man called and reduced my dole money to six shillings a week old money because my father had the audacity to be earning 6s 8¼d for a shift of 8½ hours. . . My years on the dole killed any ambitions I might have had; I became a zombie. I walked miles and miles putting in miners' loads of coal for one shilling when I could. I could be well remembered in those days as the only man to sign on three times a week at the Labour Exchange at the corner of Green Street and Church Street, wearing a bowler hat. I was twenty-one years of age in 1931 and my twenty-first birthday present from my mother was a fourpenny packet of ten Woodbines. . .[36] They were only the good old days if you had a home, a job, and a family, but for me they were the bad old days. . .".

Poverty led to inadequate feeding. It is impossible to say how much actual malnutrition there was because of "a lack of satisfactory standards by which to assess the state of nutrition in a given individual."[37]

It is accepted that: "no one can seriously doubt that the working classes on the eve of the Second World War were better fed, better clothed and better housed than their parents had been a generation before".[38] Yet there is clear proof that many simply could not afford to buy an adequate amount of nutritious foods. In 1933, a B.M.A. Committee had concluded that weekly minimum costs of diets required to maintain health (and insufficient for a man doing hard work) were: adult male 5s 10½d, adult female 4s 11d, child from 2s 8d to adult costs, depending on age. So a man, wife and three children might require to spend over £1 a week on food. Clearly many of the unemployed and low paid workers could not do this.

Evidence was offered that 10 per cent of the population and 20 per cent of children were very inadequately nourished.[39] The diet of half the nation was lacking in some essentials. In 1939, Boyd Orr was still claiming that the diet of nearly half of all Britons did not meet the standard required for full vigorous health.

Boyd Orr's findings were much criticised. But the mass evidence that numbers of poor people lacked the height, weight, better health, sounder teeth of richer people was truly enormous. Thus in 1927, in Stockton-on-Tees, when a large slum was partly cleared, 710 people were moved to a new estate, 1,298 were left in their existing homes. Death rates rose dramatically on the new estate and the investigators were convinced the cause was diets "which showed considerable quantitative and qualitative deficiences".[40] Because of higher rents, spending on food – it was argued – was cut and bad health resulted. It must however be stressed that other findings quite failed to confirm that movement from slum to new council housing had bad effects on health.

In 1931, the Committee of Newcastle-upon-Tyne's Dispensary,[41] which provided basic medical attention to large numbers of the poor, stated that it was "gravely concerned about the great increase in the poverty, sickness and malnutrition amongst the poorest classes in the City".

The City Corporation asked Dr. J.C. Spence to investigate. He selected two samples, the first of children of professional classes, the second of poor "City" children, and compared these. His conclusion was: out of 125 City Children examined, 45 (36 per cent) were found to be unhealthy or physically unfit.

Normal zones of height and weight for children were known. When children in the sample groups were examined, results were:

Weight	% above normal zone	% within	% below
Professional children	48.4	38.7	12.9
City children	11.2	33.6	55.2
Height			
Professional children	25.0	70.2	4.8
City children	1.7	51.3	47.0

Of 124 "wealthy" children, two had had pneumonia, one pleurisy, two chronic and recurrent cough. Of 125 "poor" children, 17 had had pneumonia, 32 had been or were affected by chronic or recurrent bronchitis. Five "poor" children examined had rickets, 23 were judged anaemic. But, "no signs of actual deficiency disease other than rickets and anaemia were found in the City children. There was no scurvy and none of the diseases associated with near starvation".

In 1930–31, Dr. F.C.S. Bradbury,[42] carried out a deep, thorough, scientific enquiry into tuberculosis in Jarrow. He found that while other factors such as bad housing were significant, yet the most important cause of Jarrow's high tuberculosis rate was poverty.

In 1937, Mr. J. Chuter Ede, a highly respected M.P. (later Home Secretary), was "impressed by the apparent poor physique" of the pupils when on a visit to Spennymoor Secondary School in Co. Durham. A Board of Education Medical Officer examined Spennymoor and, for purposes of comparison, Surbiton and Woking School children. It will come as no surprise that he found the latter to be better nourished.[43]

In 1939 were published results of researches into the physique of groups of public and secondary school boys. 500 boys from wealthy families were compared with 500 boys from secondary schools in Co. Durham. "At each year between the ages of fourteen and eighteen a boy of the first group is approximately sixteen pounds heavier and three inches taller than a boy in the second group . . . it is emphasised that the differences in the physical development of the two groups . . . correspond to differences known to exist in their diets."[44]

It would be difficult to find clearer evidence of the grave handicaps suffered by relatively poor children in the race of life. Yet not all the evidence points to serious dietary deficiencies, even in depressed areas. Thus, in 1934, in Newcastle, a survey of the diets of 69 working-class families was carried out.[45] There were wide variations and some important deficiencies, in the diets, but the average family intake of food supplied 2,960 calories daily per man-value, which was clearly not unreasonable. It is re-iterated that food prices were so low (3½d or about 1½p for a 2 lb loaf), that anything approaching starvation must have been virtually non-existent, even on unemployment relief. But poor nutrition there certainly was, among signficant sections of the population.

Health

Health improved significantly over the inter-war years, yet large differences between regions and classes remained.

In 1920–22, expectation of life at birth of males in County Boroughs in Northumberland and Durham (Region North 1) was 49.59 years. So heavy still was the infant death-rate that expectation of life at age ten was higher than at birth – 50.85 years. In all England and Wales, male expectation of life at birth was 55.62 years, in Eastern Counties (Rural Districts) it was 62.83 years.[46]

Expectation of life at birth of females was 53.90 years in North 1 County boroughs, 59.56 in England and Wales, 64.33 in Eastern Counties Rural Districts.

In 1930–32, of every 1000 boys born in North 1's County Boroughs, 96 failed to survive their first year, in Eastern Rural Districts the corresponding figure was 57.22.[47]

The very significant infant death rates also revealed the influence of social class on health.[48]

Table 11 *Infant mortality between the Wars*

Social class of father	Rate per 1000 legitimate live births		Per cent of ratio for all classes	
	1921–23	*1930–32*	*1921–23*	*1930–32*
All classes	79	62	100	100
Class I	38	33	48	53
II	55	45	70	73
III	77	58	97	94
IV	89	67	113	108
V	97	77	123	125

From the above, as from practically all health statistics covering the inter-war period, it is obvious that there was marked improvement but that large inequalities remained.

Did the Great Depression of the early 1930s adversely affect the health of Britons? The official view was quite clear: it did not. The Chief Medical Officer, Ministry of Health, wrote thus in 1933: "we cannot escape the conclusion that there is, at present, no avilable medical evidence of any general increase in physical impairment, in sickness or mortality, as the result of economic depression or unemployment".[49]

A whole barrage of facts seemed to prove him right. But many remained sceptical. For example, under a headline, "Whom the Gods Love. . . "[50] a 1935 article compared actual death-rates in the depressed areas with those which would have resulted had "standard" death rates of the rest of the country applied. For females, numbers were:

Table 12 *Female deaths in depressed areas, 1930s*

Age groups	Standard deaths	Actual deaths	per cent surplus
0–14	6,985	9,107	30
15–44	7,347	9,110	24
45–65	12,817	15,546	21
65 over	22,773	27,442	21
Total:	49,922	61,205	23

Unfortunately, officials could reply that northern industrial areas had for long suffered from higher than average mortality rates. Yet, the Medical Officer of Health, Hebburn, (on Tyneside), wrote in 1935, "It is curious to notice, in this area, which has suffered severely from poverty, that not one of the returns of the death certificates indicate that malnutrition has played any part as a primary or contributory cause of death".

Yet "personal contact with mothers and children . . . convinces me that serious under-nourishment does exist, whether we get to know of it by statistical methods".[51]

12.3 Protest

In a free society, with well established institutions existing to further working-class interests, the unemployment and poverty of Britain in the 1919–39 period were bound to provoke strong protest and action. This they did.

19th century attitudes were changing. Already, in the early years of the 20th century: "the attitude of suspicion towards government action . . . was slowly dissipated . . . the possibilities of democratic control were enhanced by the growth of general education and the diffusion of political awareness".[52] One view is that the impact of the Great War "was on the whole in the direction of strengthening the faith in collective action".[53]

Thousands of young men who survived the War had lost much of their former deference. Those who had suffered so much, often now expected a better deal. They were led to so believe by wily politicians who promised them "a land fit for heroes".

Labour, with a new Constitution (committing the Party to Socialism, to common ownership of the means of production), with a mass circulation newspaper, the "Daily Herald" became a main party. Particularly on "Red Clydeside", the I.L.P. received dedicated support and in election after election retained a small band of left-wing M.P.s. The Communist Party, established in Britain in 1920, received zealous support from a small minority. To thousands of left-wingers the years immediately following the Great War were "Days of Hope".[54]

The Trade Union movement registered important advances over the period 1914 to about 1922. Membership increased from over 4 million in 1914 to above 8 million in 1920. In 1921, the General Council of the T.U.C. was formed to "co-ordinate industrial action". Mergers produced the large modern unions – the Amalgamated Engineering Union in 1921, the Transport and General Workers Union in 1922. During the Great War, the shop stewards had increased in numbers and influence, while militancy was not lacking in areas such as Clydeside and South Wales. In 1918 and 1919 even police in London and Liverpool went on strike: their Union was defeated and some officers dismissed.

But certainly not all Union Leaders wished for strife. Harry Gosling, President of the T.U.C. said in 1916, "We are tired of war in the industrial field. The British Workman cannot quietly submit to an autocratic government of the conditions of his own life . . . would it not be possible for the employers of this country, on the conclusion of peace . . . to agree to put their businesses on a new footing by admitting the workmen to some participation, not in profits but in control".

Tragically, his suggestion was not taken up, though the Industrial Courts Act of 1919 did set up machinery through which with the consent of both unions and employers, disputes might go to arbitration.

But acute depression in 1921 led in the stormiest years yet experienced in British industrial relations history. Working days lost in disputes which had been nearly 41 million in strike-torn 1912 rose to nearly 86 million in 1921 and topped 162 million in 1926.

In both years, trouble centred on the coal industry. In 1921, the pits, controlled by Government during the War, were handed back to the owners, in spite of the fact that a majority of the Government-appointed Sankey Commission had recommended nationalisation. The owners, faced with losses, determined to cut costs by lowering wages. The miners refused to accept reductions and a dispute closed the mines from April to June 1921. The miners felt betrayed by the other two members of the so-called Triple Alliance – the Railwaymen and the Transport Workers – who did not support them, and they had to accept defeat.

In 1925, with falling exports, owners proposed to cut pay and lengthen the working day. A dispute began in May 1926: the T.U.C. and its constituent unions supported the miners, so on 4 May 1926 the coal stoppage became a General Strike. Workers called out (a minority of all at work) gave complete loyalty to their unions but on 12 May, T.U.C. leaders called off the strike, failing even to ask for simple undertakings concerning re-instatement of strikers. The miners remained out until November when they had to accept defeat.

True, there was no very serious upheaval in May 1926: in Plymouth strikers played against police in a much-publicised football match. But over the whole country there were 1,389 cases of actual disorder. Some careers were utterly ruined when first offenders went to prison for example for putting obstacles on railway lines or when strikers were not re-instated. In the case of a miner this might well mean losing house as well as job.

In 1927, a Trade Dispute and Trade Union Act considerably weakened the trade unions and the Labour Party, since it declared illegal sympathetic strikes, or strikes aimed at coercing the government, forbade established civil servants to join a union affiliated to the T.U.C. and ruled that trade unionists must contract in to make political payments to the Labour Party. Total trade union membership fell from 5.2 million in 1926 to 4.8 million in 1928. The Slump brought the number down to not much above 1914 levels – 4.39 million in 1933. A steady recovery then set in and 1939 membership was nearly 6.3 million.

The unions were seriously defeated in 1926. Sir Alfred Mond,

I.C.I. Chairman, met with Ben Turner, Chairman of the T.U.C. General Council, in 1928 in a series of talks on fundamental industrial problems. Though no concrete results emerged, these meetings were symptomatic of new attitudes. Walter Citrine became Secretary of the T.U.C. in 1926 and, in that key office, became very influential over the remainder of the inter-war period. He emphasised the role of the Trade Unions in attempting to maintain and improve their members' standards of life and working conditions under the existing social system and under whatever government was in power. The other most powerful Union Leader to grow in stature over those years was Ernest Bevin of the Transport Workers. One of his dreams was realised when the new Transport House was opened in Smith Square in 1928. It housed not only the T. and G.W. Offices but those of the T.U.C. and Labour Party also.

After 1933, total Trade Union membership and that of some individual unions climbed. By 1937, the T. and G.W.U. with 650,000 members, was said to be the largest trade union in the world. Much of this expansion was in new industries and areas where traditional unionism had been weak. Problems arose: there were demarcation disputes between different unions and the seeds of much future trouble were sown as a number of unions recruited in, for example, one car plant. There were strikes in the Thirties for union recognition or against new piece-work proposals. But compared with years before and after the Great War, or even with the late 1970s, the Thirties were a decade of comparative industrial peace. Only 960,000 working days were lost in disputes in 1934 and though this figure climbed to over 3.4 million in 1937 this was still but a small fraction of 1919–22 figures.

At Trade Union Congresses of 1932 and 1933, important statements concerning the role of the unions in future socialised industries were adopted. Management and and unions would negotiate about wages and working conditions: existing Union rights, such as the right to strike, were to be maintained.

Unparalleled economic depression, 1931 salary cuts, continuing grave social problems, overseas wars, persecution of Jews in Central Europe, and, above all, the inexorable drift to World War, ensured that the Thirties were a decade of much ferment, of anxious, bitter political protest. Much of this came from the

Left. The Communist Party was small but very active. Members were particularly successful in South Wales where they moved into many responsible positions in the Miners' Federation. Very naturally, there was deep discontent in the areas of high unemployment. There were quite serious disturbances in Birkenhead and Liverpool in 1932. Unemployed workers formed their own organisation and organised marches and demonstrations, the most famous "Crusade" being that from Jarrow to London in 1936. There were some unpleasant and bitter election contests, particularly that at Seaham Harbour, Co. Durham in 1935.

In intellectual and academic circles, the foundation of the Left Book Club by Victor Gollancz in the mid-Thirties was significant. The Club, with around 40–60,000 members sold, at cheap rates, two new books a month to members. Usually, these books followed a strong Marxist line. On the shelves of many students' rooms in the thirties, these distinctive books were prominent. Edited by Kingsley Martin, the "New Statesmen and Nation" had much influence.

Yet, not all left-wingers were mere theorists. Hundreds went to fight with the International Brigade for the Spanish Government against Franco in Spain, and they suffered heavy casualties. In committed political circles in Britain, the Spanish Civil War aroused very strong feelings.

Protest was not confined to left-wingers. For example, the writer Henry Williamson, who like so many others was clearly affected by his terrible experiences on the Western Front in the 1914–18 War, became a very critical Fascist farmer: "Rats, weeds, swamps, depressed markets, labourers on the dole, rotten cottages, polluted streams, political parties and class divisions controlled by the money-power . . . this was the real England of the period of this story of a Norfolk farm".[55]

Apart from clear political protest and trade union action, over the interwar period, complaints, suggestions, plans for reform came in vast numbers in widely separated fields. There was a campaign for much-needed Family Allowances, in which Eleanor Rathbone was the leading figure. Women continued their fight for equality. They gained the vote, and the right to be awarded degrees at Oxford and Cambridge. They continued to advocate equal pay, still denied them in professions such as teaching, though not in official appointments in the medical profession.

Under the very energetic leadership of Marie Stopes, some worked against continuing strong opposition for the dissemination of family planning information and clinics.

Increasing numbers of, though by no means all, doctors, supported the advocates of birth control. In 1928, a speaker at the B.M.A.'s Annual Meeting stated that: "the health of many poor women is being destroyed by overwork and over child-bearing. In such cases it is our duty to see that child-bearing is modified and that her conditions of life are relieved".[56]

Many scientific investigations into diet, nutrition, health provided clear evidence that much was wrong and in need of improvement. In 1937, reference was made to broadcast talks on nutrition given by Sir Robert McCarrison and Dr. McGonigle: "both were 'seditious' in that they cause discontent with a social order which, though passing, is still with us".[57]

Around 1934, Dr. C.F. Walker of Sunderland[58] investigated possible causes of chorea (or St. Vitus Dance). Many of the 188 patients in his survey had quite appalling home backgrounds. For example: 60 were in families of six or more children: 40 in conspicuously damp and/or draughty accommodation; 44 were troubled by serious noise, e.g. "In the tenement flat above are ten children", "neighbours very noisy all night. Much fighting", "very noisy street swarming with children". 31 lived in over-crowded homes, e.g. "Six persons living in one room with two beds"; 65 in families so poor that they were "living seriously below the level of subsistence". Truly, grim realities of life in a depressed area were here brought to light. Books, stories, plays, articles dealt with every sort of social and economic problem. Here are mentioned only W. Greenwood's "Love on the Dole" and A.P. Herberts' "Holy Deadlock", the latter dealing with the problems of divorce.

Perennial debates on how to bring up and educate children were conducted with usual vigour. "Progressive" schools were founded.

12.4   Change, improvement, advance

Over the inter-war years, health as measured by statistics improved, families continued to shrink in size, average living standards rose, the national housing stock was much enlarged, social services were improved, the volume of holidays taken and of leisure activities increased. Some detail in support of these claims follows:

The significant infant death rate thus fell:

	1891–1900	1901–10	1911–20	1932
England and Wales	153	128	100	65

By 1939 it was down to 50.4.

Total death-rates per 1000 had dropped from 21.4 in 1871–80 to 12.0 in 1932.

Central to this lowering of death-rates was the increasing control over the slaughter brought by formerly murderous infectious diseases. Death-rates from some of these had collapsed as follows:[59]

England and Wales, Deaths per 1 million

	1871–80	1921–30
Typhoid fever	320	11
Smallpox	240	1
Scarlet fever	720	23
Whooping cough	510	114
Respiratory tuberculosis	2130	813
Measles	380	109
Diphtheria	120	84

As already stated in this work, the sulphonamides were introduced in the 1930s and for the first time, doctors had an effective treatment of previous mass killers such as pneumonia. After the introduction of Prontosil in 1935: "The results in puerperal sepsis, pneumonia and meningitis were dramatic. . . "[60] Many lives of mothers were saved. Miracle cases were reported: "A case of meningitis with mastoiditis, supervening on scarlet fever, the outlook apparently hopeless. Almost as a despairing measure, Prontosil Rubrum was given . . . in huge doses. . . "[61] Recovery followed. In V.D. clinics, many hours of formerly very unpleasant treatment were saved as the new drugs were effective, for example, against gonorrhoea.

Perhaps astonishingly, health improved even in the most depressed of regions, Relevant figures for the industrial North-east were:[62]

Sunderland	Average 1920–24	Average 1935–39
Death-rate per 1000 population	15.1	13.2
Infant death-rate per 1000 births	104.0	78
Co. Durham (Administrative area)		
Death rate	12.99	11.9
Infant death-rate	100.0	67
Gateshead		
Death-rate	14.6	12.5
Infant death-rate	111.0	66.0

Even in Jarrow the infant death-rate fell from an averge 101.63 in 1929–31 to 81.74 in 1936–38, still appallingly high by national standards.

Health improvement over the inter-war period arose from a large number of interlocking causes among which may be mentioned: smaller families; improvement in the environment particularly in housing; generally rising standards of living with opportunities for leisure and exercise; better social and health services; tighter official control over health dangers; steadily improving medical care. Some of these factors have been, or will be, further mentioned elsewhere in this work. Here a note is now added on the very important matter of smaller families.

The average number of live births to couples married in stated periods were:

Period of marriage	Average number of live births
1900–09	3.37
1925–29	2.19

Average annual numbers of births in Great Britain fell from 866,000 in 1922–24 to 689,000 in 1934–36, before recovering to 703,000 in 1937–39. In the Thirties, authoritative books, forecasting a serious fall in population, remain as a perennial warning against the dangers of demographic prophecy.

Since large families suffered from higher than average death-rates, this reduction in size of family was an important factor accounting for reduction of death rates.

Young women writers and intellectuals appreciated the importance of the changes, (though they overestimated the breadth of their adoption): "The emancipation of women was a big thing, important to women of all social classes. The new attitude to love and sex, marriage and divorce, and the dissemination of knowledge about contraception and the setting-up of birth control clinics . . . was a liberation both physical and spiritual".[63]

Another London-based young writer: "in the Twenties, after the birth of our second child, I went and got fitted with a Dutch cap. . . It was the main method used at the North Kensington Clinic."[64]

Birth control clinics were not limited to London: Co. Durham had nine by 1938. But numbers attending were still very small – 607 mothers in Co. Durham.[65]

In a research project in London[66] in the late Thirties, 500 women, "respectable young citizens of the working-classes generally between twenty and thirty years of age", were questioned. 264 had used some form of birth control. Methods were:

entire continence	in	4 cases
coitus interruptus	in	177 cases
a male condom	in	35 cases
a cap	in	20 cases
soluble pessaries	in	21 cases
post-coital douche	in	4 cases

So the very ancient method of withdrawal was still the main one used.

100 women admitted to attempts at abortion, 19 had succeeded. In two cases where a wife had been warned that "another confinement would kill her", no advice on family planning was given.

It was considered that the investigation showed "that birth control has been accepted in principle as a desirable thing".

Yet, not only from surveys, but also from personal reminiscences, it is clear that spread of the use of reliable contraceptives was slow. In a 1981 radio series – "Milltowners" – an elderly Northern lady recalled, "You were frightened of letting them have owt, because you were afraid of expecting again, you never enjoyed sex because you were frightened of having more children".[67] The Registrar General found it startling that in 1939 "nearly 30 per cent of all mothers today conceive their first-borns out of wedlock".[68]

Though divorce remained comparatively rare, (7,621 marriages were dissolved in England and Wales in 1938), A.P. Herbert's Act of 1937 added desertion and insanity to adultery as grounds for divorce.

Work

In the inter-war period, the average industrial employee put in a 5½ day, about 45 hour week. Just after the Great War had come a significant reduction in hours – from about 9 to 8 a day. Saturday morning work was still very general – though, by 1939, not universal. Shops and post offices were open on Saturday afternoons. Shop assistants still worked very long hours – up to six or seven p.m. on weekdays, (except on the weekly half-day), and to eight or even nine on Fridays and Saturdays. Right at the end of the Thirties, a paid week's holiday became general – 11 million workers received a paid holiday in 1939.

Workers moved into new industries, very often located in the Midlands and South-east and into service occupations. From 1921 to 1934, numbers in London and the South-east grew by nearly 14 per cent, those in South Wales actually fell by 5 per cent. In 1939, there were some 23 million occupied persons – insured and uninsured workers, employers, managers and the self-employed – in Britain. About 9½ million were in manufacturing, 1.1 million in mining and quarrying, 1.07 million in agriculture, forestry and fishing – totalling 11.7 million in "productive" industries. Some 1.5 million were in transport and communication; 3.7 million in distribution, commerce, finance, 2.9 million in "personal" largely domestic services and 3.2 million in other services – including the professions, public services and armed forces.[69] These "service" industries occupied some 49 per cent of the working population and this was not the full story since in productive industries were many clerks, drivers and so on not directly engaged in production.

After his 1933 tour, Priestley wrote of the executives, the workers and the gap between them, "the masters of the machines and the servants of the machines. It is not here a question of the capitalists and the proletariat, the bosses and the workers. The men I call the masters of the machines may not have a penny of capital and they are workers too".[70]

A contemporary noted the dangers of recruiting the executive class, like potential officers, straight from higher education establishments with the "spread" of the idea of a cadet class, an officer class, of youths from the polytechnics and colleges and universities, recruited to step direct into higher posts requiring a better education . . . every cadet so introduced into a concern blocks the way of advancement for the youths who come in straight from the elementary school".[71]

By 1935 the hundred largest enterprises in the U.K. were responsible for 24 per cent of manufacturing net output. Often these enterprises owned many plants and, over the whole manufacturing sector, there were huge disparities in plant size. Working from the so-called "Florence median", (half of employees are to be found in plants greater than this size and half in smaller plants), the median plant in 1935 employed 250 and the central 50 per cent of all employees worked in plants employing 70 to 750 people. In vehicle manufacturing the Florence median was 1,250, in timber and furniture 50.[72]

There were opportunities for rising entrepreneurs in modern technological industries: electrical goods, electronics, hydraulics, aircraft and so on.[73] Expanding retail and service industries also created many openings.

Of well over 16 million females aged 14 years and over in England and Wales in 1931, 5.6 million were at work.

In 1919, Parliament had passed the Sex Disqualification (Removal) Act: women were not to be barred from any profession or employment on grounds of sex. "By 1931, only thirteen out of every hundred girls of eighteen were living in idleness. The rest were already at work or were preparing to undertake it".[74] But in 1931, while 46 per cent of women aged under 25 were at work, their proportion fell to 13 per cent for the

35 to 45 age groups and 10 per cent for those women aged 45 to 55. Most women made a career of marriage. Of all women at work in 1931, the proportion who were married was 16 per cent. Of married women the proportion "occupied" was only 13 per cent.

Just after the Second War, a historian asked: "What is there for the woman who has passed her fortieth birthday? Is her place still the home?"[75] He quoted H.G. Wells: "These millions of under-occupied citizens have votes, control expenditure and exercise great influence on the general body of opinion. If they are to be left to themselves . . . the world is creating for itself a force of ignorance, prejudice and self-satisfaction. . ."

While many housewives would not have agreed that they were among "the under-occupied", here was a social problem recognised not only by Wells, but also by many others.

Of the women at work in England and Wales in 1931, a massive 1,934,000 were in personal services of all kinds – still largely domestic service: 582,000 were in textiles, and 56,000 in agriculture. But the "new" 20th century occupations now engaged large numbers: 605,000 in commerce, finance, insurance; 577,000 clerks and typists; 394,000 in professional and technical occupations: 27,000 administrators, directors, managers.[76]

In teaching and nursing women predominated. In England and Wales in 1931, (in full-time equivalents), there were 138,670 female and 15,173 male nurses; 121,990 of the women were single, only 6,652 married and 10,028 widowed or divorced.[77] There were practically 200,000 women teachers compared to 84,000 men, 79,364 women Civil Servants, (235,775 men). The numbers of qualified women medical practitioners rose from 1,253 in 1921 to 5,391 in 1931 – still not then 10 per cent of the total on the Medical Register.[78]

Standards of living

In spite of mass unemployment and much poverty, the real standard of life of the majority of the British people rose appreciably over the inter-war period and was considerably higher than it had been before 1914. In 1900 and 1936, Seebohm Rowntree conducted social surveys in York: the "second survey in 1936 showed that the standard of life of the workers was 30 per cent higher than in 1900".[79] Percentages of the working class population of York living in primary poverty had been cut down from 15.46 to 6.8. Decline in the size of families and rise in real wages were among the chief causes of this improvement.

It can be argued, of course, that York was certainly not in an economically depressed area, but statistics relating to national consumption portray a switch to more expensive and nutritious goods and to luxury items of expenditure. The vast quantities of foods sold could not have been eaten by a limited class. The average intake of calories per head per day in the U.K. rose from 3,057 in 1909–13 to 3,139 in 1924–28 to 3,246 in 1934. The annual consumption per head of certain foods as a percentage of 1909–13 was:[80]

	1924–28	1934
Fruit	149	188
Vegetables (other than potatoes)	130	164
Butter	100	157
Eggs	115	146
Cheese	128	143
Meat	99	106
Potatoes	93	101
Wheat flour	94	93

Other evidence of a switch to foods with relatively high income – elasticity of demand is conveyed by statistics relating to total annual consumption.[81]

	1920–22	1937–38
Potatoes (tons per head)	0.083	0.074
Fresh milk (million galls)	848	1000
Cream (million galls)	3.22	9.19
Eggs (million)	3,915	9,385
Soft drinks (million galls)	1.72	5.79
Sugar, chocolate, confectionery (million tons)	1.06	1.53

Consumption of coffee, sugar and tobacco in lbs per head in the U.K. rose as follows:[82]

	Coffee	Tea	Sugar	Tobacco
1913	0.62	6.69	83.22	2.10
1929	0.76	10.16	91.97	3.24
1933	0.70	9.36	92.32	3.22
1938	0.72	9.09	100.51	4.00

Masses of varied statistics prove that the majority were better off. An index of average real earnings rose from 100 in 1920 to 118 in 1938. True, owing to Great War restrictions, taxes, depression and availability of other leisure pursuits, drinking diminished.

Quantities of beer charged with duty in the U.K. fell from 37.1 million barrels in 1900 to 15.8 in 1918 and 12.9 in 1933, before rising to 18.0 in 1938. British spirits paying duty dropped from 34 million gallons in 1900 to 8.5 million in 1933, rising to 9 million in 1938.[83] A clear indication of calamitous economic depression in Durham came when even some of that County's pubs applied for reductions in rating assessments.[84] It was conceded that not only "the lower spending capacity of the masses" but also rival attractions such as picture houses, clubs, cheap bus trips, caused difficulties for the pubs.

The vastly important late 19th century revolution in retailing, which brought mass consumption by making great quantities of goods readily available, continued.

In 1919, Sainsbury had 123 branches: by 1938 this number had risen to 244. Even in 1932, 14 new branches were added. Their shops became bigger, goods offered more varied, with deliveries to branches speeded by motor vehicles. As elsewhere, prices in the depression were very low: "Back bacon, tea and Australian butter all at 8d (3p) a lb", said one poster.[85] Expansion of large firms,[86] for example of those of Home and Colonial and Liptons, continued in the inter-war period. In the grocery and provisions trade, 125 firms had 7,130 branches in 1915. By 1939, 157 firms had 13,110 branches. Co-operative Societies continued their rapid expansion: membership rose from 4.1 million in 1919 to 8.5 million in 1939: retail sales from just over £100 million in 1915 to £220 million in 1935. Licensed tobacco dealers increased in numbers from 365,000 in 1921 to 530,000 in 1939; newsagents from some 40,000 in 1914 to 45,000 in 1938. Consumption per head of chocolate and sugar confectionery rose by an estimated 55 to 60 per cent between 1920 and 1938.

Those concerned by the very sorry state of the nation's teeth had no cause to rejoice at the rise in sugar consumption but other results of changes in fashion and of developments in mass retailing, were more favourable to health. A school medical officer in Newcastle in 1921: "was greatly impressed with the sensible and hygienic clothing worn by a great number of the girls . . . corsets of the old type, stiffly boned in some few cases still continued to be worn. This is due entirely to the mother's conservative ideas of dress, as evidenced by the child's invariable reply".[87] Another expert wrote: "One observation admits of no doubt, that children were cleaner in 1931 than in 1921. Vermin infestation . . . diminished and the clothing worn was better and cleaner. . ."[88]

The shops offered ready-made clothes for men, dresses and artificial silk stockings for women at cheap prices. With some truth, later executives of Marks and Spencers were to claim that their stores had taken working-class men from neck scarves to shirts.[89] Marks and Spencer's turnover grew from just under £2½ million in 1929 to nearly £23½ million in 1939. The Company opened 129 stores between 1931 and 1935.

The growth in retailing becomes clear when it is noted that the distribution trades employed 1,661,000 workers in 1920–22, 2,436,000 in 1937–38. For consumers with any money it was indeed a golden age. All goods in Woolworths were priced at 3d or 6d (1¼p or 2½p); it was possible to buy, say, a bucket for 6d. Millions in the Northern towns bought a twopenny fish and a pennyworth of chips. A snack in a Student's Union, (tea plus beans on toast) cost 6d.

A striking example of entrepreneurial flair was that which introduced Penguin Books in the Thirties. Cheap paperbacks were now available to, and bought by, millions. There had been cheap classics before, but they did not have the same sales of Penguin. Now for 6d, the price of a pint of beer, it was easy to buy a book.

Indeed, far more leisure was enjoyed by far more people. This was the peak age of the cinema, with the introduction of the

Talkies but before Television. By 1939, some 20 million people were going each week to see films. One survey in Liverpool revealed that 40 per cent of people went to the cinema once, and 25 per cent twice a week. On Saturday evenings it was immensely difficult to gain admission to the new "Gaumonts" and "Paramounts" which offered warmth, deep plush seats, chocolates and teas plus organ music with the films.

Rival attractions included the popular dance halls, of which the larger were staffed by resident bands. Indeed, this was the peak age of the big bands and on radio and records, Henry Hall, Ambrose and others entertained audiences of millions. In 1934, Rochdale, for example, gained its first purpose-built dance hall with resident band and restaurant.[90]

Association Football attracted vast crowds. Over a million, for example, attended the opening matches of the 1926 season. The main news story in a Northern paper in July 1926, "England in danger of defeat",[91] referred not to the coal-strike but to a cricket test against Australia. The inter-war years were those of Hobbs, Sutcliffe, Bradman, Verity, Larwood.

There was great emphasis on healthier living, with a growing cult of outdoor exercise, particularly in the Thirties. Each weekend, routes from the towns to the Pennines and open spaces, were thronged with lines of cyclists and train or bus loads of hikers. By 1939 over a million people a year were staying at Youth Hostels Association accommodation. There was growing emphasis on physical education in schools: the Women's League of Health and Beauty, (often altered to "of Healthy Beauties"), had 166,000 members by 1939.

There was indeed vast evidence that many patterns of life were changing very rapidly. By the end of the Thirties there were 2 million private cars. 15 million people took holidays by the seaside: Butlin's first holiday camp was opened at Skegness in 1937. Of those without cars, increasing numbers travelled cheaply on the new bus-routes. The railway network still retained its 19th century comprehensive coverage of the country and thousands escaped from the cities each weekend on cheap trips from, say, Newcastle to the coast.

Housing

One of the most important, health-bringing, happiness-giving improvements of the inter-war period was the vast house-building programmes which, particularly in the Thirties, changed the face of much of Britain, especially, but certainly not only, in the South-east.

Statistics were very impressive: for the whole inter-war period the figures for new home constructions were:[92]

(In thousands)	*England and Wales*	*Scotland*	*Great Britain*
Built by local authorities	1,163	230	1,393
By private enterprise	3,029	106	3,135
Total:	4,192	336	4,528

So, 4½ million new dwellings were constructed. The number of families was estimated to have risen by 3½ million so there was a considerable – and admittedly much needed – improvement in housing conditions. Most of the new development was private enterprise housing for sale and much of it was in the large new suburbs of the Midlands and South-east, where, by the 1930s a new semi-detached house could be purchased for £300–£400. A deposit of £25 might secure possession: the mortgage rate on the borrowing was 4½ per cent by 1935. Over 1.6 million new houses went up in the South-east over the inter-war period.

But that improvements affected all classes and regions is confirmed by the evidence. In 1933, the Ministry of Health called for local authority plans to clear slums within five years. From 1934 to 39 some 250,000 slum houses were demolished, over 450,000 repaired. New construction averaged 334,000 dwellings a year between 1935 and 1939. By 1937, the very authoritative P.E.P. could write: "the housing problem seemed to be on the way or on the verge of solution. Those who most needed houses were at last beginning to get them".[93]

In the North-east, for example, there was much house-building and slum clearance. Even in Jarrow, 1,640 council and 118 private houses were built between 1920 and 1938 and a further 135 houses were being built at the end of 1938.

There were difficulties. Rent and rates on new council housing were not light: around 7s 9d a week rent plus 3s 9d rates in Newcastle. Over 11s a week was a good deal to pay out of a wage of £2. But many people were very anxious to move into the new housing and were generally pleased with it, while much official opinion echoed that expressed by the M.O.H. Gateshead, 1938: "life in a slum is a vicious circle in which the highest of human aspirations may quickly be submerged in a general hopelessness". He added that following rehousing: "Mental outlook, hygienic behaviour and family pride all undergo a marked change for the better".[94]

Council houses were built to laid-down standards. Normally new houses in the inter-war period were equipped with flush toilets, bathrooms, kitchens. There was also much improvement of existing houses. In 1922, Gateshead had under 6,000 water closets compared with over 18,000 ash closets and 1,400 privy middens and open ash-pits. In 1925, the Council decided on mass-conversion to water-closets: some 6,000 being installed in 1925 alone. By 1936 practically every house in the borough had a water-closet.[95] The townspeople's gain was the Tyne's loss: river pollution was much increased.

Over the same period, South Shields, (1176 water-closets installed in 1924), and large mining areas of County Durham switched to improved sanitation. By 1933, over 18,000 houses in Easington Rural District had water-closets.

By 1938, even a number of Rural Districts in Co. Durham, for example, had piped water supplies to most villages. In this they were well ahead of the truly rural areas of the country, though in 1934 Government did make available £1 million for the improving rural water supplies. Similarly, thousands of parishes still lacked sewerage in 1938.

Particularly in the Midlands and the South-east, the face of England was much changed between 1919 and 1939. Priestley, leaving London on the Great West Road noted "the line of new factories on each side . . . decorative little buildings, all glass and concrete and chromium plate" . . . making . . . "potato crisps, scents, toothpastes, bathing costumes, fire extinguishers. . ."[96] Orwell's fictional George Bowling, re-visiting Lower Binfield, scene of his boyhood, found: "Houses, shops, cinemas, chapels, football grounds – new, all new. . . . All these people flooding in from Lancashire and the London Suburbs, planting themselves down in this beastly chaos. . ."[97]

In the section which follows, it will be demonstrated that there were significant improvements in some important social services.

12.5   Social and health services and education

Welfare and helath

By 1914 the foundations of the Welfare State had been laid. Children at state schools were medically examined; the poorest children might receive meals; Old Age Pensions and National Insurance against unemployment and illness were introduced; beginnings had been made to the provision of Health Visitors and of clinics for mothers and babies.

This latter provision was greatly enlarged over the inter-war period and provided an important contribution to the significant fall in the infant mortality rate. In 1914, Government grants were made available for local maternity and child welfare work. The Maternity and Child Welfare Act of 1918 conferred on local authorities wide powers.[98] By 1918, there were 1,278 Maternity and Child Welfare Centres and 2,577 Health Visitors (including part-timers).

Increasingly from 1919 to 1939, local authorities made provision in this vital sphere. Most certainly all was not well. Until just before 1939 and the use of sulphonamides, the maternal mortality rate remained stubbornly high. Particularly in the 1920s, proportions of expectant mothers, and of mothers and babies, attending clinics were often low. Thus, in Sunderland, a borough with relatively highly developed welfare services, 1,436 children were on the welfare centre registers in 1920. About 80 per cent of young children did not attend.

Already however, by 1920, a very close watch was kept on the newly born. In Sunderland in 1920, there were 5,414 births; 5,015 babies received a Health Visitor's call. Enquiries were made into each still-birth and each infant death. There were 13,201 revisits to infants under one year old, 15,991 to children aged one to five. Similar work went on in every area.

By the end of the inter-war period, in a town such as

Newcastle-upon-Tyne, most mothers and infants received skilled attention. In 1938, there were 4,617 births in Newcastle. 3,319 expectant mothers attended ante-natal clinics; 4,513 newly born babies were visited by Health Visitors. Of 3,860 infants who, in their first year, were consistently followed up, 2,638 attended centres. Health Visitors continued to visit children under five. In all they paid over 77,000 visits.

At the Newcastle Welfare Centres, 3,751 individuals made 22,596 attendances in 1920: 10,577 made 137,404 attendances in 1938.[99]

In Middlesborough, the infant death-rate fell from a horrendous 135 per thousand, (nearly one in seven), in 1920, to 72 in 1938. In that town in 1924, at no less than 109 confinements a "handy woman" still attended at the birth; neither a doctor nor a trained midwife was present. By 1938–39, the municipal maternity hospitals plus municipal midwives, (appointed throughout the country following reform in the 1930s), were covering over half the total births. It was not easy to become a midwife then: fees at Bishop Auckland's County Maternity Home, (first in the North of England)[100] were 40 guineas for untrained girls and 25 guineas for trained nurses taking the midwifery course. But the law stipulating professional attendance at childbirth was enforced – 30 unqualified women were warned in Co. Durham in 1925 alone.

In all areas, including the most economically depressed, the life saving work went on, though rural areas lagged far behind the towns in provision of clinics. But in 1938, at Co. Durham's 79 child welfare centres, 7,346 babies under one year, nearly 19,000 infants and 6,515 expectant mothers attended.

At the age of five most children proceeded to state schools. There they were under the supervision of the School Medical Service. Basic tasks of this service were to carry out three inspections during the child's school career. Co. Durham in 1938, examined 57,905 pupils. "One of the very strong claims of the School Medical Service is its magnificent opportunity for discovering diseases of a serious character in their earliest stages".[101] Sometimes, discoveries were tragic: "A girl aged seventeen, who intended to become a teacher was found to be suffering from active pulmonary tuberculosis".[102] More commonly, inspections revealed, and clinics treated, infestation, skin complaints, problems of eyes, teeth, throats. Newcastle clinics in 1921 treated 87,465 children with "minor ailments", including 16,214 cases of vermin or impetigo of the head, 19,720 of sore eyes, 20,238 of running ears, 20,366 of septic sores and 10,877 of ringworm.

There were continuing deficiencies in the school dental services – shortages of staff and continuing non-co-operation by some parents. But the volume of completed work was enormous. For example, in Newcastle in 1936, 6 dentists inspected 25,000 of the city's 41,000 school children, treated 8,529 with 7,641 fillings and nearly 16,000 extractions. Similarly, eye care was steadily improved: 2,330 were provided with glasses in Co. Durham in 1938. Large numbers of tonsil and adenoid operations were performed: 192 in Newcastle in the last 3 months of 1929 alone.

A comparison of official reports on the health of the child for, say, 1921 and 1936, reveals a considerable widening of the range of treatment offered by school clinics.

Two other significant improvements in the schools which had marked relevance to child health deserve emphasis. Again, particularly in the 1930s, there were developments in physical education: organisers and specialist staff were appointed, gynm-nasia often built, playing fields laid out. Though, especially in County areas, the age of mass school feeding did not come until the Second War, yet in the towns there were large increases in the Thirties in numbers of children taking milk and meals. In 1933, in Jarrow, 1,170 children received 88,000 breakfasts and 166,000 dinners. In 1938 – though provision of breakfasts had ceased due to diminished demand – 91,000 dinners were supplied and over 2,500 Jarrow children were receiving free milk. In Gateshead a systematic attempt was made to feed under-nourished school children. In 1938 over 16,000 were examined and nearly 7,000 recommended for extra nourishment. 398 were given milk once a day, 5,048 milk twice a day, 516 milk and meals.[103] Virol was given with free meals. A watch was kept on progress and intake of food stepped up if necessary.

As already stated, working people were insured against unemployment and sickness. By 1938 National Health Insurance covered 12 million males and 6.1 million females for basic doctoring and sickness benefits. The latter were administered by no less than about one thousand Approved Societies – the great

Insurance Companies, friendly Societies, Trade Unions – varying in membership from less than 50 to over 2 million. Large numbers of the insured paid extra contributions to help cover costs of treatment to eyes, teeth and other benefits. By 1939, membership of some such schemes bringing added benefits[104] was: Dental 12 million, Nursing over 6 million, Ophthalmic over 10 million, hospital treatment 1.6 million, convalescent homes, nearly 11 million. Coverage was often far from complete.

In their Out-patients Departments and their Wards, the hospitals continued to provide attention and care to all who needed them. "However uninteresting the patient's disease, however lengthy the treatment required, some form of institutional care was always available if nothing finer than a workhouse sick ward".[105] With the Local Government Act, 1929, the Poor Law system ended and the work of the Guardians was transferred to the large local authorities. So Poor Law hospitals and medical care of outdoor paupers passed to County Borough and County Councils.

Over the inter-war period, hospital provision grew:[106]

		Hospital Beds		*England and Wales*
Voluntary hospitals	Year 1921	56,550	1938	87,235
Public hospitals	Year 1921	172,006	1938	175,818
		228,556		263,053

Per 1,000 population, beds increased from 6.03 to 6.41 over the period 1921 to 1938.

The voluntary hospitals, especially those linked to a medical school, often remained the most prestigious. Doctors gave their services free to poor patients and charged fees to those who could afford to pay and/or were covered by insurance. Much valuable local control remained. Particularly after municipalisation in 1930, many public hospitals were greatly improved. Thus, Newcastle's former Poor Law Infirmary became the Newcastle General Hospital. Its work load greatly increased: there were 596 operations in 1930, 3,388 in 1938. It established a reputation for advanced neurosurgery. Other hospitals provide similar records of advance. Continuing improvements in clinical work culminated in the already mentioned use of the sulphonamides and the discovery of penicillin.

It is always easy to level criticism at medical services. Many family doctors simply did not have the time nor the facilities to provide first-rate care.[107] Hospitals were often desperately seeking funds; their buildings were frequently old and quite inadequate. Over the whole country, provision of medical services varied greatly. Until the introduction of the new chemotherapy in the Thirties, quite common diseases such as pneumonia or accidents such as rusty nail through the hand, might well be fatal. Care of teeth and eyes was often shamefully neglected.

Yet, apart from those who could pay, the vast majority of people seem to have been covered, one way or another, by the wide range of services, while no urgent case would have been turned away by the hospitals.[108] Thus, in Gateshead, not the best endowed of towns, out of a 1938 population of some 117,000:[109]

47,169	were covered by National Health Insurance
8,466	by Public Assistance Medical Services.
15,500	by the Public Medical Service for dependents of insured persons and others unable to pay fees
19,590	patients were treated at the Dispensary
5,260	were in-patients at hospitals plus unknown number of out-patients
1,524	cases were nursed by the Gateshead District Nursing Assoc.
1,031	babies were delivered by midwives

There is overlapping here and many areas had not Gateshead's widespread arrangements to treat groups such as dependents of uninsured. After 1925, in Gateshead, doctors operated a scheme under which subscribers paying a small weekly sum were entitled to ordinary medical practitioner treatment. In many Northern industrial araes, there were doctors' clubs and arrangements to treat miners, steel-workers, (for example) and their families. There is the clearest evidence that some doctors were highly regarded,[110] that the best of them gave an individual service seven days a week, 365 days a year, and that even under the system of outdoor medical relief, a doctor allegedly neglecting a patient could be in serious trouble. In Sunderland in 1933, a doctor working for the P.A.C. with an enormous work-load, was accused of neglecting a sick child who tragically died. He was nearly dismissed from his post but independent witnesses said the mother had taken her very sick child out of doors.[111]

In Newcastle, in the 1930s, a domiciliary medical service for the sick was inaugurated on the open choice method. Patients could choose a doctor from the list of those willing to undertake this work: doctors by 1938 were paid 25s (£1.25p) per patient per year. This was very generous, though it must be remembered that many on outdoor relief were the old and/or chronic sick.

The above examples are given to reveal the clear dangers of generalisation when applied to Britain's Health Service in 1939.[112]

Pensions and poor relief

Non-contributory old age pensions had been paid since 1909. In 1925 came a significant enlargement with the Widows', Orphans' and Old Age Contributory Pensions Act. A national scheme of contributory pensions was inaugurated. Widows were covered – a great advance for previously many had suffered terribly on the deaths of bread-winners. Those with young children had sometimes been forced to put them in the workhouse so that mothers might seek work.

Large numbers continued to draw poor relief, administered after 1931 by the local Public Assistance Committees. Not only the uninsured, but also considerable numbers of sick or disabled, inadequately provided for by insurance or compensation schemes, sought extra help. In Co. Durham alone, in the week-ending 4–6–38, 520 workers on compensation sought or received extra relief. In 1939, 1,156,000 people (including dependents) were on domiciliary relief and 169,000 were in institutions.

The handicapped

As always, there were inadequacies, but the quality and amount of provision for the handicapped and mentally sick improved and increased over the decades before 1939.

In 1938, there were 71,875 registered blind persons in England

and Wales. The Blind Persons Act 1938 lowered from 50 to 40 years the age at which a blind person could receive a pension. In 1939 over 27,000 blind persons received such pensions.

Local authorities assisted blind persons in need: in Co. Durham and Northumberland, for example, in the 1930s, incomes of unemployable blind persons over 21 were made up to £1 a week. Voluntary associations helped with training and advice for the blind. A great boon by the Thirties was the advent of wireless. Licences were issued free to the blind and "Wireless for the Blind" appeals were among the most successful of those broadcast.

The Education Act 1921 provided for attendance of deaf children at special schools. Thus, in Newcastle in 1930, 150 children were in residence at the Northern Counties Institution for the Deaf and Dumb. This and other voluntary institutions had a good record of keeping in touch with former pupils.

The Elementary Education (Defective and Epileptic Children) Act of 1899, later embodied in the 1921 Education Act, empowered local authorities to make provision for crippled children. By 1937, there were 130 special schools for 13,000 children while at 335 clinics orthopaedic treatment was available. As in other spheres, between local authorities provision varied greatly and in many areas it was clearly quite insufficient.

Under the Lunacy Act of 1890, county and county borough councils were made responsible for the public asylums. By 1914, there were 140,446 "notified" insane persons in asylums.

One of the few advantages brought by economic depression was that it brought into mental nursing needed recruits.

The Mental Treatment Act of 1930 enabled preventive measures to be taken in the early stages of mental illness through the use of hospital out-patient clinics and by making possible voluntary hospital treatment.

For the mentally handicapped not in institutions, local authorities provided some supervision. Thus in 1929, in Co. Durham, 93 health visitors supervised 1,318 mental defectives. Indeed over the period 1914–39, there was "a swing away from the concept of permanent detention and a desire to find means of integrating patients . . . with . . . society".[113]

Voluntary organisations, such as the Central Association for Mental Welfare gave important service.

Scope of total provision

By 1938, the pattern of social and health services was still patchy, piecemeal, ill-co-ordinated. Yet provision was large. Over 15 million were covered by unemployment, 19 million by health, insurance, 20 million for pensions. An expert could write: "the British state had committed itself to the maintenance of all its citizens according to need as a matter of right. . . Britain had attained a defacto national minimum. An edifice had been built, shambling and rickety, without an architect".[114]

Education

Over the 1919–39 period there were steady but significant improvements in the education system, coupled with strong disappointment at the absence of more rapid progress. At the end of the Great War, Fisher's Education Act raised the school leaving age to 14 without exemption. Repeated efforts to raise it to 15 came to nothing. Change would have been implemented from 1–9–1939 but Hitler took a hand. Fisher also established the Burnham Committee which formulated national scales of pay for teachers.

A plan to establish Continuation Schools for young people aged 14–18 fell victim to an economy drive (the Geddes Axe) after the War. But spending on education was considerably increased. Expenditure of Local Authorities on education rose from £30.6 million in 1913 to £98.0 million in 1938. Falls in school rolls and in prices after 1920 meant that expenditure per pupil increased quite dramatically over the inter-war period: by some 60 per cent in primary, and 100 per cent in maintained secondary schools.[115] The most important improvement came in class size – still very large, but at least practically all classes over 60 had gone by 1938 while an attack was being successfully launched on classes over 50.

In 1926 Sir Henry Hadow's Consultative Committee issued a Report, "The Education of the Adolescent", advocating that pupils in England and Wales should be transferred to some form of post-primary schooling at eleven. By 1938 many Authorities had built Senior Schools for the 11–14 age groups, though all-age elementary schools were still extremely common. All too often, buildings had been erected in the 19th century: in 1932 two thirds of school children went to schools built before 1900.[116]

One important development in English education over the period was the growth of the secondary (grammar) schools. Percentages of the 12–14 age group receiving secondary education grew from 7 .5 in 1911 to 20.6 in 1938. Most grammar school pupils paid modest fees, but, by the early twenties, about a third received free places.[116a]

In 1931, an estimated 10,000 private schools taught some 400,000 pupils. Some were excellent, some were small establishments of doubtful standards, staffed by often reluctant teachers to whom no other career was available. In the twenties, down from Oxford with a poor History degree, ("I cannot say that your Third does you anything but discredit, especially as it was not even a good one"[117] wrote his Dean), Evelyn Waugh went to a remote private school at £50 a term. By the Thirties, scholastic agencies were advertising such posts at £80–£120 per year in return for long hours of slavery.

By 1938–9, there were 50,000 full-time students (including about 11,500 women) at British Universities. For the very brilliant there were scholarships – Open Scholarships to Oxbridge, 360 State Scholarships by 1938, a few awards to other Universities. Intending teachers, (and they had solemnly to undertake to teach) had their fees paid and were given a maintenance award. With varying generosity local authorities issued scholarships, grants and loans. Students in Education Departments were maintained by State and Local Authorities: most of the future doctors, engineers, dentists, lawyers, came from middle-class homes and were paid for by parents. There were University developments of vast importance: in atomic and economic sciences at Cambridge, the growth of biochemistry at universities such as Liverpool, the appointment of internationally famous social scientists to the L.S.E. and so on. Thousands of graduates left each year to perform useful professional work. I.C.I. was recruiting chemists; about half the doctors practising around Newcastle were trained at King's College in that city, and must have come into contact with very grim realities. Their work in clinical medicine was made more effective by advances in basic sciences.

Yet, considering they were citizens of one of the World's

richest countries, most Britons in 1939 were still very badly educated. Here, surely, was a major failing of modern Britain. At the 1921 Census, per 1,000 people, the following numbers were in full-time education in Co. Durham.

Age	Males	Females
6–13	947	941
14	315	318
15	79	94
18	13	20
20	8	11
21–24	8	2

(The higher percentage of women in education at ages 14–20 can be accounted for by the predominance of girls among intending teachers and the fact that Co. Durham's heavy industry recruited males).

At the beginning of 1942, Government registered 16 and 17 year olds. Of 835,000 boys only 67,000 were still at school.[118]

The quality of the education provided in grammar schools and Universities was high: for an advanced industrial nation, quantity was insufficient. On the other hand, the educational system produced the scientists, the airmen, the submarine detectors and the makers of that vast amount of advanced scientific equipment needed to fight from 1939–45. As Trevelyan put it in 1941: "If we win this war, it will have been won in the primary and secondary schools".[119]

Social Services Expenditure

Despite cuts in public expenditure in the early 1920s and again in 1931, spending on social services climbed over the inter-war period. With fluctuations, social services spending per head at constant prices (1910=100) rose from 60 in 1890 to about 500 in 1940.[120] A 1933 book chronicled a rise in total social services expenditure from £94.57 million in 1913–14 to £369.65 million in 1929–30. Thus, spending on Education's Special Services (medical inspection, school meals, special and nursery schools) rose from 3s 4d (17p) per child in 1913-14 to 16s 4d (82p) in 1930–31.[121]

Even in hard hit areas, local spending rose. That of Sunderland Borough[122] was £766,096 in 1926–27, £1,838,302 in 1938–39. Spending on Sunderland's Municipal Hospital was £22,204 in 1933–34, £44,126 in 1938–39. Newcastle's school medical services cost £8,016 in 1920–21, £18,783 in 1938–39.

Staffs increased. County Durham increased its health visitors from 54 in 1920 to 112 in 1938. South Shields Health Department employed 9 clerks in 1924, 15 in 1938.

Further, over much of the inter-war period prices fell heavily and a pound bought much more not less. The internal purchasing power of the pound (1920=100) was 143 in 1923 and 173 in 1932, before falling with economic recovery and rising prices to 159 in 1938.

As Winifred Holtby wrote to her mother: "when I came to consider local government, I began to see how it was in essence the first-line defence thrown up by the community against our common enemies – poverty, sickness, ignorance, isolation, mental derangement and social maladjustment."[123] Over the inter-war period such defences – both national and local – were much strengthened.

13. THE SECOND WAR[1]

13.1 A turning-point

Over the past century, main movements in British history have been gradual, continuous, slowly cumulative. But some outstanding events brought rapid, dramatic change. Foremost among these was the Second World War of 1939–45.

Like the Great War, this dug a deep gulf between those who experienced its full horrors[2] and those who escaped them. Some were scarred for life.

Experiences were sometimes horrifying, tragic, heroic, more often they were boring, frustrating, exhausting. Particularly in 1940, the nation was virtually united in a grim fight for survival. "We're in the final and we're playing at home" was chalked on one city wall. In contrast to the Britain of 40 years later, that was a time of marked consensus and cohesion.

The War vastly increased the knowledge which people of different classes and regions had of each other and lessened class inequalities. There were mass evacuations from vulnerable areas and an immense movement and mixing of troops, war-workers and others. Very large numbers, drawn from all classes, spent many days and nights in danger: "the wall between the living and the living became less solid as the wall between the living and the dead thinned".[3] There was no room for class divisions among the crew of the hunted bomber over Germany. Millions shared not only perils but also the same relaxations, for example, they listened to Tommy Handley in I.T.M.A." While it would be utter folly to deny that class differences survived,[4] yet conscription, rationing, heavy direct taxation did apply to all sections of the community.[4a] In face of a great common danger, there was a measure of real equality of purpose, effort, sacrifice.

There was an immense rise in expectations – always so crucial a factor – plus an awakened interest in, and willingness to discuss, serious political and social problems, coupled with a strong determination never to return to the evils of the Thirties – particularly to the dole. In a quite remarkable profession of faith in 1940, the "Times" stated: "If we speak of democracy, we do not mean a democracy which maintains the right to vote but forgets the right to work and the right to live. If we speak of freedom, we do not mean a rugged individualism which excludes social organisation and economic planning. If we speak of equality, we do not mean a political equality nullified by social and economic privilege. If we speak of economic reconstruction, we think less of maximum production (though this too will be required) than of equitable distribution".[5]

Many of the thousands of young people, thrust together in war service, were interested in Britain's plans for her future. The Army mounted a huge programme of adult education with its Army Bureau of Current Affairs, (A.B.C.A.) and varied lectures and courses.

The working class gained greatly in power and influence: "it was in 1940 that the organised working class . . . was for the first time brought into a position of partnership in the national enterprise of war – a partnership on equal not inferior terms, as in the First World War."[6] Labour Party leaders were given posts in Churchill's War Cabinet, and Ernest Bevin directed national manpower from his key post of Minister of Labour and National Service. Nationally, and locally, the T.U.C. and the Unions were consulted on all important aspects of production, direction of labour, working conditions and other matters. Total trade union membership rose from just under 6.3 million in 1939 to 8 million in 1944.

While the massive output of Britain's industry shows that survival of such customs cannot have been too widespread, yet, even in the direst perils of war, it proved impossible to end some restrictive practices: in the shipbuilding yards at Newport, fitters had long worked in pairs though clearly one skilled man was normally sufficient. The "Ministry issued directions, but the men refused to obey them . . . at the end of the War the Newport fitters were still working in pairs".[7]

Once again, the economic position of many working people

was greatly improved by war. From 1940, there was practically no unemployment. From October 1938 to July 1941, average earnings were up by over 40 per cent while official cost of living rose by 28 per cent. True, much of the increase in earnings accrued from well-paid overtime work and involved an obvious loss of leisure, but many people were better off.

As in the First War farming prospered. It has been calculated that between 1938 and 1949 farmers' incomes increased seven-and-a-half fold.[8] This time, the prosperity did not vanish with the coming of peace. It remained after 1945 and brought a very important change to the countryside.

The role of Government was greatly increased. Spending and taxation were hoisted on to higher plateaux from which post-war descents were small and/or temporary. Ministries, Departments, staffs multiplied. Britain fashioned a controlled, planned, siege economy with a rationed people. True, most economic organisations remained in private hands but the degree of state management and control was so vast that in real respects, a Socialist economy was formed. "During the latter years of the war, the government was consuming three fifths of the national product, while taxation took over a third of the national income: . . . the flow of most goods and services was governed at all important stages by direct controls. A third of consumers' expenditure was subject to rationing: and all imports and most building were subject to licence. Controls over materials and labour governed what could be produced".[9]

For the first time in modern British history, Government made use of the Budget, of public finance, as a means of controlling the whole economy. Before 1940, peace-time Chancellors of the Exchequer had considered it their duty simply to balance the books – to raise enough revenue to meet expenditure. Now in a time of very heavy inflationary pressures, with many incomes rising and many goods in very short supply, a major aim of the Budget was to mop up spending power through direct taxes plus enforcement and encouragement of saving.

Vital welfare provision came in the War years. For this, and other reasons, public health, as measured by key statistics, improved – a truly amazing achievement.

Britain poured out vast quantities of wealth and effort in the Second World War. She emerged impoverished and weakened.

True, Germany, Japan and others were in a far worse plight, but the century of British hegemony which followed Trafalgar and Waterloo was now decisively over. The U.S.A. and the U.S.S.R. were the new superpowers.

For all these clearly important reasons, the Second War was an important turning point.

13.2 Costs

Service losses (300,000 dead) were lower than in the 1914-18 struggle, (in Russia it was a very different story). British Army fatal casualties in the Second War were 145,000 contrasted with 677,515 in France and Flanders alone in 1914–1918. The Air Force, as will be shown, was very dangerous for some, but on one 1940 fighter airfield, 35 men and women stayed on the ground for each fighter pilot who took off.[10]

Service – like civilian – experiences varied enormously. Many were stationed in safety in Blackpool, Cyprus and Ceylon. Others experienced terrible dangers and hardships, sometimes extended over years. By 1945, some young men who survived had burned themselves out and never recovered.[11]

From particular branches of the services, very high proportions did not return. The leading authority considered the submarine "the most dangerous of all services".[12] In a mere 5 months of 1942–43, 11 British submarines were lost in the Mediterranean. Bomber Command lost 55,573 aircrew: 38,462 of these from the R.A.F., the others from Commonwealth and Allied Forces. "It is important to stress the extraordinarily high calibre of the human material that came to Bomber Command. The majority had matriculated. . . . ." (in 1980 terms, they had good "O" levels). Physical and other tests were generally strict.[13] The loss of so many picked men is dreadful to contemplate. For, of every 100 recruits to Operations Training Units, 51 were later killed on raids, 9 killed in crashes in Britain, 3 badly hurt in crashes, 12 captured and 1 shot down but escaped. Only 24, (less than one in four) escaped death, capture or serious injury.[14]

Of 58 pilots selected at random from the list of those who saved this country in 1940, 21 were killed in the Battle of Britain, or later.[15]

In the advance from Normandy to Germany, 1944–45, a battalion of The Gordon Highlanders (which landed with just under 600 men), had over 1,000 casualties (killed and wounded). "I shall never get over the sadness of these losses".[16]

Over 30,000 merchant seamen perished in one of the most crucial of the war's battles – to keep open the sea lanes.

Thanks to new drugs, techniques and surgical skills, the sick and wounded received far more effective medical attention than in any previous war. Less publicised was the treatment of the mentally afflicted, but it deserves mention since it revealed significant advances in knowledge and humanity. While in the First War, soldiers who broke under the strain were sometimes cruelly shot for cowardice, in the second conflict such severity was not practised and treatment of those who had breakdowns was much improved.[17] True, airmen who broke under the hideous strain of the terrible flights over Germany which were statistically almost certain to bring their deaths, were branded as "lacking moral fibre" (LMF), demoted, disgraced, or worse. But the forces did make much use of psychiatrists in the treatment of the mentally ill, and, for example, in the selection of Army Officers.

The Second War thrust millions of British civilians into the front line. An estimated 71,000 metric tons of bombs, (including over 6,000 tons of flying bombs and rockets) fell on Britain. Over 60,000 civilians were killed and well over 200,000 injured.[18]

Many died of accidents which would not have happened in peace-time. Because a blackout of lights was ordered to frustrate enemy raiders, road casualties mounted in the early days of war. In the four months September–December 1939, over 1,700 more than the pre-war average were killed on the roads.[19] Some thousands of babies and children perished in accidents attributable to war-time conditions, (on the other hand, as will be pointed out later, there was much saving of infant life). But the majority of the tragedies and upsets resulting from war were not as final as death. Thousands of young couples were separated for years. Many experienced long worry and frustration. Marriages broke up, sometimes with recriminations. Many servicemen's families experienced deep economic hardship for, in 1940, a private's wife with one child received around 30s a week. Finding suitable accommodation was often a great problem. The Army

Authorities received tragic letters: thus a sergeant with 18 years' service, transferred from India, had a wife and three children living in a one-room garret with room for only one bed, so the husband slept elsewhere on leave. The wife of a sick prisoner-of-war theatened to write to the German doctor in charge of the sanatorium where her husband was a patient asking that he should not be repatriated.[20]

To use a term not then in widespread use, there was a large rise in the number of one-parent families. Not only were many fathers away with much impact on the upbringing of children, but also the number of illegitimate births increased: in England and Wales they averaged roughly 41,000 a year from 1941–44 as compared with 26,000 in 1939 and 40.[21] Sometimes the father had been sent abroad (the proportion of legitimate births occurring within the first 8 months of marriage fell steadily to 1943). Though many thousands of British girls married American or Commonwealth servicemen (there were some 70,000 "G.I. brides"), and, after the War departed for a new life in North America, many a girl was left holding the baby as, for example, in Sussex villages where Canadian troops were stationed.

Of some their marriages, of others their homes, were wrecked. In Britain, well over 4 million houses sustained some degree of damage from air attack. 220,000 were destroyed or damaged beyond repair; many others were rendered uninhabitable for long periods. (The reader might pause to consider the upset resulting from the sudden destruction of his or her house). Already by June 1941, roughly 2¼ million people had been driven out of their homes for short or long periods. Areas near vital and easily located docks suffered terribly. London's East End was shattered by September 1940. In Bootle in 1941, only one house in ten escaped damage, nearly a fifth were destroyed or rendered uninhabitable: about a quarter of the people were homeless, a third of the retail shops went. On Clydebank, three quarters of the homes were unfit to live in after heavy 1941 raids. In Plymouth, in April 1941, 30,000 were made homeless and thousands trekked out of the city each night.[22]

Attitudes of ordinary citizens caught up in the war varied enormously. A youth of 18 wrote down his 1940 London experience with clear exhilaration.[23] But as the long years passed a more prevalent attitude became that of a young married woman: "The months dragged on into years, and even the most resilient of us began to realise that our youth was being drained away, and that those precious years of our late teens and early twenties would be lost for ever".[24]

Not all Britons shared the hardships, dangers and sacrifices of war. In the safe areas: "The hotels are filled with well-to-do refugees, who too often had fled from nothing. They sit and read and knit and eat and drink, and get no nearer the war than the news they read in the newspapers".[25] Citizens who should have set an example lived by the old rule: "Do as I say, not as I do". Up to April 1942, in one town 37 prominent citizens, including the vicar, ministers of two churches, the town clerk, the billeting officer, the chairman of the billeting committee and others, had not billeted one evacuee. To a town which said it had no room for war workers, the Ministry of Health sent its own investigators who found that between them 25 councillors had 76 habitable rooms to spare.[26]

Conventional views of legality, property, morality, were again much shaken by total war. With massive destruction of life and property going on all around them to many servicemen, "winning", looting, stealing, seemed unimportant. From the wounded Raleigh Trevelyan, under morphia, were stolen his watch, flask, lighter and wallet.[27] Perhaps this disgusting case was exceptional but personal acquisition of service property was widely regarded as no particular crime, while looting of enemy property was widespread. It is not surprising that many acquired a casual attitude to what in peace-time would have been regarded as crime.

Many British losses in the Second War were more tangible and material. At the end of the War, the U.K. Merchant Fleet was some 30 per cent less than at the beginning. By 1944, (excluding munitions), exports were only 13 per cent of their 1935 volume. External capital assets valued at over £1,100 million had to be sold off, while there was an increase in overseas debts of £2,879 million. Gold and dollar reserves were much reduced.[28]

Capital equipment and household goods could not be replaced. Perhaps capital depreciation totalled some £1,700 million. On the railways, for example, locomotives and track were worn out on a system which came under immense strain. Ton-miles of freight carried rose from over 16 million in 1938 to over 24 million in

1944, passenger miles from nearly 19 million in 1938–39 to 32 million in 1944. By 1946, "even good quality sheets etc., are feeling their age, whilst the cheap goods normally purchased by working-class families are merely shreds and tatters, and, in the case of blankets, have worn so thin that all warmth has vanished".[29]

London County Council bought practically no new school furniture over seven years. Books were often worn out. The schooling of many was severely interrupted and curtailed by evacuation and bombing. In April 1941, in England and Wales 290,000 school children were not receiving full-time education. Male teachers on war service were replaced by married women or by older teachers who would normally have retired. Class size climbed: by 1944 nearly a third of Sheffield's classes had over 50 children. Standards in London, for example, clearly fell. Testing of Army intakes in 1946 and 1947 provided disturbing evidence of clear falls in scholastic attainment.[30]

True, there were some economic gains to be set against the heavy losses. Value of net agricultural output at constant prices rose by some 35 per cent while large-scale mechanisation meant that the farmers' 60,000 tractors increased to 190,000 over the war years. New Government factories built to produce aircraft or munitions and equipped with modern machine tools could, in 1946, be converted to peace-time uses. There had been much development of high-technology industries – aircraft, radio, radar. Executives and workers had learned new skills and techniques. Yet, in the main, Britain emerged from the War a much poorer country.

Over six war years, experiences had varied immensely. Some furthered their careers or improved their businesses and prospered. But, as the Americans were informed in 1944: "The British civilian has had five years of blackout and four years of intermittent blitz. The privacy of his home has been periodically invaded by soldiers or evacuees or war workers requiring billets . . . nearly every man and every woman under fifty without young children has been subject to direction to work, often far from home. The hours of work average fifty-three for men and fifty overall; when work is done, every citizen who is not excused . . . has had to do forty-eight hours a month duty in the Home Guard or Civil Defence. Taxation is probably the severest in the world, and is coupled with continuous pressure to save. The scarce supplies must be shared with hundreds of thousands of United States, Dominion and Allied troops".[31]

Very many Britons had six very hard years and six years is a long time.

13.3   Other social and economic effects

Following the immense movement and mixing of Britons in the Second War, many facts, some extremely disturbing, came to the personal attention of millions. In September 1939, nearly 1½ million people – children, mothers, severely handicapped persons, teachers – were moved from vulnerable to safe areas. Many of these evacuees came from areas in London, Merseyside, the North-east, and central Scotland with some of the worst housing and most pressing social problems in Britain. Following their arrival in rural areas, "complaints arose from all quarters in a volume amounting to outcry. Against some of the mothers of young children they were extraordinarily intense and bitter."[32] These feckless mothers, it was strongly alleged, could not control children who were often dirty, verminous, bed-wetting, used to sleeping on the floor, unused to wholesome meals; sometimes defiant, destructive, foulmouthed.

Many evacuees returned home in the quiet months of 1939–40, only to move again with the heavy bombing of 1940–41 and (from South-east England) with the flying bomb and rocket attacks of 1944–45. As usual, it was the failures and complaints which received the publicity. Yet, in 1943, 154 householders in Bognor, for example, had not been without evacuated children since 1939, and 33 had kept the same children over those years.[33]

Evacuation was but part of a vast movement of citizens. Since, under National Registration, names and addresses had to be notified, it is known that in England and Wales alone there were some 34,750,000 removals over the war years.[34] Administrative changes had to follow, for Local Government boundaries with localised responsibility often ceased to have relevance – who was to pay for dental treatment of London children sent to the Counties? Government made arrangements for doctors to be paid for treating unaccompanied evacuated school children.

Despite the immense demands of war, there were improvements in welfare services. This was one reason for the astonishing improvement in public health, as judged by key statistics.

In English and Welsh schools in 1939, nearly 160,000 dinners were served each school day. By early 1945, this figure had risen to 1,650,000. One in seven was free, the others cost parents 4d to 5d (2p) a meal. In July 1940, about a half, in February 1945 nearly three-quarters of schools in England and Wales served milk. After 1940, all children under five, plus expectant and nursing mothers could buy a daily pint of milk at 2d, less than half the normal cost. The milk was free to those with low incomes. This scheme was a great success; by September 1940, 70 per cent of around 3½ million mothers and children entitled to cheap or free milk were getting it. Children and expectant mothers were also supplied with cheap or free orange juice and cod liver oil, (or vitamin tablets).

Before 1939 many children had died tragically from diphtheria. There had been immunisation but provision was patchy and outbreaks severe. In 1936 (a bad year) there were 397 cases with 30 deaths in Sunderland, for example; but, between 1940 and 1945, nearly 7 million children were immunised against diphtheria.

Not only the young benefited from improvements in welfare. In 1940, the Old Age and Widows' Pensions Act enabled old age pensioners and widows in need to apply for supplementary allowances. By 1945, £60 million was being paid out under this scheme.

In the last months of the War, an important reform came with the introduction of Family Allowances for which Eleanor Rathbone, who had campaigned for years, must be given the main credit. Since large families were a major cause of poverty, this was a significant step towards the elimination of what Shaw had called the greatest of crimes.

What could be implemented in wartime was but a tiny fraction of what was proposed for the coming days of peace. Proposals and plans for economic and social betterment were on a large scale. In 1940 the Barlow Royal Commission on the Distribution of the Industrial Population advocated national action to affect the distribution of industry and people. Among ameliorative measures recommended was the building of new towns. In 1942

Beveridge recommended a comprehensive insurance scheme
which would abolish serious want. In 1944, Government accepted
"as one of their primary aims and responsibilities the maintenance of a high and stable level of employment after the
War".[35] Proposals were advanced for widespread reform of the
health service. Immediately after the War, valuable research was
conducted into the state of the nation's hospitals and on each
region, detailed findings were published.

But the remarkable achievement came within the war years.
Health, in general improved. The revealing infant death rate fell
considerably after 1941, an amazing success in the midst of total
war.

Number of infant deaths under age 1 per 1000 births[36]

Year	England and Wales	Scotland
1939	51	69
1941	60	83
1944	45	65
1945	46	56
1946	43	54

That older civilians shared in the general improvement in
health is clear from the following mortality figures:

*Death rates per 1000 – England and Wales (civilians, excluding
war deaths)*

	MEN			WOMEN		
Year	45–55	55–65	65–75	45–55	55–65	65–75
1938	10.2	23.1	53.7	6.97	15.2	38.8
1945	9.0	22.2	50.2	5.85	13.2	34.5

These improvements came in spite (cruel cynics might say
because!) of a large reduction in numbers of family doctors,
many of whom were on war service. Their ranks were reduced by
a third and ten per cent of those remaining at home were aged
over 70.

There were many reasons for better health: full employment,
heavier wage packets, provisions under rationing of a scientifically determined nutritive diet, (including a more nutritious loaf as

more of the wheat went into bread), new and very effective drugs, and, health-giving welfare provision for vulnerable groups. Very important too, was the fact that health improvement is cumulative. By 1939, for example, rickets was becoming comparatively rare,[37] so mothers had less difficulty giving birth to healthy children since they themselves did not suffer from deformed pelvic structures – one possible legacy of rickets.

Not all was rosy. There was an increase in tuberculosis in Scotland, a rise in numbers of sickness benefit claims by insured workers, some evidence of much taking of pills and medicines. Certainly, however, the infant mortality returns, in particular, were conclusive proof of a general rise in standards of living, health and welfare provision. Obviously, babies are particularly susceptible to any changes in standards.

But between 1939 and 1945 the overriding consideration was victory. To achieve this, under the direction of new – (Economic Warfare, Food, Shipping, Aircraft production) – and of often vastly expanded existing Ministries, the British carried through a degree of economic mobilisation for war perhaps unequalled in any other warring nation. From mid 1941 to 1944, the United Kingdom was devoting over half its national income to war expenditure which, according to American findings, was a higher percentage than in any other major combatant. By 1944, 55 per cent of the labour force of the U.K. were either in the Forces or in civilian war employment, as compared with 40 per cent in the United States. Out of a total British labour force of 23.5 million, 5.2 million were in the Forces and 7.8 million in civilian war employment. The degree of economic mobilisation – judged by percentages of the work force in the Forces plus munitions – was greater than in 1918.[38]

In sharp contrast to most peace-time experiences, there simply were not enough workers. Well-known economic teachings concerning scarce means and the allocation of resources among competing ends now came into their own. But now it was not the operation of market forces which determined which means satisfied which ends. Now manpower and material resources were allocated by planning and direction in a planned economy. It was a very major departure from peace-time practice.

True, particularly in the early years of the war, very many continued in their normal peace-time jobs as miners, bank clerks, shop assistants and so on, much as if nothing had happened. As part of pre-war planning, a Schedule of Reserved Occupations had been constructed and those listed as being on essential work were not called up. Even in the darkest days of 1940, Ernest Bevin relied considerably, and certainly at first, on a softly-softly approach, based on generally consent, to labour direction. To July 1941, no more than 2,800 individual direction of workers to particular jobs had been issued.[39] There was an obvious great gap between degrees of direction endured by those called up and those left in civilian life.

Bevin was helped by Hitler's invasion of Russia in 1941 which turned militant Communist shop stewards into fervent supporters of the war effort. Certainly, economic nets were further pulled in after 1941. The Essential Work Order laid down that no employee of a scheduled undertaking could leave or be sacked, (except for serious misconduct), without official permission. Under the Registration of Employment Act, 1941, men and women within stated age limits had to register for some form of war work. By the end of 1947, nearly 6 million workers in 30,000 undertakings were covered by the Essential Work Order. Also in 1941, for example, women aged 21–30 were given the choice of going into an Auxillary Service, Civil Defence or essential industry. Increasingly, workers had to move into essential industries as non-essential firms, unable to obtain steel, timber, cotton and so on, had to close down.

As in the First War, large numbers of women moved into the vital engineering industries which employed 411,000 women in 1939, over 1½ million in 1943. Also, as in the First War, there were great improvements in industrial welfare. A 1940 Order stipulated that in a factory employing over 250, Inspectors could require the appointment of a welfare officer. The B.B.C. provided "Music while you work". Trouble-free production was considerably ensured by the setting up of Joint Production Committees – made up of employer and union representatives – which covered 3½ million workers by 1944.

Certainly, statistics of war production were most impressive. In 1941 alone, output from British factories included over 20,000 military aircraft, 143,000 tons of bombs, nearly 5,000 tanks, 110,000 heavy vehicles and nearly 17,000 guns.[40] R.G.D. Allen calculated that, from 1939 to 1943, Commonwealth forces were supplied with war equipment worth 100,000 million dollars. Practically 70 per cent of this came from the U.K.[41] Though over a life span, the world had been repeatedly assured that German was much in advance of British science, technology and industry, yet in the Second War, British aircraft, radar, submarine detection, action against magnetic mines, code-breaking and so on, were at least a match for the Germans.

But in one important sphere, production was disturbingly disappointing. "The industry that came nearest to defeating Bevin, and everyone else was mining".[42] Statistics show the truth of this statement.[43]

Year	Saleable output of mined coal (tons)	Av. numbers of wage-earners	Output per wage-earner per annum (tons)	Total absenteeism %
1938	226,993,200	781,000	290.4	–
1944	184,098,400	710,000	259.2	13.6

In full employment conditions, mining was unpopular. Numbers of workers fell: though over 20,000 "Bevin boys" were conscripted into the pits. Clearly some miners took advantage of their new power. The dreadful legacy of bad labour relations, often depressing housing and environmental conditions, aliena- tion, resentment, could not be banished by exhortation and a doubling of miners' earnings between 1935 and 1944.

Fortunately, coal was a major exception. By 1943, the total mobilised labour force in industry, Civil Defence, the Forces, was 3¾ million over the 1939 figure. Of the nation's war effort it has been written: "the Government mastered the difficulties and the people took the strain".[44]

Real spending on consumer goods and services was much reduced. In 1944, as compared with 1938, all consumption was down by 16 per cent. Spending on motoring fell by 95 per cent, on a range of household goods, (1944 as compared with 1935), by 82 per cent. In the U.S., on the other hand, consumption in an economy restored to full employment went up. At 1938 prices, examples of U.K. spending in stated years were:[45]

	1939	1944	
Food	1307	1120	£ million
Household goods	274	100	
Clothing	444	275	
Private motoring	113	8	

Many incomes rose as more people worked longer hours at rising pay rates. Goods available fell in quantity. Many foodstuffs, (meats, bacon, sugar, butter, cheese, tea, sweets and others) were rationed as was clothing. Many goods were practically unobtainable – petrol, prams, tropical fruits, tinned goods and a whole host of household goods.

Rising incomes and falling supplies of consumer goods produced a classic inflationary situation of "too much money chasing too few goods". In 1939 "Times" articles on "How to Pay for the War" (which became a 1940 book), Keynes advocated forced saving. To a modified extent, his proposals were implemented in a savings scheme known as "Post-war credits", enforced deductions from income to be repaid after the war. Much heavier reliance was placed on penal direct taxation: after 1941 the standard rate of income tax was 10s in the pound.

It was indeed a much planned, controlled, siege economy. Britain's achievements and social cohesion under such an economy were very great, but it must be stressed that there was one overriding objective – victory, and that, to achieve this, citizens were prepared to obey the rules and accept sacrifice.

Appendix to Chapter 13

A critical analysis of Britain's industrial performance in World War II is ruthlessly developed in Corelli Barnett, *The Audit of War. The illusion and reality of Britain as a great nation.*, Macmillan 1986.

It is conceded that the degree of mobilisation, and the mountain of production, were vast. 700 major ships of war, over 5,000 lesser naval craft, 4½ million tons of merchant ships,

100,000 aircraft, including over 10,000 heavy bombers, over 150,000 pieces of artillery, 25,100 tanks, 900,000 wheeled vehicles, nearly 4m machine guns were produced.

But this output was only possible because of vast American aid. American food, materials, equipment, to the value of over 27 billion dollars came to Britain in 1941–45, under the lend-lease scheme. It is indeed disturbing that a leading industrial nation such as Britain should have had to import over 65,000 American machine tools in 1940 and 41 and that Britain in 1941 was totally dependent on America for over 20 types of advanced machine tool. Between 1940 and 1944 Britain also imported from N. America (for example) over 14½ million tons of steel.

Well-known failings of British industry are again castigated: falling coal output, the failures in tank design and production which meant that two-thirds of the tanks with British armoured divisions in Normandy in 1944 were American Shermans: slackness in ship repair yards; managerial inefficiencies; trade union conservatism and bloody mindedness. Symptoms of the "British disease" which was to gain notoriety over subsequent decades were clearly evident, says Barnett. Where there were vast increases in output, as in aircraft, they were gained by drafting in hundreds of thousands of extra workers. Output per worker remained below that attained in the U.S. or Germany.

All of which is undoubtedly true, though it has to be set against the undoubted triumphs; that in 1940, for example, before U.S. aid arrived in bulk, British radar and planes and organisation did thwart the Luftwaffe, that very much British equipment – specially equipped tanks, an artificial harbour etc – did help towards the success of that 1944 Normandy invasion and so on.

Barnett criticises what he calls the "New Jerusalemers" – those who advocated vast improvements which were to come in a Britain clearly facing huge economic and industrial problems. He selects these "New Jerusalem" advocates – Beveridge, Archbishop Temple and others. He does not emphasise that, particularly in the Forces, there was in 1939–45 a strong mass movement in favour of radical reform. Millions of young people were herded together in ships, camps, airfields. Some were in great danger. Of course, many were just not interested in health service changes, export potential or Balance of Payment problems. But many were. Compared with any time before or since there was an immense, inquisitive, interest in serious, political debate. Large numbers were convinced that they had had a raw deal before, and were going to get a better one after, the hardships and sacrifices of the War.

The educational system, in particular the lack of technical training, is much blamed by Barnett for the poor performance of British industry. He is not alone. But awkward questions do arise. Why, for example, has farm production been so successful? Modern farming is very scientific. Farmers and farm workers are not normally trained in colleges, but are the "practical men" so berated by critics of industry's preference for the practically trained over the University man.

14. BRITAIN IN A CHANGED AND CHANGING WORLD

14.1 Outline

Victorious but impoverished, economically weakened, and relatively much less powerful, Britain emerged in 1945 into a vastly changed and rapidly changing world. The triumphant Grand Alliance rapidly dissolved, to be replaced by a deep division between the West and the Communist bloc headed by the U.S.S.R. Astronomical sums devoted to armaments provided one undoubted fuel injection system to the continuing world inflation.

With the significant exception of the Russian Empire, (now the enlarged U.S.S.R.), European Empires, gained in the centuries of scientific and technological superiority, disappeared. In 1939 the British Empire and Commonwealth still embraced about a quarter of the World. By 1979 only a few small Dependencies to which for one reason or another it seemed difficult to grant independence remained. It was a truly enormous change.

In 1973, a decision of historic importance was taken when Britain, which had for centuries expanded over the oceans and still had Commonwealth attachments, joined the European Economic Community.

The post-war world saw much rapid change and conflict. Britain, with an open economy and world-wide interests, was particularly vulnerable to dislocations following, for example, Iranian revolution, Middle East war, United States recession. With too great cost in scarce resources and over too long a time, Britain attempted to fulfil a world power role for which she no longer had the economic and military strength.

Certainly it is hard to over-emphasise the reality that what happened to the British economy, to the plans of ministers and so on, was much determined by overseas happenings over which Britain no longer had any control.

Very clear evidence that this country was no longer a world power came with the Suez fiasco of 1956 when Egypt nationalised the Canal. Britain and France intervened militarily but withdrew in face of world, particularly American, hostility.

In the 19th century, Britain had the power to keep the peace and to guide developments over a large part of world. After 1945, that power had gone.

Dramatic evidence of a fundamental shift in economic power came in 1974. Oil which had been costing around £8 a ton in 1973 cost £32 a ton by mid 1974. This was but the first of a series of jackings-up of oil prices, (from which by 1980 the U.K. was actually a substantial benefactor since she was a producer). The same could not be said, however of commodity prices, which rose by some 50 per cent in 1973. Traditional high dependence on imported primary products has continued to make the U.K. economy very vulnerable.

In 1945, with main competitors Germany and Japan defeated and occupied, Britain was in a very favourable economic position. But Germany and Japan rapidly rose from the ashes to massively overtake Britain in production and exports. Their percentage shares of world manufacturing exports were:

	1958	1978
West Germany	18.5	20.8
Japan	6.0	15.7

Over this period Britain's share was nearly halved from 18.2 to 9.5, while that of the United States fell from 23 to 15. High-grade exports from rich countries such as Sweden and cheap goods from some Third World countries such as Hong Kong, Korea, Taiwan, entered very competitive markets.

14.2   End of Empire and world power: the European Community

At Yalta in early 1945, Churchill met on equal terms with Roosevelt and Stalin to decide Europe's fate after victory. In the

economic sphere, Keynes assumed that the international monetary arrangements he was helping to set up at the end of the War,
would be under American and British direction. But over the
decades after 1948, Britain's power, influence and Empire waned
with great rapidity.

Already, by the end of the War, relative decline was obvious.
The U.S. Navy was far, far more powerful than the Royal Navy.
The U.S.S.R. was clearly the other superpower. Already, before
1939, there had been strong nationalist movements in India and
Egypt. The latter country gained virtual independence in 1936,
though British troops remained. But in 1945, few foresaw such a
rapid end to the British Empire. Yet, over the next twenty years
over 500 million people in Asia, Africa, the Caribbean, gained
independence. Here was surely one of the most important
changes in modern world history.

Often, British rule had been a brief episode. True, the British
were in India for around two hundred years, though even there
much of the sub-continent was ruled for about one century. But
in Africa, the Sudan, Kenya, Northern Rhodesia, much of
Nigeria, were ruled by British for only some 60, Tanganyika for
little over 40, years.

Britain's going was clearly necessary and inevitable. To that
small minority of Britons actually engaged in colonial government, the end of Empire was clearly of major personal concern.
Some stayed on, their terms and conditions of service guaranteed
by British and local governments: some returned home to start a
new life. In 1980 over 30,000 pensioners or their dependents were
eligible for membership of the Overseas Service Pensioners'
Association.

For the services of Britons, in particular of the qualified,
overseas demand continued to be brisk as development schemes
were implemented. By the 1970s, rich Middle East oil countries
were offering lucrative contracts to thousands of expatriates. But
these now went out as paid servants to foreign governments.

The end of the Empire personally affected, and sometimes
saddened, a small minority of Britons. Others were openly
pleased that what they had advocated had been achieved. Most
simply did not care. "Coming home in the mid-1960s was a
depressing experience for many ex-colonials and their wives.
They came back to an England where the public image of

colonialism and the colonial servant was very different from their own. Even more wounding was "the complete lack of interest in what had happened in Africa in the last fifty years".[1] Such was one view, which takes no account of the fact that some, particularly, perhaps, the wives and mothers, were glad to be back in their own land with all its advantages.

In the years following 1946 it might have been easy for a victorious and much-praised Britain to have assumed the lead in the economic unification of battered West Europe. But immersed in their own national problems, British ministers missed opportunities taken up by others. In 1952 was established the European Coal and Steel Community, in 1957 the European Economic Community. Britain joined the Community in 1973. In 1975, in their first national referendum, just over two-thirds of those voting wanted Britain to stay in.

Joining the Market was the subject of keen debate and cause of acute division before and after 1973. Pro-marketeers emphasised advantages of belonging to a protected, rich expanding market of some 250 million people. Such a boost was particularly valuable, it was claimed, to the high technology modern industries. Anti-marketeers dismissed such promised dynamic effects as "a pious hope".[2]

Before and after Britain's joining, very much criticism was directed against the Community's Common Agricultural Policy. For Britons, their own well-tried and successful agricultural policies were very much saner and more beneficial. In simple terms, Britain had long bought much of her food on competitive world markets. Since the world prices were often lower than those which would guarantee British farmers reasonable incomes, additional deficiency payments were made to British producers who received guaranteed prices negotiated in an annual review. The consumer could buy relatively cheap New Zealand butter, Ausrtralian apples, Canadian wheat. The farmers were aided.

The Community protected its farmers by preventing imports from low-price countries. If at resulting high prices, supply exceeded demand, surpluses were bought up and stood in butter "mountains" or wine "lakes". As a percentage of world market prices, community support prices by 1969–70 were: Hard Wheat 230, Barley 203, Maize 159, Rice 186, Butter 613. In 1973, 200,000 tons of butter were sold, at a give-away price, to Russia.[3]

As might have been forecast, Britain became the largest net contributor to E.E.C. funds. The Common Agricultural Policy absorbed very much of Market spending. Britain is a mainly industrial country with relatively few farmers, so gains to her people were less than were gains to Irish or French.

Britain's net E.E.C. budget contribution rose from £150 million in 1976 to £780 million in 1979. Following most energetic British protests, the Community agreed in June 1980 to refund to Britain £1,570 million in 1980 and 1981. Britain agreed that food prices should be further increased.

Criticism of the Community was strong. Raised food prices and the huge cost of agricultural support were main grounds. While conceding that British exports to the E.E.C. were up to £2,000 million a year more than they would have been had past trends continued, economists pointed to the much larger increase in imports from the E.E.C. – up by £4,500 to £6,000 million more than might have been expected.[4] Yet, by the first half of 1980, 43 per cent of Britain's visible exports were to, and 41 per cent of imports came from, the E.E.C. Operations of the vast multi-nationals, such as Ford, were planned on a European scale.

Yet, through the 1970s, Britain was not a whole-hearted participant in E.E.C. polices. She did not join in linked currency arrangements. The Government "felt it more prudent to keep a low profile". [5]

This brief summary has concentrated on economic issues but in a violent and dangerous world political reasons for joining a European bloc are strong. Yet, loss of sovereignty and Parliamentary supremacy, inevitably consequent on membership, have aroused opposition. So, too, have the weakening of economic and other ties with Commonwealth countries such as Australia and New Zealand.

15. THE POST-WAR CONSENSUS

15.1 Keynes and Beveridge

The twenty or so years after 1945 were one of the most successful periods in Britain's economic and social history. With full employment, rising living standards, better social services, most people truly "had never had it so good." As already stressed, much of the prosperity was due to factors quite outside Britain's control: world economies and trade boomed and Britain's went up with them.

At home, an important new consensus was thought out by intellectuals and implemented by politicians. However violent their verbal onslaughts when in opposition might be, once in office politicians followed much the same policies as had their opponents. Indeed, in the 1950s, the term "Butskellism", (Butler was a leading Tory and Gaitskell leader of the Labour Party), was coined to describe this underlying agreement and continuity. The mixed economy was considerably managed, the Welfare State enlarged, the Unions mollified, industrial strife avoided.

Of course, much of this was not new. The economy had been vastly controlled in two World Wars, the Welfare State had been developing for decades. But in peace-time before 1939, British governments had not attempted to stabilise or control the economy as a whole by budgetary means. In 1945–51, Labour much increased the size of the public sector and of provision by the Welfare State. The Conservatives did little to dismantle their main constructions.

Among those responsible for the thinking and planning that lay behind the post-war economic and social structure, two men stand out – J.M. Keynes and W. Beveridge. "There can be no doubt, I think, that Keynes is generally recognised as the predominant figure among economists of this century", wrote a Scandinavian economist.[1]

In his most influential book, "The General Theory of Employment, Interest and Money", Keynes argued that the economy, left to itself, might not produce full employment, but might find equilibrium at less than full employment and stay there.

In a free market economy, entrepreneurs produce goods and take on labour only when they can sell the goods at a profit. Keynes assumed, (and it was a reasonable assumption in 1930s conditions) that on the supply side, firms were producing efficiently. The main determinants of output and employment therefore came from the demand side. Firms could only produce, and provide employment, if there was a demand for their products. If total demand was insufficient, then there was depression and unemployment.

This was the central, key, assertion of Keynes, for it followed that slump and unemployment could be cured by increasing demand.[2]

In 1936 there was depression and unemployment. In 1939 there was much risk of demand inflation. Keynes, as already indicated, advocated control of demand through obligatory savings.

Here, then, were the basic ideas of Keynesian demand management which were to be explained in economics textbooks on both sides of the Atlantic and be implemented by modern Governments in London, Washington and other capitals.

Yet Keynes's theories had critical weaknesses. The "General Theory" paid insufficient attention to Britain's external position and to the fundamental economic problems of structural unemployment, to the decline of Britain's basic industries and the resulting depressed areas with high unemployment. It is arguable that a general expansion of demand after 1936 would have produced inflation and would not have provided work for unemployed miners in South Wales or shipyard workers in Jarrow.

But, until the late 1950s, Keynes's ideas held almost undisputed sway. There then came a successful counter-attack from the monetarists led by Milton Friedman, about which more later. But in 1979 to many economists and others, (particularly in Cambridge), Keynes was still a very major source of inspiration.

Beveridge

In an immensely favourable climate of opinion, with the mass of Britons yearning for and expecting drastic social changes after their sufferings, William Beveridge seized the opportunity to propose comprehensive reform of the variegated and incomplete social welfare provision. "Social Insurance and Allied Services – Report by Sir William Beveridge", was published at the end of 1942. It advocated a full scale attack on the five evil giants on the road to prosperity – want, ignorance, squalor, idleness and disease – through the establishment of a comprehensive system of social insurance for the whole community, full employment, family allowances and a national health service. Beveridge's own plan was mainly concerned with insurance. In return for weekly contributions, citizens when in need were to receive benefits as of right, without means tests. Approved societies were to go, the system would be administered and uniformly applied by the State.

Beveridge was not simply concerned with making payments to those in want. He had long been struck by the need for social cohesion which was gravely threatened by poverty and excessive inequality. Achievement of cohesion would be assisted if there were a common freedom from the evils of want.

The Report received a cold reception from some leading politicians, civil servants and others.[3] Yet there was a welcome from thousands of Britons, starved of hope over more than three mainly disastrous war years.

Keynes was not the only economist to advocate management of the economy to avoid evils such as mass unemployment. By 1945 very many had been converted to the need for the further abandonment of laissez-faire and the need for intervention.[4] Similarly, numerous and cumulatively massive were the investigations into, and suggestions for, reform of social and health services.

15.2   Mixed, managed, economy and welfare state

With a large Parliamentary majority until 1950, Mr. Attlee's Labour Administrations of 1945–51 supervised impressive economic recovery, added largely to the public sector, much extended the coverage of the Welfare State. The loyalty of most industrial workers was retained through difficult years. Though Labour lost the 1951 Election, practically 14 million people voted Labour as against 11½ million in 1979 when the electorate was much larger.

Particularly under the direction of Sir Stafford Cripps, (Chancellor of the Exchequer 1947–50), continuing austerity was imposed at home through high direct taxation, rationing and controls, while emphasis was rightly placed on recovery of the basic economy. "You will see, then, that as long as we are in this impoverished state, the result of our tremendous efforts in two world wars, our own consumption requirements have to be last in the list of priorities. First, are exports . . . second is capital investment in industry; and last are the needs, comforts and amenities of the family".[5] Perhaps only a generation schooled in the hardships of war could have been induced to accept such an economically sound, but undoubtedly Puritan, policy.

Achievements were considerable. As early as 1948, (1938= 100) industrial production had reached 117 and the volume of exports 138. The volume of personal consumption had been held down to 103 and of imports to 81. Home investment took 15 per cent of national income in 1948 as compared with 12 per cent in 1938. The immense war-time blessing of full employment was preserved. Unemployment percentages were only between one and two per cent from 1946 and 1951.[6]

Government had to take the lead, but there was an impressive array of voluntary restraints: on dividend payments, industrial advertising and most important, from 1948 to 1950 on the wages front. Over 2½ years from early 1948, wage rates rose by only 5 per cent and retail prices by 8 per cent. Compared with 1970s figures, here were most impressive achievements. High taxation and resulting revenues covered total Government expenditure: there was no Public Sector Borrowing Requirement in those years which in so many respects were vastly more difficult than the 1970s. Typical of very hard economic decisions which had to be taken was that to hold down much-needed house building to around 200,000 new dwellings a year, mainly for the councils.

Naturally, there was strong opposition from Conservatives and very bitter complaint from middle class people who could no longer easily find servants, whose incomes were heavily taxed and whose basic foodstuffs were still rationed. But compared with 1900–1914, or the 1920–30s, these were years of industrial peace and greater social cohesion as the evils of mass unemployment and degrading poverty were removed.

Yet though economic achievements were impressive, at the time, certainly, problems and difficulties seemed greater still. A large loan borrowed from the Americans in 1945 rapidly evaporated. The oft-repeated post-war Balance of Payments problem raised its ugly head. There was a deficit of £450 millions on the current balance in 1947. In 1949 came a large devaluation of the pound: down by 30 per cent to 2.80 dollars to the pound. By making exports cheaper and imports dearer, this helped the overseas balance. Unfortunately, this latter was again thrown into deficit by the Korean War of 1950, with its resulting upsurge in the prices of raw material imports. It must be emphasised that Britain, along with the rest of Western Europe, benefited from the immense injection after 1948 of American economic assistance under the Marshal Aid programme.

The economic structure which emerged in the years 1945–51 was that of a "mixed" or "social" economy in which, first, was an enlarged public sector, second the private sector was complex and much controlled, third, a very large slice of income generated by output was appropriated by the State for social uses.

Labour nationalised basic industries and services – "the commanding heights of the economy". Taken into public ownership were the Bank of England, (which many were surprised to find still in the private sector), coal, gas and electricity, railways, and large-scale road transport, steel, cable and wireless. These undertakings were bought out from their previous owners and placed under State Boards. Administrative arrangement varied greatly among nationalised undertakings: some, like coal, had a strong Central Board, others like gas and electricity distribution had de-centralised Regional Boards. Day to day running of the concern was left to the Board, but in major matters of policy, investment, pricing, relevant Government ministers felt bound to intervene and relations between Ministers and Board chairmen have not always been happy.

Nationalised industries were among Britain's largest. They

controlled vital sectors of the economy in fields of energy, communications, transport. But most economic undertakings remained in private hands, and by the second half of the 20th century, the structure had become immensely complex. Within the private sector there were, for example, trustee savings banks, building societies, Co-operatives, pension funds and insurance companies (including mutuals and friendly societies) all of which have legal structures quite distinct from any classic capitalist form. Capitalist institutions included companies, partnerships and other businesses, all varying greatly in size. All branches of the economy had been brought under growing legislative and official control and under public scrutiny. Increasingly, from 1945 to 79, newspaper, radio and television reporters probed into any dark places in the economy.

Giant firms, headed by the vast multinationals, increased their share of industries' output. In U.K. manufacturing net output, the share of the hundred largest enterprises rose from some 22 per cent in 1949 to around 40 per cent by 1970. That large British establishments increased their share of offered employment is clear from the following table showing percentages to total employment offered by establishments within the stated ranges[7].

No. of employees	1935	1961
11–99	25.6	30.1
100–499	39.1	31.2
500–999	13.9	14.2
1000–over	21.4	34.5

The output, wealth, power and importance of the largest firms form one outstanding reality of the modern world. In 1979, Unilever's sales were worth £10,249 million, (far more than the national income of many states), while their employees world-wide totalled over 300,000. Such great companies reap vast advantages in key fields such as finance, product price determin-ation, specialisation, economics of scale, training and provision of amenities, (for example, I.C.I.'s medical facilities at Billingham are extremely good). In important respects these vast multi-nationals can make a nonsense of national barriers since they move vast sums of money from one country to another or in the case of vehicle producers such as Ford plan their operations on a

Europe-wide basis, moving engines, parts and vehicles from one country to another.

Increasingly, shares in capitalist concerns in Britain have been bought by Pension Funds, Insurance Companies and other Institutions. Here is a great change in the pattern of ownership from Victorian times when the rich individual investor was far, far more important.

Yet, small firms remain very numerous and important.

In 1971, the Bolton Committee published its report on small businesses in manufacturing, retailing, wholesale trades, construction, the motor trades and road transport, catering and miscellaneous services. In each of these the "small" business was "defined": e.g. in manufacturing it had less than 200 employees, in retailing less than £50,000 a year turnover, and so on. On these definitions of small firms, there were 820,000 of them supplying 14 per cent of gross national product. If agricultural and the professions are included, numbers rose to 1.25 million and percentage of g.n.p. to 19. So small firms remained a very impressive segment of the British economy.

The 1960s and 70s saw many company mergers. For example, Arnold Weinstock became Managing Director of G.E.C. which took over Associated Electrical Industries and English Electric. Leyland, Austin and other firms merged into what became B.L.

Hundreds of thousands of small firms remained but the accumulative continuing triumph of large companies did cause concern and did lead to questions as to whether Britain's economic and social climate had become unfavourable to the foundations and growth of small businesses.

By the late 1970s it was calculated that of all those at work in Britain, 8 per cent were employers or self-employed: 9 per cent were working for central and 12 per cent for local government; 8 per cent were with public corporations and 63 per cent were working in the private sector.

Most of the economy, therefore, remained in private hands. Increasingly, however, income created by that economy was taken by the State and used for social purposes – defence, education, social services and so on. By the 1970s, the public sector was responsible for around half of all national spending.

In spite of very difficult world and domestic economic situations, the post-war Labour Government not only did much to shape the mixed economy of the post-war decades but also greatly enlarged existing welfare state provision.

1945–50 saw a spate of major social reforms. The new Ministry of National Insurance – set up at the end of the War – co-ordinated much social provision. Family Allowances had already been introduced. An Industrial Injuries Act replaced the Old Workmen's Compensation Acts, dating from 1897. Benefit payments were governed by the degree of disability and it became easier to claim damages after accidents.

The important National Insurance Act provided income or grants in sickness, unemployment, retirement, widowhood, maternity, death. Devised on lines drawn by Beveridge, the scheme was universal and state-administered. Under the Ministry a thousand local offices had to be found and staffed. On 5.7.1948 the vast scheme was put into operation.

To many, the most important, radical and beneficial of all these reforms was the setting up of the National Health Service in 1948. A 1944 White Paper laid it down that: "The proposed service must be 'comprehensive' in two senses – first that it is available to all people and, second, that it covers all necessary forms of health care".[8] Such aims were very ambitious indeed.

True, as already explained in this work, there was in Britain before 1948 a vast array of assorted health provision; but a great lack of comprehensive and uniform coverage. Now, in 1948, health care became free to all. Existing voluntary and local authority hospitals were taken over and – apart from the few who remained in private practice – doctors, dentists, opiticians, were paid by the state for services to patients. Those who preferred to pay for private treatment could still do so.

A huge, previously unsatisfied demand, particularly for services of dentists and opticians, became evident. Many thousands of women, for example, benefited from free treatment of gynaecological conditions which had plagued lives of so many poor housewives. The Health Service gave enormous and popular benefits.

In 1951, Conservatives once more returned to power, in which they remained for 13 years. In the main they accepted and retained changes brought in by Labour. Full employment and the Welfare State, remained. Total N.H.S. expenditure, for example, rose from £499 million in 1951 to £1130 million in 1964.[9]

Industrial relations remained reasonably harmonious. Serious attempts were made by Ministers to work with the Trade Unions. To a T.U.C. appeal when cuts in Adult Education were threatened, Churchill himself composed a reply which deserves repetition:[10] "There is perhaps no branch of our vast educational system which should more attract within its particular sphere the aid and encouragement of the State than adult education. How many there must be in Britain who thirst in later life to learn about the humanities, the history of their country, the philosophies of the human race, and the arts and letters which sustain and are borne forward by the ever-conquering English language. . . I have no doubt myself that a man or woman earnestly seeking in grown-up life to be guided to wide and suggestive knowledge will make the best of all pupils in this age of clatter and buzz, of gape and gloat".[11]

In the main, then, both main parties accepted Keynesian policies of management of a mixed economy, the Welfare State, powerful free trade unions with which consultation was necessary. To aims and methods of economic management attention is now turned.

15.3   Economic policy: aims and means

Policy implies aims. Main aims of British economic policy over the two to three decades following the Second War were: Full (or a high level of) Employment; Growth; a stable currency; a Balance of Payments surplus and a more equitable income distribution among individuals and regions in this country and over areas of the World economy.

Obviously, lists of, and emphasis placed on particular, aims varied. Some added care for the environment, a subject on which increasing numbers felt deeply. Others were not much interested in a fairer distribution of income, believing that taxation was already too high for the good health of the economy. But there was much agreement that the above mentioned five were over-riding aims in this, as in other similar, economies. Thus reported the authoritative Radcliffe Committee on the working of the Monetary System.[12] "We may in summary list the objectives in pursuit of which monetary measures may be used.

1. A high and stable level of employment.
2. Reasonable stability of the internal purchasing power of money.
3. Steady economic growth and improvement of the standard of living.
4. Some contribution, implying a margin in the balance of payments, to the economic development of the outside world.
5 A strengthening of London's international reserves implying further margin in the balance of payments".

Naturally, a committee concerned with monetary management placed emphasis on London's financial importance. A more general view was taken in 1964, when a "Joint statement of Intent of Productivity, Prices and Incomes" was signed by representatives of the T.U.C., the Labour Government, and the Association of Chambers of Commerce. Opening words of this statement were:[13]

"The objectives
The Government's economic objective is to achieve and maintain a rapid increase in output and real income combined with full employment. Their social objective is to ensure that the benefits of faster growth are distributed in a way that satisfies the claims of social need and justice. . .
Essential conditions for the achievement of these objectives are a strong currency and a healthy balance of payments".

Full employment

"The Government accept as one of their primary aims and responsibilities the maintenance of a high and stable level of employment after the war".[14] These were the opening words of the significant 1944 White Paper. It was added, and the forecast was correct, that: "There will, however, be no problem of general unemployment in the years immediately after the end of the war in Europe . . . it will be a period of shortages".
Governments, while naturally claiming credit for the continuation over more than two decades of a high level of employment,

did not have to try hard to achieve this. Unemployment was no
serious problem between 1945 and the 1960s. Indeed, unfashionable industries and services, short of labour, offered work to
many thousands of immigrants. World economy and trade
boomed: Britain benefited. At home, continuing high spending
on defence[15] and increasing expenditure on education and social
services helped. So, too, did regional policies which pushed
industries into formerly depressed areas. In the main, however, it
was general economic circumstances rather than specific government action which provided full employment. Government was
repeatedly damping down demand to avoid inflation not stimulat-
ing it to provide employment.

Growth

Increasingly, as a high level of employment seemed assured, the
main aim of policy became economic growth, or growth per
person in the output of goods and services.

Growth depends on management and workers – on the
installation of new machinery and adoption of more productive
techniques and work practices. Governments helped by taxation
policies designed to favour the ploughing back of profits into
investment in the firm rather than their distribution as dividends
to shareholders, by education and training which increased the
efficiency of workers, by aid to research, and by taking the lead
in deliberate planning to increase productivity.

The Conservative Government of Harold Macmillan, with
Selwyn Lloyd as Chancellor of the Exchequer, presided over the
setting-up of the National Economic Development Council in
1962. Top representatives of Government and of both sides of
industry met on this body to help formulate national economic
targets while Economic Development Committees – "little
Neddies" – studied the problems and opportunities of particular
industries.

The 1964 Labour Administration, with amazing confidence,
undertook to "prepare and implement a general plan for
economic development, in consultation with both sides of
industry, through the National Economic Development
Council."[16] A National Plan was indeed published, "designed to

achieve a 25 per cent increase in national output between 1964 and 1970".[17]

There is much agreement that, in the main, indicative planning has not been successful in Britain, not as successful as in, say, France. Important was the fact Governments found themselves unable to sustain growth programmes because of economic constraints which will be later detailed.

Stable prices

Back in 1934, with economic recovery, prices slowly began to rise. They have been rising ever since. The curbing of this price rise or inflation, has been a major pre-occupation of all British Governments since the Second World War and in the 1980s it is still in the economic sphere, a main pre-occupation.

Inflation has been a world-wide phenomenon. International causes have included:

1. heavy spending on wars and armaments;
2. increasing world population and growing demands on limited resources;
3. much increased spending by Governments;
4. in the 1970s, a rapid increase in the price of oil.

Within Britain, there was much learned discussion in the 1950s and 60s as to whether inflation was caused by the pull of demand or by the push of costs.[18] For many producers, the main cost is that of labour and much emphasis has been placed on rises in earnings as a prime generator of inflation. The matter is not simply of academic interest, for decisions as to the main cause of rising prices must determine the proposed cure.

It used to be widely believed that a moderate inflation was preferable to deflation since rising prices gave a boost to supply or output. Certainly, as house owners know, some people benefit from inflation, but any benefits are greatly outweighed by very harmful economic and social consequences and dangers, which include:

1. There is always the terrible risk that the inflation may get out of hand, may become raging or hyperinflation, as happened for example, in Germany in 1923.

2. Inflation harms the economy because it becomes more profitable to invest in property of which the price is rapidly increasing – grandfather clocks, paintings, gold – rather than in productive industry.

3. Inflation is socially very injust. It is like a lottery. Some draw out winning tickets: property owners of every sort, estate agents selling houses, prices of which constantly rise, members of strong Trade Unions, and so on. Others lose out – those who retire on fixed pensions, most savers, nurses who refuse to strike. A deep and dangerous sense of injustice permeates society, crime thrives.

4. In the case of an open economy like that of Britain, it is clear that if prices in Britain rise faster than in other countries then it becomes more difficult for British exports to sell abroad and easier for importers to sell foreign goods in Britain.

For all these reasons, the Authorities have moved against inflation with measures which will be described.

The balance of payments

The main aims of policy can therefore be summarised as growth with full employment and stable prices. A powerful constraint on these over-riding objectives rather than an aim in its own right, (though it can be described as such), was the need to achieve a surplus on the Balance of Payments. The problem of the Balance of Payments arises because imports of goods and services have to be paid for in foreign currency. An American selling a computer to Britain needs to be paid in dollars since his workers want to receive dollars. So a country which imports more than it exports runs out of foreign currency.

Not by any means always, but repeatedly, the British Balance of Payments was in deficit and deficits had to be covered by running down reserves and/or borrowing. Measures deemed necessary to remedy the Balance of Payments position are later described.

Equality

Labour has been, and is, more committed to greater economic equality than the Conservatives. Yet measures taken by both parties when in office since 1945 have in fact lessened income inequalities, since social service benefits have aided the poor more than the rich and since regional aid helped the poorer regions.

Conflicts between aims of policy

Individuals know that their aims in life can and do conflict. It is difficult to reconcile a desire for independence with a wish to marry and raise a family. Britain's economic aims, also, seriously conflicted. Incompatibilities contributed very much to problems, difficulties and disappointments and were therefore important.

Certainly not all aims were in conflict. Thus growth in output often led to growth in employment. But the following problems repeatedly bedevilled general advance.

Full employment made control of inflation difficult. First, the level of demand was high since nearly all who wanted to work were receiving pay packets. At current prices, total demand in the economy – consumption plus investment, plus Government spending plus demand for exports – was repeatedly higher than total supply – home output plus imports. There was therefore a constant tendency for prices to rise, as always happens when demand exceeds supply. (We may note, too, the obvious danger that imports would also rise).

Second, full employment meant that workers were placed in a strong bargaining position. In a 1958 article,[19] A.W. Phillips gave the not surprising information that particularly in decades before the First War, when unemployment had been low in the booms, wage rates had risen much more than when unemployment had been relatively high in the slumps.

Labour is not homogeneous but highly differentiated. Long before full employment is reached there are acute shortages in particular fields. Through the post-war decades, to obtain labour, employers in, for example, the engineering industry were under pressure to offer inducements such as bonus payments and overtime working.

An important development progressed. Earnings rose faster and moved considerably higher than negotiated wage rates. In other words, if the wage-rate were £1 an hour or £40 a week, actual earnings at the end of the week might be £50. The tendency for earnings to thus move ahead was christened "wage drift": the changes in the amount by which earnings (excluding overtime pay) exceed negotiated wage rates.[20] Thus, from 1952 to 1959, hourly wage earnings rose at an average 5.8 per cent a year, standard wage rates by 5.0 per cent a year.

In an admittedly complicated situation, full employment placed workers in a favourable position from which to bargain. Wage rates and earnings rose. This was a factor threatening price stability.

Two other aims conflicted, with harsh effects on achievement. Economic growth conflicted with the need to secure a favourable balance on overseas account.

Each time that Government launched an expansion pro-gramme designed to get the economy to grow, then this country sucked in imports and the Balance of Payments was in deficit. Government then restricted demand, thus curtailing growth. The whole dismal repeated process was known as "stop-go". Why did it happen?

Growing output demanded increasing raw material imports. Rising income purchased greater quantities of foreign manufac-tured goods. A disturbing feature of the British economy in the second half of this 20th century has been that the average and marginal propensities to import – that is the ratio of imports to gross domestic product and the percentage change in imports associated with the percentage change in incomes – have been relatively high.[21] The inability of successive Governments to sustain expansionary policies has been one reason for Britain's relatively undistinguished growth performance.

Undoubtedly, then, there have been persistent clashes in aims and these seeming incompatibilities have had dire results.

Means of policy

How did the Authorities attempt to realise their aims? The sheer difficulty of their task must again be stressed. Overseas factors were mainly outside their control. At home they had to operate in a free society in which comment and protest focused on any undesirable consequences of policy and in which millions of individual consumers and savers, thousands of firms and very powerful institutions such as trade unions and multi-national companies made their own economic decisions. Government hoped to harness, guide and chivvy along the horses, but if those animals were really awkward, then the stage coach's journey was not a happy one.

There were difficulties inherent in the uncertainties of economic forecasting and resulting from the actual behaviour of the economy. The Authorities were attempting to get the economy to grow in roughly a straight upward line. What actually happened was that between 1955 and 1968, for example, industrial production expanded either rapidly over particular periods or not at all. Thus, between the 3rd quarter of 1958 and the 1st quarter of 1960 industrial production rose by over 9 per cent per annum: between 1960 and 1963 there was no growth. Fluctuations were much due to swings in investment and exports, particularly to rises and falls in public investment.

It is true that over the post-war decades, slumps were of nothing like the magnitude which they had attained in pre-war days. But ups and downs had not disappeared. The Authorities attempted to iron them out by stabilising the economy. From collected statistics it could be seen how the economy was behaving and forecasts of future trends could be presented. But it was like driving a car with only a view in the mirror to help.

If figures showed that the economy had slipped into recession, the Authorities took action to boost output and employment. But it might well be the case that economic activity was turning up anyway so official action merely heightened the boom. Similarly Government might take action to break a boom just when recession was beginning. The fall in activity was thereby made more pronounced.

The instruments used by the Authorities to stabilise, manage or control the economy were fiscal and monetary measures plus controls such as those in regional and incomes policies. Ad hoc measures such as those designed to remove a deficit on overseas accounts might also be adopted.

Fiscal policy

Over the decades after the Second War, the fiscal weapon was the main one employed. "There is probably no country in the world that has made a fuller use than the United Kingdom of budgetary policy as a means of stabilising the economy".[22]

There were private and public sectors. If private sector activity was depressed, the vast scale of Government revenues and spending made it possible to pump in extra funds. Personal and corporate taxes could be reduced, whereby consumers and businesses would have more to spend. Spending could be increased. Consumption might be augmented through improvements in the social services. There were marked fluctuations in public investment which rose by over 20 per cent between early 1963 and early 1965, but fell between 1960 and 1963.

On the other hand, if boom and inflation were raging, Government could increase taxes (thus reducing amounts left for consumption), and reduce public expenditure.

Under Labour (1945–51), emphasis was placed on controls and fiscal policy. Monetary weapons were scarcely employed. Bank Rate continued at the very low 2 per cent of the War years and was still only 2½ per cent in 1951–52. The Conservatives after 1951 gave more weight to monetary instruments.

Monetary policy

Traditional pre-1939 monetary weapons were Bank Rate and Open Market Operations, affecting interest rates and, (through purchases or sales of Government stock), the level of bank deposits. Bank Rate was raised from 2½ per cent in 1951 to 7 per cent in 1957 before falling to around 5 per cent in 1960.

In the 1950s and 60s, additional measures were implemented. Banks were asked to limit lending or advances to customers. Such advances create deposits which are money. From time to time, the commercial banks were asked to hand over "Special Deposits" to the Bank of England. They had to transfer funds to the Central Bank, thus reducing their ability to lend.

In the British, as in similar, economies many cars and consumer durables are bought on hire purchase. The Authorities brought in hire purchase restrictions to restrict demand. They might, for example, stipulate that a third of the purchase price should be paid when goods were bought and the other two-thirds paid over a maximum of two years. Over the short term, certainly such hire purchase restrictions proved effective in cutting demand, though they did hit a restricted number of valuable industries.

Discussion concerning the efficiency of monetary instruments continued and, indeed, continues. The Radcliffe Committee was sceptical, "Though we do not regard the supply of money as an unimportant quantity, we view it as only part of the wider structure of liquidity in the economy. It is the whole liquidity position that is relevant to spending decisions". Moreover money circulates and "we cannot find any reason for supposing, or any experience in monetary history indicating, that there is any limit to the velocity of circulation". In words which might have been more frequently quoted around 1979, the Committee warned: "Monetary measures are aimed at the level of demand, but by their nature they are incapable by themselves of having an effect sufficiently prompt and far-reaching for their purpose, unless applied with a vigour that itself creates a major emergency. They are not so much a policy in themselves as a part of one general economic policy which includes among its instruments fiscal and monetary measures and direct physical controls".[23]

The 1959 Radcliffe Report's cautions and qualifications regarding monetary policy probably helped to secure the general dominance of fiscal measures and direct controls in 1960s economic management. But by 1970 interest in, and debate on, money were very evident. To Professor Milton Friedman must be given the main credit – or blame – for attaching to money and control of the money supply a dominating significance of inflationary situations.

Direct controls, very widely employed in the war and immediate post-war years were much reduced in numbers and effect partly before 1951 and greatly after the Conservative victory in that year. But important controls remained.

Regional policies

As part of regional policy, location of industry was controlled. The Distribution of Industry Act 1945 delineated Development Areas which were aided. An effective form of help was that provided by the Town and Country Planning Act 1947 which stipulated that an industrial workplace of more than 5000 square feet had to have the Board of Trade's Certificate before planning permission for its erection could be given. Planning controls of development and building in general have been, and remain, the subject of vast controversy, praise and blame. Strictly from the economic point of view – which need not, of course, be overriding – growth would have been somewhat faster had there been no environmental controls.

Prices and incomes policies

Policies to control income and prices – the most important of economic controls in the post-war period – deserve description and comment.

Price controls were not new. What were new in modern Britain were the systematic attempts over the thirty years after 1948 to control incomes. In Prices and Incomes policies the main – but not only – emphasis was on the control of incomes.

Arguments for – and against – controlling incomes in a modern industrial economy such as the British, are very strong indeed.

In 1970, of total domestic income (wages, salaries, profits, rent), of over £43,000 million, income from employment totalled over £30,000 million. Year after year powerful unions asked for wage increases. In the last resort, management had to pay up or risk a costly strike. Management generally paid up knowing that in an inflationary situation in which all major firms were likely to be similarly affected, prices could be raised. Firms reckoned up the cost of producing goods, added a mark-up to give them profit and fixed the selling price. Cost of production was therefore a key variable and, generally, the major item in cost of production was wages and salaries. If inflation was to be controlled, it was argued, wages and salaries must be controlled.

How on earth, replied critics, do you satisfactorily control the wages of workers in thousands of occupations with different responsibilities, skills, output? Some industries are dying, others growing. Was it not sensible to pay more in the new, dynamic industries which the economy needed? In any case, said some, if Government managed the economy sensibly there could be no inflation and no need for income control. Some trade unionists naturally resented the atrophy of their wage bargaining function and resented the limiting of wages while some incomes – they argued – remained untouched.

With trade union co-operation, Labour in 1948 brought in a wage freeze. As already stated, it was successful until the 1950 Korean War sent many prices soaring.

From 1956 to 1963, the Conservatives, without resorting to statutory controls made serious efforts to limit pay rises. A pay pause was announced in 1961. Advisory bodies, the Council on Productivity, Prices and Incomes and the National Incomes Commission – were set up. Reports were issued. Co-operation was not forth-coming from the T.U.C. and it cannot be said that their voluntary attempts at incomes policy were markedly successful.

Wilson's 1964 Government embarked on full-scale prices and incomes controls embodied in legislation. A National Prices and Incomes Board, under Aubrey Jones as Chairman, was set up. It considered proposed or actual increases in prices and pay, in the light of "norms" and criteria laid down by Government. In 1966 a complete price and wage freeze was enforced. This was followed by a period of severe restraint. The "freeze" was successfully applied, there were few known attempts to contravene it. But by 1968 the "ceiling" for wage and salary settlements had been raised to 3½ per cent, while in fact, settlements at the end of the 60s were running at a considerably higher figure. Strict pay control had broken down.

Meanwhile the Prices and Incomes Board had issued numerous reports carrying much information and decisions of continuing interest.

Heath came into power in 1970. The Conservatives had said there would be no incomes policy but as a much-used cliché put it, they executed a U-Turn and controlled pay and prices with varying degrees of severity. Three stages of incomes policy were introduced, beginning with a freeze. In 1973, miners refused to accept the limit laid down. Heath appealed to the country early in 1974. He lost seats and Mr. Wilson came back into office. The Labour Administrations, 1974–79, drew up a Social Contract, and operated in closest co-operation with the Unions. Government gave the Unions considerable benefits in labour legislation strengthening union and workers' rights: unions gave Government their backing for laid-down limits to wage rises. Voluntary restraint on pay worked well until 1978–79 when in a winter of discontent it was rejected by considerable groups of workers. In 1979, the Conservatives came in with pledges not to introduce another incomes policy.

In general, incomes policies, 1948–78, worked well in their

early stages. Then pressure built up against the restricting dam, which broke with a resulting flood of high wage and salary settlements.

Governments resorted to direct controls to restrain imports and/or remedy an unfavourable Balance of Payments position. In limited fields imports have been banned, (for example, some imports of early potatoes were stopped in 1980), or reduced. In 1964, a surcharge of 15 per cent was levied on imports of most manufactured goods. It was reduced to 10 per cent in 1965, dropped in 1966. In general, however, British governments, committed to less restriction on world trade, tied by membership of the E.E.C. and wary of provoking retaliation, have been reluctant to impose import controls which have been strongly advocated by some economists, industrialists and workers.

Faced with recurrent overseas deficits, the Authorities resorted to deflation, to restrictions on private capital outflows, cuts in overseas Government spending, and, in the last resort, to devaluation. Since a significant proportion of national income was spent on imports, cuts in that income meant lower imports but a fall in domestic income also meant unemployment.[24]

Devaluations were resorted to in 1949 and 1967. They were successful in that they improved the Balance of Payments by reducing imports and boosting exports. But the cost of living rose since imports were dearer while Britain had to export a greater volume of goods to recover the same numbers of dollars.

In the early 1970s, fixed exchange rates were abandoned. Until North Sea Oil came on stream to strengthen a petro-currency, the pound floated down. In late 1972 it had under 60 per cent of its 1971 exchange value. It rose from 1.70 in February 1977 to nearly 2.40 dollars to the pound in late 1980 before falling again to 1.50 by March 1983.

Other problems and achievements of the post Second War economy are described in the following section.

15.4   Economic achievements and problems

The twenty or so years after 1950 constitute one of the most successful periods in Britain's economic history. Some 98 per cent of the work-force were in jobs. Rates of growth of output and productivity, low in comparison with some other countries, was very good with reference to late 19th century and early 20th century experience, since they averaged between two and three per cent per year, sufficient, at compound interest, to double the quantity of goods and services available, or standard of living, in 20 to 30 years, or over a generation. Statistics relating to key variables clearly reveal this to have been the period of most rapid economic advance in modern Britain's story. From 1951–73 Gross Domestic Product increased by 2.8 per cent a year, domestic gross reproduceable assets by 3.2 per cent, real wages per man-hour by 3.5 per cent, output in manufacturing by 3.2 per cent, total factor productivity in manufacturing by 2.4 per cent. Apart from considerably increasing her domestic capital stock, Britain again invested overseas. Net overseas assets rose from £0.7 billion (liabilities) in 1951 to £7.4 billion in 1973.[25]

Farming

From 1939 to 1979 farming constituted one of the most dynamic and successful sectors of the economy. By 1952, farm output was 50 per cent higher than the pre-War level. It continued to increase: at 1975 prices it was £4,378 million in 1968, £5,022 million in 1978.[26] With one of the lowest percentages of the labour force in agriculture among world economies, (387,000 of a total working population of over 26 million were engaged in agriculture, forestry and fishing in 1978), Britain's farms supplied around half of the nation's food. Percentages of total intake provided by home output, in 1975–7, were:[27]

Milk	100	Potatoes	95
Poultry meat	99	Barley	93
Eggs	98	Beef and veal	85
Cheese	64	Wheat	56

Nationally, the average farm grew bigger, the degree of mechanisation was very high, crop and milk yields rose, falling numbers of workers produced rising output in the best traditions of modern growthmanship![28]

In Great Britain in 1977, of 230,000 holdings comprising 16½ million hectares, (hectare = nearly 2½ acres), 144,000 holdings or over 9 million hectares were owned or mainly owned, 86,000 comprising over 7 million hectares were tenanted.[29] Some land is directly farmed by landlords and it is still true that "a remarkably large part of Britain is owned by a remarkably small number of people."[30] 21 dukes still owned 400,000 hectares. But, with over half the holdings farmed by owner-occupiers, the change from 19th century practice was dramatic.

Holdings have become larger. In England and Wales, land in holdings of 500 acres or more increased from 2,663,000 to 3,917,000 acres between 1949 and 1964.[31] In Britain holdings of some 300 to 500 acres increased in number from 12,270 in 1964 to 13,179 in 1975 and those of 500 acres and more from 5,747 in 1964, to 8,236 in 1975. Smaller sized holdings decreased in numbers. By 1977, U.K. farms had 519,000 tractors, nearly 58,000 combine harvesters and a vast array of cultivators and assorted machinery. By 1978, over 13.6 million cattle, nearly 30 million sheep and lambs, 7.7 million pigs and 137 million poultry provided milk, meat and eggs. Higher yielding varieties, fertilisers and chemicals lethal to pests and weeds, have sent up yields. Between 1947 and the mid 1970s, wheat yields rose on average by some 3 per cent a year and barley yields by some 2 per cent.

True, modern farming methods – particularly the keeping of large numbers of birds and animals in sheds, the vast use of chemicals, the removal of hedges – are the subject of bitter, continuing controversy. But the productive success of modern British farming since the Second War is remarkable.

Retailing

Other examples of success may be found in retail trading and in financial services. In 1939, shopping still meant a visit to a corner shop or larger store where groceries, for example, were sold by a proprietor or by one or more assistants working – in the larger stores – at specialist counters. Of course, in very many stores or shops in 1979 it still meant much the same. But for millions the weekly shop now involved a visit to a self-service supermarket where a trolley was pushed round, loaded with goods, which were paid for at the check-out. In 1950, Sainsburys opened their first self-service store (refrigeration in the open-top cabinets needed much study). By 1969, 101 Sainsbury's supermarkets were each taking an average of over £24,000 a week.[32] In 1961, Sainsbury's stores went over to a 5-day week. Saturday closing at 4 also helped staff whose hours of work had been vastly reduced compared with those of predecessors in 1913 or 1938.

Marks and Spencers had 239 stores in Britain by 1966. They served some 8 to 10 million people a week and sold about 10 per cent of all clothing.[33]

Tesco had a turnover of over £1,600 million by 1979–80 and was planning to increase its selling areas to 8 million square feet by 1983–4.[34]

Small shops continued to exist in rapidly falling, but still large numbers. In 1979 there were still 338,210 single outlet retailers.

The standard of living

Surely a main criterion by which to judge the success of an economy is the extent to which it provides its people with a satisfactory standard of living – hard though that may be to define. Certainly, average British living standards did rise dramatically over the thirty or so years after 1945. Rostow's "age of mass-consumption"[35] had definitely arrived. By 1974–75, percentages of U.K. households with the listed goods were:

Car	56.4	Washing machine	70.5
(2 or more cars)	10.5	Refrigerator	83.6
Central heating	44.9	Television	94.4
(full or part)		Telephone	50.7

To many, the motor vehicle was the most obvious benefit (and curse!) – brought by dispersed prosperity. Numbers of motor vehicles in Britain rose to over 9 million by 1960, nearly 15 million by 1970. Private cars made up 11½ million of the 1970 figure.

Advances in living standards, in education and social services, receive further attention later, but one output statistic of predominant relevance may here be mentioned. Between 1951 and 1970 (inclusive), 6,600,000 houses and flats were built in the U.K.

Many workers strongly sensed that they were living in what for them was a more congenial age. A novelist with personal knowledge, wrote of a Midlands factory: "The thousands that worked there took home good wages. No more short-time like before the War, or getting the sack if you stood ten minutes in the lavatory reading your "Football Post" – if the gaffer got on to you now you could always tell him where to put the job and go somewhere else". The hero's father was happy at last, as he deserved to be happy, after all the years before the war on the dole. "The difference between the war and after the war didn't bear thinking about".[36]

In spite of failings and difficulties,[37] shortly to be outlined, Britain remained a relatively rich country.

Further, before going on to point out how much more efficiently some other economies have performed, it is necessary to issue a warning concerning the monstrous difficulties found in comparing standard of living. To most British houses, the morning delivery of bottled milk comes as an accepted benefit. It is unknown in nearly all other countries, even in Western Europe. On the other hand, some comparisons – for example, bills for electric or other heating are not heavy in Africa! – are less favourable to Britain.

Problems and failings

Yet the relative failings, heavy difficulties and repeated problems of the economy must be stressed. Interlocking and inter-reacting factors included:

1. Britain's rate of economic growth was lower than that of competitors;
2. Many sections of British industry failed to compete satisfactorily with foreign industry;
3. Government took a growing annual share of economic resources;
4. The country's commitments, at home and abroad, were too great for the economy to bear;
5. Inflation continued;
6. Balance of Payments problems were recurrent.

The following figures show annual percentage growth rates of real national income, in total, per employee, and per head of population, in the stated countries between 1950 and 1964.[38]

Country	National Income	Per employee	Per head
U.K.	2.6	2.0	2.2
Germany	7.1	5.3	5.9
France	4.9	4.7	3.8
Netherlands	4.9	3.7	3.5

Japan's rate of growth of real national income, 1950–64, was 8.7 per cent per year.

Some reasons for relative foreign successes are obvious. Following the Second War, many countries started from a low level of economic performance which could be, and was, rapidly improved. Again, in other countries it was still possible to transfer from agriculture to industry the large numbers which were no longer available in Britain. It is also clear that the share of total resources devoted to investment was lower in the U.K. than in other Western countries. Between 1955–68, investment took an annual average 16.4 per cent of gross national product in the U.K., 29.4 per cent in Norway, 24.2 per cent in West Germany, 21.6 in France, 23.8 in Austria. Social, institutional and other factors are so important that raising the investment ratio is not always sufficient to raise the rate of growth, but a high rate of investment is necessary for a high rate of growth.

While it is dangerous to generalise about anything as variable as "the quality of management", there is evidence that American management, for example, was more effective. In 1958 and 1961, American subsidiaries in Britain earned substantially higher profits than did U.K. competitors.

Other evidence merely adds to difficulties of diagnoses. Hours of work fell far less in Britain between 1950–62 than in Germany and most other West European economies. A high proportion of British women went out to work – in 1960 nearly half of those between 15 and 64 were employed, relatively a very high proportion. The British labour force, judged by years of schooling, was about as well educated as other European working populations. It will be shown that higher education was much expanded.

Industrial relations

Contrary to widely held opinion, as judged by the numbers of working days lost in strikes, British labour relations, though worse than in Japan and Germany were better than in some advanced countries. Over the decade 1968–77, annual average of working days lost through industrial disputes per 1000 employees in mining, manufacturing, construction, transport, were:[39]

U.S.A.	1,340	Italy	1,914
Canada	1,893	W. Germany	53
Japan	241	U.K.	850
France	308		

Yet Britain's relatively slow growth is an uncomfortable fact of which there are deep-seated causes. Since 1945, compared with the much more economically successful Germans, British industry has not developed institutions and attitudes which further co-operation and productivity advances. In Germany, workers elect representatives to an internal works council which plays a leading role in determining company policy. These works councils are consulted at an early stage of proposed technological change. All employees seem to agree on the obvious advantages of a steady rise to joint prosperity free from excessive inflation. In Japanese controlled factories in Britain, managers and workers seem to work hard together without the "them" and "us" legacies of British plants, where wide discrepancies in starting hours, amenities, sick-pay, holidays, "perks", and so on frequently help to divide executive from production workers.

It can be argued that keeping up with rapidly growing economies with their unnecessary luxuries does not matter.

Swimsuit manufacturers lamented in 1979 that British women under 35 bought new swimsuits every two years while West European women bought four in five years![40] But in technological economics a relatively slow rate of growth does lead to an increasing failure to modernise and compete and does lead to other problems.

Thus, growing concern has been caused by the steadily increasing quantities of manufactured goods coming into Britain. To Victorian industrialists it would have seemed incredible that they should clearly fail to compete, on a truly massive scale, in their own home market, with overseas competitors. Yet this has happened. The ratio of imported manufactures to gross domestic product rose from 5.1 per cent in 1957 to 13.3 per cent in 1972. The share of all manufactured goods in imports rose from 31.3 per cent in 1957 to 57.4 per cent in 1972.[41] Half these manufactured imports were in a semi-manufactured state, but the whole trend is unmistakable. Between 1961 and 1970, imports of all manufactured goods rose from £1,531 million to £4,572 million: included are rises of finished manufactures from £556 to £2,072 millions. True, exports of British manufactures over the same period rose from £3,258 to £6,806 millions. Clearly, however, the rise in imports of manufactures was faster. The problem continued and indeed became more acute.

Public expenditure

Between 1951 and 1976 while National Product rose at a compound rate of 2.8 per cent a year giving a total percentage increase of 102, the cost of public policy rose by 4.3 per cent a year giving a total increase of 185 per cent.[42]

The growth of public expenditure was only one of a number of demands which, in total, the British economy found very difficult to meet. Repercussions of the domestic commitment to full employment have already received a mention. Abroad, Britain still sought to play a significant (though diminished) role in World affairs. This involved the maintenance of military bases, and of considerable diplomatic and cultural activity. Aid to less developed countries was running at over £200 million a year by the early 1960s. Britain resumed her traditional role as an exporter of capital – investment abroad averaged over £300 million a year between 1958 and 1966, though considerable foreign investment in Britain offset much of this. London remained a very major financial centre attracting and holding large funds which could be, and were moved in a variety of unfavourable economic circumstances. For some decades after 1945, Britain was also the centre of the Sterling Area, (mainly the Commonwealth countries) – and held the foreign balances of the whole area with consequent benefits, risks and pressures. It is very obvious that all the above added up to a very heavy load of commitments which only a strong economy could shoulder.

Remorselessly, inflation continued, though at a rate which, until the 1970s, was very modest. Retail prices rose by almost exactly 50 per cent over the ten years 1950–59 and by a further 50 per cent over the 1960s.

One consequence of over-commitment was that the Balance of Payments ran into periodic deficits. On current account, these occurred in 1946 and 47, 1951, 55, 60, 64, 65, 66. As already stated, corrective measures, harmful to growth, had to be implemented.

Low productivity

At the root of Britain's economic difficulties lay a relative failure, the importance of which surely cannot be over-emphasised, the failure of much of industry to match productivity levels attained in industrial countries compared with which Britain had once been more efficient. In the years after 1945, report after report pointed to higher productivity levels in investigated American industries, later the dismal comparisons were often made with European (particularly German) and Japanese industries. Thus a chemical study found output per production worker in the United States up to 85 per cent greater than British productivity. Another study comparing productivity in comparable plants in Germany and Britain found that German output per head was between 4 and 29 per cent higher in printing, from 6 to 27 per cent higher in chemicals, up to 20 per cent up in shipbuilding.[43]

It is difficult to exonerate management since: "the average workers cannot influence the amount or quality of production very much, the supervisor can exert distinctly more influence, the department manager can hamper or enhance the work of his department considerably, and so forth. It is the design of products, the organisation of their production, the inspection and quality control operations; and marketing technique that matter rather than the individual output of the particular employee. All this is management's concern".[44]

For a complex variety of reasons in Britain a circle was established of relatively low output per head leading to slow growth of total output not conducive to a further rapid rise in productivity. In the social sciences, these vicious circles do prove to be of great importance.

Main economic achievements and problems over the period following 1945 have been outlined. Perhaps last words here may be left to the team of North American experts who surveyed the British economy in the 1960s:[45] "In many ways, Britain's economic performance since World War II outstrips any earlier period in the last half century. Her rate of growth, her attainment of full employement are, in the perspective of history, fit objects of pride. . ." Yet compared with some other West European lands, "the U.K. economy has grown less rapidly and has been plagued with crises in international payments and by fitful movements of prices and employment."

16. SOCIETY

16.1 Demographic trends

Over centuries up to the 18th, British, (like World), population growth was very slow and erratic. Both birth and death rates were high. Then, over the 19th century, death rates were slashed and Britain's population quadrupled. The birth-rate fell after the 1870s but remained above the still falling death-rate. So, at a slower pace, the rise in numbers continued over most of the 20th century. But, by the mid-1970s, a significant development was clear. Britain's population was roughly stationary. The 1981 census revealed an increase of a mere 150,000 or 0.3 per cent over the 1971 figure.

In thousands, census figures were:

Year	U.K.	England and Wales	Scotland	N. Ireland
1931	46,038	39,952	4,843	1,243
1951	50,225	43,758	5,096	1,371
1961	52,709	46,105	5,179	1,425
1971	55,515	48,750	5,229	1,536
1981	Great Britain – 54,129 (does not include N. Ireland).			

Britain's population increase of a mere 0.3 per cent over the 1970s decade contrasts strongly with increases between 1971 and 1977 in the Third World: 17.9 per cent in Brazil, 13.6 in India, 22.9 in Kenya and so on.[1]

The Death-rate

The U.K. death-rate per 1000 fell for males from 18.4 in 1900–02 to 12.9 in 1930–32, to 12.1 in 1977. For females, falls were from 16.3 in 1900–02 to 11.5 in 1930–32 to 11. in 1977.

If, through the employment of sophisticated statistical techniques, allowance is made for the changed age-structure, i.e. that there were increasing numbers of old people in the late 20th century, then the standardised male death-rate shows falls from 20.7 in 1930–32 to 17.6 in 1950–52 to 15.3 in 1976. For females, falls were from 16.4 in 1930–32 to 12.1 in 1950–52 to 9.2 in 1976.[2]

It has been calculated that the standardised mortality rate in England and Wales, (1950–52=100), fell from 335 in 1871 to 235 in 1901–10 to 86 in 1971.[3]

Most important, life-saving slashing of the infant mortality rate must again be strongly emphasised. Deaths of infants under age one per 1000 live births in the U.K. were:

1900–02	142	1940–42	59	1977	14.1
1930–32	67	1970–72	18		

Maternal deaths, (deaths of mothers due to child-birth), fell from 4.71 per 1000 live births in 1900–02 to 4.54 in 1930–32 to 0.13 in 1977.

The vast saving of life implicit in the above-quoted death-rate figures has meant that far higher proportions than in former generations of middle-aged and old people now live in Britain. It is again stressed that: "Medicine has done nothing to affect the length of human life, it has only reduced the numbers of premature deaths from disease".[4]

One modern calculation is that, with individual variations, the average age of death in an ideal society would be around 85.[5] In 1871–80, the average Briton could only expect to live for half this period. By 1975–77, expectation of life was practically 70 years for men, 76 for women.

It follows that increases in numbers in older age groups have been vastly greater than in the population as a whole.

Age (U.K.)	1901	1971	(thousands)
45–64	5,706	13,384	
65–74	1,278	4,713	
75 Over	531	2,594	

It is clear that numbers of those aged 75 and over have been multiplied five times over a life-span during which total population has increased by roughly a half.

Totals of men and women over retiring age, (60 for women, 65 for men), have increased from 6,662,000 in 1961 to nearly 9½ million in 1977.

The Birth-rate

It was a quite dramatic fall in the birth-rate which, in the 1970s, put a stop to population growth. We noted that the rate fell steadily from 1877 to the 1930s. It rose in the 1940s reaching a peak of 20.7 per 1000 in 1947. It fell to 16 in 1950–52 then rose considerably in the 1960s, peaking again at over 18 in 1964 before falling off sharply in the 1970s to as low as 11.6, (in Gt. Britain) in 1977. The Northern Ireland rate remained higher – still 16.5 in 1977.

Clearly, a major cause of the falling birth-rate in the 1970s was that an effective contraceptive, the Pill, plus sterilisation and legal abortion were available.

One main result of family planning was that by 1976, over 80 per cent of births in England and Wales were of first or second children. The following figures reveal the diminishing numbers of large families.[6]

Table 13   *England and Wales: fall in family size 1961–76*

Legitimate live births (thousands)			*Distribution by birth order (percentage)*	
Birth order	*1961*	*1976*	*1961*	*1976*
First	278	211	37	42
Second	229	195	31	39
Third	121	64	16	13
Fourth	58	20	8	4
Fifth	28	7	4	1
Sixth and over	32	6	4	1
Total	746	504	100	100

Class differences in birth-rates remained but lessened. Whereas for marriages of the 1920s, manual groups had some 40 per cent more children than non-manual groups, for marriages of the 1940s this excess was down to 20 per cent.

A 1967 Act made it possible for large numbers of women to obtain legal abortions. Each year from 1971 to 1977 there were over 100,000 such operations in Britain. Obviously, here was another powerful reason for the fall in the birth-rate. To 1980 and beyond abortion was still a subject of the strongest controversy.

Governments supported family planning. In the 1970s practitioners issued the Pill free to women. Voluntary organisations were aided: for example, in 1979, the Family Planning Information Service received a grant of £155,000 while in 1980 Government agreed to increase the grant to the regional work of the Family Planning Association from £68,000 to £120,000.

Yet, in spite of the great increase in knowledge and use of reliable contraceptives, problems remained. In 1980, the Minister of Health announced the illegitimate births among girls under 16 were about 1,400 a year. From 1974 to 1976, in England and Wales, 14,739 schoolgirls under 16 became pregnant, 10,273 of these pregnancies were legally terminated. Medical opinion portrayed the stark tragedies: "these young girls are more likely to have complicated pregnancies"; "tension and discord within families"; "loss and disruption of education"; "the risk of later attempts at suicide".[7]

Migration

It has already been stressed that particularly in pre-1914 years, emigration from Britain was heavy, but that in the depressed and dangerous 1930s, the tide turned. In England and Wales net outward flows of 5,620,000 between 1911 and 21 and 170,000 between 1921 and 31 turned to a net inward flow of 757,000 in 1931–51. In the austere post Second War Years there was considerable emigration to Australia and Canada, but from 1951–61, England and Wales registered a net gain of 387,000. Scotland has lost numbers very heavily through the 20th century, the net loss, 1901–66 being 1,486,000.

By the late 1950s an important new phneomenon was

becoming obvious. By 1958 there were an estimated 210,000 non-white people from the Commonwealth in Britain. In the three years 1960–62, net emigration amounted to around 388,000 people, mainly from the Commonwealth. The Commonwealth Immigrants Acts of 1962 and 1968 restricted the flow. According to official figures for movements into and out of the U.K., since the mid-1960s more people have left than have come to this country. Thus, in 1964–65, 230,000 came in, 281,000 went out: in 1970–71 there were 227,000 immigrants, 266,000 emigrants. The same picture held for every year from 1964 to 1977, though the gap narrowed. In 1976–77, 181,000 came in, 208,000 went out. Official figures are not very reliable in this sphere, but it was calculated that in the late 1970s: "The average *net* outflow of migrants over the last decade has been estimated . . . as 50 thousand per year".[8]

A section on the considerable social challenges posed by immigration appears later.

Within the United Kingdom, the inter-war movement of population from old industrial regions in the North and West to newer industrial or residential areas in the South and East continued, though it was claimed that regional policy much slowed down the movement. Within all areas, there was a movement out of great cities into outer and rural areas and New Towns.

Over the 20 years 1951–71, net migration from England North of Sheffield was 530,000, from Wales 44,000, Scotland 646,000 and N. Ireland 156,000. East and West Midlands gained 190,000, the South-east 502,000, the South-west 323,000 and East Anglia 162,000.[9] Around the 1960s, four major growth areas could be identified: East Anglia, the East Midlands, the South-west and the Outer South-east (i.e. the South-east away from London).

As might have been expected, it was largely the young and vigorous who moved – with depressing consequences for problem areas. In 1971, 21 per cent of the population, but 30 per cent of inter-regional migrants, were aged 25–44. There were exceptions, the South-west attracted not only young workers to the Bristol area, but also many retired people. 42,300 aged 60 and over moved to the region in 1966–71.[10]

Since 1945, there has been a great increase in an important movement already obvious in earlier 20th century years, namely the movement out of large towns into outer and rural areas with consequent commuting. True, the proportion of urban dwellers in England and Wales, (defined as those living in urban administrative districts), hardly changed, being 78 per cent in 1911 and in 1971. But in the 6 English conurbations, 38 per cent of the population lived in 1951, 33 per cent in 1971. Numbers in English conurbations fell from 16,794,400 to 15,928,000 in 1971 while numbers in Rural Districts rose from 8,193,400 to 10,568,300. In Scotland, population of the huge Clydeside conurbation fell by 32,000 but numbers in districts or counties also fell. Taking the U.K. as a whole, the 1960s saw a considerable rise in rural district but a fall in conurbation numbers.

Between 1951 and 1971, the resident, economically active, population of some major cities declined as follows: Manchester by 28.3 per cent, Liverpool by 22.8, Newcastle by 24.3, Glasgow by 16.1, Birmingham by 11.1, Bradford by 6.6.

By 1961, 36 per cent of all people at work in England and Wales, and 35 per cent in Scotland, lived outside the local authority area in which they worked. From 1921 to 1961, in England and Wales, numbers travelling to work in another area, increased by 115 per cent.[11] Clearly, here is a well-known but important feature of modern population distribution. Preliminary 1981 census figures revealed dramatic falls in numbers in nearly all main cities. Over the decade 1971–81 losses were:

	Fall in numbers	*Percentage decline*
Inner London	535,179	−17.7
Glasgow	219,155	−22.3
Liverpool	99,807	−16.4
Manchester	94,691	−17.4
Birmingham	91,053	−8.3
Salford	36,156	−12.9
Newcastle-upon-Tyne	30,602	−9.9

Rural counties such as Norfolk, Suffolk, Northamptonshire, Cornwall, West Sussex and those along the Welsh border took in the migrants and their numbers increased by more than 10 per cent over the decade.

16.2   Families and households

Marriage

"Marriage, a home of your own, and two children (about 1.3 of them boys) remain the feminine ideal"[12] such were the findings of a 1976 survey, confirmed by the fact that, is in the late 1970s, by the age of 40, 95 per cent of women and 91 per cent of men had been married.

That more women married, and married at earlier ages, in the 1960s than in earlier generations is clear from figures comparing 1961 and 1921:[13]

Proportions of women ever married per 1000 pop. England and Wales

Year	Under 20	20–24	25–29	30–34	35–39	40–44	45–49
1921	18	274	590	790	796	821	832
1961	66	579	844	890	902	903	895

In 1967, the Registrar-General wrote, (of England and Wales): "the mean age at marriage for spinster brides fell by about two years from 24.41 to 22.54 years between 1951 and 1966 . . ." whereas during the period 1901–1935 . . . "it stood between 25.37 and 25.81 years".[14]

It is not here claimed that earlier marriage was necessarily a social advance. In earlier generations, couples often "walked out together" and/or were formally engaged[15] for years before economic circumstances seemed sufficiently favourable for them to marry. This still happens, as, for example, when couples continuing with higher education wait to marry. But the statistics do reveal a marked trend around the 1960s towards earlier marriage. These early marriages were more likely to end in divorce. Of all women marrying in 1967, 12 per cent had divorced 10 years later: of women marrying at ages under 20 this percentage was 19.[16]

Divorce

One outstanding feature since the Second War has been the marked rise in the number of divorces, particularly following the implementation after 1971 of the Divorce Law Reform Act 1969 which made the "irretrievable breakdown" of a marriage the main criterion for divorce. So United Kingdom divorces climbed, with fluctuations, from 31,000 in 1951 to 125,000 in 1972 to 136,000 in 1976.

Divorce is the legal recognition of a fact – that the marriage has broken down. It may be preferable to the martyrdom of a disastrous marriage. Many divorcees remarry: by 1980 around a half of people getting divorces in any one year were married again within five years. Unfortunately, by 1977, there were over 20,000 divorces involving an already divorced person.[17]

Yet, it seems utter folly to deny that massive unhappiness, upset and tragedy result from the hundreds of thousands of divorces accomplished every few years in modern Britain. Overwhelmingly, couples do enter marriage with happiness, high hopes and forethought. Of a comprehensive 1970 survey it was said: "All the young women in our survey . . . had thought enough about marriage by the age of sixteen to be completely articulate about what could make or mar a marriage and the qualities to be hoped for and the defects to be feared in a husband".[18] Failure is not pleasant and in an undertaking as important as marriage it can bring much unhappiness. In particular divorce can bring great economic difficulties to separated partners and to the re-married with existing obligations.

Of 127,000 divorcing couples in 1976, 79,000 had between them 152,000 children under 16. Such children are effectively separated from their mother or father, (usually from the latter) and unhappiness may result. In Gt. Britain the number of one parent families rose from 570,000 in 1971 to 750,000 in 1976. In 415,000 cases in 1976, the lone parent was a separated or divorced woman. By 1976 well over a million children were living with one parent only, though for many, single parenthood was only an intermediate stage between two marriages.

Women at work

In the second half of the 20th century there was a large rise in the number of women going out to work.

Employees in employment (millions)[19]

Year	Total	Men	Women	Women as per cent of total
1959	21.0	13.8	7.2	33
1978	22.2	13.1	9.1	41

The most dramatic increase has been that of married women at work – 4 million more by 1976 than in 1951. Figures for the total labour force, (people available for work, including self-employed and unemployed) of Gt. Britain were:

Labour force estimates	1951	1976
Men	15.6	15.9
Women – Married	2.7	6.7
Other	4.3	3.2
Total Women:	7.0	10.0
Total	22.6	25.9

By 1979, 49 per cent of all married women were at work or looking for work: this percentage rose to 61.3 among married women aged 45–59. These are dramatic changes.

A large proportion, (41 per cent in 1977), of women at work were part-time workers. They are heavily concentrated in service industries, female employment in which rose by 12.4 per cent between 1959–76. By 1977, just over half the workforce in services was female. It is expected that women's employment will be heavily reduced by the advent of microprocessors, but, up to 1979, their increased participation in employment was a truly major economic and social development.

Households

The great majority of households in 1971 were "married couple households" i.e. headed by a married couple. But there were significant minorities of one parent, one person and other households.

At the 1971 Census,[20] England and Wales had 16.6 million households, with an average 2.87 people each. 11.7 million were married couples, 1.1 million lone parents, 3.0 million one-person,

and 0.9 million other households. In 4.7 million of married
couple households the head of the family was aged between 45
and 64 and in 1.7 million cases age was 65 or over.

2 million of the 3 million people living alone were women over
60 or men over 65.

In Gt. Britain in 1971, half of the households consisted of one
or two people – a proportion rising in the 1970s and estimated at
53 per cent in 1976. Here is another very significant factor. We
still often think of the average household as being father, mother,
about two children. In fact such households are now a decided
minority.

The number of one parent families increased by a third
between 1971 and 1976 when they made up over a tenth of all
families with dependent children. 660,000 of the 750,000 lone
parents in 1976 were women, of whom 130,000 were single,
185,000 separated (married), 230,000 divorced and 115,000
widowed.

In previous centuries, the number of widows was much greater,
of divorcees much, much less.

Changes in family

Couples marry at an earlier age, are often together longer, have
fewer children, get divorces more easily, than used to be the
case. In general men help much more with the house-work and
baby-minding than did their grandfathers. Some developments,
(comfortable houses and, in particular, television), have brought
the family together for longer periods. Others, (women going out
to work, parents going out together for drinks, meals and so on),
have diminished time spent together by all members of a family.

The family survives as the basic institution in British society.
There is immense study of the family, help from the Authorities
and voluntary agencies, (e.g. child allowances), great interest
shown by many parents in the upbringing and education of their
children, as evidenced, for example, by the success in many
centres of voluntary play-groups and parent-teacher groups. Not
only has the nuclear family survived but some surveys showed
that even when children had married they still often maintained
very close contact with parents.[21 & 22]

True, these surveys were of working class families, many of

whose members lived near together. Enquiries among mobile class executives and professionals might well have revealed a different picture. But above-mentioned facts do show that easy generalisations that the family had lost its cohesion were far from universal truth.

However, other enquiries have revealed the unhappiness among old people resulting from the departure of their young.[23] As often, the evidence is mixed.

16.3 Ethnic minorities

In 1931, of every 100,000 people in England and Wales, 96,345 had been born here. The population was remarkably homogen-eous. By 1966 the figure of over 96,000 was down to 92,227: the British nation now included a considerable minority who had themselves, or whose parents, had been born in the West Indies or the Indian subcontinent or in other overseas countries. According to official estimates, which in this field are not reliable,[24] there were 2 million people of New Commonwealth and Pakistani ethnic origin in Britain by 1979. Here was fact of significance which commands attention.

Immigration was not new. In the 19th century, numbers of Irish had moved into Britain, then another part of one United Kingdom of Gt. Britain and Ireland. By 1901, there were over 45,000 Irish born people in Liverpool where their descendants are an obvious constituent of the population: by 1961 there were 90,000 Irish in Warwickshire. Even in the depressed 1930s, Irish immigrants could still find work because they were mobile and willing to take hard, dirty jobs. In the years before 1914, quite considerable numbers (perhaps around 45,000) of East European Jews fled persecution to settle in Britain – considerably in the East End of London. Another influx of European Jews came over in 1933–39. They included large percentages of middle-class professionals and business people who were a great asset to depressed Britain. These European immigrants – some from very different backgrounds and cultures from that of the host country, particularly in the case of poor Jews from East European ghettoes who came here before 1914 – have merged almost completely into the native British nation and some have prospered mightily.

After 1945, tragically displaced Europeans – including well over 100,000 Poles – settled in Britain. In full employment years just after the Second War, the British Government, for perhaps the first and last time, actively encouraged immigration, in this case of displaced Europeans needed to swell the British labour force.

In 1951 there were 1.6 million people living in Britain who had been born outside the U.K. Of these, only 0.2 million were born in the New Commonwealth. By 1971, 3 million residents had been born outside the U.K. 1.2 million in the New Commonwealth.

A book published in 1954[25] put the total number of black people in Britain at 50,000. Before that time, they had been concentrated in four main ports, one of which was Liverpool, with around 500 Negroes in the 1930s. During the Second War over 300 West Indian technicians and trainees came to Merseyside and industrial Lancashire. They were volunteers who came under a British Government scheme to recruit labour for war production. A case-study of their experience found: "one fact stands out beyond all others: the clearly marked in group/out group delineation which exists between white and coloured people".[26] It is interesting to note that after around 1943 the arrival of large numbers of American troops, including whites from the Southern States with strong racial views, "led to a serious deterioration in the state of racial attitudes".[27]

The British Nationality Act 1948 allowed passport holders from colonies and those with passports from independent Commonwealth countries to enter Britain. So, in the full-employment 1950s, immigrants arrived in substantial numbers to take jobs which, often, natives were not rushing to fill: there were vacancies by the thousand in hospitals, London Transport, Black Country foundries, West Yorkshire mills.

In 1956 nearly 47,000 coloured immigrants came, numbers which fell with recession to 21,600 in 1959. Now Commonwealth immigration reached a peak of 136,000 in 1961 and 94,000 in the first half of 1962.

Controls were enacted. The Commonwealth Immigrants Act 1962 restricted the right of free entry by Commonwealth citizens who had to obtain an employment voucher before gaining admission. By the late 1960s official coloured immigration figures were:

Employment voucher holders		Dependents	Others
1967	4,716	50,083	2,849
1968	4,353	42,036	3,771

By the Commonwealth Immigrants Act 1968, U.K. passport holders seeking to enter Britain from a Commonwealth country had to show a "close connection" (which was defined) with Britain. The Immigrants Act 1971, gave the "right of abode" in Britain to "patrials" who were defined in the legislation.

Between mid-1966 and 1978, according to official estimates, numbers of people in Britain of New Commonwealth and Pakistani ethnic origin rose from 886,000 to 1,920,000. Births exceeded deaths by around 40,000 a year. Restricted immigration, mainly of dependents continued, but fell to some 30,000 in 1977–78.

So a country which in 1949 was peopled overwhelmingly by white, native-born citizens had by 1979 absorbed something like 2 million immigrants and their children from cultures as diverse as those of West Indians, East African Asians, Pakistani, Hindus, Chinese and others. It was indeed a vast, challenging change.

The basic problem was graphically portrayed by Conrad who, in his terrible story "Amy Foster", told of a young immigrant from Eastern Europe, ship-wrecked on the English coast en route to America. "He was different; innocent of heart, and full of goodwill, which nobody wanted, this castaway, that like a man transplanted from another planet, was separated by an immense space from his past and an immense ignorance from his future. . . ." Marriage to a local servant-girl brought incomprehension and "The supreme disaster of loneliness and despair".[28]

True, attitudes had changed vastly since 1900. Education, travel, television, and so on have widened horizons. This is a free country in which thoughts, words, actions varied immensely. Ordinary daily experience shows that many people of diverse origins do mingle freely and with reasonable content in the streets, shops, educational institutions, hospitals, of Britain's towns. Some Britons have gone out of their way to welcome immigrants, have formed voluntary groups to assist them.

But very many Britons were opposed to immigration. Enoch Powell received massive popular support around 1968 when he denounced immigration and uttered dire warnings concerning its consequences.[29] In practice while denouncing Powell, Labour and Conservative ministers deemed it wise to tighten immigration controls and to emphasise to the electorate that they were so doing.

Only a minority joined or actively supported the National Front which openly campaigned against ethnic minorities. Of over 29 million votes cast in October 1974, only 113,579 were for Front candidates. But there was much expressed animosity.[30] In years around 1980 there were increasing numbers of attacks by white youths on coloured people and of muggings of whites by black youths. By 1979, an American Magazine was writing of "Britain's Race Crisis".[31]

Grounds for concern included the following:

Immigrants came to work in Britain. They were young: in 1971, 41 per cent of the blacks in Britain were aged under 15 and another 49 per cent were aged between 15 and 44. Corresponding proportions for Britain as a whole were 24 and 39 per cent.[32] By 1971, about half a million black people were employed. Many were in manufacturing industry, where many found work in metals, clothing and footwear.

Unfortunately, employment opportunities, particularly in manufacturing industry, diminished gravely in the 1970s. School-leavers found it increasingly difficult to find work. Unemployment among non-whites, especially West Indians, was even higher than among whites. Already in 1977, before the sharp rise in numbers of workless around 1980, well over 30 per cent of non-white males were unemployed in Liverpool.

The outlook was indeed dismal, since new technology was denying work in the unskilled and granting opportunities only to those with professional or technical qualifications. Some immigrants, e.g. doctors, had such, but many had not for they had come from Asian villages or Caribbean Islands where modern technology was in short supply.

Among black children educated in Britain another serious problem arose. In the main, West Indian children have performed relatively poorly in Britain's schools.[33] Discrimination has made it even more difficult for often poorly qualified applicants to get jobs in a shrinking labour market.

Non-whites have concentrated considerably in particular

regions and areas. Many have moved into the run-down centres of the great conurbations where poor accommodation could be rented or bought cheaply. Such areas contain far higher than average numbers of houses built before 1919 and/or houses lacking or sharing in at least one basic amenity.

In 1971, nearly two-thirds of West Indian immigrants were in the South-east and 15 per cent in the West Midlands. Nearly half of those born in India were also in the South-east and nearly a fifth in the West Midlands. Of those born in Pakistan, over a third were in the South-east, a fifth in the West Midlands, nearly a fifth in Yorkshire. On the other hand, Wales, the South-west, East Anglia, the North and Scotland had very low percentages of coloured immigrants.

By 1977, births to mothers born in the New Commonwealth and Pakistan were over 40 per cent of all births in London Boroughs of Brent and Ealing, over 30 per cent in boroughs such as Newham, Leicester, Slough.[34] By 1979, it was reported that in one district of Peterborough with a heavy concentration of Asian immigrants, 3 primary schools had the following proportions of children of immigrants on their rolls: 175 out of 201 in School A, 253 of 295 in School B, 196 of 281 in School C.[35]

By 1979 there was in some areas a much discussed and tragic gulf between the police and black youth – tragic because the maintenance of law and order should be desired and sought by all, particularly, perhaps, by minorities who stand to lose much if crime and violence reign.

There have been health problems – for example rickets and vitamin deficiency – among some immigrant groups, particularly Asians. In some London Boroughs, social service departments have received into care a disproportionate number of black children. A relatively high proportion of West Indian families have a single parent.[36]

Anti-discrimination legislation was enacted: it was a radical departure from British legal tradition in that Britain has no written constitution to guarantee equal rights. The Race Relations Act 1965 made unlawful discrimination in such places as hotels and places of entertainment. Conciliation machinery was to be operated by a Race Relations Board.

The Race Relations Act of 1968 was concerned with discrimination in employment. A Community Relations Commission was established.

The Race Relations Act 1976 set up the Commission for Racial Equality which replaced the existing Board and Commission. A more widespread and determined effort was codified to attack racial discrimination.

To diminish urban deprivation, which harmed blacks and whites, a battery of measures was taken: the Urban Programme 1968, Community Development Project 1969, Urban Deprivation Unit 1973 and the Comprehensive Community Programme 1974. Funds, research, attempts at amelioration – clearly insufficient in the light of later developments – were channelled into the inner cities. Spending on the Urban Programme grew from under £30 million in 1976/77 to £98 million in 1978/79. Under the Community Development Project neighbourhood developments were established in areas such as Hillfields in Coventry.

Under section 11 of the Local Government Act 1968, local authorities with large numbers of immigrants in their areas could claim grants. Educational Priority Areas were delineated: teachers in them were given extra pay. The Housing Act 1974 enabled Authorities to give grants for housing improvements in action areas.

Not all statistics and observations relating to ethnic minorities are depressing. In the important sphere of housing, many are buying their own homes or are being housed by the Authorities. It appears that in England in 1977, over 60 per cent of Asian households had bought or were buying their houses. About 40 per cent of West Indian households lived in Council accommodation. While housing of blacks was on average worse than that of whites, yet the overwhelming majority of their households had sole use of basic amenities.[37]

In towns such as Leicester, numbers of Asians have prospered: "For all these Asians Leicester is home . . . life in Leicester is good, safe and comfortable. As Satwinder Singh put it: 'There is plenty of money in Leicester. . .' ".[38]

Many immigrants did find work in Britain between 1961 and 1971, the number of non-U.K. born males at work rose by 359,000 and of females by 249,000.[39]

The Health Service relied heavily on immigrant labour. In the late 1970s, some 18,000 registered doctors in the U.K. were born outside Britain and Ireland: About half were from India and Pakistan. In England, 20 per cent of G.P.'s, but over 50 per cent of Senior House Officers and Registrars in hospitals were born outside the U.K. and Irish Republic. Similarly in 1976 over 16 per cent of all nurse learners were born overseas. In certain areas, high proportions of hospital ancillary staff were born overseas: 34 per cent of domestic staff and 31 per cent of catering staff in the case of one Health Authority.[40]

Up to 1979, immigrants were prepared to make great sacrifices to get into Britain and many of those already settled wished to bring in spouses and relatives, so conditions cannot have been hopelessly bad. Yet, that most certainly much remained to be done became depressingly clear when in 1980 and 1981 very severe and destructive rioting occurred in Bristol, Brixton,[41] Southall and other areas. "Let there be no doubt, though", wrote R. Dahrendorf in 1982, "that coming to terms with its new citizens . . . is the single most difficult and important task before British society today".[41a]

16.4   Work, income, standards of living

Employment and unemployment

From 1940 to the late 1960s the overwhelming majority of Britons who wanted to work could find jobs: except in exceptional and short-lived circumstances, the unemployment percentage did not rise above 3 per cent and in most years was considerably below this figure, especially in England. Percentages of the insured population of Great Britain who were out of work were between 1.1 and 2.2 per cent in the 1950s, rising slowly in the 1960s to 2.6 per cent by 1970. Rates in Wales, Scotland and Northern Ireland were consistently higher than the English rate, as the following figures make clear.

Unemployment percentages

Year	England	Wales	Scotland	N. Ireland
1950	1.0	2.7	2.5	6.1
1959	1.8	3.8	4.4	7.8
1970	2.4	4.0	4.3	7.0

Within England itself there were considerable regional variations, but even in Development Areas, unemployment was a mere fraction of terrible 1930s figures. Thus in 1959, (a depressed year), rates at mid-June were 4.2 on Merseyside, and 3.0 in Northern Areas. Since in a number of years, (for example in 1965–66), numbers of unfilled vacancies were higher than numbers of unemployed, it is repeated that for a generation after 1940, Britain enjoyed the enormous boon of full employment.

The situation began to deteriorate about 1967. The U.K. unemployment rate, which had been 1.6 in 1961 was up to 4.1 by 1975 and 6.2 by 1978. By August 1980 there were 2 million out of work and unemployment was again a serious economic and social problem.

It may be emphasised that the above figures relate to registered unemployment. Many married women in particular, and others who would like to work do not "sign on" as unemployed. Official estimates are that the registered unemployed account for about 80 per cent of unemployed men, 75 per cent of unemployed single women, and 50 per cent of unemployed married women.

On the other hand, in the 1970s about 3 per cent of employees interviewed in surveys had more than one job. They either worked for someone else or in a self-employed capacity in a subsidiary occupation. Further, in Gt. Britain in 1978, average overtime of 4.2 hours was being worked by all male employees aged 18 and over. 56.8 per cent of male manual workers received overtime pay and they worked an average of no less than 10.2 overtime hours.

Just as the published unemployment statistics have underestimated the full extent of worklessness, so published numbers do not tally with real numbers of vacancies since many employers do not trouble to notify openings to the Department of Employment.

The maintenance of high levels of employment over some decades after the Second World War deserves emphasis. Investigators found that in York "the reduction of unemployment to negligible proportions had been a factor of considerable importance in the reduction of poverty from its comparatively high level in 1936 and to the low level we found in 1950".[42] As late as the 1970s, surveys found that 90 per cent of men aged 18–24 had not had any spell of unemployment in the previous 12 months. It was still very different from the 1930s.

The total labour force of Gt. Britain increased as follows: – (millions)[43]

Women	1951	1961	1971	1975
Married	2.7	3.9	5.8	6.6
Other	4.3	3.9	3.4	3.2
Men	15.6	16.1	15.9	15.8
TOTAL:	22.6	23.8	25.1	25.6

In 1977, 43 per cent of U.K. women of working age were at work. This is a very high figure, corresponding percentages in Germany, France, Holland, Italy, and the U.S.A. ranged between 22 and 41. However, it must be strongly emphasised that 41 per cent of U.K. women at work in 1977 were working part-time.

Of a U.K. employed labour force of just under 25 million in 1978:

2.3 million worked for Central Government (include H.M. Forces)
3.0 million for Local Authorities
2.1 million for Public Corporations
17.5 million, as employers, self-employed, employees, in the private sector.

So about 30 per cent worked in the public, about 70 per cent in the private, sectors. In Central and Local Government, women outnumbered men workers, though many were part-time.

We noted that in the inter-war period there was a decline in numbers employed in old stable industries, with growth in numbers engaged in newer engineering, vehicles and other sectors. There was also a continuing enlargement of service employment. These tendencies continued in the post-war decades.

Full employment Britain of the 1950s and 1960s was heavily dependent on engineering, metal goods, vehicles and services. Coventry was still immensely prosperous with its car factories offering some of the highest engineering wage rates in the country. The dramatic plunge in fortune came there in the late 1970s. 1956 employment distribution was as follows:

Table 14 *Distribution of employees, Gt. Britain 1956*[44]

Industry	Total Employees, May 1956 (000s)
Agriculture, forestry, fishing	683
Mining, quarrying	862
Manufacturing	9,150
Building contracting	1,419
Gas, electricity, water supply	379
Transport and communications	1,698
Distributive trades	2,408
Insurance, banking, finance	478
Public administration and defence	1,310
Professional services	1,685
Miscellaneous services	1,619
Total:	21,700

The 1970s saw considerable falls in numbers engaged in manufacturing: from 1969–1978 total manufacturing employment fell over a million. This important development is given further emphasis in Section 17.1.

Over the century covered in this work there has been a continuous growth in numbers employed in professional and non-manual occupations. Social consequences have been very important. The traditional 19th century manual workers have declined in numbers and relative importance. Mention trade unionists and we still tend to think of miners, dockers, car workers. By 1974, however, 4,222,000 trade unionists were white collar workers. Their numbers had considerably more than doubled between 1948 and 1974, over which period male manual trade unionists had actually fallen in numbers by 6.8 per cent.

Further reference will later be made to the expansion of professional classes, staffed by products of a much enlarged higher education sector.

It has been claimed that the rapid absolute and relative growth of white collar employment between 1911 and 1966 was: "The most striking characteristic of the occupational structure".[45] Over that period, non-manual employment increased by 176 per cent from 18.7 per cent to 38.3 per cent of the labour force.

Between 1931 and 1971 numbers in major occupational groups in Britain changed as follows:[46]

Changes in numbers in occupational groups, 1931 to 71

		1931		1971	
				(thousands)	
1.	Employers and proprietors	1,407		622	
2.	White collar workers	4,841		10,405	
	(a) Managers, administrators		770		2,085
	(b) Higher professionals		240		928
	(c) Lower professionals, technicians		728		1,880
	(d) Foremen, inspectors		323		736
	(e) Clerks		1,404		3,412
	(f) Salesmen, shop assistants		1,376		1,364
3.	Manual workers	14,776		13,343	
4.	Total occupied pop.	21,024		24,370	

20th century growth of numbers in professional occupations, particularly in the period since the Second War, has been quite remarkable. Examples make this clear. Between 1951 and 1971 numbers rose as follows in the named professions.

Accountancy	from	32,424	to	76,610
Nursing	from	235,397	to	438,980
Teaching	from	313,235	to	688,220
Social Welfare	from	22,151	to	61,240
Scientific	from	119,977	to	201,280

In some professions – nursing, teaching, social welfare – women have long predominated. In others such as the scientific they have made great advances. In the major churches, only men can enter the priesthood. In law and accounting, (for exmaple) men still vastly outnumber women.

There is entrenched discrimination, as convinced supporters of the women's cause point out. But there are real problems, very worthy of debate. Some jobs can be quite horribly demanding, and it is often very difficult indeed to combine caring for a young family with a heavy full-time job.

Accepted arrangements in marriage will have to change much if women are to gain equality in the labour market.

Income and wealth

In 1977, percentages of total weekly income arising from the stated sources were as follows:[47]

Wages and salaries	Self employed	Invest- ments	Annuities and Pensions	Social Security Benefits	Rent	Other Services
72	5.9	3.0	2.5	11.4	4.2	1.0

Wages and salaries

So income from employment is easily the main form of income received by most Britons. It accounted for over 80 per cent of weekly incomes of households with £100–£200 a week in 1977. The wealthy, with incomes of £200 or more a week were more likely to receive income from self-employment (14.9 per cent of their receipts) and/or from investments (6.2 per cent). The poor, with household incomes of less than £40 were very heavily dependent on social security benefits.

In 1978 the national income, or net national product of the United Kingdom, was £124,525 million.[48] After providing for stock appreciation, main income paid to the factors of production was as follows: (£million) –

Income from employment	98,156
Income from self-employment	12,492
Gross trading profits of companies	13,968
Trading surpluses of public corporations and Government enterprises	5,187
Rent	9,843

Allowances for wearing out of capital have to be set against profit and rent totals: in 1978 this allowance for capital consumption was £18,310 million. Nearly 80 per cent of net national income (98 of 124 thousand million) went into wages and salaries.

Since the Second War, in Britain as in other industrialised
countries, labour has taken – in the form of wages and salaries –
a greatly increased share of the national income. This trend was
already evident before 1939, there was a considerable upward
leap in the 1939–45 War. An authoritative set of calculations
was:[49]

Distribution of U.K. national income

Year	Wages and salaries %	Rents %	Profits, interest mixed incomes %
1870–79	48.7	13.1	38.2
1905–14	47.2	10.8	42.0
1930–39	62.0	9.7	29.2
1940–49	68.8	4.9	26.3
1950–59	72.4	4.9	22.7

In the 1960s and 1970s there was a rapid increase in share of
national income going to labour. One calculation was that the net
wage ratio, (proportion of net national income going to wages
and salaries) rose from 74 per cent in 1959–61 to 77 per cent in
1969–70 to 82 per cent in 1974–5.[50] Only Sweden, (81 per cent)
and Norway (77 per cent) had so high figures in 1974–5, though
the average for 17 industrialised countries rose from 61 per cent
in 1959–61 to 72 in 1974–75.

Here is a most significant development. It had been held by
economists that the share of labour in national income was
roughly constant. This is known as "Bowley's Law" after the
statistician, A.L. Bowley, (1869–1957), who formulated it around
the 1920s. On pre-1914 evidence it was a very reasonable
generalisation. By 1979 it had to be abandoned.

So average earnings rose. In the 1950s (1950=100) weekly
wage earnings rose to over 180 in 1959 while retail prices went up
to 150 and industrial productivity barely touched 130. Almost
exactly the same story was repeated over the 1960s: weekly wage
earnings up to over 180, retail prices barely up to 150, industrial
production around the mid 130s. At constant 1975 prices, male
manual workers' average earnings rose from £31 a week in 1951
to £54 in 1977. The proportionate increase gained by women
workers was even greater.

Yet, in the 1970s those working for themselves were more likely than employees to get really rich.[51] In the mid 1970s there were 1.8 million self-employed, 7.2 per cent of the work force. They had an average income of just over £4000 a year compared with under £2,400 for employees. But in 1974 the top 1 per cent of the self-employed had an average income of £34,528 compared with the mere £10,097 received by the top 1 per cent of employees. Stockbrokers, lawyers, accountants had the best chances of joining this wealthy minority. It must be added that part of these high receipts must be termed a return on capital ploughed into the business and is not labour factor income.

After an examination of employment over the period 1906–60, an expert concluded: "The outstanding characteristic of the national pay structure is the rigidity of its relationships".[52] Certainly in 1978 as in 1906, higher professionals and managers received more than lower professionals and foremen who in turn received more than skilled manual and clerical. Some relationships were astonishingly stable. Earnings of male unskilled manual workers, expressed as a percentage of average earnings, were almost the same throughout the period 1913–14 to 1978. As a percentage of the median for male and female employees, wages of the male lowest decile, (or poorest tenth), were 68.6 in 1886 and 68.6 in 1974, of the female decile 64.3 in 1938, 69.1 in 1974.

Yet between 1914 and 1978, the gap between the highest and lowest earnings narrowed markedly. In 1913–14, male higher professionals were receiving over 300 per cent of average earnings, and managers over 200 per cent. By 1978 they got less than twice average earnings. Foremen had moved above lower professionals and skilled manual had moved much closer to them in pay.[53]

Figures for movements between 1913–14 and 1960 confirm this trend and show that some of the largest relative increases were gained by women (see table on next page).

In the 1976–77 tax year, 28½ million received an income, (married couples are here counted as one). If we recall the old Army order – "Tallest on the right, shortest on the left: Size": we can line up the 28½ million with those with the highest income at one end and those with the smallest at the other. Then, if we

Average earnings, 1913–14 to 1960[54]

	Men 1960 as % of 1913–14	Women 1960 as % of 1913–14
Higher Professional	620	–
Lower Professional	546	680
Manager etc.	925	–
Clerks	689	949
Foremen (or women)	898	1,056
Skilled manual	804	898
Semi-skilled manual	842	678
Unskilled manual	849	1,000

divide this line into 10 equal parts, we find that in 1976–77, before tax:

The top	tenth, income	over	£5,924	received 26.2 per cent of all income
The second	"	"	£4,743	" 16.1 " " " " "
The ninth	"	"	£944	" 2.7 " " " " "
The bottom	"	below	£944	" 2.5 " " " " "

The effects of taxation on this distribution were surprisingly small. After tax the top tenth received 23.2 per cent of all income, the ninth tenth 4.5 per cent, the bottom tenth 3 per cent.[55]

Of growing importance over the decades to 1980 were benefits on top of pay received by employees. All full-time employees benefited from national insurance contributions paid by the employer. Paid holidays, sick pay, pensions were other important gains for large numbers. By 1979, large numbers of non-manual workers had the use of a company car and other "perks". Usually, the more you earn, the larger percentage you get on top of pay. By 1977, it was reckoned that managing directors and general managers received a whole battery of "fringe" benefits worth some 36 to 37 per cent of their average paid salaries.

Looking at the total pay scene since the Second War it seems clear that in the 1940s there was a marked reduction in inequality. One set of calculations found that in 1938 the top 5 per cent of income receivers, (tax units), took 29 per cent of

income before and 24 per cent after tax. By 1957 these figures
had fallen to 19 per cent and 15 per cent.[56]

But over nearly 30 years, 1949 to 1976–77, changes in income
distribution were not large. Before tax share of total income
taken by the top 10 per cent fell, but the middle 11 to 50 per
cent, not the bottom half, benefited.[57]

Of income receivers	*Per cent of all income taken*	
	1949	*1967–77*
Top 10 per cent	33	26
Next 11–50 per cent	43	50
Bottom 50 per cent	24	24

That low pay remained a major cause of relative poverty must
be emphasised.

Wealth

Wealth is a stock, income a flow. By wealth we mean marketable
assets or property: house, land, shares, insurance policies,
deposits in banks or building societies, and so on.

Figures and facts about income and wealth must be viewed
with caution. In Britain, most occupied people work for wages or
salaries, which are generally accurately known. But there is a
"hidden" or "black" economy which grew considerably in the
1970s. Some worked for pay or made profits which, for obvious
reasons, they did not declare to the authorities. Estimates of the
size of the black economy varied greatly: certainly, some
thousands of millions of pounds were involved.

Figures about wealth are likely to be less accurate than those
about income. We simply cannot know what wealth is stored in
over 20 million British homes. But the vast amount of
information leads to a clear conclusion that throughout the 20th
century, wealth in Britain has been very, very unevenly
distributed.

According to one set of calculations, the richest 1 per cent in
Britain owned more marketable wealth in 1976 than the bottom
80 per cent in that year.[58]

The top	1	per cent owned	25	per cent of wealth			
The next	2–5	”	”	”	21 ”	”	”	”
The next	6–10	”	”	”	14 ”	”	”	”
The next	11–20	”	”	”	17 ”	”	”	”
The bottom	80	”	”	”	23 ”	”	”	”

It is true that the picture was dramatically changed if occupational and state pension rights were reckoned as wealth. Then total wealth in 1976 leapt from £274 to £505 thousand million, and shares in that wealth altered as follows:

The top	1	per cent owned	14	per cent of wealth			
The next	2–5	”	”	”	15 ”	”	”	”
The next	6–10	”	”	”	11 ”	”	”	”
The next	11–20	”	”	”	15 ”	”	”	”
The bottom	80	”	”	”	45 ”	”	”	”

Wealth is much more unevenly distributed than income because it can be inherited, increased by marriage, amasssed over a lifetime. A large proportion of rich Britons owe their wealth to inheritance. According to a 1970s survey[59] between a half and two-thirds of people leaving £100,000 or more in the 1950s and 60s had fathers who left at least £25,000. Researchers[60] established that of "top wealth leavers", persons in the top 0.1 per cent leaving around half a million pounds or more, about half the men and two-thirds women had fathers who left over £50,000 at 1956 prices (worth £250,000 in 1980 money).

There was evidence that rich men married rich women. 26 per cent of "top" wealth holders' had both fathers and fathers-in-law who left over £100,000.

Yet wealth in Britain was less unevenly distributed in the 1970s than it had been in the inter-war period or in 1911–13. The estimated percentages of total personal wealth held by the stated proportions of the adult population fell as follows: (strictly 1961 and 1971 figures cannot be compared with previous figure as they were calculated on a separate basis, but all the statistics show an unmistakable trend).

Percentages of total wealth owned [61]

	1911–12	1936–38	1960	1961	1971
Richest 1 per cent owned	60	56	42	32	26
Next 2–5 ” ” ”	18	23	33	23	21
Next 6–10 ” ” ”	5	9	8	–	–
Bottom 95 ” ” ”	13	21	25	45	53

There is evidence that the richest (in the top 1 per cent) gave or left wealth to members of their families, (often in the next 2 to 5 per cent), so that the share of wealth held by the latter rose from 1911–13 to 1960.

While again statistics for the years 1966 and 1976 are not completely comparable, they do reveal similar trends.[62]

Percentage of total wealth owned

	1966	1976
Top 1 per cent	31	25
Next 2–5 ” ”	24	21
Next 6–10 ” ”	13	14
Bottom 90 ” ”	32	40

One important factor making for less inequality over the years 1960–76 had been changes in the relative importance of ingredients of total wealth – house, life assurance policies, shares and so on. Company shares became less important – they made up 21 per cent of wealth in 1960, 10 per cent in 1976. Homes, building society deposits, life assurance policies, became more important. Very relevant were the facts that (1960=100) the price of homes was nearly 600 in 1977, the price of company shares up to less than 200. So since individual share-holders were generally rich, while home-ownership was widespread – over half Britain's homes were being, or had been bought, by occupiers by the late 1970s – here was a significant development making for less inequality in wealth ownership.

Inequalities have diminished, but it is perhaps strange that heavy taxation did not reduce them further. However, estate duties could be avoided while continuing inflation vastly increased the money value of property.

Standard of living

While a significant minority of the population continued to exist in relative poverty, most Britons experienced a large rise in their standard of living between 1950 and the 1970s. As Socialist Naomi Mitchison wrote in 1979: "Few of my readers will know poverty as it was half a century ago. As people's expectations go up the poverty line goes up too . . . the disadvantaged and miserable have become news. They were not news then".[63]

Food and drink

"The poorer a family the greater the proportion of its total expenditure that must be devoted to the provision of food" – so states Engel's Law. From 1870–1914, working people spent between a half and two thirds of their wages on food. By the mid 1970s only about a quarter of total spending of an average British household went on food.[64]

However, diet does remain an important component of standard of living. Quantities of food per head, which had had to fall in War and post-war years were back above pre-1939 levels by the 1950s. By 1955, average intake of calories per day, which had fallen from 3000 in the 1930s to 2,880 in 1947 had risen to 3,120.[65]

As income rose after 1950, there was a continuing move away from the relatively cheap, starchy, filling foods such as bread and potatoes. Consumption of bread fell from the equivalent of about 2¼ large sliced loaves per person in the early 1950s to a little over 1 loaf in 1978. Each person ate, on average, 1.8 kilos of potatoes and potato products in 1951, 1.25 kilos in 1978.[66]

As more women went out to work and reluctance to slave in the kitchen grew, so convenience foods accounted for a higher proportion of spending on food – a quarter by 1970. Easily prepared foods and drinks which could be consumed in front of the television set were particularly popular.

Food buying and eating habits changed considerably. In 1970 only about 4 per cent, but by 1978, 41 per cent of householders had a deep-freeze. Amounts of frozen vegetables brought nearly doubled between 1970 and 1975. Between 1957 and 1978, factory farming plus deep freezers brought an eightfold increase in quantities of poultry eaten. There was evidence that diet was becoming somewhat healthier and more adventurous. By 1977, about one eighth of bread eaten was brown and wholemeal. Mediterranean foods were eaten following foreign holidays while Chinese, Indian and other restaurants grew in popularity, but it was reckoned that in 1970 every man, woman and child of the population drank an average four cups of tea a day.

Relative to many other goods, drink became cheaper over the period 1950–79. To buy a pint of beer a manual worker on average earnings would have had to work 34 minutes in 1950, 18 minutes in 1977. In bulk barrels (each of 36 gallons) production and consumption of beer in the U.K. increased as follows:[67]

Year	Production	Consumption
1959	25,444,000	26,543,000
1979	41,195,000	41,700,673

Per head of population, beer consumption rose from 147 pints to nearly 215 pints in 1979. At constant 1975 prices total spending on beer rose from £1,572 million in 1959 to £2,808 million in 1979. At current prices, U.K. consumers spent £4,822 million on beer in 1979. Numbers of U.K. licensed premises rose from 123,000 in 1946 to nearly 156,000 in 1975. Clubs went up in numbers from over 17,000 to over 30,000: off licences from 24,000 to nearly 36,000.[68]

Wine and spirit rose even further than beer consumption; wine drinking up four-fold from an average 2½ bottles a year per adult in 1951 to 9½ bottles in 1978. Spirits consumption roughly doubled over this period, reaching over 1½ litres per head per year by 1976.

At constant 1975 prices, an index of spending on tobacco (1975=100) rose from 102 in 1963 to 106 in 1973 before falling to 96 in 1976. No doubt, most of the fall resulted from the adverse publicity received, on health grounds, by cigarette smoking. However, around 45 per cent of men and 40 per cent of women still smoked in the late 1970s. About 60 per cent of men had done so in the early 1950s. By the early 1980s, consumption of tobacco was heavily falling.

From 1963 to 1977, at constant prices, spending on clothing and footwear climbed slowly but steadily, reaching over £5,000

million by 1975. The figures do not disclose major fashion
changes – particularly in women's clothing – which included the
1960s mini-skirts, the demise of full length stockings and the
popularity of tights, the use of plastics, the informal dress,
(sweaters and denims), of both men and women. In the 1970s
women were spending about half as much again as men on
clothes.[69]

Housing

For more than a decade after 1945 there was a severe shortage of
houses in the U.K. Shortages persisted, and persist, in certain
areas – particularly in London and other large cities. But by 1977,
it could be claimed that: "We have more and better houses in
relation to the numbers of households than ever before."[70] In
1951, when many thousands of couples and others were still
trying desperately to find a house, there were 13.8 million
dwellings for a British population of under 49 millions, giving an
average 3.5 people to a dwelling. By international or historical
standards, this density was low and by the late 1970s was down to
2.7. The typical British house with around three bedrooms often
now has to shelter only one or two people.

Indeed, as the following figures prove, after about 1960, there
were crude surpluses of houses in Britain in the sense that there
were more dwellings than households.

Great Britain: Population, households, dwellings (millions)

	1951	1961	1971	1976
Population	48.9	51.3	54.0	54.5
Households	14.6	16.2	18.5	19.3
Dwellings	14.0	16.3	19.0	20.1
Crude surplus of dwellings	0.6	0.2	0.5	0.8

Such statistics must be read with critical caution. The fact that
there are holiday and/or weekend cottages in rural retreats, does
not help those searching for a home in Camden.[71] But masses of
figures reveal the great growth of the housing stock since 1945.
Between 1960 and 1974, the total U.K. stock of dwellings rose
from over 16 to 20 million. Between 1966 and 1970, a period of

rapid augmentation of housing stock, there was a total annual net gain of 276,000 dwellings; slum clearance and other losses cost well over 100,000 dwellings a year, but the local authorities and New Towns were building 185,000 and the private sector 200,000 a year.

Nature of dwellings and of occupation changed much, as the following figures demonstrate:

Percentages of households: Great Britain

Year	In terraced houses	Semi-detached	Detached	Flats or tenements
1947	45	30	13	12
1977	28	32	22	17

In 1947, 26 per cent of households lived in owner-occupied accommodation, 13 per cent rented from local authorities, 62 per cent rented privately. By 1973 changes were great. Of dwellings in Britain 52 per cent were owner-occupied, 31 per cent rented from local authorities or New Towns, only 17 per cent rented privately.

However, marked regional variations persisted. In 1977, over 40 per cent of Scottish households lived in flats or maisonettes. In 1974, 33 per cent of Scottish dwellings were owner occupied and 54 per cent rented from local authorities.

We are here concerned with social changes of significance. Around 1900, probably some 90 per cent of households lived in accommodation rented from private landlords. By the early 1970s this percentage had shrunk to under 10. Landlords provided housing when it paid them to do so. In the 19th century, investment in house property to let seemed safe and profitable. But rent controls, high costs of repairs and alterations needed to meet increasingly stringent official health and safety requirements, rising house prices, these and other factors, conspired to bring about the gradual exit of landlords. They have received much bad publicity, but many young people, for example, have been glad to rent accommodation when they have moved, as students or workers, into new areas.

The growth of owner-occupation deserves comment. By the 1970s the half of households who were owner-occupiers, fully or partly owned a valuable asset. From 1950 to 1980 buying a house was a very sensible economic move. The purchaser usually borrowed from a building society money which was falling in value to acquire a real asset which was increasing in value. From 1946 to 1978, while retail prices went up sevenfold, house prices multiplied about 12½ fold.

From 1803 to 1963 income in kind rising from home ownership was taxed under Schedule A. This imposition was dropped while mortgage interest qualified for tax relief. There were therefore powerful fiscal factors adding to the popularity of home buying. One authority calculated that by 1978 over £5000 million a year was being borrowed to finance purchase of houses. "This is capital guzzling".[72] Tax relief plus subsidies to public housing were costing the Authorities a total of over £5000 million by 1973.

Certainly, numbers of dwellings had increased while quality and amenities had improved. By 1962, about 52,000 planning applications to build garages and 85,000 applications for other building were successful. By 1975–6 numbers of applications for extensions and improvement were up by nearly 90 per cent. A truly enormous "Do it yourself" industry arose. Households spent £1 billion on "D.I.Y." products in 1978. Nearly 1 million kilometres of wallpaper and 110 million litres of paint were bought.[73] Resulting labours and frustrations are surely beyond description!

Amenities increased, overcrowding diminished. In 1951, some 38 per cent of British households lacked, while a further 8 per cent shared, a fixed bath, 8 per cent were without, 15 per cent shared, a toilet. By 1977 some 90 per cent of households had sole use of basic amenities – fixed bath or shower, wash basin, sink, hot and cold water, toilet. Unfortunately, persons living alone – probably most were aged, were often less favourably placed. In 1964 in England and Wales, over 60 per cent of people living alone lacked at least one basic amenity.

Up to the Second War and beyond almost all British houses could be very cold in winter. The coal fire in the kitchen or living room was often the sole, limited source of warmth. In the 1960s and 70s central heating was installed in the typical new, and in many older houses. By 1964 eleven per cent, by 1977 over half, the houses in Britain had full or partial central heating.

By 1977, the vast majority of Britons were far better housed than ever before in their history and, in total, British housing compared very favourably with that of most other countries. Only 3 per cent of householders lived at a density of more than one person per room. Yet, among the 20 million dwellings, there continued to be many which were disgracefully bad. In 1975, 43 per cent of houses had been built since 1945, 23 per cent between 1919 and 1945, 34 per cent before 1919. By the 1970s, richer countries such as Germany were building houses at a much faster rate than Britain.

Great blunders were perpetrated by planners. Unfortunately, planning was very much left to architects and traffic consultants. Social scientists and the needs and wishes of communities were often much ignored. Thus, around the 1960s, large tower blocks of flats were built. Whole districts were cleared, though many houses could have been renovated. One published survey revealed that of some 91,000 houses destroyed between 1967 and 1971 in Greater London, 54,000 had been described as being in "good" or "fair" condition.[74] Sadly, they just happened to be in areas scheduled for re-development.

Homelessness and vagrancy have not disappeared. Indeed the mass media have given them great publicity. But the very significant step has been taken whereby local authorities are obliged to find some kind of accommodation for the homeless.

Consumer durables

While food, clothing and shelter remain basic needs, any concept of the standard of living of modern industrial communities embraces far more than these. Since 1950 practically all British households have acquired one or more of a range of gadgets. By 1956 some 40 per cent of households had a black and white television set: by 1978 some 96 per cent had sets – nearly 60 per cent colour – which they had bought or rented. Only 8 per cent had refrigerators in 1956, but around 90 per cent by 1978. By this date, about three quarters of households had a washing machine and well over half had a telephone. Unfortunately, while not much more than 40 per cent of all households lacked a phone, nearly three quarters of the old poor, who much needed a phone, were without one.

By 1977, around 57 per cent of households had the use of a car. At the end of 1978 there were nearly 18 million vehicles on Britain's roads: nearly 14 million private cars, 1,700,000 goods vehicles, nearly 1,300,000 motor cycles, 110,000 public vehicles. Over 2 million new vehicles were registered in 1978. Over 1,600,000 driving tests were conducted.

Advantages brought by the millions of private vehicles were great: so were the costs. Public transport declined in quantity and often in quality. Public road transport was calculated to total 83,000 million passenger kilometres in 1951, 53,000 million in 1977. Controversial recommendations of Lord Beeching were implemented in the 1960s and Britain's rail network cut by some 20 per cent. By 1978 roughly 5 times as much freight went by road as rail. Yet in that year British Rail still carried 172 million tonnes of freight and 30,700 million passenger kilometres.[75]

In 1977, 6,614 were killed, 81,681 seriously and 259,768 slightly injured on Britain's roads. Air pollution and noise were so severe that in certain urban areas the welfare of residents was grossly diminished. "I live with my wife in a GLC tower block. This is situated at the intersection of two motorways. . . Directly below us an overground Metropolitan line crossing two busy British Rail lines. . . The noise is sickening. We live day and night with the unceasing thunder of motor vehicles. It is impossible to read, think or listen to music . . . we sleep fitfully . . . our air is contaminated by fumes and lead . . . our block, which is similar to many others in this area was consciously planned and built with foreseeable results".[76]

Affluence

Modernisation and higher living standards brought bad as well as good results. Affluence had many factors; one was packaging. Immense quantities of cardboard, paper, plastic encircled the goods sold in shops, though customers had managed without most of such wrappings as recently as the Second War years.

As late as 1960, two-thirds of holiday spending was at home, about a third abroad. By 1971, around half was abroad. Holidays taken abroad increased from 3.5 million in 1960 to 7.25 million in 1971. However, in 1970 and 1971, around 34 million holidays a year were still taken in Britain.[77] Even in recession, in 1979–80 tour operators reported record bookings with five million Britons departing on overseas package holidays in 1979, and the top 30 tour operators having a record turnover of £644 million. Consequences of this mass mingling of European peoples during the summer months were varied and considerable. For many Britons, horizons were widened.

Continuing poverty

"The poor are always with us". In the 1950s, there was a widespread belief that this age-old saw was no longer applicable. Obviously greater affluence, agreement that Britons "had never had it so good", social surveys all seemed to agree that the Welfare State had abolished poverty. The survey of York conducted by S. Seebohm Rowntree and G.R. Lavers[78] revealed that only 2 per cent of working people in that city were below the poverty line. A well-known 1950s text on social conditions said of the York survey that: "its main conclusion that poverty has been much reduced in incidence, is not open to question."[79]

But in the 1960s and 70s, researches by B. Abel-Smith, P. Townsend and others, much shattered the comforting view that poverty had virtually disappeared: (again it must be stressed that to define poverty is monstrously hard). Figures relating to 1960, show that of those in poverty, 7 per cent were poor because of unemployment, 40 per cent because of old age and sickness, 40 per cent because of inadequate wages and 10 per cent because they were in fatherless families.[80]

The theme of a massive study published in 1979 was that: "Poverty can be defined . . . only in terms of the concept of relative deprivation . . . individuals, families, and groups in the population can be said to be in poverty when they lack the resources to obtain the types of diet, participate in the activities and have the living conditions and amenities which are customary or are at least widely encouraged or approved, in the societies to which they belong".[81]

The case studies which abound in the work reveal the continuing vast chasms in income, possessions and life-styles between the fortunate and the unfortunate in British society. By the state's supplementary benefit standard, 6.1 per cent of the sample in households, 9.1 per cent in income units, were in poverty. According to these findings, from 3.3 to nearly 5 million were poor. An additional 21.8 per cent in households and 23.2 per cent in income units, were on the margin of poverty.

When other standards or definitions were employed, even higher percentages and numbers in or near poverty were discovered.

The work of Townsend and others provided a valuable corrective to the view that the age-old problem of poverty had disappeared in late 20th century Britain and clearly revealed that not all Britons inhabited the lush world of the Sunday and glossy monthly magazines. Indeed, soon after the appearance of Townsend's major work, the steep rise in unemployment added to the numbers in relative poverty. The continuing relative decline of Britain's manufacturing competitiveness which, in the 1970s, had become a factor accounting for absolute industrial shrinkage, must add to difficulties in this, as in other spheres.

16.5 Class

Classes are "groupings across society, broadly recognised by members of that society, involving inequalities, or, certainly *differences*, in such areas as power, authority, wealth, income, prestige, working conditions, life styles and culture. . ."[82]

Class is not a simple, but a most complicated social reality. Even before 1914 some never recognised it. John Buchan's father "did not know the meaning of class consciousness"; while Buchan's "own upbringing had made any kind of class feeling impossible".[83] Others found it difficult to ascertain class bases of an actual social group. At an Edwardian ducal house party, the hero in a novel found: "This organisation puzzled him, for, so far, he could perceive no common factors between all these people; neither high birth nor wealth nor brains seemed to be essentials. . . Why some people qualified and others did not, he could not determine".[84]

Back in the 19th century, individuals with firm Victorian convictions might find themselves in conflict with other members of their own class. Domination of the village by squire and parson has been much described. A fascinating account of one Victorian village, records of which have survived, shows squire and parson at loggerheads.[85]

Many of the middle classes, with their emphasis on individual effort and worth have denied the importance of class. Modern American sociologists, in particular, have announced the demise of class in complex, open, modern societies with their very many gradations. Such views have been echoed in Britain where many believe that class has ceased to be a phenomenon of leading significance. "Politicans take note, the class war is over", reported one commentator in 1980, following publication of results of a public opinion survey showing that a mere 5 per cent considered "class distinction and snobbery" to be one of the causes most to blame for our problems.[86]

On the other hand, a host of modern analysts and writers, academic and non-academic, Marxist and non-Marxist have recognised the continuing significance of class.[87]

While recognising the existence of other complicating groups, Marx was clear that in industrial, capitalist, economies, two main classes existed: first, the owners of the means of production, that is the capitalists or bourgeoisie; and second, those who had had to sell their labour-power to the capitalists, namely the workers or proletariat. Conflict was inevitable as industrial concentration widened the gap between capitalists of increasing wealth and workers who became poorer, (whether Marx meant relatively or absolutely poorer is not clear).

Marx's views were based on his studies of early British industrialisation when gulfs and conflicts were wide and harsh. Developments since Marx's day which have very greatly changed realities while not destroying foundations of, class structure, include:

1. Improvements in working conditions, and, in particular, of standards of living. Class differences in consumption patterns have been much affected, especially in this 20th century. The transistor, television set, washing machine, of an upper class are often no different from those of a working class household;
2. Growth of trade unions has enabled many working people to negotiate from strength to improve pay and conditions;
3. Political enfranchisement of the working classes much changed the nature and application of that state power which Marx saw as merely a tool in the hands of exploiting

capitalists. The 20th century British state has much interfered with laissez-faire capitalism and much improved the lot of unfortunate citizens;

4. For the above and other reasons a large revolutionary working-class consciousness never developed in the industrial areas of Britain as it did in many continental countries. Here is another clear difference between British and European developments;

5. Early capitalism has much changed. Major industries were nationalised. Others were dominated by large corporations considerably owned by institutions such as insurance companies and pension funds, and managed by career executives;

6. Central and local government, public and private corporations require the services of a vast bureaucracy of administrators and executives. Welfare state, large scale business, technology, the media, demand vast quantities of professional expertise supplied by doctors, nurses, teachers, tax inspectors, accountants, engineers, scientists and a host of others. A huge "service class" has developed. Considerably recruited on merit, (a University or equivalent education is frequently a necessary qualification), salaried, and often much protected, this huge class is an important phenomenon;

7. A vastly expanded educational system provides opportunities for students to achieve, (though those from fortunate backgrounds have vast advantages), and provides careers for large numbers of those who have themselves succeeded in the system. In key respects in Britain's comprehensives and polytechnics, for example, class is not an important phenomenon. Education has joined property as a determinant of class position and attainment of educational qualifications is not limited to any one class;

8. Technological advance has led to much shrinkage of the manual working class. The middle classes have greatly expanded. The lower middle class includes a large army of women – often married, perhaps to husbands of another class – who have no strong class affiliations and who greatly complicate a picture of simple class hierarchy;

9. Sadly, in the inner cities, an underclass, composed of alienated blacks and others, and re-inforced by heavy unemployment, was making its presence felt in the early 1980s.

Convinced Marxists and others counter much of the above analysis pointing to continuing existence of very wide gaps in British society and to the continuing power and influence of these with property, wealth and privilege. While vast changes had occurred since 1870, yet in 1979, as in 1870, three main classes could still be differentiated. Society could be compared to a layer cake, with chocolate on top, jam in the middle and cake at the bottom.[88] Though dividing lines were very inexact and complexities abounded yet three main classes – upper, middle and working, still existed in 1979.

Into this 20th century an upper class has continued to exist through a "blend of a crude plutocratic reality with the sentimental aroma of an aristocratic legend."[89] Late 20th century aristocracy may prefer to remain "invisible" in a society much devoted to advocated ideals of equality of opportunity, while lifestyles have often changed very dramatically as owners of great stately homes live in a few rooms, open the rest to paying visitors, and even, on occasion, clean the shoes of guests.[90]

Again growth in numbers of middle class groups must be stressed. Examples of percentage distribution of economically active population, makes clear the fall in unskilled and rise in service class numbers.[91]

Table 15 *Economically active population distribution in percentages: examples*

| | 1931 | | 1951 | | 1971 | |
	Males	Females	Males	Females	Males	Females
Unskilled manual	17.9	7.5	13.8	7.9	8.2	6.4
Self-employed and higher grade professionals	1.7	1.0	2.8	1.0	6.1	1.4
Administrators and Managers	4.5	1.6	6.8	2.7	9.9	3.3

Yet while percentages of unskilled have dramatically declined, the working class remained large and important to 1979. In country villages, agricultural and council workers gathered in the bar while the better-off frequented the saloon, but the masses of working people were to be found in London and the great industrial cities. Contrasts between middle class Solihull, for example, and mainly working class Sunderland, were still dramatic, with Solihull having far more owner-occupiers, car-owners, students going on to higher education, Conservative voters, and so on.

By 1966, a sociologist could slot the 25 million economically active into the following classes:[92]

Class	Percentage in that class
Upper middle	11.5
Lower middle	31.5
Skilled working	25.4
Semi and Unskilled working	31.6

(So small are upper class numbers that this analyst, like some others, prefer to merge them with the upper middles).

Enormous difficulties arise in devising any such classifications. Observers may discern many layers: Wynford Vaughan Thomas noted that Swansea "has as many layers as an onion, and each one of them reduces you to tears."[93] Classes may embrace utterly divergent groups: for example Polytechnic lecturers and Norfolk farmers would probably be placed in the middle class but two groups differing more in attitudes, leisure activities and so on, it would be hard to imagine.

So there are a number of classifications. Assuming that: "*Social class is a grouping of people into categories on the basis of occupation*"[94] the most used categorisation is that of the Registrar-General, based on the Census.

From 1911 to 1971 the Registrar-General grouped the tens of thousands of occupations under five heads:

1. Professional, etc.
2. Intermediate
3. Skilled
4. Partly skilled
5. Unskilled

Since 1971 this division has been slightly modified into:

1.	Professional etc.	e.g. accountant, clergyman, doctor
2.	Intermediate	e.g. pilot, farmer, nurse, school teacher
3.(N)	Skilled non-manual	e.g. clerk, secretary
3.(M)	Skilled manual	e.g. bricklayer, miner (under ground)
4.	Partly skilled	e.g. barman, docker, bus conductor
5.	Unskilled	e.g. labourer, office cleaner.

This is the division which is normally used in social surveys into the effect of class on health and so on. But there are other divisions. Much quoted is that consulted by market researchers, advertisers, Gallup pollsters:

A.	Higher managerial, professional, administrative
B.	Lower managerial, etc.
C.1	Skilled, or supervisory, or lower non-manual
C.2	Skilled manual
D.	Unskilled manual
E.	Residual, including state pensioners.

This is a clear division, corresponding with realities. Thus, in the Army, Lt. Cols. and above go into Class A, Captains and Majors into B and so on.

In 1971, in percentages, economically active and retired Britons could be allotted to the Registrar's divisions as follows:

	I	II	III(N)	III(M)	IV	V
Male	5	18	12	38	18	9
Female	1	17	38	10	26	8
All	4	18	21	28	21	9

Much analysis proves conclusively that up to the 1960s and 70s, class differences remained wide and pervasive. For example members of upper, were more likely than members of lower, groups:

To survive birth and their first year;
To live longer;
To retain their teeth;
To be owner-occupiers and live in detached houses;
To stay at school longer and move into higher education;
To read papers such as the "Times", to be interested in Rugby
  Football and golf;
To drink at home.

Again it must be emphasised that British classes are not castes. There has been much change over this 20th century. There is much movement – many rises and many descents – from one class to another.

In the Second War, Orwell was writing: "In 1910 every human being in these islands could be placed in an instant by his clothes, manners and accent". But: "after 1918 there began to appear . . . people of indeterminate class . . . the technicians and the higher paid skilled workers, the airmen and the mechanics, the radio experts, film producers, popular journalists and industrial chemists. They are the indeterminate stratum at which the older class distinctions are beginning to break down".[95] The 1939–45 War hurried along change. Working people acquired more affluence and sense of importance, strengthened by Labour victory in 1945.

In the "affluent" 1950s and "permissive" 1960s very much changed. Consumption patterns of all classes considerably moved together as, for example, T.V. dominated leisure (though there were class differences in viewing habits). 1960s youth rejected hierarchy and found heroes in North country pop groups, footballers or writers.

In the late 1960s[96] Cambridge sociologists undertook a major survey of then relatively affluent Luton car workers. Contrary to a much accepted view, they found that the "affluent worker" had not become middle class. However, in many respects, he had abandoned traditional working-class attitudes. He no longer shared in the close kinship and neighbourhood patterns of earlier working class culture. The home became the centre of many leisure activities. Trade Unions and Labour Party were given conditional support while they seemed to be helping the worker.

A fluid society was emerging. Deep researches conducted at

Oxford in the 1970s showed that: "Britain is not a society in which individual position in the class structure is fixed at birth".[97] On the other hand, so great are the advantages of being born to upper class parents that large proportions of sons remain in the top classes. Similarly, most sons of working class fathers remain in the working class.

In this Oxford survey Goldthorpe divided the working population into 7 classes. It was found by the research team that nearly half of those surveyed, whose fathers were in Class I were themselves in Class I. But 8.4 per cent of those whose fathers were in Class VI and 6.9 per cent of those with fathers in Class VII had risen to Class I. Well over half those whose fathers were in Class VI and VII were themselves in Classes VI and VII.[98]

With changes in economic structure, there had been considerable mobility. One in five men whose fathers were in manual work had moved into white-collar jobs. Economic expansion plus greater educational opportunities had brought more "room at the top" and meant that the upwardly mobile outnumbered the downwardly mobile.

Most certainly there are cycles of advantage and disadvantage in modern society, yet men born into the same social class, even brothers, can experience very different career patterns.

At work, women are bunched in relatively lowly-paid non-manual groups. Single women can do well, being more likely to be upwardly mobile than single men. Marriage brings to women both upward and downward mobility. Working women add to and complicate the class affiliations of families and weaken class solidarities.[99]

It could be that the rise of huge organisations is creating a meritocracy with a class structure more pronounced than the older order. Projecting himself into the 21st century, one writer[100] described the hierarchy of large-scale organisations such as his European Atomic Authority with its 222 salary grades.

To sum up: class has much changed but remains. Classes are not castes. Edges are very blurred. Contradictions abound: a cleryman, ex-public school and Oxbridge, placed in Class I by the Registrar-General and in the middle class by public opinion is now much worse paid than many manual workers. A village may be a class-ridden centre of dreadful snobbery, or a reasonably democratic community with energetic individuals of lowly class origins running councils, Institutes, Associations.

Yet, over recent 20th century decades, hundreds of media interviews during industrial disputes have clearly shown bosses and men with the very different accents and attitudes of classes still in much conflict.

16.6   Public provision

The social wage

In 1979 in Britain it was still easily possible to point to groups which were poor, afflicted, disadvantaged. Yet, over the years 1945 to 1979 such groups had been helped by the community in an increasingly generous way.

By the middle 1970s the social wage, (i.e. the value of public and social services of direct benefit to the citizens) averaged around £1,000 a year, for each worker. The following list does not include items such as defence which could be reckoned to be a benefit.

	Public expenditure 1973–4 *£ million*[101]
Housing	2,740
Other environmental services	1,517
Law, order and protective services	1,017
Education etc.	4,307
Health and personal social services	3,707
Social security	6,460
Price restraint and transport subsidies	430
Total	20,258

It is agreed that these benefits were mainly paid for in taxes and that some paid out far more than they received. The unmarried, the childless couples (or couples whose children were at work) were often in this position. Children, the old, the sick and handicapped, and so on, benefited.

On following pages, examples of major developments, are selected for description.

Education

20th century Britain has vastly expanded her state educational system.

As measured by national income statisticians, (excluding transfer payments such as student grants), current U.K. educational spending thus increased:[102]

Year	Spending at current prices £m	Spending at 1948 prices £m	Index of real spending 1948 = 100	Current spending as per cent of national income
1920	65.1	100.2	47	1.2
1935	92.7	158.4	74	2.4
1950	272.0	263.0	122	2.7
1965	1,114.9	451.4	210	4.1

At current prices, spending on goods and services in national education rose from £1,355 million in 1968 to £6,467 million in 1978:[103] (the 1978 pound had a third of the real value of the 1968 pound).

British education is mainly provided by Local Education Authorities, controlled, supervised, inspected and much grant-aided by Central Government, Local provision has important results, including the facts that educational spending is easily the main demand on the rates, (amounting to nearly half in East Northants in 1980–81), and that Authorities have always varied considerably in their organisation and spending.

Before 1945, pupils attended state elementary schools from age 5 to 14. In England and Wales before the Second War, especially in rural areas, they often went to the same school for the 9 years, though by 1939, many areas provided Senior schools for the 11–14 year olds. Some of these gave excellent schooling. A minority of fortunate pupils "won scholarships", (or their parents paid modest fees), to Grammar schools where they stayed till around 16 or 18. It was possible, though difficult, for a poor child to go to University. There were Open and State Scholarships (360 of the latter in 1938), Local Authority awards, and help for intending teachers – on sworn promise to teach. But practically all intending doctors, dentists, lawyers, engineers were paid for by parents. Only quite rich families could hope to put a son or daughter into Medicine, since the fees for five or six years at Medical School, plus, often, the cost of a practice and equipment, barred all but the rich.

The 1945 Butler Act promised secondary education for all. Normally this was organised in a tripartite system in Secondary Modern, Technical and Grammar Schools. A clear majority went to Modern, a minority to Grammar Schools and a small number to Grammar/Technical or Technical Schools. Usually, pupils were selected at about age 11.

The school leaving age was raised to 15 in 1947, and to 16 in 1972–3. In the 1960s and particularly in the 1970s, Labour administrations implemented their party's proposals that secondary schools be made comprehensive. In 1971, 3 pupils out of 10 in England and 6 out of 10 in Wales and Scotland were in comprehensive; by 1978 these proportions were 8 and 9 out of ten.

Strong argument concerning advantages and failings of comprehensive education still raged in 1979 and beyond. "Black Papers" of academics and letters from businessmen and others denounced alleged falls in standards.

Yet in many respects progress was clear. Ladders leading upwards were much widened. In 1900 a very bright working class girl in a village probably at the age of 13 went into the local Hall as a servant. In 1980 she could go to University.

However, still in 1979 it was mainly the children of "service class" parents i.e. of professionals, managers, administrators, who sought University places. Over half the students admitted to Universities in 1978 came from this class. In 1980 A.H. Halsey, and others published results of a mammoth 1972 survey which they had conducted with J.H. Goldthorpe, some of whose researches have been noted. Of course, by 1972, there had not been time for the expansion and changes of the 1960s to be reflected in survey findings. In the whole educational system, state plus independent, class inequalities were very marked.

Class inequalities at different stages of the educational system[104]

Father's class	Percentage attending selective Secondary schools	Percentage obtaining "O" Levels	Percentage obtaining "A" Levels	Percentage going to University
Service	71.9	58.1	26.9	20.1
Intermediate	39.6	24.2	6.9	4.6
Working	23.7	11.8	2.8	1.8
All	35.0	21.8	7.3	5.1

The type of school attended proved to be of great importance: "If we take boys of *identical* social origins and intelligence, the ones sent to more prestigious secondary schools ended up with substantially longer school careers and substantially improved chances of obtaining O- and A-levels".[105]

In 1980, the Labour Party Conference committed the Party to an attack on private, non-state schooling in Britain. Of the independent school system R.H. Tawney wrote:[106] "It is at once an educational monstrosity and a grave national misfortune. It is educationally vicious, since to mix with companions from homes of different types is an important part of the education of the young. It is socially disastrous for it does more than any other single cause, except capitalism itself, to perpetuate the division of the nation into classes of which one is almost unintelligible to the other."

The case against attacking the independent schools is also very powerful. Some are very good indeed: for example, Oundle School is particularly strong in the Mathematics, Science and Computer studies which this nation needs.

U.N. and European Conventions, ratified by past British governments stipulate that parents have the right to educate their children outside the state system. So we wait developments with interest, for here surely, is an interesting example of the problems and difficulties involved in bringing about a major change in a modern state.

Expression of concern at the state of national education is no new phenomenon. Less common has been the documentation of success as, for example, in primary education.

Certainly, the amount of schooling – especially in adolescent years – has increased as have numbers of teachers with consequent improvement in the pupil-teacher ratio. Percentages of 17 year old Britons still at school rose from 12.02 in 1962 to 21.17 in 1977. State school teachers in the U.K. increased in number from 412,944 in 1970 to 537,381 in 1977. Pupils per teacher in England fell from 22.5 in 1970 to 19.8 in 1977. School leavers with 2 or more GCE A or 3 or more Scottish H passes rose from under 83,000 in 1966–7 to 113,000 in 1976–7.[107]

Higher education was greatly expanded, particularly after the Robbins Report of the early 1960s which recommended increases in full-time places in higher education from 216,000 in 1962 to 390,000 in 1973. After 1945, existing Universities grew, (Sheffield for example, up from about 800 students in 1938 to 7,600 in 1978); new universities were founded: advanced technological institutions were upgraded. Full time students, who had numbered a mere 50,000 in 1939 were up to 188,900 by 1966/67 and 289,000 by 1978. 30 existing Technical and similar colleges became Polytechnics around 1970 and have given opportunities to many thousands of students, as have much developed Technical and similar colleges.[107a]

Since 1970, the Open University, with 72,000 part-time students in 1978, has given tens of thousands the opportunity to learn and to graduate as well as providing B.B.C. programmes which interest many who are not registered students.

Degrees by the non-University sector were vetted by the Council for National Academic Awards (CNAA) which in 1976 awarded nearly 13,000 degrees.

Over the decade 1968 to 1978, full time U.K. students increased in numbers as follows: (in thousands)[108]

| | Men | | Women | |
	1967/68	1977/78	1967/68	1977/78
Universities				
Undergraduates	115.9	139.1	47.6	82.0
Post-graduate	20.4	21.4	6.3	10.2
Further Education				
First degree	16.8	50.0	4.9	27.9
Teacher-training	29.5	19.7	78.8	52.0
Other courses	32.5	37.9	11.5	23.4
Total:	215.1	268.2	149.1	195.5

Marked rises in numbers of women will be noted as too, will be the fact that their totals fall far short of those of men.

National Health Service

One does not have to be a brilliant economist to forecast that if demand is great and expanding, if price is low or non-existent, then it will be difficult for supply to meet demand.

Perhaps the most widely read of modern European writers commented thus: "A new law has been added to the famous Rights of Man; the Right to Life . . . and already one glimpses the Right to Health. Free medicine, free care foreshadow it, as free studies foreshadow the Right of Knowledge".[109]

Increasingly, as the 20th century passed, citizens were not prepared to tolerate pain, suffering, discomfort which very many in previous generations had had to bear with resignation. Cure or palliation has become possible for formerly disabling or killing conditions: insulin, artificial hipjoints, heart or kidney transplants, treatment for many forms of cancer are but a few examples of well-known advances. So demand for medical care, and pressure on resources, have increased. It is again necessary to emphasise that numbers of care-demanding elderly have risen.

So family practitioners are often under great pressure. About 9 million new out-patients a year – in the 1970s – flocked to hospital waiting-rooms. Some 16 per cent waited over an hour to be seen after their appointment. Waiting lists for admission, particularly for non-urgent cases, were often long. One survey, (which did not differentiate between urgent and non-urgent cases) found that 45 per cent of in-patients were admitted after less than a month's wait, but six per cent had to wait over a year.[110]

Similarly, patients' experiences of family practitioner services varied considerably. In some conurbations, it was not always easy to contact the family doctor at week-ends and holidays, since use was made of temporary stand-in doctors covering for the practitioner. On the other hand, in many areas, group practices provided round-the-clock service, supported by a range of local staff, and able to refer to laboratories, specialists, hospitals.

The 1970s saw discussion of, and changes in, the necessarily large – but some thought too cumbersome – administrative structure of the Service. Management and industrial relation problems were vast since about a million full-time equivalent people were employed by the NHS in the late 1970s. Like education, health services were very labour intensive. It was not easy to adequately raise the pay of so many employees. The winter of 1978–79 saw serious and sad industrial disputes which dislocated some hospital services.

By the late 1970s, the NHS was employing a huge army equivalent to over 200,000 of ancillary workers, domestics, catering staff, laundry workers, drivers, stokers and many others. 70 per cent were women. "A forgotten army where training and role development is concerned", said the Confederation of Health Service Employees.[111] Yet many were found in one study to like the job and, in general, there were no shortages of recruits.

The NHS seemed typical of a number of British institutions in that while there was grumbling, there was also satisfaction and some pride in achievement. After a large investigation, the Royal Commission considered in 1979 that "we need not be ashamed of our health service and that there were many aspects of it of which we can be justly proud" and "the NHS has achieved a great deal and embodies aspirations and ideals of great value."[112]

Certainly between 1949 and 1979, resources devoted to the NHS were much increased:[113]

Year	Total N.H.S. Spending £ million	N.H.S. Spending as per cent of Gross Domestic Product
1949	433	3.95
1959	788	3.71
1969	1,773	4.49
1977	6,897	5.59

Index of N.H.S. expenditure at constant prices
1950=100

1949	90.8
1959	117.8
1969	160.2
1977	208.8

Growth in number of doctors 1949–78 (whole-time equivalent)

	1949	1977
Hospital doctors – England and Wales	11,735	28,397 (England)
		1,648 (Wales)
Scotland	1,900	4,737
General medical – England and Wales		18,000 22,327
Wales		1,394
Scotland		2,000 3,089

Numbers of nurses, midwives and health visitors increased from 272,630 in 1971 to 335,081 in 1977, though it must be pointed out that the working week became shorter and holidays longer.

Growth in numbers of scientific and technical personnel was very great indeed. Examples are:

Grade	1957	1977
Biochemists and physicists	337	1,627
Psychologists	153	965
Dark room technicians	877	1,428
Medical laboratory scientific staff	2,942	15,878
Medical physics technicians	125	1,767
Physiological measurement technicians	579	2,149

Housing and environment

Very many of 56 million Britons live in crowded urban conditions where public provision of housing, roads, amenities and control of nuisances and pollution have long been, and are, of crucial importance to the quality of life of ordinary citizens. Here we come across weaknesses of conventional economics and of national accounting. It would be possible for a chemical firm to be adding a net product of £1 million a year to national output but to be diminishing health and enjoyment worth well over a million a year if it were pouring noxious material into air or stream. It is not easy to measure the economic value of environmental protection, but its importance has grown in modern societies.

To most people, their home and surroundings form the

important aspect of the environment. Housing has already received attention in this work. By the mid 1970s, some 6 million U.K. houses were rented from local, or New Town, authorities. Tenants did not pay the full economic rent needed to cover the rising costs of building.

New public housing by the mid 70s was subsidised by £900 a year per house. By the late 1970s, the authorities were spending £5,000 million on housing, mainly on construction and subsidies.

In 1978, roads (including lighting same) cost £1,696 million. While traffic congestion and pollution still constituted quite hideous problems on many roads, while Central London was authoritively threatened with complete traffic standstill within a few years, yet advances have been great. Surely Britain is one of few countries in this world where practically every village is approached by a tarred road. More obvious to many was the development of the motorways. The first main motorway was opened in 1959. By 1977 there wre about 1,400 miles of motorway and rather more miles of dual carriageway trunk roads.

After 1945, strong efforts, (they were not new) were made to plan and improve cities, abate pollution and preserve the countryside.

Urban reconstruction was often the subject of acute controversy and recriminations. In London, Coventry and other shattered cities, bombed areas were re-built. Then in the 1960s and 70s the centres of Birmingham, Newcastle-upon-Tyne and other cities were vastly changed as urban motorways and great new shopping centres were constructed. At great cost, traffic flows were assisted.

An interesting and valuable venture was the development of New Towns after 1946. 32 were established; though labelled "new" many were expansions of existing settlements. They were carefully planned to relieve congestion in conurbations by providing balanced communities with homes, work, amenities. The 2 million people living in New Towns by 1974 must generally have found that they provided far warmer and more convenient houses, far more pleasant surroundings, than those known to their grandparents in 1938. Washington was a vast improvement to Durham pit villages, Milton Keynes on East London. Peterborough has planted many thousands of trees and laid out excellent leisure areas.

Some other towns have vastly expanded, often under "overspill" arrangements with conurbations. Basingstoke had around 18,000 people in 1950, 80,000 in 1980.

Pollution from motor vehicles grew as did noise from traffic and transistors. But air and water pollution were much diminished; there were important successes. Smoke abatement was enforced so that while little or no change was noted in suburbs, average monthly hours of bright winter sunshine increased by a half in Central London between 1958 and 1967. Changes in Sheffield and Manchester were great; progress was slower on Tyne and Wear-side. In Manchester: "'Marvellous difference' said a park official. . . 'at one time nothing grew but these old poplars: now we've got roses and flowering cherries – right here in the centre – and all sorts of bedding-out stuff'. And he beamed with satisfaction at a stunning blaze of geraniums and petunias".[114]

Developments were strictly controlled in National Parks such as the Lake and Peak Districts and carefully watched by people and planners in all rural areas. Environmental impact assessment became an in-concept.

Social Security Benefits

In spite of repeated, and sometimes no doubt justified, charges of meanness and inadequacy, British authorities paid out £3,170 million in 1968, rising to £14,946 million in 1978, in social security benefits.[115] True, £10,506 million of the 1978 total came from the National Insurance Fund, mainly financed by contributions of £5,425 million from employers and £6,631 from insured persons (mostly employees). The Fund provided the following payments:

	£ million
Retirement pensions	7,353
Widows' and guardians' allowances	517
Unemployment benefit	667
Sickness benefit	681
Invalidity benefit	854
Maternity benefit	114
Death grant	16
Injury benefit	53
Disablement benefit	219
Industrial death benefit	32
	10,506

The preponderant cost of retirement pensions, bound to increase as the elderly live longer, is obvious.

Other benefits were:

	£ million
War pensions and allowances	322
Child benefits	1,574
Supplementary benefits	2,096
Other non-contributory benefits	448
	4,440

These are large sums, there have been great increases: for example, retirement pensions cost £1,550 million in 1968, £7,353 million in 1978; family allowances (or child benefit), £270 million in 1968, £1,574 million in 1978. It is repeated that, roughly, the 1978 pound had a third of the value of the 1968 pound: even so, increases were large.

In the 1960s and 1970s came significant additions to social security and allied provision. The important Supplementary Benefit Acts 1966 to 1975 introduced supplementary allowances and pensions to replace national assistance and non-contributory old age pensions. In place of the Ministry of Pensions and National Insurance and the National Assistance Board, (which were abolished) there were established a Ministry of Social Security, (later merged into the Department of Health and Social Security), and an independent Supplementary Benefit Commission to administer the complicated procedure of awards of benefit. The object of supplementary benefit was to provide a safety net to ensure that everyone had a minimum income on which to live. The benefit was paid to those who, for one reason or another, were unable to work full-time, because they were unemployed, old, sick or had family responsibilities.

In 1971 an attempt was made to tackle another large cause of poverty, namely low wages. Those in full-time work, with children, could claim an addition to income called family income supplement.

By 1973, under the Supplementary Benefit Scheme, over 4 million people (2,675,000 recipients with 1,347,000 dependants) were receiving benefits. 1,747,000 of these were old people.

By the 1970s an impressive list of benefits was available. Under the national insurance scheme, contributory benefits included unemployment, sickness, invalidity and maternity benefits; retirement and widow's pension plus death grant.

Non-contributory benefits included invalidity and very old person's pension, attendance, guardians' invalid care and mobility allowance. Special provision was made for those injured or disabled at work or in War.

Into the difficult 1970s, spending on social security continued to increase. A critical survey conceded that such expenditure nearly tripled between 1973/4 and 1978/9. In real terms the increase was 30 per cent. At constant prices the disabled and long-term sick had 47 per cent more spent on them. The 1974–79 Labour Government, it was claimed, "paid more attention to the disabled than any preceding government."[116] In 1975 and 1976, non-contributory invalidity pensions, mobility allowances and invalid car allowances were introduced.

Rises in retirement pensions were higher than increases in the cost of living, while in 1975 an ambitious new pension scheme under which pensions were to be related to earnings was introduced. These index-linked and earnings related pensions will be paid after 1999.

In the late 1970s family allowances were paid to the first child, previously only the second and subsequent children had been eligible. The family allowance was replaced by a child benefit scheme. Expressed in 1978 prices, the combined value of family plus tax allowance for a married couple with two young children rose from £3.54 in 1946 to £3.84 in 1979. As often, there was much complaint that such additions were quite inadequate to meet modern costs.

It is very clear that only a relatively rich, successful economy with high output can afford this much-needed provision.

16.7 Leisure

After 1945 Britons had more leisure hours and more money to spend on them. Mass observation and household survey investigators questioned them about their activities and results were published.[117] Often these merely confirm what common observation tells. Thus in 1977 in the 4 weeks prior to the interview, main activities were visiting or entertaining relatives and friends, going out to meals or drinks, listening to records or tapes, and so on. There was a huge range of interests. Thus in 1977, 320,000 belonged to the Youth Hostels and 30,000 to the Ramblers' Association, 180,000 to the Caravan Club, 50,000 to the Pony Club, 52,000 to the Royal Yachting Association, 29,000 to the Cyclists' Touring Club, 11,000 to the British Gliding Association, 700,000 to the National Trust, 450,000 to the English Golf Union.

Large numbers fished, raced pigeons and took part in a whole host of specialist activities and interests.

It has already been made clear that numbers going on holidays, and numbers going out for drinks and meals increased (there was also an increase in drinking at home). The number of licensed premises in the U.K. went up as follows:[118]

Year	Full on-licence pubs and hotels	Restricted on-licences	Clubs	Off-licences	Total
1946	81,445	n/a	17,322	324,215	123,032
1965	75,439	6,313	25,316	29,900	136,968
1975	73,656	15,798	30,513	35,990	155,956

For home consumption, drink was readily available on supermarket shelves.

Over the post-war years, the greatest change in leisure activities was that resulting from the near-universal presence of the television set. By 1978, Britons spent the following average weekly hours in television viewing:

Age group	February	August
5–15	24	19
16–49	18–19	15–14
50–64	20	15
65 and over	22	15

The young and the old spent rather more hours in front of their sets than did those with ages in between, women rather more than men, the poorer rather more than the richer social groups. But differences were not great.

Some consequences of television can be quantified. Cinema attendances fell from an average 26 million a week in 1951 to 2 million in 1977. Also, television helped bring about falls in popular newspaper and magazine sales. Other consequences remain subjects of much argument, but it must be stressed that, while of necessity treatment here must be cursory, it is obvious that here is a new phenomenon of quite outstanding social significance.

An authority[119] thus listed consequences of the "deleterious" impact of television:

1. "reading skills amongst the young . . . have remained static or deteriorated";
2. "Serious novels and poetry have become even more a minority art form than they were before the advent of television";
3. "conversation between members of a family, and particularly between parents and children, has diminished";
4. "language through the infiltration of expletives, obscenities and clichés has become vulgarised";
5. "television has been positively and scientifically identified as a major contributor to the increase of violence. . .";
6. "to many, television has become a daily fix or habit, deterring them from engaging in the other multiple leisure activities available in a civilised society. It encourages a spectator, rather than a participant, population".

While it is impossible to entirely rebut this formidable indictment, it can be replied that every major change is likely to bring some disadvantages but also some advantages. Thus:

Television positively encourages some reading. As one example among many, following a moving serialisation of "Testament of Youth", Vera Brittain's book shot to the top of best-seller lists in 1980;

Whole families, from the oldest to nearly the youngest, do sit together to watch some pleasant programmes such as "Play School", and "Blue Peter" to which not the slightest objection could surely be raised;

Coverage of current news and affairs on British television is so full as to be repetitive. Viewers learn much. Certainly, they are moved by what they see since they have donated millions of pounds to help the starving of South-east Asia or East Africa. Dickens would surely approve of the investigative and denunciatory vigour of some T.V. current affairs teams;

Some historical, scientific and nature programmes, for example, are truly first-class and must have brought interest, pleasure and knowledge to millions here and abroad, ("The Six Wives of Henry VIII" was sold to over 70 countries), who have seen them;

The well-produced and acted sequences of the most popular shows, like "Coronation Street" – bring harmless relaxation to millions who often work hard;

In this, as in some other respects, Britons were fortunate. They did not have presented to them only those scenes and view-points that Government considered they should see. In the whole world of 1979 this was not a very common privilege.

16.8   Crime and punishment

The number of honest acts – such as handing in lost property – is not recorded, nor is the frequency of occasions on which young people, and others, help the aged and infirm to clean their homes, and so on.

On the other hand, crime statistics are recorded and facts concerning crime and violence provide riveting material for the media.

As an official 1959 Report put it: "It is a disquieting feature of our Society that, in the years since the war, rising standards in material prosperity, education, and social welfare have brought no decrease in the high rate of crime during the war: on the contrary, crime has increased and is still increasing".[120]

The final assertion in the above paragraph can be proved by a vast mass of statistics:[121]

Numbers of indictable crimes known to police:

England and Wales	1938 – 283,220	1962 – 896,424
Scotland	1939 – 60,104	1962 – 117,824
Metropolitan Area	1938 – 95,280	1962 – 214,120

Offences recorded by the police U.K.:[122]

England and Wales:
  Recorded indictable
  offences   *1951* – 547,000   *1977* – 2,463,000
Scotland: Crimes   *1951* – 83,000   *1977* –   301,000
Northern Ireland:
  Indictable offences   *1951* –   8,000   *1977* –   46,000

Many of these who committed offences were young men. Per 100,000 population the following numbers were found guilty in 1975:[123]

England and Wales, males aged Under 14   1,291
                              14 and under 17   7,229
                              17 and under 21   6,428
                              21 and under 30   2,714
                              30 and over   642
                              All ages   1,694

While the published figures are sufficiently disturbing, it must be added that they are only the tip of the iceberg, an appropriate metaphor since most crime does not come to light. One study in Brixton, Hackney and Kennington in 1972 and 1973 "implied that only about one in ten of all crimes committed in these areas were actually included in statistics of recorded crime."[124]

Particularly in the big cities, chances that law-breakers would be caught were not high. Percentages of crime cleared up by police in England and Wales fell from 47 in 1951 to 41 in 1977; in Scotland from 37.1 in 1951 to 28.6 in 1977: in the Metropolitan Area from 27.1 in 1938 to 24.6 in 1962.

Yet police forces have grown, prisons overfilled, private security firms mushroomed. The strength of U.K. police forces increased from 71,800 in 1951 to 125,000 in 1977. England and Wales figures were:

	1951	*1977*
Men	60,500	100,300
Women	1,400	7,900

The average daily prison population rose from 32,461 in 1960 to 41,791 in 1978. In 1977, in local prisons for men, the average number of inmates was 42 per cent higher than the recognised amount of accommodation. Public spending on police and prisons rose from £344 million in 1968 to £1,655 million in 1978.

Crime, violence, vandalism cause much distress and unhappiness. Their volume has increased. However, when considering the statistics, it is necessary to note that a high proportion of crime is committed by youths and young men, numbers of whom rose in the decades after 1945 as a result of relatively high birthrates and that increased numbers of police officers probably do record on their computers increased numbers of crimes, the less important of which might have gone unrecorded in previous generations.

For centuries there has existed a class of professional criminals living off the proceeds of theft or fraud.[125] In the 20th century, greater affluence and inflation brought fatter pickings. The ablest of the criminal hierarchy were not often caught and convicted and received considerable, tax-free incomes.

In recent decades, recruitment into the criminal groups has been brisk. Juveniles committed to Borstal numbered 818 in 1969, 2,117 in 1978: to detention centres 2,228 in 1969, 6,303 in 1978. 85 per cent of those leaving Borstals, three quarters of those leaving detention centres, were again convicted within two years.

It is not easy to account for the rise in crime. Earnings have risen, unemployment was low from 1940 to 1970; housing, education, social services have improved. Obviously causes of crime are very varied and include: domestic friction leading, for example, to the murder of a spouse, mental illness and social problems.

Life in modern conurbations offers little scope for healthy outdoor activity and expenditure of the abundant energy of the young. Rooted hostility to authority, particularly to the police, widespread anti-social behaviour especially heavy drinking, high rates of crime, continued, for example, in districts of Merseyside, London, the North-east and Clydeside.[126] One researcher into the activities of male youth in Sunderland found that "nearly everyone has either smashed or stolen something during the previous year."[127] The influence of the gang or group was immensely important.

In this, as in so many other fields, much more research is needed.

Since 1945 efforts have continued to make the penal system more humane and effective. Hanging and whipping ceased. After 1957, "diminished responsibility" could be pleaded. Determined efforts were made to separate the treatment of juveniles from that of adult offenders and to try to make sure that young offenders did not early embark on a life of crime made more likely through association with adult criminals. In 1963, the age of criminal responsibility was raised from 8 to 10 years. The special courts which dealt with juveniles might discharge them (absolutely or on conditions), fine them, put them on probation, or send them to an institution. Probation had been established by a 1907 Act and in 1970 a probation service of some 3,000 officers attempted to keep law-breakers out of further trouble. But by the late 1960s, probation was largely for adults, since the Children and Young Persons Act 1969 substituted supervision by a social worker. One of the tasks of the enlarged social service departments has been that of caring for and supervising young people who, for one reason or another, have broken the law.

Deterrence was provided by Approved Schools, by the Attendance and Detention centres set up by the 1948 Criminal Justice Act, and by Borstals.

Adult offenders might be cautioned, or fined, or put on probation, or sent to prison. Numbers in prisons have grown vastly: there were some 35,000 on an average day in 1968 in Borstals, detention centres and prisons compared with 20,000 in the early 1950s and 10,000 pre-1939.[128] By 1980, Britain's overcrowded gaols were repeatedly stated to be in a near-crisis situation.

Yet, through this 20th century, repeated efforts have been made to curtail the use of imprisonment as a deterrent. Imprisonment of young offenders has been restricted by various Acts. The First Offenders Act 1958 made it more difficult for summary courts to imprison adults not convicted since their 17th birthday. In 1968, suspended sentences were introduced and have proved popular with the courts. Compared with those in previous ages, prisoners might well expect early release. In the Second War, remission for well-behaved prisoners was increased to one-third and remained at that level. Under the 1967 Criminal Justice

Act, prisoners became eligible for parole when they have served a third of their sentences, or one year, whichever was longer. Compared with Victorian institutions a typical British prison of 1980 had seen much relaxation of discipline, much less solitary confinement, much more association.

Critics of the prison system remain and point out that, on the one hand, four out of five offenders do not offend again, no matter what sentence is imposed, while, on the other hand, prison seems to have little effect in reforming the 15 to 20 per cent of hard-core offenders. Yet society must retain the right to protect itself against those who are a clear menace and danger when they are at liberty.

Perhaps all that can be added is that prevention is better than cure, that there is no alternative to a long hard slog involving parents, schools, churches, police, social, probation and after-care services.

17. ASPECTS OF THE 1970s

17.1 The economy: end of the boom

In 1973 the boom ended: the world and Britain's economies descended into prolonged and serious recession. There was a limited upswing between 1975 and 1979 then a deepening recession and such an upsurge of unemployment that over 3 million Britons were out of work by 1982. Gross national product (1975 = 100) rose from 91.1 in 1970 to 102.8 in 1973, then fell to 100 in 1975 before rising to 108.5 in 1978. Production in manufacturing industry (1975 − 100) fell to 95.4 in 1980 (and continued to fall to 88.4 in 1982).

Only oil production (up from 333,000 tonnes in 1972 to 103,424,000 in 1982) rescued Britain from serious trouble with her Balance of Payments and government revenues. Even here there were nasty stings. The jacking-up of the pound's exchange value – for sterling had become a petrocurrency – made exporting harder and importing easier. Oil exports increased income, helped the Balance of Payments, and enabled Britain to pay for those imports of manufactured goods which put workers on the dole.

It is not surprising that the post Second War boom is associated with domestic consensus and social advance. Much harsher 1970s and early 1980s saw the ending of consensus, a far tighter grip on Government spending, and far sharper divisions within society.

The world economy

The recession after 1973 was a world phenomenon. Leading industrial countries witnessed serious falls in their rates of growth.

Causes of world recession were complex but note must be here taken of the very steep rise in commodity prices in 1973. By the end of that year they were 50 per cent above their average 1972 level. Then came an additional great blow: following the Arab-Israeli war of October 1973, the Arab producers who controlled oil prices through a cartel (the Organisation of Petroleum Exporting Countries or OPEC) vastly raised the oil price. The U.K. price of Gulf oil which had been 2.40 dollars a barrel on 1st Jan. 1973 was 11.30 dollars a barrel on 1st Jan. 1974.

It was reckoned that whereas in 1972, total world trade in food, raw materials, fuel was worth some 150 billion dollars, in mid-1974 the same amounts of food, raw materials, fuel cost some 320 billion dollars. The extra cost to the U.K. of importing a constant amount of fuel and raw materials was calculated at over £5,000 million.

Oil exporters accumulated astronomical surpluses, creamed off from consumers whose real purchasing power was then reduced. In 1974 these producers' surpluses were around 60,000 million dollars and by 1977 they totalled some 150,000 million dollars. These developments greatly changed the fortunes of a world economy which had been making much progress since 1950. Inflation accelerated: growth ceased. Over the two years 1973–75, inflation in all O.E.C.D. (the world's rich, advanced Western-style) countries averaged 26 per cent, ranging from 13 per cent in Germany to 44 per cent in the U.K. World industrial production, which had risen by 6–7 per cent a year through the 1960s and 8 per cent a year in 1971–73, stagnated in 1974 and fell by 10 per cent in 1975.[1] For a still large trading nation like Britain these were most serious developments. Yet in accounting for Britain's economic woes, it would be wrong to attach too much weight to extraneous factors such as the oil price rise. Further, as overseas primary producers complained, the prices of Western manufactured exports rose too. The U.K. prices of the cheapest Mini was £638 in 1970, £2,684 in 1980. In fact, whereas from 1967 to 1975 import prices climbed faster than those of exports, from 1975 to 1978 this tendency was reversed. Unit value index numbers (1975=100) were:[2]

	1967	1975	1978
Imports (f.o.b.)	35	100	146.4
Exports (f.o.b.)	42.9	100	155.1

Oil

That North Sea Oil made a large contribution to the credit side of the Balance of Payment is clear from the following statistics.[3] Relatively minor items have been omitted so the table is not complete:

1976–79 Balance of Payments: current account £ million

	1976	1977	1978	1979
Visible balance of which	−3911	−2239	−1493	−3312
Oil balance	−3947	−2771	−1999	−780
Non-oil balance		+1039	+1579	−2449
Invisible balance	−2709	+2015	+2425	+875
Current balance	−1202	−224	+932	−2437

Britain's poor economic performance

From 1945 to 1970, Britain made a modest success in achieving main aims of economic policy.

In the 1970s, performance was much worse, growth slackened to come to a stop at the end of the decade, unemployment rose, inflation became serious. Particularly by 1970–80, recession had become an international problem. In September 1980, the unemployment rate in the European Community was 6.5 per cent, with 7.1 million out of work.

British administrations (and most Britons) still regarded inflation as their major economic problem and took steps to moderate it. Unfortunately, but very predictably, their anti-inflation measures made recession and unemployment worse.

Britain's record with regard to inflation, though good in comparison with some South American states, Iceland or Israel, was poor when compared to that of most other industrial nations, as the following examples show:[4]

Percentage Annual Change in Consumer Prices

Year	U.K.	U.S.	Japan	W. Germany	France	Italy
1970	6.4	5.9	7.7	3.4	4.8	5.0
1973	9.2	6.2	11.7	6.9	7.3	10.8
1975	24.2	9.1	11.8	6.0	11.8	17.0
1976	16.5	5.8	9.3	4.5	9.6	16.8
1978	8.3	7.7	3.8	2.6	9.1	12.1

Cost inflation

Faced with such a dramatic rise in import costs as that of 1973, an economic dictator could have frozen money wages and imposed a deflationary package designed to cut real income, consumption and imports. Then general inflation could not have occurred.

But Britain was a free country, for which blessing she paid a high price. The miners struck for much higher pay which they gained in 1974. Many others gratefully rushed over the flattened walls of official pay restraint policy. Serious cost inflation ensued: the retail price index (Jan 1974 = 100) was at 134.8 for 1975, 204.2 at the end of 1978. Prices in mid-1975 were up by a quarter of their level of a year before. By 1978 the pound retained only a third of its 1968 purchasing power. The rise in earnings was quite out of line with the rise in output. One set of figures for total U.K. output increases (1975=100) shows a rise from 93.6 in 1970 to 105.5 in 1978.[5] Even in the 3 years to the end of 1978 when inflation was abating and Government had an agreement with the unions to dampen down wage increases, earnings rose by 42.8 per cent.[6]

True, the pace of inflation much slackened after 1975. By 1978 it was down to under 10 per cent before gathering speed for another leap to over 20 per cent in 1980.

To reduce the growth of inflation, Government restrained the growth of public expenditure, raised the interest rate, and allowed the pound's exchange value to rise.

Bank rate, or Minimum Lending Rate, which had been 5 per cent in 1971 rose very sharply in the later 70s: it was 12 per cent in early 1977, varied around that figure till 1979 when it was pushed up to 14 then 17 per cent.

In 1972 the pound was allowed to float, or find its own level, on the foreign exchange. It had exchanged for 2.40 dollars from 1967–71; it was down to under 2 dollars by 1976, hitting a bottom of 1.57 dollars in October of that year. High interest rates and North Sea oil helped push it up until by 1980 it again stood at 2.40 dollars to the pound, before another prolonged and heavy fall.

Clearly, high interest rates were an additional burden to businessmen who had to borrow though the important point must be made that if inflation is running at 20 per cent, an interest rate of 19 per cent is a negative rate. In real terms, the borrower, not the lender, is gaining.

Further, the stronger pound helped reduce the cost of imports – including those of raw materials for industry.

It cannot be said that fiscal policy was deflationary since the public authorities continued to borrow in order to cover expenditure. While it is true the real value of borrowings was falling, yet the Public Sector Borrowing Requirement, (the annual amount by which spending exceeded tax income and had to be borrowed), remained large, as the following examples show:[7]

Financial Year	Current prices	1975 prices	P.S.B.R. as per cent of GDP
1969–70	−509	−993	−1.1 (Some repayment)
1974–75	7,993	9,583	9.1
1975–76	10,586	10,142	9.6
1976–77	8,519	7,228	6.7
1979–80	9,964	5,795	5.1

So there was considerable borrowing in the 1970s, as contrasted with the late 1960s. Keynesian teachings upheld the wisdom of borrowing in recession. The obvious difficulty was that – in the main – such borrowings tended to make inflation worse. This is the simple crux of the matter and accounts for the fact that British and other Governments – rightly or wrongly – have felt unable to take really effective fiscal and monetary measures to drastically reduce 1980s mass unemployment.

Declining growth rate and rising unemployment

That over the 1970s Britain's growth performance was poor is clear from the following table:[8]

Average annual growth of Gross Domestic Product or Gross National Product

	1967–73	1973–78
U.K.	3.4	1.1
U.S.	3.5	2.4
Japan	10.2	3.7
France	5.6	2.9
W. Germany	5.3	1.0

It is very clear that both in boom and in recession, Britain's growth rate was lower than that of other main Western economies.

U.K. unemployment rose as

follows:	1971	1973	1975	1977
Total (000)s Unemployed	792.4	618.8	977.6	1483.6
Unemployment rate	3.5	2.7	4.1	6.2

In 1979–80 a very steep rise brought the number out of work to over 2 million by the Autumn of 1980. By early 1982 a record total of over 3 million were registered unemployed.

By the late 1970s, then, unemployment was once again a very serious problem in Britain. Many thousands who wanted to work could not find it. This was a new phenomenon to that half of the nation born after 1940 and it hit many very hard, though, for some, generous redundancy payments, for example in the steel industry, and far more generous social provision than that obtainable by means tested benefit recipients of the 1930s, softened the blow of worklessness.

Mass unemployment returned because there was a world recession, Britain's economic performance and growth rates were poor, deflationary measures such as public expenditure cuts and high interest rates added to problems, the high birth rate of the 1960s brought large numbers of young job-seekers on to the labour market, human was replaced by machine labour.

Regional, occupational and age disparities continued. With a 1978 national unemployment rate of 6.1 per cent, the North, Wales and Scotland registered over 8 per cent and the North-west 7.5 per cent: the South-east and East Anglia had less than 5 per cent. The recently very prosperous West Midlands had 5.6 per cent, a figure which was rapidly growing.

Of 1,209,000 out of work in Great Britain in June 1977, 874,000 were manual workers of whom 431,000 were general labourers. Unskilled workers were hard hit by unemployment.

The old found it hardest to get back to work. In 1978, of 132,000 unemployed men aged over 60, 61,936 had been off work for more than a year.

But in spite of large official efforts to find them work, or training, many young people could not find jobs. In September

1980, 208,000 school-leavers, 91,000 more than a year before, were still without work.

It must be noted that through 1970s years of rising unemployment, there remained vacancies not only for skilled people, such as tool-setters and computer staff, but also as late as 1978 – in unpopular occupations such as "bus conductors, coal miners, policemen and security guards".[9]

Employment

Manufacturing employment fell dramatically, Government and service employment grew over the decade.

Table 16   *U.K. Employment 1969, 1978*[10]

Employees (thousands)	1969	1978
All manufacturing industries	8356	7298
Agriculture, forestry, fishing	491	387
Mining and quarrying	437	343
Construction	1463	1269
Gas, electricity, water	405	350
Transport and communication	1560	1446
Distributive trades	2711	2734
Financial, business, professional, scientific services	3742	4829
Catering, hotels, etc.	708	895
Miscellaneous services	1284	1519
National and local government	1467	1636

Deindustrialisation[11]

Employment in Britain manufacturing industry fell by a third (34.1 per cent) between 1966 and 1981. No other major industrial country underwent anything approaching this scale of deindustrialisation. Indeed, over the same period Japan's industrial labour force grew from 15.8 to 19.8 millions.

Total employment in U.K. manufacturing rose to 1966 then remorselessly fell. Total figures (with examples of declines) were:

	1960	1966	1974	June 1981
Total manufacturing	8,850.5	9,163.1	7,871	6,041
Metal manufacture	617.1	623.0	507	326
Mechanical, instrument and electrical engineering	2,048.9	2,376.9	1,980	1,530
Vehicles	919.8	853.2	792	636
Textiles	901.8	810.8	585	364
Clothing and footwear	591.7	554.2	427	313

Causes of falling employment were varied and included switches to Government and service work and automation, (though Japan which adopted automation more than any other country increased industrial employment). But the basic cause was highlighted by many very disturbing statistics. Thus, the ratio of the value of imports to output, or import ratio, in the vehicles industry was 0.073 in 1970, 0.363 in 1979, an increase of nearly 400 per cent over the decade. Corresponding changes in electrical engineering and in clothing and footwear over the decade were 128 and 155 per cent.

Shares of each of six major industrial countries in exports to each other were:[12]

	1963	1974
U.K.	14.4	9.7
Germany	23.6	25.0
France	14.3	16.1
Italy	10.5	11.4
U.S.A.	28.7	23.7
Japan	8.3	14.1

In the following countries, manufactured imports as a percentage of the domestic market were:

	1969	1974
U.K.	10.2	16.7
Germany	13.4	11.8
France	12.1	14.3
U.S.A.	3.7	4.7

Thus, there is very much proof that many of Britain's major industries were not competitive – that imports were rising faster, and exports rising more slowly, than those of other similar economies. Purchase of cars made in Japan did not provide work in Coventry. One basic cause of growing unemployment was relative industrial failure.

Industrial performance

The following table[13] clearly reveals other major industrial nations expanding far faster, and controlling inflation far more successfully, than Britain, (though it will be noted that British expansion, particularly of exports, was by no means small).

Table 17 *Economic indicators: Percentage changes, 1969–79*

	U.K.	U.S.A.	Japan	W. Germany	France	Italy	Sweden
Gross domestic product	25	32	80	38	49	49	26
Output of manufacturing industries	7	37	69	31	45	40	21
Exports of goods and services	54	91	205	93	130	93	53
Consumer prices	225	98	137	61	132	225	126
Output per person hour in manufacturing	33	34	96	54	69	54	–

Among many explanations, one basic weakness leading to poor performance must be firmly emphasised. For a variety of reasons, the average Briton in industry did not produce as much as the average American or West European.

It was no new situation. L. Rostas had calculated that in 1935–39, in a sample of manufacturing industries, output per American worker was 2.2 times as much as that of a British worker. By 1978 the gap was even wider.[14]

By 1980 it was very reasonably asserted that: "Low productivity is the central issue of our political life, as it underlies all the others, it is the issue of our national future".[15] Certainly, in an open economy heavily dependent on trade, continuing relative decline must be disturbingly serious.

Yet, in the midst of all this gloom concerning Britain's economic position it is necessary to consider many divergent points of view. Briefly stated, some are:

In 1980, Britain was still a rich country, enduring penalties of affluence. In the late summer of 1980, after the disappointing decade described above, and in the midst of recession, Britons "enjoyed" a Bank-holiday . . . "by mid-morning more than 33,000 cars an hour were leaving London on 25 main roads . . . police reported a true bank holiday bumper-to-bumper situation on approach roads to most popular seaside resorts".[16] Britain might be forgiven for believing that increased income was not sufficient recompense for the loss of accustomed life-style and work practices.

An economy is like a forest. Some trees are old and dying, some encrusted with parasites, others are young, vigorous, fresh green. In the 1970s there were vast numbers of firms and many sectors in the British economy. They varied immensely in size and efficiency. In all manufacturing industries, 117,849 units employed over 7 million workers.[17]

There was a great range still of activities, including some which were highly skilled, modern, technology-based. Thus, in the mid-1970s, chemicals employed 428,100 and sold over £6,000 million of output a year, of which £2,170 million were exported. Instrument engineering (scientific and industrial instruments, watches, clocks, and so on) employed 153,900 and sold £883.9 million worth of goods, of which £523.6 million were exported. Electrical and Electronic Engineering employed 768,000 and had sales of over £5,500 million.[18] Even in sharp recession in 1979–80, many aircraft and highly skilled electronic firms continued to expand and recruit labour.

Many branches of the huge sector were highly efficient. There is very wide recognition that this was true of the great retail chains. Through the 1970s changes in retailing structure were marked and rapid. It is not here claimed that they were wholly beneficial since many customers lost the valued services of corner or village shops.

Details were:[19]

Table 18 *Structure of retailing, 1971, 1976*

	Businesses number 1971	Outlets number	Persons engaged 000s	Turn over £m	Businesses number 1976	Outlets number	Persons engaged 000s	Turn over £m
Total retail trade	368,222	509,818	2,852.6	16,949	261,958	391,136	1503.4	34,160
Single outlet retailers	338,210	338,210	1,339.7	7,076	231,111	231,111	996.4	11,609
Large multiple retailers	1,386	87,642	1,136.3	7,739	1,410	81,355	1,115.4	17,548
of which Co-op socs:	313	16,480	173.3	1,215	236	11,117	155.2	2,414

It will be noted that, compared with other large multiple retailers, the Co-ops which had made such rapid progress in the 19th century, now lost ground in the much changed economic environment. A further point of interest is that of all forms of retail trading, mail order business made the most rapid advance in the 1970s. Counting their 1971 sales as 100 by 1978 they had moved up to 334.

As already stated, Britain gained largely from exports of services. The 1978 credit balance in financial and similar services was some £2,800 million.

Over the decade to 1978, though some 1½ million acres were lost to agriculture, yet output went up: final agriculture output (at constant 1975 prices) was £4,378 million in 1968, £5,022 million in 1978. Yield per hectare of wheat rose from 3.55 to 5.26 tonnes, of barley from 3.44 to 4.19. In 1978, British farmers kept well over 13 million cattle, nearly 30 million sheep, 7,700,000 pigs, 137 million poultry. With over half a million tractors and nearly 58,000 combine harvesters in 1977, plus a vast array of assorted cultivators and other machines, the common complaint of too little investment could not be levelled against farmers. Again, structural change was under way. Farms were getting bigger: holdings of 500-plus acres increased in numbers from 5,747 in 1964 to 8,236 in 1975.[20]

Finally, an economy which could sell abroad goods worth over

£35,000 million in 1978 could not have been wholly uncompetitive.

17.2 Paying for the welfare state

In 1978, total U.K. public expenditure was over £71,000 million.[21] As a proportion of the National Product, public spending had risen from 34 per cent in 1951 to 49 per cent in 1976. Average percentage growth of public expenditure, 1951–76, was 4.3 per cent. Over the same 25 years, gross domestic product grew by an average 2.8 per cent per year.[22]

Relative to national income, Britain's public spending was not the highest in Europe, nor was it much out of line with similar Western economies. Sweden's public authorities spent 54 per cent of National income in 1976, in France the figure was 41 per cent, in Germany and Italy 46 per cent.

Further, there were continuing clear needs for increased spending on the Health Service,[23] child benefit, education, housing, the old and in other spheres.

But what proportion of total national income should Government spend? Government spending is mainly paid for by taxes. So income of people at work can be divided into two piles – take-home pay and taxes (including National Insurance Contributions). By the early 1980s, some 40 per cent of National Income was being taken in taxation. A combination of low tax thresholds, low pay, very complicated social security arrangements, meant that some workers were nearly as well off or actually better off, not working than working.

Through the late 1970s and into the 80s British governments strove to cut public expenditure. By 1980 a distinguished economist was arguing: "Public expenditure reductions must be seen as representing a normal and continuing process".[24] It was not a view which gained universal agreement.

17.3 Dispute, protest, violence, unease

Compared to many countries, Britain in the 1970s (with the significant exception of Northern Ireland), was a peaceful and tolerant land in which many citizens, including this writer, never saw a serious act of violence or even an industrial picket line, except on television. In very many British local communities, acts of co-operation and helpful kindness far, far outweighed those of confrontation and protest. Yet, in comparison with other post-war decades, the 1970s saw an upsurge of violence and unrest.

Ulster

When most of Ireland gained virtual independence in 1922, Northern Ireland contracted out. The million Ulster Protestants wanted to remain part of the United Kingdom. Unfortunately for them, many in the Irish Republic strongly desired a united Ireland for which some were prepared to fight. Within Ulster itself a sizeable minority of Catholics have supported not Britain but the Irish Republic.

In 1969, as often, trouble boiled over when reform was being attempted. The British Government sent in the troops, who were at first welcomed by all who valued their safety. Then the killings began. In 1972, the worst year, 468 died from violence in Ulster. The death rate dwindled, the intractability of the problem did not. Into the 1980s there was no sign of an effective lasting settlement in Northern Ireland.

The I.R.A. attempting to sicken Britons of the Irish involvement, spread terror in the mainland. In 1974, 44 died in bomb blasts. 21 in crowded Birmingham pubs. Nine were killed in 1975 and one in 1976.[25]

Protest and violence in mainland Britain

Compared with the armed patrols, the almost daily horrors of Ulster, violence and protest in mainland Britain were limited. But in a free society, marches, demonstrations, protests were frequent.

Their frequency and volume had grown in the 1960s with student unrest in the Universities, marches by supporters of the Campaign for Nuclear Disarmament and vast gatherings, (50,000 around Grosvenor Square in 1968), to protest against American involvement in Vietnam. In the later 1960s and the 1970s there were clear signs that the demonstrations were becoming nastier.[26]

In June 1974, a man was killed at a political demonstration in
Red Lion Square, London – the first man to be killed since 1919
in such a demonstration in England, Wales or Scotland. The later
1970s saw further very ugly riots when opponents tried to break
up National Front marches and meetings. Again, at Southall in
1979 there was a tragic death. In a frightening episode in Bristol
in 1979, the police abandoned an area to rioters for some hours.

Violent events, (followed by much discussion of causes and by
apportionment of blame), were seen by millions on their
television screens and thus entered the homes of citizens on an
unprecedented scale.

Industrial unrest

Industrial unrest escalated in the 1970s: days lost in disputes,
under 4 million in 1955, were over 24 million in 1972, higher still
in 1979.

Strikes had major economic and social consequences: miners'
strikes such as that of 1974[27] wrecked pay policy and Mr. Heath's
chances of remaining in power, put miners back on top of the
industrial pay league and much raised the price of coal.

The February 1972 strike was accompanied by violent mass
picketing. 1972 also saw violence at a construction site at
Shrewsbury after which three men were sent to prison. In the
saddening "winter of discontent", 1978–79, much dislocation of
public services resulted from industrial action of hospital and
council workers. Throughout the decade, the car industry was
repeatedly disrupted, while among major strikes were those of
postmen in 1971, engineers in 1979, steel workers in early 1980.

Viewers could sit at home and watch the violent mass
picketing, as at a small London business, Grunwick, in 1977.

Governments tried to legislate for better industrial relations. In
the late 60s, Mr. Wilson abandoned an attempt to reform the
Unions – "In Place of Strife" – in face of opposition. Mr. Heath
did pass an Industrial Relations Bill to change laws relating to
unions, to picketing and so on. The attempt failed and Labour
enlarged power and immunities of unions. After 1979 Conservatives again legislated to reduce immunities and strength.

Unease

In 1979, 79 per cent of those questioned in a survey thought Britain a reasonably good place to live in, but 55 per cent thought things had got worse over the past decade.[28] Many letters to the media showed a sense of unease.

What seemed as advances to some was evidence of deterioration to others. Some welcomed, others were distressed by changes in the field of personal relationships, the family, expression.

In politics there was clear dissatisfaction with performance of the two main, leading to a rise of minority, parties.

Even the marked rise in living standards between 1950 and 1970 did not bring universal content.[29] Then, as already noted, the boom ended with resulting hardships of redundancies and business failures.

It could be maintained that the media stress the gloomy and ignore constructive and hopeful aspects of Britain's story. Decaying, inner city areas receive more attention than New Towns. Again, it was left to an American, Kingman Brewster, to call the Open University "the greatest single innovation in education in the Western World of the last four decades".[30] There is a tradition, noted by Orwell,[31] that British intellectuals should not be nationalistic.

This having been said, grounds for concern remained.

17.4   End of consensus

From 1940 to around 1970 main political parties and most Britons were broadly united in pursuit of central foreign, defence, economic and social policies.

In the 1970s this consensus evaporated. Keynesian policies no longer seemed appropriate. If more demand was pumped into an ailing economy, would not this fuel inflation and imports, feather-bed inefficient concerns and finance restrictive practice?

With the Conservative victory in 1979, monetarism considerably supplanted Keynesianism as the guiding economic philosophy. The key propositions of monetarism according to its highest exponent – Milton Friedman – were that "*inflation is always and everywhere a monetary phenomenon*"; that "there is a consistent though not precise relation between the rate of growth of the quantity of money and the rate of growth of nominal income (i.e. money income)".[32]

To monetarists, then, the most important variable in the economy is the money supply i.e. notes, coins, bank-deposits. Other economists do not agree that this is a realistic interpretation of a complex situation. Sir John Hicks held that: "the critical question is not a monetary question. . . The crucial question concerns the behaviour of wages; it is not a matter of the working of financial markets but of the labour market. . . It is cost inflation . . . which upsets the monetarists' case, creating a problem for which his prescription is quite inappropriate. . . Only by a combination of measures . . . could a solution be found".[33]

Many pointed to obvious consequences, in a period of recession, of making credit dearer and scarcer, to the inevitability of even higher unemployment and lower output.

Supporters of the monetarist emphasis credited their policies with some success in that by late 1980 the rate of inflation had fallen, a gain purchased in high cost in output, profit, jobs.

Like the preceding Labour administration, Conservatives after 1979 attempted to cut back public spending. Through the 1980s, public spending on a percentage of national income did decline. But cuts in particular sectors did rouse strong opposition. Evidence accumulated that the gap was growing between the affluent majority on the one hand and considerable minorities of relatively less well-off on the other.

It seemed clear after 1980 that the consensus of around 1940 to the 1970s was no longer here.

18. CONCLUSION

18.1 Limited scope of the work

An attempt has been made to chart economic and social evolution over the last century. The task is truly enormous. To add to existing masses of material, new books, articles, sources constantly appear. Thus, for example, in November 1986 "The Economic History Review" could list over 1,300 publications, published in 1985 alone, on the Economic and Social History of Britain and Ireland (by no means all of course dealt with the last century, but many did).

So drastic selection is inevitable and omissions grievous. In this work, important tributaries feeding main streams of development have been ignored. So practically nothing has been said on art, architecture, ballet, music, opera, the press, the theatre, and other topics. Another sad omission has been the failure to give due credit to that vast host of voluntary agencies which were so often the forerunners and later the helpmates of official bodies.

18.2 Continuity and change in modern Britain

Over the century covered in this work, Britain experienced much stability and continuity. Queen and Parliament, "The Times" and the Law Courts, Winchester Cathedral, T.U.C., country pubs and cottages were there in 1870 and remained in 1979, together with thousands of other structures, institutions, customs, recreations. In contrast to what happened in so many other countries, for three centuries since the 17th, Britain has avoided violent revolution, civil war and enemy occupation with hideous memories and divisions never to be laid to rest.

The case for stability

The powerful but much neglected case for tradition and stability has been thus stated: "As long as human beings need rules and categories and institutions and as long as they cannot create these for themselves just when the occasion arises and for that occasion only, they will cling to traditions. . . .

"The fact that certain beliefs, institutions and practices existed indicates that they served those who lived in accordance with them. . . . These traditions were not so crippling that human beings could not live under them. Nor did they prevent the human race from accomplishing great things".[1]

Constant, drastic change is perturbing and unsettling. It causes much unhappiness and worry, particularly to the old and the very young who need and relish stability, routine and the continuation of accepted customs and ways of life. The loud complaint of a baby being weaned is known to many!

Nor is there any certainty that change will bring clear improvement. Tower blocks of flats which replaced rows of houses in so many British cities, around the 1960s, were often centres of unhappiness, violence and vandalism, unsuitable for children, and so on. On a wider world stage, there are areas of the former British Empire, racked by civil strife and/or gross mismanagement, which were clearly better off under British rule, (admittedly it was inevitable and right that this should come to an end).

Practically all progress brings costs and disadvantages. Cars give mobility and enrichment of lives: they also bring death, injury and massive pollution. Radios inflict noise: television which, like radio brings entertainment and enlightenment may also waste a myriad hours. Computers help managers, researchers, shoppers: they can also put many out of work. The great increases in British farm output since 1940 (which have brought the amazing turn-round that a large importer of temperate foods in 1939, had some considerable export surpluses in the 1980s), have involved the destruction of miles of hedgerows and much wild life. One could go on for many pages!

That general conservatism was still a powerful factor in Britain was confirmed in the political sphere between 1979 and 1987, when the Conservatives won three consecutive general elections, (admittedly without gaining majorities of votes cast). In 1987, a main reason for their success was the undoubted fact that most – certainly not all – Britons had continued to improve their standard of living. Allied to this factor was another. People desire security and esteem for themselves and for their families. A clear method of gaining security is to acquire property – finance and/or real estate. Over the past century, since the days of Lord Salisbury, Conservatives have successfully garnered allegiances among increasing numbers moving into the propertied classes. By the 1980s, 60 per cent of British householders owned, or were buying, their dwellings.

But the need for change

So there has been much continuity and the case for reasonable stability is strong. On the other hand, there is very powerful evidence that Britain has suffered because of the retention of quite outworn and/or positively harmful institutions, customs, ways of thought. For example:

1. Until well into this century, in an industrialised, modernising society which needed all the trained talent it could muster if it was to remain in the top rank, Britain wasted the brains and abilities of huge segments of her youth. It was possible for a poor boy to reach the top. William Robertson enlisted as a trooper in the cavalry in 1877 and climbed to be Chief of the Imperial General Staff. But such cases were very rare exceptions, not common examples. Normally a boy in the Yorkshire coal-field, or a girl in Norfolk, went into pit or service, however bright they were. Robert Roberts's local school did not equip him to gain entrance to the local Technical College.[2] His sister was bright and of very good character, but a Grandmother regarded such qualities mostly as a guarantee that the girl would pass out of school at age 12 and enter the mill. A father unwilling to cut his heavy spending on beer was fully in agreement.[3] To strengthen the conservatism of wealthier rate-payers, there was much working-class opposition to extended education of the young.

2. Denial of opportunities to proceed beyond very elementary schooling was but one of many grievous handicaps suffered by

the majority of Britons until recent decades. While it is repeated that it was not a caste system, yet differences between those born in a manor and those born in a cottage were indefensibly great.

3.   Britain gained but also paid a terrible price for being the first to industrialise. Large industrial towns grew without conscious planning and necessary amenities. Public health provision was long lacking. Change was desperately needed in this huge sphere.

4.   Opposition to what now seem reasonable reforms, was often bitter, extreme, long successful. The very lengthy fight for women's emancipation proves the point. In particular, it is strange to read of the refusal of a Liberal Government to grant votes to women in those stormy pre-1914 years.

5.   Class cohesion – them versus us – vitiated much of industrial relations. In this late 20th century, Germans and Japanese have demonstrated the success of methods of co-operation and consensus. With that confidence in superiority which the British once had, Japanese have moved into factories in Britain's old industrial areas and – with physical jerks, uniforms, common canteens, plans and procedures discussed by all the staff – have attempted to teach the "backward nation" their ways.

6.   As has been stressed on previous pages in this work, with constantly increasing velocity and mass, modern science and technology have changed and are changing work, life-styles, administration, finance and so on. It is horribly difficult, but very necessary, for government, law, administration, social services, to attempt to rapidly adapt to changed circumstances. It is easy to say this, but sometimes whether and how to implement change perplexes. Should the Christian Churches change doctrines and practices held or followed for nearly two thousand years?

In Britain, there has been continuity and change. This is clearly seen in very many villages.[4] If a 1870 resident could return, he would probably see the same church, hall, pub, many of the same cottages, the village school, a number of great grandchildren of people he knew, and so on. But, there might no longer be a resident parson, the Hall could be a home for the elderly, older children and many residents would leave the village each morning, the road would be busy with cars, television aerials would top every cottage.

Examples of change

In previous chapters, reform and change have been described in detail. Here, a mere outline is given of some important changes, which, over the past century, have affected the British nation.

Loss of Empire and world power   In 1913, the British Empire included about a quarter of the World's surface. Britain was the leading naval power, main centre of finance, still a main manufacturing country. It was inevitable that this situation should change. The puzzling question is not why Britain lost an Empire, but how it came about that a small country off the coast of Europe ever came to dominate a quarter of the world. After 1919, Britain, faced with the rise of local nationalisms, no longer had the power to hold the Empire together.

A main mass of the British people were never vastly interested in the Empire and were not acutely concerned when it was dissolved. One fact is very clear. Since 1947, most Britons have enjoyed standards of life and welfare which were denied to the majority of previous generations in the days when a quarter of the world was coloured red on the map

Loss of industrial pre-eminence   In 1870 Britain was easily the main exporter of manufactured goods. By 1980, Britain's share of world exports of manufacturers was a mere 9.7 per cent, compared with Japan's around 15 per cent and Germany's nearly 20 per cent.

By 1985, the Japanese – despite, or perhaps because of – the total lack of an overseas Empire, through the application of modern technology, education, investment, consensus and hard work, had no less than 20 per cent of the world market for industrial exports, compared with Britain's 7.8 per cent.

Indeed, by the mid 1980s, a situation had arisen which would have seemed unbelievable to previous generations. Britain's imports of manufactures were worth more than her exports. North Sea oil and large invisible earnings from banking, insurance, returns on investments, tourism and so on helped pay for such imports.

However, it must be strongly stressed that world trade and that of Britain rose strongly in post 2nd World War decades. By 1985,

British exports were worth £78 billion.

Also, Britain has accumulated vast investments overseas. Much is made in the media of foreign acquisitions of British factories. In 1985 alone, while total overseas investment in the U.K. was £3619 million, U.K. private investment abroad was £14,585 million.[5] (Not all agree that is a good thing that funds which could provide modern factories for Merseyside go overseas).

The switch to a mainly service economy   Between 1971 and 1984, numbers employed in manufacturing fell by over 2½ million, nearly a third – a shattering reduction bringing much human upset. Service industries took on an extra 2 million between 1971 and 1979. By 1984, of 11.8 million males and 9.3 million females in employment, 6.2 million males and no less than 7.4 million females were in service industries and trades. Of 2.4 million self-employed, around 1.5 million were in services. Among reasons for the growth of service industries were the large growth of provision for holidays and leisure and the rise in numbers of overseas tourists coming to the U.K. By 1986 nearly 14 million foreign visitors were spending about £5 billion in Britain.

Social consequences of these vast economic switches were considerable. The typical British worker was ceasing to be a manual worker employed in field, pit or factory. By the 1980s, 40 per cent of male and well over half of female employees were non-manual workers.

Women at work   In Victorian villages and in heavy industrial areas such as the North-east, Clydeside or S. Wales, men went out to work – often to heavy manual labour – women stayed at home. Except in areas such as Lancashire cotton towns, it was relatively uncommon before 1939 for married women to go out to work. Indeed, very many women teachers, civil servants, (then including postal workers) had to resign on marriage.

By contrast, in 1976, 10 million women were employed, no less than 6.7 million were married. 61 per cent of married women in the age group 45–59 were economically active. But it is important to add that 41 per cent of working women in 1975 were part-time workers.

So very many women have won economic independence, though often at high cost in stress and strain. If their marriages are unsatisfactory they are easily ended. Obviously, couples where both are working enjoy a higher standard of living.

Again, social consequences of economic change have been great.

Rise in prices Very roughly, it took £20 in 1984 to buy what £1 would have bought in 1938. True, most people earning £3 a week in 1938 would have earned very much more in 1984. But not all were winners. Further, it must be repeated that if British prices rise faster than those of competitors, then, we, a trading nation, lose out. The pound has lost much of its exchange value: it was worth well over 4 dollars in 1914: about 1.6 dollars in mid 1987.

Demographic changes After 1870, birth and death-rates fell. Families became smaller. On average, people lived longer, and for the first time in history, a relatively large segment of the population of late 20th century advanced societies is aged over 60. Indeed, as average expectation of life steadily rises to about 80 years, clearly one quarter of the people will be aged 60–80.

In the U.K. in 1901, only 784,000 males and 1,025,000 females were aged over 65: by 1981, corresponding figures were 3,229,000 and 4,921,000.

So, for the first time in history, a relatively large army of the old has been retained. Economic and social consequences are vast. Pensions and health care cost more. The survival of many widows helped create the 1981 situation in Britain when of 19.4 million households, 4.2 million were of one person only, 6.2 million of 2 people.

Though it is sadly true that a significant percentage of the elderly do degenerate into tragic senility and/or are afflicted with crippling conditions, yet millions are now presented with opportunities to abandon work and, for around 20 years, to enjoy varying forms of leisure, to travel, to take up education, reading, painting and so on.

It may even be that the poverty of Britain's old has been exaggerated. An authoritative 1986 article[6] stated that in 1982, couples over pension age had an average of about £88 a week disposable income, single men had about £55, single women about £50. Admittedly, those solely dependent on the state retirement pension were hard done by, but 70 per cent of married couples aged 65–69 had occupational pensions. As often with averages, there was a wide spread. In 1982 the bottom fifth of married couples had £57 a week, the top fifth £152. Single women ranged from £32 for the bottom to £77 for the top fifth. It was asserted that, measured in real terms, pensioners' disposable income tripled between 1951 and the early 1980s. The article aroused some controversy.

Marriage and Divorce   Overwhelmingly, Britons still marry. In the late 1970s, 95 per cent of women and 91 per cent of men had been married by age 40. By 1976, 3 out of 10 marriages were re-marriages by one or both partners. In 1984 alone, there were 158,000 U.K. divorces. 72 per cent of decrees in England and Wales were granted to wives, often because of alleged unreasonable behaviour by the husband. Divorces in England and Wales in 1984 directly affected nearly 149,000 children, who often – for a period at least – became children of one-parent families.

Leisure   Over the century covered in this work, the length of the working day and week has been steadily reduced. By 1984, normal basic weekly hours of male employees were 38.2, of women 36.6 (in spite of heavy unemployment, manual men still worked an average 5.1 hours of overtime). By the 1980s, 4 or more weeks of paid holiday was very common.

Such conditions would have seemed incredibly ideal to 1870s employees with 10-hour days, Saturday morning work and no paid holidays.

On the other hand, considerable numbers in the 1980s did still continue to work for very long hours and/or in jobs involving great stress and strain.

Between the wars, cinema, radio, football matches and dance floors occupied much leisure time. Since the Second War, leisure has been increasingly dominated by television. Viewing figures are quite staggering. It is stated[7] that in the first two months of 1985, for example, average weekly time spent watching television in the U.K. was 26 hours by men, 31 hours by women. (Admittedly in August 1984, summer viewing was 9 hours less by men, 12 hours less by women). The old watch more than the young: less well-off classes more than the better-off. It may well be that for hours television sets are left on with no one watching with much attention, if at all. But vast correspondence to T.V. Channel authorities, responses to appeals and so on do demonstrate beyond doubt the hold of the riveting attractions for many of television.

Yet there is a truly vast spread of other leisure activities: going to sport or race meetings, DIY, gardening, drinking and eating out, going to the cinema, visiting great houses, fishing, pigeon racing, growing prize leeks and so on, and so on.

In 1984, it is reckoned that Britons took some 50 million holidays. No less than 16 million was spent abroad (over a third in Spain). Here is another vast post-2nd War development and change. Before 1939 only a relatively few rich went to the Mediterranean.

Religion It has been calculated that in 1980, about 7.4 million people in the U.K. (a sixth of the adult population) were Christians.[8] There were more Catholics than members of the Church of England. Compared with Victorian times, Christian churches have seen a great decrease in numbers and influence.

Another huge and growing change has been the very rapid growth in the numbers of those belonging to non-Christian religions: in 1980 there were 600,000 Moslems, 150,000 Sikhs and 120,000 Hindus. Again, the change from pre-1939 days is very great indeed.

Some are convinced that the decline in organised religion is a powerful factor partly accounting for the growth of crime, vandalism and anti-social behaviour in modern Britain.[9]

18.3 Some problems

An open economy subject to severe competition in a difficult world

In the relatively small United Kingdom live 56 million people. Britons can only continue to be an advanced nation with a high average standard of living if they can sell goods and services at home and abroad and import essential and additional goods and services. Competition is very severe: From other advanced economies, (which have often moved ahead of Britain in the application of modern technology, and in industrial organisation), and from newly industrialising economies such as Hong Kong, Taiwan, S. Korea, which, with their cheap labour, can undercut Britain in textile and other industries.

While advances are numerous and widespread, this modern world does not provide an easy course on which to run. The peoples of the 160 or so Sovereign states occupy a vast range on the stairway of development. There are nations which can put men into space and have enough weaponry to destroy mankind: other peoples live with such illiteracy, poverty, inequality, famine, corruption and maladministration that – to all intents and purposes – they might be societies of centuries ago. At least a dozen wars – great or small – are being waged at any one time. Utterly innocent people are taken hostage or blown up in pursuit of causes. Civil wars, changes of government, bankruptcy, can virtually close what were important markets.

Britain no longer has Empire and power to impose peace over large areas. It may well be that for too long after the Second War she retained a military presence in overseas areas when she no longer had the economic base essential to a world power. However, with each passing decade from 1946 to 1980, involvement, commitment and presence overseas were remorselessly curtailed.

Northern Ireland

Within the British state, in N. Ireland, a condition of controlled civil war has existed since 1969. A majority of Protestant "Loyalists" want to remain within the U.K.: a considerable minority clearly support those who are fighting to merge Ulster into the Irish Republic. In such situations a settlement means that someone wins and someone loses. Meanwhile, with increasing impatience and resigned irritation, many mainland British – angry at the continuing haemorrhage of blood, money, effort and reputation – increasingly long to get rid of a seemingly impossible problem.

Productivity

As has been stressed in previous pages, during this 20th century Britain's economy has grown at a slower rate and industrial productivity per worker has been lower than in other comparable countries. Here lies a root cause of relative economic decline.

Multiple problems resulting from technological change

In recent decades, automation and mechanisation have, with increasing momentum, continued to reduce demand for human labour. In spite of great expenditure on roads, more vehicles have brought greater congestion. Retail outlets have become larger, computerised, often situated near great urban centres, accessible by car. Rural areas, particularly in the South, have attracted commuters who have pushed up house prices well beyond the reach of locals, for whom few council houses were being built in the 1980s. Science has boosted farm output: combined with EEC pricing policy this has brought large surpluses or "mountains" of food products.

Such are but a few of the many problems generated by the continuing advances of science and technology.

Run-down areas

Since about 1970, the marked decline of traditional and other industries has left many areas with high unemployment and a blighted environment. Housing shortage and/or decay, crime and vandalism, have added to the problem of the "inner cities" – much publicised by the late 1980s. The plight of Merseyside and other similarly afflicted conurbations received much attention, but it was not only a problem of the inner cities but rather of all those towns and villages left behind as the majority of Britons marched on to greater prosperity. Political and technological changes played their part. Parts in the East and South coasts gained, for they were facing Europe and could easily handle containers, lorries, people going to the Continent. Liverpool lost out. Motorways around London and other cities took away traffic and trade from the centres, boosted areas on the peripheries.

Greater London, between 1971 and 1977, lost over 270,000 jobs in manufacturing industry – in engineering, paper, printing and publishing, timber, furniture and a whole host of enterprises.[10] Areas of Scotland, Wales, the North, Midlands were even harder hit and had not London's compensation of over

100,000 jobs (1971–1977) added to service employment.

This "inner city" problem was much bound up with unemployment and the presence of racial minorities – to which concerns we now turn.

Unemployment

From 1870 to 1914, there was considerable unemployment in the slumps, approaching full employment in the booms. From 1915–19 there was full employment. Between the Wars, unemployment was heavy and prolonged. From 1940 to about 1970, there were again low levels of worklessness. After about 1970, unemployment became a very serious problem, with over 3 million out of work by 1986–7.

Major causes of this high unemployment rate have been indicated. They are:

(a)   there was a serious world recession after 1973 which affected all W. European countries;

(b)   machines of all sorts, (and in particular in recent years, computers) have replaced humans;

(c)   Britain suffered worse than other industrial countries, because her industries were frequently less competitive, with marked overmanning in some;

(d)   After 1979, Government gave top priority to reducing inflation, not to maintaining full employment;

(e)   Temporarily high exchange values of a pound boosted by North Sea Oil production and, in particular, high interest rates made life hard for British manufacturers.

At terrible cost in jobs, firms and industries were harshly pruned. Fortunately, by 1987 there were signs that the worst was over. Unemployment was falling.

Ethnic minorities

While exact numbers of non-white people in the U.K. are not known, one set of figures shows that of Gt. Britain's 1985 population of 54.2 million, 51.2 million were white, nearly 2.4 million non-white, 637,000 "not stated".[11] Numbers of non-whites are growing rapidly. In 1985, births per thousand women aged 15–44 were 58 among mothers born in the U.K. 210 among others born in Bangladesh and Pakistan. However, birth-rates among women born in Caribbean or Asian countries have fallen considerably since 1971.

Is there a problem here? Those who hold that a human being's race is not a factor of significance do not think so. But the following factors need to be borne in mind.

(a)   Black people came to Britain to find better-paid work and a higher standard of living. Unfortunately, after about 1970, unemployment grew.

(b)   Immigrants much grouped together in inner cities, which have problems already mentioned.

(c)   Unfortunately, experience of other societies with white majorities and considerable non-white minorities, shows that difficulties do exist. They have so existed in the U.S. Even of favoured New Zealand, with only 3.3 million people (1986) in an area at least as large as the U.K., with no huge cities, with traditions of good race relations, outstanding Maori soldiers in the Second War, multi-racial Rugby, and so on, even there, we are told, Maoris are an underclass, who, for example, make up a quite disproportionately high fraction of the prison population. The country's "multi-racial future does not look entirely encouraging", is the pessimistic verdict given by one writer.[11a]

(d)   While organisations and individuals in the host society helped and welcomed immigrants, the latter were met with much hostility and alarm. There was some downright racial prejudice. There was, too, much fear that Britain's old society and ways of life were under threat. In 1968, Enoch Powell spoke out against immigration and forecast bloodshed. He received about 100,000 letters, less than a thousand opposed him. Most of the letter writers were not racialist, even using that over-worked term in a broad sense. Out of a sample of 3,347 letters, 1128 feared for British culture, 839 feared for British culture with a special emphasis on liberty, 204 pointed to the strain on the social services.[12]

(e)   There has been unpleasantness and far worse in the cities. Non-whites have been insulted and attacked. Many white Britons feel that their very valuable and now time-honoured right to much free speech is being curtailed. Escott,[13] in 1881, boasted that: "free play is allowed to every mind and to every tongue. . . . . To coerce the multitude is too often to consolidate sedition". Admittedly, here is a difficult issue. No-one could defend propaganda such as that put out by the Nazis against the Jews. But reasoned and reasonable comment about racial issues should surely be allowed.

(f)   Many West Indian children, in particular, have done badly in Britain's schools. Immigrants arriving in the 1960s sent children to schools affected by dramatic re-organisation, shortage of good teachers in still full-employment Britain, changes in approaches to discipline, much truancy and poor performance.

(g)   What kind of education should be given to non-white children in Britain? This problem is bound up with a major issue. What sort of society is Britain becoming – still British, or multi-cultured?

From the 17th to the 20th centuries, Britain absorbed large numbers of Huguenots from France, Jews from Eastern and Central Europe, Poles and others after the Second War, and Irish. There were shows of hostility and difficulties, but it can surely be claimed that these groups merged into British society in which many individuals from very poor backgrounds prospered. It is often very difficult to discover that a person's ancestors were French, Jewish, Irish and so on.

On the other hand, some Welsh, for example, have retained over many centuries their language and culture, plus a strong sense of nationalism.

Will the immigrants who came to Britain since 1945 and their children, merge into British society like the Jews or Irish? Informative articles on 17–19 August, 1987, in the "Times" pointed out that there were around a million Moslems in Britain. Would they merge into British society or would they increasingly isolate themselves in their own strong faith, educational system, customs?

Should the main emphasis of national and local policies be on creating one society based on British culture, or should a multi-cultured society be accepted? These are huge questions and should be frankly discussed in an atmosphere free from accusations of the all-embracing charge of "racism".

Surely, one simple fact ought to be clear. The English language is not only the main language of Britain but also the most important world language. It is, therefore most reasonable that English should be given over-riding priority in British educational institutions.

(h) Compared with very many societies in this imperfect world, Britain is free, democratic, open and tolerant. If people cannot live peacefully together here, it is not easy to see where they can. But realities of 1980s strife in the Punjab, Sri Lanka, S. Africa, Middle East, N. Ireland, even Fiji, plus memories of murderous riots in Britain's own inner cities, must banish complacency. Very much has been done but not all trends are uniformly helpful. In 1987 there were signs that self-chosen apartheid was coming to parts of England's school system.

Crime and disorder

Everything is relative. In 1987, a British teacher thus described[14] experiences of the Martin Luther King school in New York, where she was for a time a tutor. She entered through heavy steel doors, and was given a pass. There were no windows at ground level. Armed guards were stationed. During lessons classrooms were locked. She knocked on the re-inforced glass and collected two students who went for tutoring. Another person had to be in the room with her. (Yet, she obviously quite enjoyed the work).

No doubt, it can be a very different story in Maine, Minnesota or Oregon and it is certainly very different in Britain.

But statistics relating to crime, prison population, expenditure on law and order, (as has already been demonstrated in this work), have shown vast rises since 1946. In 1985, in England and Wales, notifiable offences recorded by the police included 871,000 cases of burglary, 539,000 cases of criminal damage, 121,000 cases of violence against the person, 21,000 sexual offences, 1,884,000 cases of theft and handling stolen goods. Between 1971 and 1985 numbers of recorded offences more than doubled, as they did in Scotland and N. Ireland. Very many cases are never reported.

Surely there is no need to emphasise that here is a problem.

The level of public spending

In 1984–5, public spending in the U.K. totalled £129.6 billion. A total working population of 27 million had to find the best part of £5,000 each per year to cover this spending. Argument as to how moneys should be raised can be brisk, as in 1987, when Government proposed to replace domestic rates in England and Wales by a community charge or poll tax.

Yet, the spending of vast sums has not, of course, stilled the voices of those many calling for more, often with excellent reasons. The Health Service costs more as expensive kidney machines, drugs, and so on, ease suffering and prolong life. Salaries of public sector workers go up. Defence equipment annually costs ever more astronomical sums, and so on. The annual Autumn battle to limit demands of spending Departments of Government has become a Downing Street ritual.

Some problems of the Welfare State

We have seen that the ground floor of the Welfare State was constructed in early 20th century years. Constant additions followed, with a spate of building occurring in 1945–51. Soon the main fabric will be at least half a century old, a long time in a rapidly changing modern world. Reasoned discussion of reform is needed. Costs of the vast enterprise have already received much attention. Another perennial problem, endemic in all states, is that posed by the large bureaucracy recruited to run the Welfare State. Very fallible human beings, even when engaged in caring activities such as social or medical work cannot be trusted without stringent checking to exercise the great powers which some modern legislation has given them for example in the case of deprived or assaulted children. 1987 witnessed a most disturbing enquiry in Middlesbrough where consultants and social workers had arranged the taking into care of a considerable number of children, alleged to be victims of sexual assault. Sufferings of families concerned were appalling. One was reminded of witch-hunts in 17th century Europe or Massachusetts. "The road to Hell is paved with good intentions". It is not disputed that assaults on children constitute a sickening national problem.

Trade Unions

From high points in numbers, power and influence in the late 1970s, Trade Unions suffered severe falls in membership and influence in the 1980s, as recession, drastic falls in numbers in old, unionised, heavy and manufacturing industry, and Conservative legislation, drastically slashed their numbers and power.

In this field, Britain has a long way to go to reach the position of the U.S.A. where under a fifth of the work force are in Unions, but there is a tendency for developments in advanced states to progress in a similar fashion. Rapid technological development means that those with the required skills in computers, or whatever, are in a very strong bargaining position and may not feel the need for a union.

However, in 1986, nearly 10 million working people were members of unions affiliated to the T.U.C. Unions and supporters clearly thought that much work was still needed to recruit and organise low-paid workers in for example catering. Problems, concerning the legislative framework within which unions and industrial relations operate remain and will continue.

Divisions within the nation

As already stated, most Britons are better off than they were, but some are not. The North has suffered more than the South in drastic economic upheavals so the division is often stated, in shorthand terms, to be the "North-South divide". In fact, practically all areas have some affluent, some poor people. There is still suffering and deprivation in an increasingly rich society: able people thrown on the economic scrap-heap at age 40 or younger through no fault of their own; old, feeble survivors in cold rooms; mentally or physically ill people whose conditions can still not be cured. The latest horror is, of course, Aids.

As societies advance economically and choices multiply so divisions occur. Some seek money, others learning or to help others. Some read widely, others never open a book. Some listen to classical music and watch serious plays, others prefer pop music and T.V. "comedies". There is an immense gap in attitudes, thinking and life-styles between, say, the average young Polytechnic lecturer and a Norfolk farmer or shopkeeper.

Sad divisions on racial grounds, which do exist, have already received mention.

From a now lengthy, depressing list of problems, which could be much extended, we now turn to happier themes.

18.4 Some advantages and advances

Improved standards of living

Compared to the vast majority of people in this poor world, most Britons are very well off. The total value of income-generating production of goods and services i.e. the Gross National Product, was £277.8 billion in 1984. True, this was considerably lower than the National income of W. Germany, for example, (equivalent to 546 billion dollars in 1985 against Britain's 401 billion), but it was vastly higher per head than that of most countries.

From 1856 to 1973 the average annual rate of growth of Britain's Gross National Product was 2 per cent.

Since the Second World War, growth has been relatively fast, though it much slowed around 1980. At 1980 prices, Gross Domestic Product rose from £148 billion in 1961 to 215 billion in 1973 – a growth rate of some 3 per cent a year. Between 1973 and 1984 growth slowed to around 1 per cent a year. Counting 1980 as 100, GDP rose from 48 in 1951 to 96 in 1976 to 110 in 1985. At 1980 prices, GDP per head rose from £2226 in 1951 to £4465 in 1985.[15] Very roughly, then, we can say that Britain was twice as well off in 1985 as in 1951.

Other facts give support to claims that material standards of living have greatly improved. For example, percentages of householders having the following were:

	1956	1985
Car	25	61
TV Set	40	98 (85 colour)
Video Set	–	26
Refrigerator	7	97
Washing Machine	19	82
Telephone	16	79

Growing popularity of foreign holidays, eating out, garden equipment, alcohol, provided further evidence of higher spending.

Housing

The U.K. housing stock totalled just over 14 million dwellings in 1951, nearly 22½ million in 1985. Owner occupation vastly increased: from just over 4 million in 1951 to nearly 14 million in 1985: an increase from 30 to 62 per cent of dwellings.

By 1984, 97 per cent of households in Gt. Britain had sole use of a bath or shower and 97 per cent sole use of a water closet. 61 per cent had central heating.[16]

Sadly, local authority housing bore much of the brunt of Government's drive after the late 1970s to cut public spending. New construction of council dwellings, which had averaged 152,000 a year from 1961–70, slumped to a mere 29,000 in 1985. Private sector completions were 154,000 in 1985 compared to 198,000 a year in the 1960s.

The statistics provide a complex, indeed contradictory, story. On the one hand, by 1980 the number of dwellings exceeded the numbers of households by nearly a million. (Sometimes reasons for houses standing empty were reasonable: as when the occupant died and it was unclear what was to happen to a property. Some people had second homes. Other reasons were less clear). On the other hand, there was a large problem of sheer homelessness. After the 1970s, Local Authorities were under an obligation to provide accommodation for the homeless, and in 1985 nearly 109,000 homeless households were accepted by local authorities in Britain.

Again, it is a picture of dire contrasts. There are in Britain, miles of suburban houses with their well-kept lawns. There are also towns like Bradford where for example, by 1987, most of the city's 55,000 Moslems "are packed into acres of Victorian homes and overflowing schools".[17]

Statistics relating to the whole country, however, make it clear that the number of dwellings relative to population has increased, and amenities within houses have vastly improved, over this century. Compared to most societies in the World, British households had small numbers: 3.09 in 1961 2.56 in 1985 were the averages. Over half of households in 1981 (i.e. over 10 million) consisted of one or two people. There is homelessness: there is, clearly, great under-utilisation of the existing housing stock. Purpose-built accommodation for the elderly is being provided and is much needed.

Better social services

Briefly, examples of improvement are here given: details abound on previous pages.

The Victorians relied on individual and family work, thrift, self-help, supplemented by the work-house or outdoor relief for the desperately poor and/or sick. (It is repeated that most people around the world in this late 20th century still do not have such institutions and benefits which have been so strongly criticised by some British historians and others).

Compensation for injured workmen was introduced at the end of the 19th century. Between 1905 and 1914, some poor schoolchildren were fed and all were medically examined and if necessary, received treatment. The very old were granted pensions. Sick manual workers received medical attention, under an insurance scheme. Some were insured against unemployment too.

Between the Wars, sickness and unemployment insurance schemes were vastly improved. Widows were granted pensions.

After the 1939–45 war, expensive additions were added to the Welfare State: the National Health Service, more comprehensive insurance cover for childbirth, sickness, unemployment, old age. In subsequent decades the handicapped gained much more aid. Numbers employed and spending on the social services increased dramatically after about 1950. Manpower in the social services (education, health welfare, social security) increased from 769,000 in 1931 to 1,188,000 in 1951, to 1,978,000 in 1971. Even between 1976 and 1983 totals employed in health and personal social services increased by nearly 13 per cent.[18]

It is obvious from many details given earlier in this work that British social services were vastly expanded over the century up to 1979.

Higher levels of educational attainment

In England and Wales, before 1870, children of the wealthy were educated at independent schools from which some went on to University. Children of the poor often received some schooling at voluntary schools maintained by the Churches. After 1870 Board schools, maintained from the rates, supplemented this work. By 1900, schooling was compulsory and all children aged 5 to 12 or 13 went to school. After 1902, secondary schooling for those who could pay and for a small but expanding number who won free places in competitive examinations, was expanded, as were the universities.

Between the wars, the school leaving age was 14, at which age the vast majority left school with no proper qualifications. A minority were often well educated at independent or state Grammar schools and at the universities.

Though not remarkably egalitarian or comprehensive,[19] the Scottish educational system did allow for more than the English to proceed from poor homes to higher education.

After the Second War, the school leaving age was raised first to 15, later to 16. Secondary education for all was provided, first in separate schools, later mainly in comprehensives.

By the 1980s, numbers staying on at school after 16, gaining qualifications, proceeding to higher education, have increased dramatically. Some detail has already been given. It may be added, for example, that by 1984–5, 15 per cent of boys and 14 per cent of girls leaving school had 2 or more "A" levels, or 3 or more Scottish "H" grades, 34 per cent of boys and 46 per cent of girl school leavers in England and Wales had reasonably good grades in "O" levels English or its equivalent. Sheffield University, to take but one example had around 800 students in 1938, 8,000 in 1980.

In spite of vast complaint, some advances are clear. Average class size as taught in English secondary schools in 1985 was 21.4, a figure which would have seemed truly Utopian to teachers in 1935, faced quite normally with 40, and often more, children.

Work

Shorter working weeks, longer holidays, sick pay, pensions on retirement, have been described. Machines now do much work formerly performed by humans. True, unemployment may result and people may feel that they have simply become additional parts to machines. Old craft labour with all its pride and associations has much disappeared.

But no-one need lament because no longer do workers have to toil for hours with aching backs and freezing hands lifting and trimming root crops in cold, wet, autumn fields. Digging out the foundations of a house now takes one man on a machine a day or two. Formerly a gang of men with picks and shovels worked for a week. Similar stories could be told of mines, docks, foundries and so on. There are costs, but no longer are workers so often utterly worn out by manual labour, (or indeed killed by industrial conditions), as was the case a century ago.

Improvement in women's lot

Women who have, or wish, to work had a far, far better chance of finding a job in 1980 than in 1880. Then a mere handful of women were at universities: in 1984–5 there were 137,613 at U.K. universities (in 1938–39 there were only 14,218). In 1938, only men read the News for the B.B.C.: in 1988 we take it for granted that women read much of the News and present many of the programmes on Radio and T.V.

Women who work at home are vastly helped by a battery of appliances. The washing machine in particular has cut out hours of unpleasant labour. Telephone, radio, T.V. have ended much of the isolation, and enriched many hours of domestic work. Some women, engaged in new technologies, for example, computer programming, can work at home. Others can and do study for Open University degrees.

The vast majority still marry. Those who do not wish to marry are not looked upon as having in a sense, failed, as was the case in Victorian times. If, while unmarried, they decide to have a child, few now heap censure on them. In earlier decades even of this century, they would not have been so spared. Women who decide their marriages have failed can and do obtain divorces.

Women decide when to start and finish child-bearing, an immense advance for millions.

Of course, problems and complaints persist. Britain had a

woman Prime Minister in the 1980s, but very few other Ministers and relatively few M.P.s were women. Top posts in a range of institutions and services were mainly held by men.

But contrasted with the situation a century ago, advances had been very great.

Leisure and entertainment

People have much more leisure, which, of course, they may or may not use reasonably. All must deplore the growth of heavy drinking, sheer vandalism, football hooliganism and so on. (It is little consolation to note that all advanced countries seem to suffer from similar trends).

Admittedly such activities are much concentrated in London or other towns but Britain does offer an immense range of cultural, artistic, entertainment and sporting activities: music, ballet, opera, drama, cinema, sports, athletics and so on. Millions fish, cycle, walk or run, race pigeons, etc.

British radio and television offer weekly an immense range of programmes. Some are fascinating and strongly educational, revealing the wild life of the Arctic or Amazon jungle, mysteries of outer space, new knowledge of genes, antibodies and diseases, the skill of surgeons revealed in films of operations. Coverage of news and current affairs is immense.

Apart from the usefulness of daily weather forecasts, watched or heard by millions, accompanying maps and information must educate.

True, most just wish to be entertained. Even if they watch such as "Dynasty", "Eastenders" or "Coronation Street" perhaps it is a better way to spend an evening than discussing the neighbour's latest annoyances, or waiting for Dad to come home from the pub, "activities" which may have once occupied the evenings of their grandparents.

Lessening of class differences

Class may well have still mattered in 1980 Britain: what is very clear is that it mattered far less than in 1880.

Aristocrats may continue to occupy stately homes, but often only at a cost of allowing visitors to come in droves and pay for that privilege. It is much easier for children of working class parents to climb into the middle classes, particularly up a far wider educational ladder. Service officers are selected after rigorous procedures: birth is not a deciding factor.

Drastic competition, bankruptcies, mergers have chastised firms into recruiting able executives irrespective of class. Amateurs and professionals no longer come out of separate entrances onto the playing fields at Lords – and so on.

Attitudes have changed. Before 1914, the Head of the Oxford college at which the then Prince of Wales resided was thus reported on by an undergraduate of the time: "I have never encountered a more blatant social snob. . . . . That the titled and untitled were regarded by him as sheep and goats I am quite certain".[20] Surely, a vanished outlook in such circles today!

Upward movement in a technological society continued through the 1970s and early 1980s. In 1972, 16 per cent of men of working class birth had moved up into the middle class: by 1983 the figure was 23.6 per cent. In 1972 61 per cent of those with working class parents were in working class jobs: by 1983, 52.6 per cent.[21]

Of course, it would be folly to deny the importance of good home and school, contacts, influence, money, which often, but by no means always still give some children, a start of several laps over others in the marathon of life.

Democracy, civil rights, and the rule of law

It has been very rightly stressed in this work that throughout the century covered, Britons have enjoyed much liberty and valuable civil rights.

In 1870, there was Parliamentary government, much freedom of speech and writing on political matters, freedom from arbitrary arrest in normal times, the right in serious cases to trial by jury.

These rights have continued, have been amplified and improved in important respects. In 1870 only a minority of men had the vote. In 1980, all men and women over 18 could register to vote. The government of the day could be replaced by the legalised Opposition if it lost the support of the people. Free elections, with a real choice of government, are an essential feature of democracy: opponents criticising a British government are not arrested and do not disappear. In serious cases, trial by jury is still the rule. Any voter, (except the old and others who can plead sufficient reason), may have to serve on a jury – a very important civic duty.

The powerful are not above the law, as they are in so many states. True, a rich man may hire the best lawyer he can. But the poor are entitled to legal aid. In England and Wales alone, in 1984–5, legal aid was given in 222,000 civil and 565,000 criminal cases. British police are still not normally armed and their conduct and actions are subject to strong legal constraints. There are not so many countries in this imperfect world in which policemen would be sent to prison for assaulting a citizen, as they can be in Britain.

Of course, there are imperfections and failings. Sometimes an innocent person is convicted. Much more frequently, the guilty are either not caught or are acquitted.

Longer life, better general health, less suffering

Life is our most important possession. Longer average life is the most important advance of the last century. Details were earlier given so only an outline is here necessary. For males born in 1841, in England and Wales, expectation of life was 40 years, for females 42 years. By the 1980s, the figures was 72 and 78 years respectively. Of every thousand deaths between 1848–72, in 146 cases tuberculosis was the cause. By 1981–5, t.b. was killing only one out of every thousand who died.[22] Typhoid and typhus, scarlet fever, diphtheria, and cholera, quite big killers in the 19th century, have ceased to appear as killers by the late 20th century. But it is repeated that the main cause of longer average life is the dramatic fall in the infant death rate. In 1841, about one baby in six never reached the age of one; by the 1980s, only about one in a hundred died in their first year.

Of course, problems remain. Longer lives mean more illnesses among the failing aged. Vastly increased numbers die of cancer and heart diseases. Terrible illnesses such as multiple sclerosis remain essentially unconquered. The rich are healthier than the poor. Much illness is still self-inflicted, caused by smoking, drinking alcohol to excess, eating the wrong foods.

But warnings are being heeded. 52 per cent of British males aged over 16 smoked cigarettes in 1972, 36 per cent in 1984. Corresponding figures for women were 41 and 32 per cent.

Very much suffering and incapacitation have been eased – for example, through modern dentistry, care and treatment of eyes, hip replacements, care of feet, hearing aids, apart from the wonders of spectacular surgery which can remove a patient's failed heart and replace it with a sound organ.

Higher standards of living, medical science, environmental and personal health services have brought about the fall in mortality and improvements in health which have made an outstanding contribution to the advancement of human welfare over the last century.

18.5 In conclusion

It is very right and our bounden duty to remember that the freedom and the advances so taken for granted by so many Britons in the 1980s were preserved at terrible cost.

A historian of the RAF Benevolent Fund tells how: "A Flying Officer had been killed in the First World War before he was able to marry the mother of his child. Between the wars the mother became a teacher, refusing to allow the father's family to educate her son. The boy went to college and was killed in 1940 during the Battle of Britain. . . . . . ."[23]

Lines on a Second World War memorial stone express it all:[24]

> "When you go home
> Tell them of us, and say,
> For your tomorrow
> We gave our today".

REFERENCES AND NOTES

(Words italicised in a quotation in these references are in italics in the original.)

Preface

1. G.M. Trevelyan, *English Social History*, Longmans, 1944, p. viii.
2. E. Shils, *Tradition*, Faber & Faber, 1981.
3. J. Harris, *William Beveridge A biography,* O.U.P., 1977, p. 2.

Chapter 1. History

1. D.S. Landes, *The unbound Prometheus*, C.U.P., 1969, pp. 554.
2. S. Pollard, *Peaceful conquest. The industrialisation of Europe 1760–1970*, O.U.P., 1981, Preface.
3. But in the 17th century around a quarter or third of English households contained servants normally living in as part of the family.
4. See P. Laslett, *The world we have lost*, Methuen, 2 ed. 1971 e.g. p. 86 and *Family life and illicit love in earlier generations*, C.U.P., 1977, e.g. pp. 61, 177, 218.
5. T.H.S. Escott, *Social transformations of the Victorian age. A survey of court and country*, first pub. 1897, Folcroft Library Editions, 1973, p. 403.
6. G.B.A.M. Finlayson, *The 7th Earl of Shaftesbury 1801–1885*, Eyre Methuen, 1981, e.g. p. 103.
7. Escott, op. cit., p. 401.
8. O. Chadwick, *Victorian miniature*, Hodder & Stoughton, 1960, and ed. H.B.J. Armstrong, *Armstrong's Norfolk Diary*, Hodder & Stoughton, 1963.
9. See E. Bédarida, *A social history of England*, 1851–1975, Methuen 1979, p. 147.
10. A. Macfarlane, *The origins of English individualism*, Blackwell, 1979, much stresses medieval origins of individual private property, etc.
11. 20th century Prime Minister Baldwin wrote of cousin Kipling: "We have common Puritan blood and he said a thing I have often acted on. When you have two courses open to you and you thoroughly dislike one of them, that

is the one you must choose, for it is sure to be the right one". A. Wilson, *The strange ride of Rudyard Kipling*, Secker & Warburg, 1977, p. 323. Reading of the Bible and of classics such as "Pilgrims Progress", was widespread into the 20th century. The Great War references to the "Slough of Despond" were frequent and apt. P. Fussell, *The Great War and modern memory*, O.U.P., 1977, p. 139. Baptists retained many Puritan traits. Into the 19th century, a Baptist family, the Whitakers, near Salisbury Plain, devoted time and energy to social work. Children of "the master" were taught in Sunday school by their father's employees, Marjorie Reeves, *Sheep bell and ploughshare*, Moonraker Press, 1978, p. 137. 20th century Akenfield Baptists held "the doctrine of Cromwell's saints" so considered – writer, R. Blythe, *Akenfield*, Penguin, 1972, p. 69. Clearly ramifications of Puritanism long remained enormous.

12. T.K. Derry and T.I. Williams, *A short history of technology*, O.U.P. 1960, pp. 112, 28, 139.

13. J. Morris, *Pax Britannica, the Climax of an Empire*, Faber & Faber,1968, p. 443.

14. J.B. Priestley, *English Journey*, pub. 1934, Penguin, 1977, p. 372.

15. F.M.L. Thompson, *English landed society in the 19th century*, Routledge & Kegan Paul, 1963, p. 25.

16. Thus, in 1763, rich Thomas Coutts married a servant of his brother and his wife was accepted in top circles. Edna Healey, *Lady Unknown. The Life of Angela Burdett-Coutts*, Sidgwick & Jackson, 1978, p. 22.

17. e.g. N. Nicolson, *Mary Curzon*, Weidenfeld & Nicolson, 1977, p. 87 shows care for his estate shown by Lord Scarsdale.

18. P. Thane in ed. R. Floud and D. McCloskey, *The economic history of Britain since 1700*, 2. C.U.P., 1981, p. 213.

19. e.g. E. Waugh, *Brideshead revisited*, Preface to 1960 edition. Penguin 1962, p. 8. Recalling 1944, Waugh wrote in 1960, "the English aristocracy has maintained its identity to a degree that then seemed impossible".

20. R. Williams, *The long revolution*, Chatto & Windus, 1961,pp. x–xi.

21. S. Johnson's *Journey to the Western Islands of Scotland*, ed. R.W. Chapman, O.U.P., 1970, p. 125.

22. K. Anderson, *Family structure in 19th century Lancashire*, C.U.P., 1971, p. 43. The description of Preston which follows is condensed from Anderson.

23. Ivy Pinchbeck, *Women workers and the Industrial Revolution, 1750–1850*, pub. 1930, Virago 1981, e.g. p. 311, et. seq.

24. e.g. F. Engels, *The condition of the working class in England*, pub. 1845, Granada 1969, with introduction by E. Hobsbawm.

25. E.P. Thompson, "Time, work-discipline and industrial captialism", in ed. M.W. Flinn and J.C. Small, *Essays in Social History*, O.U.P., 1974, p. 39. Attempts to impose time-keeping and discipline were by no means always successful. "Saint Monday" was widely taken as a holiday after weekend drinking. At a C.W.S. footwear factory in Leicester in 1874, 40 per cent of riveters were absent every Monday from March to June. W. Hamish Fraser, *The coming of the mass market*, 1850–1914, Macmillan, 1981, p. 78.

26. e.g. by J.L. and B. Hammond, *The Bleak Age*, etc.

27. J.M. Keynes, *Essays in Biography*, first pub. 1933, Mercury Books, 1961, p. 106.

28. Helen Forrester, *Twopence to cross the Mersey*, pub. 1974, Fontana/Collins, 1981, p. 168.

29. J. Saville, *Rural depopulation in England and Wales, 1851–1951*, Routledge & Kegan Paul, 1957, p. 5.

30. J. Foster, *Class struggle and the Industrial Revolution: early industrial capitalism in three English towns*, 1974, quoted in R.J. Morris, *Class and Class consciousness in the Industrial Revolution*, Macmillan, 1979, p. 36.

31. J. Caird, 1852, quoted Pollard, *op. cit.*, p. 32.

32. J.P. Kay, 1832, quoted Morris, *op. cit.*, p. 10.

33. N. McCord, *Free Trade*, David & Charles, 1970.

34. C.K. Harley and D.M. McCloskey in ed. Floud & McCloskey, *op. cit.* p. 61.

35. A.J. Imlah, *Economic elements of the Pax Britannica*, Russell & Russell, 1969, p. 191.

36. In million dollars worth, 1960 from U.K., 1,726 from Germany, in 1913. W.A. Lewis, *Growth and Fluctuations 1870–1913*, Allen & Unwin, 1978, p. 121.

37. Chadwick, *op. cit.* pp. 86–7.

38. Molly Izzard, *A heroine in her time. A life of Dame Helen Gwynne-Vaughan 1879–1967*, Macmillan 1969, p. 131. It is interesting to note that Dame Helen "All her life . . . . harboured a dislike of the mercantile ethos, which found its expression in a faintly contemptuous attitude towards business-men" (ibid., p. 44).

39. M.J. Wiener, *English culture and the decline of the industrial spirit, 1850–1980*, C.U.P., 1981, e.g. p. 9.

40. G. Orwell, "The Lion and the Unicorn" in *Collected Essays etc.*, 2 Penguin, 1970, pp. 75–6.

41. M. Bragg, *Speak for England*, Coronet 1978, p. 13.

Chapter 2. Land and people

1. See J. Hillaby, *Journey through Britain*, Paladin 1970. The author walked from Cornwall to Northern Scotland.

2. J. Clapham, *An Economic History of Modern Britain, Vol. 2*, C.U.P., 1952, p. 99.

3. *ibid.* p. 122.

4. ed. J.W. House, *The U.K. Space*, Weidenfeld & Nicolson, 2 ed. 1977, pp. 306–7.

5. *Bank of England Quarterly Bulletin*, Sept. 1979, pp. 283–4.

6. Guy Gibson, *Enemy Coast Ahead*, Pan, 1955, p. 246.

7. Nan Fairbrother, *New Lives, New Landscapes*, Penguin, 1972.

8. T.H.S. Escott, *England, its people, polity and pursuits*, Cassell, Petter, Culpin, 1881, p. 9.

9. *Kilvert's Diary*, ed. W. Plomer, Penguin, 1977, p. 127.

10. Ed. N. & J. Mackenzie, *The diary of Beatrice Webb, Vol. I*, 1873–1892, Virago, 1982, p. 43.
11. A.E. Dingle, "'The monster nuisance of all': Landowners, Alkali manufacturers and air pollution, 1824–64", *Ec. Hist. Review*, xxxv, 4, 1982, p. 529.
12. Ed. E. Royston Pike, *Human documents of the age of Forsytes*, Allen & Unwin, 1969, p. 238.
13. J.B. Priestley, *English Journey*, first pub. 1934, Penguin 1977, e.g. p. 316.
14. Only 24 of 74 people buried in Northants parishes of Deene and Deenethorpe, 1871–82, were 70 and over – *Parish Church Magazines 1871–82*, ed. R. Sismey, 1980.
15. In mid 19th century Preston, 47 per cent of children died before age five – "There is evidence . . . . parents usually grieved heavily. . . ." Anderson, *op. cit.*, pp. 34, 69.
16. R. Mitchison, *British population change since 1860*, Macmillan, 1977, p. 50.
17. Quoted in *On the State of the Public Health 1932*, H.M.S.O., 1933, p. 17.
18. R.C. Smith, *A study of present day scarlet fever in Darlington*, M.D. Thesis, University of Durham, 1934, p. 110.
19. e.g. in 1928, at Scunthorpe, a Medical Officer of Health wrote: "One is struck in many instances by the disgust and annoyance expressed by many mothers, especially those who have already several children, when they discover they are again pregnant" *Medical Officer*, 19.9.1928, p. 119.
    Many letters written to Marie Stopes in the 1920s clearly reveal the desperation of mothers anxious to avoid further births, ed. Ruth Hall, *Dear Dr. Stopes*, Penguin, 1981, e.g. p. 16.
20. F. Thompson, *Lark Rise to Candleford*, Penguin, 1973, p. 165. But, as often, evidence is mixed. In the mid 19th century it was said that in Durham, women farm workers usually saved for marriage rather than send much to parents. Anderson, *op. cit.*, p. 86.
21. B.R. Mitchell and P. Deane, *Abstract of British Historical Statistics*, C.U.P., 1961, p. 50.
22. ed. A.H. Halsey, *Trends in British Society since 1900*, Macmillan, 1972, p. 465.
23. Michison, *op. cit.*, p. 63.
24. B.B.C. Programme, *Scientifically speaking*, Radio 4, 10.7.79.

Chapter 3.   Some main strands of evolution 1870–1979

1. Landes, *op. cit.*, p. 331.
2. Quoted R. Rose and C. Peters, *Can government go bankrupt?*, Macmillan, 1978, p. 154.
3. N. Shute, *The Far Country*, Pan, 1967, p. 87.
4. R.C.O. Matthews, C.H. Feinstein, J.C. Odling-Smee, *British Economic Growth, 1856–1973*, O.U.P., 1982, p. 498.
5. *ibid.*, p. 70.
6. *Annual Report of Chief Inspector of Factories, 1931*, H.M.S.O., 1932, p. 52.

7. e.g. E.J. Mishan, *The Costs of Economic growth*, Penguin, 1969.

8. *Medical Officer*, 12.5.1928, p. 209.

9. P. Thompson, *The Edwardians*, Paladin, 1977, p. 322.

10. Newcastle-upon-Tyne, *School Medical Report, 1937*, p. 53.

11. ed. R. Floud and D. McCloskey, *Economic History of Britain since 1700*, vol. 2, *1860 to 1970s*, C.U.P., 1981, p. 388.

12. R. Gough, *The History of Myddle*, ed. D. Hey, Penguin, 1981, p. 24.

13. Of a sample of 70 inventions, mainly of the period 1900–50, over half came from independent inventors, ed. T.I. Williams, *A History of Technology*, VI.I, p. 34. Oxford 1978, (referring to J. Jewkes et al., *The sources of invention*, Macmillan, 2 ed. 1968).

14. Newcastle, *Health Report, 1938*, p. 108.

15. A. Maurois, *The life of Sir A. Fleming*, Penguin, 1963. Main credit for the production of penicillin as a life saving drug must go to H. Florey. See G. Macfarlane, *Howard Florey, The Making of a Great Scientist*, O.U.P., 1979.

16. In the 1930s a Sunderland surgeon recalled: "A woman about forty-five . . . . had a son . . . . whom she had never seen. . . The cataracts were successfully removed under the influence of cocaine, and she saw her boy for the first time". W. Robinson, *Centenary History of the Durham County and Sunderland Eye Infirmary*, 1936.

17. ed. Williams, op. cit., VII, II, p. 1299. A very early X-ray photograph of 1896–7 is reproduced on that page.

17a. Techniques of blood transfusions were much improved in the Great War. An American from Harvard showed how to avoid clotting. Lyn Macdonald, *The Roses of No Man's Land*, Michael Joseph, 1980, p. 95.

18. e.g. "George Potter was singularly productive in retirement. He remained remarkably fit and was able to catch up with much writing. . ." "Times" obituary of Prof. G.R. Potter, 21.5.1981.

19. A 1937 report on malnutrition listed 232 references, L.J. Harris, "The incidence and assessment of malnutrition", *Medical Officer*, 27.11.1937 to 18.12.1937.

20. ed. Williams, VI, I., pp. 298–99. Estimated numbers of horses in Britain: 1900 3.3m. 1924 1.9m of which 753,000 used in farming. 1950 number used in farming 347,000. After 1958 numbers used in farming were so small they were not recorded.

21. Advances in veterinary science are described in I. Pattison, *John McFadyean, Founder of Modern Veterinary Research*, J.A. Allen, 1981. In 1897 nearly all Queen Victoria's dairy cows were found to be tubercular, *ibid.*, p. 115.

22. ed. William op. cit., p. 676. Average height of women had been assumed to be 5 feet 6 inches, instead of correct 5 feet 3 inches.

23. ed. C. Singer et al., *A History of Technology*, v, O.U.P., 1958, p. 590.

24. ed. Williams, *op. cit.*, p. 551.

25. Landes, *op. cit.*, p. 265 and footnote.

26. ed. Singer et. al., *op. cit.*, p. 614.

27. ed. Williams, VI, *op. cit.*, p. 361.

28. ed. Singer, et. al., *op. cit.*, p. 676.

29. e.g. Clive Jenkins and B. Sharman, *The collapse of work*. Eyre Methuen, 1979.

30. D. Judd, *Radical Joe*, Hamish Hamilton, 1977, p. 10.

31. Bragg, *op. cit.*, p. 333.

32. ed. Singer et. al., *op. cit.*, p. 418.

33. quoted *Economic History Review*, 2 series, XXXII, I, 1979, p. 151.

34. R. Roberts, *The Classic Slum*, Penguin, 1973, p. 146.

35. L. Woolf, *Downhill all the way*, Hogarth Press, 1967, p. 178.

36. Jennie Lee, *This Great Journey*, Macgibbon & Kee, 1963, p. 105.

37. ed. Singer et al., *op. cit.*, p. 209.
At the very beginning of this 20th century, boys at Eton were rationed to one candle a week each, before gas was fitted. Julian Huxley, *Memories*, Allen & Unwin, 1970, p. 42.

38. Of interest in this matter is O.Y. Gasset, *The Revolt of the Masses*, Unwin 1961.

39. quoted W.H.B. Court, *A concise economic history of Britain*, C.U.P., 1965, pp. 175–76.

40. S.J. Prais, *The evolution of giant firms in Britain*, C.U.P., 1976, pp. 4, 8, 61.

41. F. Whellan & Co., *History, Topography and Directory of Northampton-shire*, Whittaker & Co., 1874, p. 196 et seq.

42. J.B. Jefferys, *Retail Trading in Britain 1840–1950*, C.U.P., 1954, p. 61.

43. ed. J. Burnett, *Useful Toil*, Allen Lane, 1974, p. 221.

44. Prais, *op. cit.*, p. 51 et. seq.

45. *History of the TUC, 1868–1968. A pictorial survey of a social revolution*, TUC, 1968, p. 12.

46. C.M. Trevelyan, *Grey of Fallodon*, Longmans, 1940, p. 176.

46a. "The lamps are going out all over Europe: we shall not see them lit again in our life time".

47. R. Dudley Baxter, *National Income. The United Kingdom*, Macmillan, 1868, p. 33.

48. D.A. Hamer, *John Morley, Liberal Intellectual in Politics*, O.U.P., 1968, p. 49. Morley emphasised "character". "Character alone is real" he thought, *ibid.*, p. 41.

49. T. Hardy, *Tess of the D'Urbervilles*, first pub. 1891, Macmillan, 1963, p. 450.

50. Whellan, *op. cit.*

51. Quoted in *Report of Royal Commission on the Distribution of the Industrial Population*, H.M.S.O., 1950, p. 11.

52. H. Perkin, *The origins of modern English society, 1780–1880*, Routledge & Kegan Paul, 1969, p. 117.

53. D.C. Marsh, *The changing social structure of England and Wales, 1871–1951*, Routledge & Kegan Paul, 1958, p. 94.

54. *Census*, England and Wales, 1921, County Durham, H.M.S.O.

55. ed. Halsey, *op. cit.*, p. 256.

56. ed. House, *op. cit.*, p. 192.

57. G.M. Young, *Victorian England. Portrait of an age*. O.U.P., 2 ed, 1953, p. 21.

58. From "Chant-Pagan" in *A choice of Kipling's verse* made by T.S. Eliot, Faber & Faber, 1963, p. 224.
59. J.K. Galbraith, *A Life in our Times*, Houghton Mifflin, 1981, p. 3.
60. Harold Owen, *Aftermath*, O.U.P., 1970, pp. 71–73.
61. Quoted by K. Middlemas, *Times*, 15.2.1980, p. 16.
62. Perkin, *op. cit.*, p. 402.
63. J.S. Mill, *On Liberty*, World Classics, O.U.P., 1948, p. 24.
64. Young *op. cit.*, p. 150.
65. e.g. S. Sturt, "The wheelwrights Shop" in ed. J. Burnett, *Useful Toil*, Allan Lane, 1974, p. 320.
66. Around the 1870s, a cavalry officer needed a private income of some £500–600 a year. R. Holmes, *The Little Field-Marshall, Sir John French*, Cape, 1981, p. 22.
67. Around 1970, 86 per cent of officers of the rank of Major-General and above had been to public schools (e.g. P. Abrams, *Work, Urbanisn and Inequality*, Weidenfeld & Nicolson, 1976, p. 213).
68. Cicely Hamilton, *Marriage as a trade*, first pub. 1909, Singing Tree Press, Detroit 1971, pp. 30–31.
69. Eva Figes, *Patriarchal attitudes, Women in society*, Faber & Faber, 1970, pp. 169–70.
70. C. Woodham-Smith, *Florence Nightingale*, Reprint Soc., 1952, p. 71.
71. V. Brittain, *Testament of Youth*, first pub. 1933, Fontana 1979, pp. 261–2.
72. C. Dickens, *Hard Times*, O.U.P., 1955, p. 23. On one Sunday in 1851, in Preston, probably not more than 20 per cent of the people went to Church. Anderson, *op. cit.*, p. 108. T.C. Smout, *A century of the Scottish people*, Collins, 1986, p. 201, describes the situation in Scotland.
73. Perkin *op. cit.*, p. 199. Henry James commented: "The most striking example, to foreign eyes, of the power of custom in England is certainly the universal church-going". H. James, *English Hours*, first pub. 1905, O.U.P., 1981, p. 70.
74. Perkin, *op. cit.*, p. 122.
75. One of the best-known of very large scale givers was Angela Burdett-Coutts. Healey, *op. cit.*, e.g. p. 162. Charles Gorden (later of Khartoum) did much to help the poor when he was stationed at Gravesend.
76. Young, *op. cit.*, p. 5.
77. R.C.K. Ensor, *England 1870–1914*, O.U.P., 1936, p. 139, footnote.
78. E. Gosse, *Father & Son* (ed. J. Hepburn), O.U.P., 1974 (First pub. 1907), pp. 132, 175 (see also A. Thwaite, *Edmund Gosse, A literary landscape*, 1849–1928, O.U.P., 1985).
79. Ensor, *op. cit.*, p. 308 (Ensor points out that the second count was far more thorough than the first, that the population had risen by half a million, so the relative fall in attendance was greater than bald figures suggest).
80. Marsh, *op. cit.*, p. 188.
81. Kilbert, *op. cit.*, p. 287.
82. J.W. Robertson Scott, *England's Green & Pleasant Land*, first pub. 1925, Penguin, 1949, p. 68.
83. R. Jefferies, *The Gamekeeper at home/The Amateur Poacher*, O.U.P., p. 48.
84. R. Browning 1812–89, *Saul*.

85. Young, *op. cit.*, p. 7.

86. *Ibid.*

87. Alfred Marshall quoted by J.H. Clapham, *Economic History of Modern Britain, III*, O.U.P., 1938, p. 416.

88. P. Larkin, 1914, quoted in P.Fussell, *The Great War, and Modern Memory*, O.U.P., 1975, p. 19.

89. E. Longford, *A pilgrimage of passion. The life of W.S. Blunt*, Granada, 1982.

90. In South Africa, Winston Churchill, surely no anti-imperialist: "Faced with the melancholy sight of the grey-stockinged feet of eighteen dead Highlanders waiting for burial . . . . found himself seized by a strange burst of anger . . . . 'scowling at the tall chimneys of the Rand' " quoted in T. Pakenham, *The Boer War*, Weidenfeld & Nicolson, 1979, p. 426.

91. G.D.H. Cole & R. Postgate, *The Common People, 1746–1946*, Methuen, 1961, p. 429.

92. J. Morris, *Pax Britannica. The climax of an Empire*, Faber & Faber, 1978, p. 219.

93. ed. Allen, *Plain Tales from the Raj*, Deutsch and B.B.C., 1975, p. 216.

94. Morris, *op. cit.*, p. 212.

95. Quoted Wilson, *op. cit.*, p. 81.

96. Roberts, *The Classic Slum*, op. cit., p. 143.

97. E.J. Hobsbawm, *Labouring Men*, Weidenfeld & Nicolson, 1968, p. 231.

98. *Ibid.*, p. 250.

99. *Ibid.*, p. 255.

100. Ed. N. & J. Mackenzie, *The diary of Beatrice Webb, Vol. 1, 1873–1892*, Virago, 1982, p. 326.

101. Kay Carmichael, "Hearts and minds: The lesson of the I.I.P.", *New Society*, 27–9–79, p. 64. The missionary zeal of early Socialists is well described in L. Thompson, *The Enthusiasts. A biography of John and Katharine Bruce Glasier*, Gollancz, 1971.
    "These people are early Christians" was the apt comment of an American lady, *ibid.*, p. 160. Glasier was strongly anti-Marx and denounced class war dogma, *ibid.*, pp. 90, 190.

102. E. Shinwell, (later Labour Cabinet Minister), said Blatchford "exercised more influence on my political outlook than any other". Manny Shinwell, *Lead with the Left*, Cassell, 1981, p. 34.
    Clement Attlee, (Labour Prime Minister, 1945–51) read Carlisle, Ruskin, and William Morris, (K. Harris, *Attlee*, Weidenfeld and Nicolson, 1982, p. 20, et seq.).

103. Clapham II, *op. cit.*, p. 482. Shinwell's recollection was that in Labour's early years "Karl Marx was rarely mentioned", *op. cit.*, p. 77.

104. Roy Jenkins, *Asquith*, Fontana, 1967, p. 18.

105. Roberts, *The Classic Slum*, *op. cit.*, p. 45.

106. Quoted in P. O'Brien and C. Keyder, *Economic Growth in Britain and France, 1780–1914*, Allen and Unwin, 1978, p. 186.

107. J.S. Mill, *On Liberty*, first pub. 1859, World's Classics, O.U.P., 1948, pp. 85–7.

108. T. Hardy, *Jude the Obscure*, first pub. 1896, Pan, 1978, p. 10.

109. R. Aldington, *Portrait of a genius but. . . .* , Readers' Union/Heinemann, 1951, e.g. pp. 172–3.
110. Kilvert, *op. cit.*, p. 17.
111. J. Motgomery, *Toll for the brave. The tragedy of Major-General Sir Hector Macdonald*, Max Parrish, 1963.
112   The list could be very long, but among fascinating pre-1914 experiences were: while at college, George Gissing stole to help a prostitute. After two disastrous marriages he lived with a Frenchwoman. Katherine Mansfield left her first husband on the evening of her wedding day. She had lovers, then went to live with Middleton Murry, whom she later married. A. Alpers, *The life of Katherine Mansfield*, O.U.P., 1982.
      J. Halperin, *Gissing, A life in books*, O.U.P., 1982. The sexual life styles of Edward VII, Lloyd George, H.G. Wells, W.S. Blunt, and others are well known. They did not conform to Victorian precepts.
113. Catherine Cookson, *Our Kate*, Macdonald, 1969, p. 15 et seq. "The cruelty of the bigoted poor has to be witnessed to be believed".
114. Poem by Emily Dickinson, quoted by Margaret Drabble, *The Middle Ground*, Weidenfeld & Nicolson, 1980, p. 223.

Chapter 5.   The economy

1. M. Blaug, *Economic theory in retrospect*, Heinemann, 1964, p. 57. See also F. Hahn, "Reflections on the invisible hand", in *Lloyds Bank Review*, Apr. 1982.
2. Whellan & Co., *History etc., of Northamptonshire, op. cit.*, p. 196.
3. Chapham II, *op. cit.*, p. 300 et seq.
4. Phyllis Deane, review of R. Church, *The dyanamics of Victorian business. Problems and perspectives to the 1870s*, Allen & Unwin 1980, in *Economic History Review*, Feb. 1981, p. 159.
5. P.Thane in ed. Floud & McCloskey, *op. cit.*, p. 222.
6. J.M. Keynes, *Essays in Persuasion*, Macmillan, 1931, p. 84.
7. T.S. Ashton, *Iron & steel in the Industrial Revolution*, Manchester Univ. Press, 3 ed., 1963, p. 159.
8. J. Burnett, *History of the cost of living*, Penguin, 1968, p. 198.
9. G. Huxley, *Both Hands. An autobiography*, Chatto & Windus, 1970, p. 9.
10. J.M. Keynes, *The Economic consequences of the Peace*, 1919, quoted F. Bedarida, *Social History of England, 1851–1975*, Methuen, 1979, p. 148.
11. Thane in ed. Floud & McCloskey, *op. cit.*, p. 215.
12. Mrs. Pember Reeves, *Round about a pound a week*, Bell, 2 ed., 1914.
13. A.G. Ford in ed. Floud & McCloskey, *op. cit.*, p. 31.
14. Thompson, *Lark Rise to Candleford, op. cit.*, p. 51.
15. G. Sturt, quoted in Burnett, *Useful Toil, op: cit.*, p. 326.
16. A house steward in Burnett, *op. cit.*, p. 192.
17. Roberts, *The Classic Slum, op. cit.*, p. 123.
18. Clapham II, *op. cit.*, p. 112.
19. A.W. Seton-Watson et al., *The war and democracy*, Macmillan, 1914, p. 313 (footnote).

20. J. Camplin, *The rise of the plutocrats*, Constable, 1978, p. 41.
21. E.J. Hobsbawm, *Industry and Empire*, Penguin, 1969, p. 56.
22. Landes, *op. cit.*, p. 215.
23. *ibid.*
24. P. Deane and W.A. Cole, *British Economic Growth, 1688–1959*, C.U.P., 2 ed., 1967, p. 216.
25. A.J. Taylor, in ed. D.H. Aldcroft, *The development of British Industry and Foreign Competition 1875–1914*, Allen & Unwin, 1969, p. 48.
26. Landes, *op. cit.*, p. 219.
27. T.H. Burnham and S.O. Hoskins, *Iron and Steel in Britain, 1870–1930*, Allen & Unwin, 1943, pp. 26–7.
28. C.P. Snow, quoted in ed. Aldcroft, *op. cit.*, p. 191.
29. *ibid.*
30. H.J. Habbakuk, *American and British Technology in the 19th century*, C.U.P., 1962, p. 151.
31. See ed. Aldcroft *op. cit.,*, pp. 223–4, 215, 200 for material in this and preceding paragraphs.
32. S. Pollard and P. Robertson, *The British Shipbuilding Industry, 1870–1914*, Harvard Univ. Press, 1979, pp. 9, 7.
33. About 1900, £100,000 was offered to Cambridge to establish a naval architecture school, but the offer was withdrawn when it was learned that students would have to qualify in Greek. *ibid.*, p. 144.
34. *ibid.*, . 146.
35. *ibid.*, . 167.
36. *ibid.*, pp. 218–19.
37. *ibid.*, p. 25.
38. D. Dougan, *The History of North-East Shipbuilding*, Allen & Unwin, 1968, p. 221.
39. Pollard & Robertson, *op. cit.*, p. 44.
40. *ibid.*, pp. 239-40.
41. ed. Singer, *op. cit.*, p. 386.
42. *ibid.*, p. 381.
43. Pollard and Robertson, *op. cit.*, p. 127.
44. *ibid.*, p. 81.
45. *ibid.*, p. 188.
46. Clapham II, *op. cit.*, pp. 86–7.
47. G.C. Allen, *The Industrial Development of Birmingham and the Black Country*, Cass & Co., 1966.
48. F. Whellan & Co., *History etc. of Northamptonshire*, *op. cit.*, p. 126.
49. Clapham II, *op. cit.*, p. 182.
50. Quoted in ed. Aldcroft, *op. cit.*, p. 183.
51. T.C. Barker in ed. Aldcroft, *op. cit.*, p. 322.
52. Landes, *op. cit.*, 1109.
53. This paragraph owes much to H.W. Richardson in ed. Aldcroft *op. cit.*, p. 278, et. seq.
54. I.C.R. Byatt in ed. Aldcroft, *op. cit.*, p. 238, et seq.
55. P. Deane & W.A. Cole, *British Economic Growth, 1688–1959*, C.U.P. 2 ed., 1967, p. 210.

56. *Census*, England and Wales, 1911, p. lxxxv.
57. *ibid.*, p. cxiii.
58. Marsh, *op. cit.*, p. 128.
59. Mitchell & Deane, *op. cit.*, p. 60.
60. Matthews et al., *op. cit.*, p. 28.
61. Deane & Cole, *op. cit.*, p. 329.
62. W.J. Ashley, *Introduction to Year Book of Social Progress for 1913–14*, Nelson, p. 9.
63. Mitchell & Deane, *op. cit.*, p. 60.
64. Deane & Cole, *op. cit.*, p. 166.
65. F.M.L. Thompson, *English Landed Society*, *op. cit.*, p. 27.
66. *ibid.*, pp. 32, 113.
67. R. Perron in ed. P.J. Perry, *British Agriculture 1875–1914*, Methuen, 1973, p. 118.
68. Thompson, *op. cit.*, pp. 322 and 322.
69. Clapham II, *op. cit.*, p. 264.
70. J.M. Keynes, *The General Theory of Employment, Interest and Money*, Macmillan 1936, p. 383.
71. 2nd Parliamentary Reform Bill, 1867.
72. G.M. Trevelyan, *British History in the 19th Century and after*, Longmans, 1937, p. 348.
73. Ensor, *op. cit.*, pp. 115, and 284.
74. ed. Perry, *op. cit.*, p. xviii. Tennyson wrote of midnight, 30th June, 1879: "Midnight and joyless June gone by,/And from the deluged park/The cuckoo of a worse July,/Is calling thro' the dark".
75. Reeves, *Sheep Bell and Ploughshare, op. cit.*, p. 70.
76. S. Saul, *The Myth of the Great Depression 1873–1896*, Macmillan 1969, pp. 22–3.
77. Reeves, *op. cit.*, p. 70.
78. ed. Perry, *op. cit.*, p. 54.
79. Clapham II, *op. cit.*, p. 283.
80. ed. Perry, *op. cit.*, p. 113.
81. M. Olsen and C. Harris in ed. Perry, *op. cit.*, p. 175.
82. ed. Perry, *op. cit.*, p. 90.
83. T.W. Fletcher, "Lancashire Livestock Farming during the Great Depression" in ed. Perry *op. cit.*, p. 97.
84. Clapham II, *op. cit.*, p. 289. The hard life of the farm labourer, even in the early 20th century, is well portrayed in Fred Kitchen, *Brother to the Ox*, Penguin, 1983, p. 37, et seq.
85. C. O'Grada, in ed. Floud & McCloskey, *op. cit.*, p. 183 et seq.
86. ed. Burnett, *Useful Toil*, *op. cit.*, p. 65.
87. Quoted Clapham III, *op. cit.*, p. 114.
88. Quoted Perkin, *op. cit.*, p. 124.
89. Burnett, *Useful Toil*, *op. cit.*, p. 139.
90. "Edinburgh Review", 1862, quoted Burnett, *Useful Toil*, *op. cit.*, p. 167.
91. Thompson, *English Landed Society*, *op. cit.*, p. 188.
92. But, because they could recruit reliable servants Victorian academics, writers, and others were freed from domestic chores.

93. Burnett, *op. cit.*, p. 185, et seq.
94. *ibid.*, p. 168 (quoting "Edinburgh Review", 1862).
95. Clapham II, *op. cit.*, p. 180.
96. *ibid.*, p. 81.
97. R. Dudley Baxter in ed. Carus Wilson, *Essays in Econ. History 3*, Arnold, 1962, p. 36.
98. e.g. S. Butler, *The way of all Flesh*, first pub. 1903, Penguin, 1947, p. 318.
99. Clapham II, *op. cit.*, p 201.
100. Clapham II, p. 207.
101. F. Thompson, *op. cit.*, p. 301.
102. Clapham III, *op. cit.*, p. 374.
103. *ibid.*, p. 377. Quoting S. Webb.
104. Quoted by H. Hamilton, *History of the Homeland*, Allen & Unwin, 1947, p. 357.
105. e.g. R. Jenkins, *Asquith*, Fontana, 1967.
106. F. Thompson, *op. cit.*, pp. 411 & 405.
107. As did the 1910 arrest of the murderer, Dr. Crippen, following much publicised wireless contact over the Atlantic.
108. Quoted Clapham II, p. 521.
109. Mitchell & Deane, *op. cit.*, p. 60.
110. The following account owes much to D.B. Jefferys, *Retail Trading in Britain, 1850–1950*, and W. Hamish Fraser, *op. cit.*
111. F. Whellan & Co., *History etc. of Northants*, *op. cit.*, p. 703.
112. Saville, *op. cit.*, p. 74.
113. Burnett, *Useful Toil*, *op. cit.*, p. 67.
114. Roberts, *op. cit.*
115. Jefferys, *op. cit.*, p. 9.
116. *ibid.*, p. 16.
117. Clapham III, *op. cit.*, pp. 244–5.
118. Jefferys, *op. cit.*, pp. 18–19.
119. B. Harrison, *Drink and the Victorians*, Faber & Faber, 1971, p. 311.
120. Ensor, *op. cit.*, p. 409.
121. Harrison, *op. cit..*, p. 311.
122. Clapham, III, *op. cit.*, p. 258.
123. Autobiographies, such as John Buchan's mention the importance for career advancement of being admitted to clubs.
124. Often entry qualifications limited recruitment to the wealthy. Thus a premium of up to £500 and unpaid work for five years were often required from aspiring solicitors.
125. G. Routh, *Occupation and pay in Gt. Britain*, 1906–60, C.U.P., 1965, p. 15.
126. B. Abel-Smith, *A History of the Nursing Profession*, Heinemann, 1960, p. 57.
127. Newcastle-upon-Tyne, *Health Report, 1887*. Appendix F.
128. H.C. Burdett, *Hospitals and Asylums of the World*, Churchill, 1893, VI.3, p. 332.
129. Sunderland, *Health Report*, 1930, p. 105.
130. Clapham II, *op. cit.*, p. 335.

131. Camplin, *op. cit.*, p. 64.
132. B.B. Gilbert, *The Evolution of National Insurance in Gt. Britain*, Michael Joseph, 1966, p. 319.
133. Reproduced in E. Royston Pike, *Human Documents of the Age of the Forsytes*, Allen & Unwin, 1969, p. 100, et seq.
134. W. Scholte, *British overseas Trade from 1700 to 1930s*. Basil Blackwell, 1952, p. 42.
135. A.H. Imlah, *Economic Elements in the Pax Britannica*, Russell & Russell, 1969, p. 94, et. seq.
136. *ibid*, p. 167.
137. Clapham II, *op. cit.*, p. 229.
138. Scholte, *op. cit.*, p. 80.
139. Clapham III, *op. cit.*, p. 50.
140. Scholte, *op. cit.*, p. 102,. et seq.
141. M. Edelstein in ed. Floud and McCloskey, *op. cit.*, p. 70.
142. *ibid.*, pp. 80 and 78.
143. H. Trevelyan, *Public and Private*, Hamish Hamilton, 1980, p. 3.
144. J. Hadfield, *The cotton export industry of Northern Nigeria*, unpublished MA Thesis, Sheffield University, 1971.
145. W.A. Lewis, *The theory of Economic Growth*, Allen & Unwin, 1955, pp. 412–13.
146. Pat Barr, *The Memsahibs*, Secker & Warburg, 1976, p. 161, et seq.
147. Clapham II, *op. cit.*, p. 250.
148. P. Kennedy, *The Rise of Anglo-German Antagonism, 1860–1914*, Allen & Unwin, 1980, p. 49.
149. Matthews, et al., *op. cit.*, p. 28.
150. *ibid.*, p. 277.
151. E.J. Phelps Brown and S.J. Handfield-Jones, "The climacteric of the 1890s: a study in the expanding economy", *Oxford Economic Papers*, 4, 1952, p. 266.
152. ed. Aldcroft, *op. cit.*, p 46.
153. Landes, *op. cit.*, p. 326.
154. Burnham and Hoskins, *op. cit.*, pp. 26–28.
155. Kennedy, *op. cit..*, p. 291.
156. D. Burn, *The Economic History of Steelmaking, 1867–1939*, C.U.P., 1961, p. 3.
157. e.g. D.M. McCloskey, *Essays on a mature economy: Britain after 1840*, Methuen 1971, p. 5. See also P.L. Payne, *British Entrepreneurship in the 19th century*, Macmillan, 1974, p. 11, et seq.
158. Charlotte Erickson, *British Industrialists: Steel and Hosiery 1850–1950*, C.U.P., 1959, pp. 12, 93.
159. H.J. Habbakuk, *American and British Technology in the 19th Century*, C.U.P. 1967, p. 216.
160. Hobsbawn, *Labouring Men, op. cit.*, p. 166.
161. Quoted ed. Aldcroft, *op. cit.*, p. 57.

Chapter 6.   Society

1. Roberts, *The Classic Slum*, *op. cit.*, p. 53.
    Of one of her sisters, Beatrice Potter wrote: "She never made a friend,
    except within her own family. . . . There is no sacrifice Margaret would not
    make for her husband and children – no effort she would grudge for her
    family. . . . 'The Family' is to her the only 'holy thing', all individual and
    all social life should be based on it". ed. MacKenzie, *op. cit.*, p. 59.
2. M. Spring Rice, *Working-class wives*, pub. 1969, Virago, 1981, p. 15

3. V.V. Ovchinnikov, *Britain observed. A Russian view*, Pergamon, 1981,
    pp. 9, 28.
4. Roberts, *op. cit.*, p. 24.
5. Reproduced e.g. ed. M. Vicinus, *Suffer and be still. Women in the Victorian
    Age*, pub. 1972, Methuen, 1980, p. 64.
6. ed. M. Vicinus, *A widening sphere*, pub. 1977, Methuen, 1980, p. XVI.
7. P. Branca, *Silent Sisterhood*, Croom Helm, 1975, p. 3.
8. Cicely Hamilton, *Marriage as a trade*, pub. 1909, Singing Tree Press,
    Detroit, 1971, p. 36.
9. Kilvert, *op. cit.*, p. 27.
10. Rebecca West (quoted *Listener*, 25.2.82).
11. Hamilton, *op. cit.*, p. 235, et seq.
12. S. Butler, *The way of all flesh*, pub. 1903, Penguin, 1947, p. 298.
13. Quoted Eva Figes, *op. cit.*, p. 158. The Victorian was indeed a privileged
    age for many husbands. Questions which Lady Catharine Boileau put to
    herself each day included: "Have I been dutiful and affectionate towards
    my dear husband this day? Have I submitted with a *cheerful humility* when
    he has thought fit to reprove me. . . ?" Chadwick, *op. cit.*, p. 68.
    But mothers of some well-known suffragettes dominated their homes.
    Hannah Webster's mother "ruled the roost": father and children fled the
    house when she went into her rages. Annie Kenney's mother was also
    clearly head of the household. A. Rosen, *Rise up women!*, Routledge &
    Kegan Paul, 1974, pp. 40–42 and *The Hard Way Up. The autobiography of
    Hannah Mitchell, Suffragette and Rebel*, ed. G. Mitchell, Faber and Faber,
    1968, p. 40, et. seq.
14. M. Allen and M. Nicholson, *Memories of an uneducated lady*, Thames and
    Hudson, 1975, p. 7.
15. Ensor, *op. cit.*, p. 170. But "one makes rash generalisations about the
    Victorians and sex at one's peril". R. Pearsall, *The Worm in the Bud*,
    Penguin, 1981, p. 22.
16. A.J. Clough, quoted Ensor, *op. cit.*, pp. 138–9.
17. H. Trevor-Roper, *A hidden life. The enigma of Sir Edmund Backhouse*,
    Macmillan, 1976, e.g. pp. 17, et seq., 279.
18. Kilvert, *op. cit.*, pp. 132, 141, 270.
19. Roberts, *The Classic Slum*, *op. cit.*, pp. 45, 51.
20. Quoted, Thompson, *The Edwardians*, *op. cit.*, p. 66.
21. *ibid*. Victorian children could be difficult, e.g. Julian Huxley, *Memories*,
    Allen & Unwin, 1970, pp. 22–3.

22. A massive number of references make it clear that corporal punishment in British schools was extremely common.
23. Allen & Nicholson, *op. cit.*, p. 37, et seq.
24. Thompson, *Lark Rise*, *op. cit.*, p. 142.
25. Roberts, *The Classic Slum*, *op. cit.*, p. 153.
26. W. Somerset Maughan, *Of Human Bondage*, pub. 1915, Penguin, 1963, p. 37.
27. Roberts, *The Classic Slum*, *op. cit.*, p. 161.
28. M. Blanch, "Imperialism, nationalism and organised youth", in ed. J. Clarke et al., *Working Class culture*, Hutchinson, 1979, p. 103.
29. He had been much impressed by his Commanding Officer in India, in the late 1870s, who had fostered "regard for and development of the human side and the individuality of the men themselves. Thus when we paraded for a field-day we generally did so at a rendezvous some two or three miles from barracks, and each man made his own way to the spot individually. . . ." (Sir R. Baden-Powell, *Indian Memories*, H. Jenkins, 1915, p. 26). How dangerous is generalisation! We usually portray the pre-Boer War army as stifling individuality.
30. P. Wild, "Recreation in Rochdale, 1900–40" in ed. Clarke et al., *op. cit.*. p. 141, describes the continuing strength of religion.
31. A.A. Thomson, *When I was a lad*, Epworth Press, 1964, p. 56.
32. Malcolm Muggeridge, *Chronicles of Wasted Time, Part 1, The Green Stick*, Fontana/Collins, 1975, p. 73.
33. Thomson, *op. cit.*, pp. 33, 58.
34. J.B. Priestley, *Instead of the Trees*, Heinemann, 1977, p. 61.
35. e.g. a photograph of Birmingham boys (1895) in I. Taylor, *The Edwardian Lady, The story of Edith Holden*, Michael Joseph/Webb & Bower, 1980, p. 15. (Edith Holden's father and others attempted to help such children).
36. Ivy Pinchbeck, *Women workers and the Industrial Revolution 1750–1850*, pub. 1930, Virago, 1981, pp. 4, 311.
37. Patricia Hollis, *Women in public 1850–1900*, Allen & Unwin, 1979, p. 53.
37a. Christine Walkley, *The Ghost in the Looking Glass. The Victorian Seamstress*, Peter Owen 1981, p. 36, et seq., 127 and 129.
38. Hollis, *op. cit.*, p. 59. (Witness from Somerset to Royal Commission on Employment of Children, Young Persons & Women in Agriculture).
39. Margaretta Greg, quoted Pinchbeck, *op. cit.*, pp. 315–16.
40. Victorian prudery could be quite incredible; "The perfect hostess will see to it that the works of male and female authors be properly separated on her bookshelves. Their proximity, unless they happen to be married, should not be tolerated". Lady Gough, 1863 quoted in M. Vicinus, *A widening sphere. Changing roles of Victorian Women*, pub. 1977. Methuen, 1980, p. 182.
41. Quoted in ed. M. Vicinus, *Suffer and be still. Women in the Victorian age*, pub. 1972, Methuen, 1980, p. 76.
42. Quoted P.M. Stearns, "Workingclass women in Britian, 1890–1914, *ibid.*, p. 114.
43. *ibid.*
44. Hollis, *op. cit.*, p. 227.
45. Ensor, *op. cit.*, p. 171.

46. Quoted by E.M. Sigsworth and T.J. Wyke, "A study of Victorian Prostitution and Venereal Disease", in ed. Vicinus, *Suffer and be still*, *op. cit.*, p. 96.

47. Rita McWilliams-Tulberg, "Women and Degrees at Cambridge University, 1862–1897", in ed. Vicinus, *A widening sphere*, *op. cit.*, p. 117. In 1897, 220 Girtonians were teaching, 62 were in other professions.

48. Our Partnership, *op. cit.*, p. 415.

49. Maud Diver, *Captain Desmond, V.C.*, Revised ed., Blackwood, 1917, p. 346. Pressures on intelligent women might be great. "Why don't you live like other people instead of pretending to be a genius" – a sister asked Beatrice Potter in 1886. Ed. Mackenzie, *op. cit.*, p. 190.

50. Branca, *op. cit.*, p. 75.

51. D.E. Baines in ed. Floud & McCloskey, *op. cit.*, pp. 147, 148.

52. Branca, *op. cit.*, p. 118.

53. A. McLaren, "The early birth control movement: an example of medical self-help". In ed. J. Woodward and D. Richards, *Health Care and Popular Medicine in 19th century England*, Croom Helm, 1977, pp. 96–7.

54. Quoted from 1875 source by Branca, *op. cit.*, p. 29.

55. ed. N. & M. Mackenzie, *op. cit.*, p. 240.

56. Hannah Michell resolved after a dreadful confinement to have only one child: *The Hard Way Up*, *op. cit.*, p. 102. Vera Brittain's *Honourable Estate*, 1930s fiction much based on fact, tells the story of a young wife who refused to have more children after a painful confinement.

57. R. Mitchison, *op. cit.*, p. 28.

58. Kilvert, *op. cit.*, p. 190.

59. "Other things being equal, smaller families are likely to receive more attention from the mother, eat better food and to be less exposed to infection within the family". *On the state of public health*, H.M.S.O., 1924, p. 24.

60. Kilvert, *op. cit.*, p. 143.

61. In 1842, a Norfolk vicar: "Drew tooth for old Mrs. Roberts. . . . I found her in great pain, upon which I drew from my pocket a pair of pincers which caused the poor old woman to shake . . . . at last broke it off. . ." Chadwick, *op. cit.*, p. 55.

62. S.R. Johansson, "Sex and death in Victorian England", in ed. Vicinus, *A widening sphere*, *op. cit.*, p. 163, et seq.

63. Routh, *op. cit.*, p. 44.

64. Mitchell & Deane, *op. cit.*, p. 60.

65. Routh, *op. cit.*, p. 3.

66. Dudley Baxter, *op. cit.*, p. 50 et seq. Hobsbawm, *Labouring Men*, *op. cit.*, p. 280 et seq.

67. Reeves, *op. cit.*, p. 86.

68. As early as 1890, Durham Coal hewers had a 7-hour day. W.R. Garside, *The Durham Miners, 1919–1960*, Allen & Unwin, 1971, p. 19.

69. Lady Bell, *At the works. A study of a manufacturing town*, (pub. 1907) David & Charles Reprints, 1969, p. 26.

70. Review in *Times* 5.1.1980 of M. Hiley, *Victorian working women. Portrait from Life*, Gordon Fraser, with photograph of South-west Lancashire Pit

Brow Women 1886.

71. G.E. Mingay, *Rural life in Victorian England*, Futura, 1979, p. 129.

72. Saville, *op. cit.*, p. 74.

73. F. Whellan & Co., *op. cit.*, p. 196.

74. R. Roberts, *A ragged schooling*, Fontana, 1978, p. 15.

75. *J.S. 100. The story of Sainsbury's*, Sainsbury, 1969, p. 33.

76. Francesca M. Wilson, *Rebel daughter of a country house*, Allen & Unwin, 1967, p. 29.

77. Burnett, *Useful Toil, op. cit.*, p. 190.

78. N. Nicolson, *Mary Curzon*, Weidenfeld & Nicolson, 1977, p. 82.

79. Wilson, *op. cit.*, p. 29.

80. C. Cookson, *Our Kate*, Macdonald, 1962, p. 15.

81. Around 1892, as many as 15,000 out of 22,000 in London docks had regular employment. D.E. Baines, ed. Floud & McCloskey, *op. cit.*, p. 164.

82. Dougan, *op. cit.*, p. 67.

83. R. Page Arnot, *The Miners. Years of struggle*, Allen & Unwin, 1953, p. 147.

84. *ibid*, p. 148.

85. Harris, *op. cit.*, p. 15.

86. **G. H. Wood, "Real wages and the standard of comfort since 1850", in ed. Carus-Wilson, *op. cit.*, pp. 140-42.**

87. Deane & Cole, *op. cit.*, p. 247.

88. Figures taken from table in ed. Floud & McCloskey, *op. cit.*, p. 125 – based on work by A.L. Bowley.

89. Dudley Baxter, *op. cit.*, p. 1.

90. Clapham III, *op. cit.*, p. 497.

91. Thompson, *The Edwardians, op. cit.*, p. 22.

92. Thame in ed. Floud & McCloskey, *op. cit.*, p. 221 quoting figures of W.D. Rubinstein.

93. T. Pakenham, *The Boer War*, Weidenfeld & Nicolson, 1979, p. 577.

94. **John Buchan, *Memory Hold-The-Door,* Hodder & Stoughton, 1940, p. 92.**

95. Jack London, *The People of the Abyss*, Re-issued by Arco Publications, 1962,. e.g. pp. 41–44, 47, 148.

96. William Booth "In darkest England and the way out", 1890, in ed. Royston Pike, *op. cit.*, p. 302.

97. Pember Reeves, *op. cit.*, pp. 80–83.

98. R. Tressell, *The Ragged Trousered Philanthropists*, first pub. 1914, Lawrence & Wishart 1955. One of the "bibles" of many 20th century socialists. Miners' leader Arthur Scargill read it, plus Jack London. "Those were the books that formed my political opinions". J. Mortimer, *In Character*, Penguin, 1984, p. 63. (quoting A. Scargill).

99. Thus 1884 saw 1,227 demonstrations in favour of Parliamentary Reform.

100. J.C. Drummond and A. Wilbraham, *The Englishman's Food*, Cape, 1958, p. 403.

101. J. Burnett, *Plenty and Want*, Penguin, 1968, p. 271.

102. Lady Bell, *op. cit.*, pp. 92, 94. See also P.M. Stearns in ed. Vicinus, *Suffer and be still, op. cit.*, p. 103, et seq.

103. "Life and Labour" in ed. Royston Pike, *op. cit.*, p 119.

104. Roberts, *The Classic Slum*, *op. cit.*, p. 112.
105. T. McKeown, *Medicine in Modern Society*, Allen & Unwin, 1965, pp. 43, 50.
106. Mitchell & Deane, *op. cit.*, p. 355 et seq.
107. J.S. 100, *op. cit.*, p. 32.
108. W. Hamish Fraser, *The coming of the mass market, 1850–1914*, Macmillan 1981, p. 162.
109. *ibid*, p. 152.
110. Roberts, *The Classic Slum*. *op. cit.*, p. 111.
111. Lady Bell, *op. cit.*, p. 3, 9, 15.
112. Pember Reeves, *op. cit.*, p. 30.
113. Smout, *op. cit.*, pp. 33–35.
114. Kilvert, *op. cit.*, pp. 87–8.
115. Robertson Scott, *op. cit.*, p. 154.
116. ed. Royston Pike, *op. cit.*, p. 238.
117. R. Page Arnot, *op. cit.*, p. 195.
118. Co. Durham, *Health Report 1920*, p. 71.
119. F.C.S. Bradbury, *Causal Factors in Tuberculosis,* National Association for the Prevention of T.B., 1933, p. 50.
120. *Census* 1921, Co. Durham, p. xx.
121. Clapham, III, *op. cit.*, p. 458.
122. *ibid.*, pp. 459–60.
123. Quoted by H.M. Dyos, *Victorian Suburb, A study of the growth of Camberwell*, Leicester Univ. Press, 1961, p. 20 (footnote).
124. *ibid.*, pp. 124–5.
125. F.M.L. Thompson, *Hampstead. Building a Borough, 1650–1914*, Routledge & Kegan Paul, 1974, p. 435.
126. *ibid.*, p. 293.
127. G. & W. Grossmith, *The diary of a nobody*, pub. 1892, Penguin, 1965, p. 19.
128. Clapham III, *op. cit.*, p. 457.
129. Quoted in *Times* review, 3.1.1980 of H. Muthesius, *The English House* (ed. Sharp) Crosby, Lockwood, Staples, Granada.
130. 1881 opinion in ed. Royston Pike, *op. cit.*, p. 24 et seq.
131. *ibid.*, p. 33 (quoting Mrs. Beeton).
132. *Census*, 1921, Co. Durham.
133. Quoted Thompson, *The Edwardians*, *op. cit.*, p. 201.
134. Harrison, *op. cit.*, p. 313.
135. Quoted Harrison, *op. cit.*, p. 362.
136. D. Parry Jones, *A Welsh Country Parson*, Batsford, 1975, p. 15.
137. Thompson, *The Edwardians*, *op. cit.*, p. 204.
138. Ensor, *op. cit.*, p. 164.
139. P. Wild, "Recreation in Rochdale, 1900–40" in ed. J. Clarke et al., *Working-class culture, studies in history and theory,* Hutchinson, 1979, p. 140.
140. Reeves, *op. cit.*, p. 155.
141. Their vanished world has been described in a work of fiction: J.B. Priestley, *Lost Empires*, pub. 1965, Granada, 1980.

142. C. Kent, "Image and Reality. The Actress and Society", in ed. Vicinus, *A widening sphere*, *op. cit.*, p. 94.
143. Wild, *op. cit.*, p. 277.
144. *ibid.*, p. 146.

Chapter 7.   Order and change

1. K. Middlemas, *Politics in Industrial Society*, A. Deutsch, 1979, p. 43.
2. F.B. Smith, *Radical Artisan. William James Linton 1812–97*, Manchester Univ. Press, 1973, p. 101 et seq.
3. Harrison, *op. cit.*, p. 24.
4. Judith Walkowitx, "The making of an outcast group" in ed. Vicinus, *A widening sphere*, *op. cit.*, p. 86 (quoting contemporary newspaper).
5. Burnett, *Useful Toil*, *op. cit.*, p. 18.
6. Escott, *op. cit.*, p. 127.
7. *ibid*, p. 129.
8. Hobsbawm, *Labouring Men*, *op. cit.*, p. 241.
9. Escott, *op. cit.*, p. 129. M.P.s did accomplish improvements in working conditions. One famous example was the enforcement of safety regulations on merchant ships after Samuel Plimsoll's 1875 outburst in the Commons. C.H. Peters, *The Plimsoll Line*, Barry Rose, 1975, p. 104, et seq.
10. Quoted Hobsbawm, *op. cit.*, p. 320.
11. *Kilvert's Diary*, *op. cit.*, p. 92.
12. Henry James wrote of: "the essentially hierarchial English society. This . . . . is the great and ever-present fact to the mind of a stranger. . . ." James, *English Hours*, *op. cit.*, p. 91.
13. A Catechism, *Book of Common Prayer*, Church of England.
14. Thompson, *op. cit.*, p. 213.
15. Young, *op. cit.*. p. 5.
16. P. Thompson,. *The Edwardians*, *op. cit.*, pp. 132–33.
17. ed. Royston Pike, *op. cit.*, p. 89.
18. Blythe, *op. cit.*, p. 166.
19. Quoted Perkin, *op. cit.*, p. 85.
20. P.H.J.H. Gosden, *Self-help*, Batsford, 1973, p. 259.
21. Figures from *ibid*.
22. N. McCord, *Free Trade*, David & Charles, 1970, p. 144.
23. A. Offer, *Property and Politics*, 1870–1914 – *Landownership, law, ideology and urban development in England*, C.U.P., 1981.
24. *ibid.*, p. 99.
25. quoted *ibid.*, p. 10.
26. Frances Pitt, *Country Years*, Allen & Unwin, 1961, p. 27 has left an account of her father, a Solicitor in Bridgnorth, Shropshire, around 1900. In a very dusty office, his clerk, in a long frock coat, wrote a copybook hand, came early and left late "to join an equally quaint . . . . sister in some mysterious backwater of our old town".
27. Offer, *op. cit.*, p. 406.
28. *ibid.*, p. 224.

29. G.D.H. Cole, "Some notes on British Unionism in the Third Quarter of the 19th century" in ed. Carus-Wilson, *op. cit.*, p. 202.
30. *ibid.*, p. 219.
31. Cole & Postgate, *The Common People*, *op. cit.*, p. 406.
32. S. and B. Webb, "History of Trade Unionism", quoted by B. Webb, *Our Partnership*, *op. cit.*, p. 20, footnote.
33. H. Pelling, *A History of British Trade Unionism*, Penguin, 3 ed., 1976, p. 95, et seq.
34. e.g. in G. Dangerfield, *The strange death of Liberal England, 1910–14*, Capricorn Books, New York, 1961 (Constable in U.K.).
35. A. Wilson, *The Strange Ride of Rudyard Kipling*, *op. cit.*, p 258.
36. Syndicalisme is the French word for unionism. Syndicalism taught that trade unions should be militant, relying on trade union, not Parliamentary, action and fighting the class war through strikes.
37. Roberts, *The Classic Slum*, *op. cit.*, p. 93, et seq.
38. A. Rosen, *Rise Up Women!* Routledge & Kegan Paul, 1974.
39. *ibid.*, pp. 201, 216.
40. Ensor, *op. cit.*, p. 459.
41. *ibid.*, p. 398.

Chapter 8.   Government

1. Imlah, *op. cit.*, p. 10.
2. P. Mathias, *The First Industrial Nation*, Methuen, 1969, pp. 462–3.
3. Mitchell & Deane, *op. cit.*, p. 414 et seq.
4. Clapham III, *op. cit.*, p. 323.
5. S. Pollard, *The development of the British Economy, 1914–67*. Arnold 2 ed., 1969, p. 34 (and footnote).
6. Mitchell & Deane, *op. cit.*, p. 416, et seq.
7. F. Whellan & Co., *op. cit.*, p. 155 (published 1874).
8. Ensor, *op. cit.*, p. 521.
9. *Country Diary of an Edwardian Lady*, *op. cit.* In vastly different Tyne Dock recalled Catherine Cookson, "from a very small child I was used to going about on my own". C. Cookson, *Our Kate*, Macdonald, 1969, p. 12. Aged about 18, Hannah Mitchell safely walked about Bolton around 1890, *The Hard Way Up*, *op. cit.*, p. 78.
10. *Report of the Chief Inspector of Factories 1931*, p. 6.
11. "Report of Dangerous Trades Committe" 1899 in ed. Royston Pike, *op. cit.*, p. 269.
12. Perkin, *op. cit.*, pp. 334–5.
13. R.M. Macleod, "The frustration of State Medicine, 1880–1899", *Medical History II*. 1967, pp. 15–40.
14. Newcastle, *Health Report 1886*, p. 18.
15. South Shields, *Health Report, 1875*, p. 17.
16. Sunderland, *Health Report 1910*, p. 67.
17. W.M. Frazer, *History of Public Health 1834–1939*, Tindall & Co., p. 58.
18. *General Report on the Sanitary Condition of the Labouring Population of*

Great Britain, 1842.

19. P.H.J.H. Gosden, *The Friendly Societies of England 1915–75*, Manchester Univ. Press, 1961, pp. 7, 34, 43.

20. A. Cox, *Among the Doctors*, C. Johnson, undated but about 1949, p. 57.

21. Perkin, *op. cit.*, p. 448.

22. *Report of the Royal Commission on the Poor Law and Relief of Distress*, CMD 4499, H.M.S.O., 1909, p. 260.

23. F. Whellan & Co., *op. cit.*, p. 150.

24. R. Pinter, *English Hospital Statistics 1861–1938*, Heinemann, 1966, p. 3.

25. R. Shannon, *The crisis of imperialism 1865–1915*, Hart-Davis, McGibbon, 1974, p. 498.

26. F. Whellan & Co., *op. cit.*, p. 196.

27. G. Huxley, *Both Hands. An Autobiography*, Chatto & Windus, 1978, p. 49.

28. R. Clark, *J.B.S. The life and work of J.B.S. Haldane*, Quality Book Club, 1968, pp. 15, 23, 25.

29. Harris, *op. cit.*, p. 20 and Sir J. Craster, *North Country Squire*, Oriel, 1971, p. 6.

30. Tragic proportions of Public School old boys perished in the Great War: 1,160 of 5,687 Old Etonians who joined up, 700 of Rugby's old boys.

31. Before 1914, conditions for teachers could be horribly hard. "I found New Street a hard chore. I always had between seventy and eighty children in my class and I taught in a kind of annexe. . . . It was terribly cold in winter. . . . The Head had a disconcerting way of bursting into the room, stick in hand . . . . 'dusting the jackets of the little perishers' ". Leah Manning, *A Life for Education*, Gollancz, 1970, p. 42, on her experiences in Cambridge before 1914.

31a. Ellen Wilkinson born 1891, went from a working-class home, through a very rare scholarship to Manchester University. Betty D. Vernon, *Ellen Wilkinson 1891–1947*, Croom Helm, 1982, p. 10.

32. ed. Aldcroft, *op. cit.*, p. 303.

33. C. Barnett, *The Swordbearers*, Penguin, 1966, pp. 215–16.

34. Quoted, *ibid*.

35. D. Jones, *In Parenthesis*, Faber & Faber, 1975, p. 139.

36. *Report of the Royal Commission on the Poor Law*, H.M.S.O., 1909, xxv, pp. 211, 547.

37. Ruth G. Hodgkinson, *The origins of the National Health Service. The Medical Services of the New Poor Law*, 1934–1871, Wellcombe Historical Medical Library 1967, p. 696.

38. e.g. Gloria A. Cadman, *The administration of the Poor Law Amendment Act in the Hexham Poor Law Union, 1836–1930*, M. Litt, Newcastle, 1976.

39. H.C. Burdett, *Hospitals and Asylums of the World*, Churchill, 1893, p. 88.

40. *Public Health and Social Conditions*, Local Govt. Board, H.M.S.O., 1909, p. 57.

41. Quoted in Hodgkinson, *op. cit.*, p. 426.

42. Cadman, *op. cit.*

43. Hodgkinson, *op. cit.*, p. xv.

44. Clapham II, *op. cit.*, p. 434.

45. Harris, *op. cit.*, p. 102.
46. J. Wilson, *History of the Durham Miners' Association*, Veitch, 1907, p. 292 et seq.
47. B.B. Gilbert, *The Evolution of National Insurance in Great Britain*, Michael Joseph, 1966, p. 103.
48. Newcastle upon Tyne, *Report of Principal School Medical Officer*, 1927.
49. Gilbert, *op. cit.*, p. 102.
50. Lady Bell, *op. cit.*, pp. 85, 86.
51. Harris, *op. cit.*, p. 198.

Chapter 9.   Outline of the period

1. Nurses saw some of the worst suffering. Often from sheltered middle class homes, girls went in 1914–18 to treat unspeakably hideous wounds and to see the deaths of many fine young men, Lyn Macdonald, *The Roses of No Man's Land*, Michael Joseph, 1980, e.g. p. 93. A good account of the most horrible battle is in P. Warner, *Passchendaele*, Sidgwick and Jackson, 1987.
2. In 16 days at Anzio in 1944, the Grenadier Guards lost 29 out of a normal establishment of 35 officers and 579 men out of 800. R. Trevelyan, *Rome '44*, Secker & Warburg, 1980, p. 70. (The Sherwood Foresters had even higher casualties). This writer's uncle, E. Longden, was killed while serving in the Guards at Anzio.

Chapter 10.   The Great War

1. A. Marwick, *The Deluge*, Macmillan, 1973, p. 290.
2. Harris, *op. cit.*, p. 260.
3. This was true of J.B.S. Haldane. See Clark, *op. cit.*, p. 35.
4. B.B. Gilbert, *British Social Policy 1914–39*, Batsford, 1970, p. 1.
5. Introduction by Peter Davies to F. Manning, *Her Privates We*, Pan, 1961. Surely one of the very best of war books.
6. Fussell, *op. cit.*, p. 66.
7. *Registrar-Generals' Decennial Supplement 1921*, pt. III p. xcviii.
8. Marwick, *op. cit.*, p. 290.
9. "I say now that nothing that has been written is more than the pale image of the abomination of those battle-fields. . . ." Sir P. Gibbs, "The Realities of War" quoted J. Terraine, *The road to Passchendaele*, Leo Cooper, 1977, Introduction. In ed. Terraine, *General Jack's Diary, 1914–18*, Eyre & Spottiswoode, 1964, it is clearly revealed that at least one regular officer was greatly careful to avoid casualties.
10. M. Middlebrook, *The First Day on the Somme*, Fontana, 1975, p. 316. The searing tragedies of those huge battles are well brought out in Lyn Macdonald, *Somme*, Macmillan 1983, e.g. pp. 97, 259, 292.
11. David Jones, *In Parenthesis*, *op. cit.*, p. xii.
12. E. Whiteing, *Anyone for tennis? Growing up in Wallington between the Wars*, Sutton Library, 1979, pp. 58–9.

13. e.g. E. Blunden, *Undertones of War*, Four Square, 1962, p. 7. Isaac Rosenburg, on the other hand, one of the greatest of that great band of First War poets, from a poor East End Jewish immigrant family, had a rough time. "I have a little impudent schoolboy pup for an officer, and he has me marked". J. Cohen, *Journey to the Trenches. The life of Isaac Rosenburg, 1890–1918.* Robson Books 1975, p. 127. Yet Rosenburg volunteered for the Army in 1915 and to return to heavy fighting and death in 1918.

14. Thompson, *English Landed Society*, *op. cit.*, pp. 331–3.

15. Matthews et al., *op. cit.*, p. 126.

16. *ibid*, pp. 129–30.

17. *ibid*, p. 28.

18. Kathleen Burk, "J.M. Keynes and the exchange rate crisis of 1917", *Ec. Hist. Review*, Aug. 1979, p. 407.

19. J.D. Tomlinson, "The First World War and British cotton piece exports to India", *Ec. Hist. Review*, Now, 1979, p. 496.

20. G.P. Jones and A.G. Pool, *A hundred years of economic development in Gt. Britain*, Duckworth, 1940, p. 324.

21. Pollard, *op. cit.*, p. 58.

22. Over just one fortnight, 17–30 July 1917, British guns in Flanders fired 4,283,550 shells. Terraine, *The road to Passchendaele*, *op. cit.*, p. 196.

23. Dougan, *op. cit.*, p. 131.

24. A.J.P. Taylor, *English History 1914–15*, O.U.P., 1965, p. 122 (footnote).

25. K.S. Lomax's in S. Glyn and J. Oxborrow, *Interwar Britain, a Social and Economic history*, Allen & Unwin, 1976, p. 90.

26. Roberts, *The Classic Slum*, *op. cit.*, p. 203.

27. Marwick, *op. cit.*, pp. 124–5.

28. Roberts, *op. cit.*, p. 204.

29. Marwick, *op. cit.*, pp. 117–18.

30. Blythe, *op. cit.*, pp. 170–71.

31. F. Owen, *Tempestuous journey, Lloyd George his life and times*, Hutchinson, 1954, p. 366.

32. Cole & Postgate, *op. cit.*, p. 539.

33. Taylor, *op. cit.*, p. 40 (footnote).

34. Harris, *op. cit.*, pp. 209, 230.

35. A.C. Pigou, *Industrial Fluctuations*, Macmillan, 1928, p. 72.

36. K. Middlemas, *Politics in Industrial Society*, A. Deutsch, 1979, e.g. pp. 18–20, emphasises that from around 1916–26 to the 1960s, Governments, determined to avoid conflict, worked with "governing institutions", i.e. trade unions and employers' organisations.

37. Vera Brittain, *Testament of Friendship*, Macmillan, 1940, p. 69.

Chapter 11.   The economy between the wars

1. S. Glyn and A. Booth, "Unemployment in inter-war Britain. A case for re-learning the lessons of the 1930s?". *Ec. Hist. Review*, 2 Series, xxvi, 3, 1983, p. 332.

2. Schlote, *op. cit.*, p. 42.
3. Taylor, *op. cit.*, p. 340 (footnote).
4. e.g. T.E. Gregory, *The Gold Standard and its Future*, Methuen, 1932, p. 42.
5. J.M. Keynes, "The Economic consequences of Mr. Churchill", 1925, in *Essays in Persuasion, op. cit.*, p. 259.
6. Pollard, *op. cit.*, pp. 121–2. References to Pollard in this and following chapters are to his *Development of the British Economy, op. cit.*
7. *ibid.*, p. 121.
8. P. Mathias, *The First Industrial Nation*, Methuen, 1969, p. 489.
9. *ibid.*, pp. 483–84.
10. A.M. Neuman, *Economic organisation of the British coal industry*, Routledge, 1934, p. 98.
11. *ibid.*, p. 40.
12. Garside, *op. cit.*, p. 314.
13. *ibid.*, p. 313.
14. Mitchell & Deane, *op. cit.*, pp. 115–17.
15. J.K. Galbraith, *The Great Crash 1929*, Penguin, 1961, p. 111.
16. E.J. Hobsbawm, *Industry and Empire*, Penguin, 1969, p. 213 (footnote).
17. Ed. H.J. Beales and R.S. Lambert, *Memoirs of the Unemployed*, Gollancz, 1934, p. 14.
18. Beales & Lambert, *op. cit.*, p. 14.
19. D.K. Benjamin and L.A. Kochin, "What went right with juvenile unemployment policy between the Wars", *Ec. Hist. Review*, 2xxxii, 4. 1979, p. 523, see also "Rejoinder" by W.R. Garside, *ibid.*, p. 529.
20. Beales & Lambert, *op. cit.*, pp. 15–16.
21. S. Glyn and J. Oxborrow, *Inter War Britain, a social and economic history*, Allen & Unwin, 1976, p. 150, (quoting Colin Clark).
22. G. McCrone, *Regional Policy in Britain*, Allen & Unwin, 1969, p. 91.
23. Whiteing, *op. cit.*, pp. 57, 59.
24. R. Fuller, *Souvenirs*, London Magazine Editions, 1980, pp. 106–7, 127.
25. *Economic Growth in the North-east of England*. Business Research Unit, Durham Univ., 1967, p. 16.
26. E. Wilkinson, *The town that was murdered*, Gollancz, 1939.
27. T. Sharp, *A Derelict Area. A study of the south-west Durham Coalfield*, Hogarth Press, 1935, p. 31.
28. *Men without work*. A report made to the Pilgrim Trust, C.U.P., 1938.
29. *ibid.*, pp. 81, 75.
30. M.P. Fogarty, *Prospects of the Industrial Areas of Gt. Britain*, Methuen, 1945, pp. 16, 33.
31. Jones & Pool, *op. cit.*, p. 298.
32. *1921 Census*, Co. Durham p. xxxv.
33. *Sunderland Echo*, 13.7.1933, and 14.1.1937.
34. e.g. Landes, *op. cit.*, p. 424, et seq.
35. *Royal Commission on Geographical Distribution of the Industrial Population*, H.M.S.O. 1938, *Minutes of Evidence*, e.g. p. 621.
36. Fogarty, *op. cit.*, pp. 177, 175.
37. Cole & Postgate, *op. cit.*,. pp. 625–6.

38. M. Bruce, *The Coming of the Welfare State*, Batsford, 4 ed. 1968, p. 236.
39. Jones & Pool, *op. cit.*, p. 281.
40. Pollard, *op. cit.*, p. 100.
41. Aldcroft & Richardson, *op. cit.*, p. 266.
42. Landes, *op. cit.*, p. 44.
43. *Northern Echo*, 20.1.1927, p. 5.
44. *Sunderland Echo*, 13.3.1937, p. 8.
45. Landes, *op. cit.*, p. 391.
46. Pollard, *op. cit.*, p. 196, et seq.
47. H. Williamson, *The story of a Norfolk Farm*, Readers Union/Faber & Faber, 1942, p. 60.
48. For criticism see P.T. Bauer, *West African Trade*, Routledge & Kegan Paul, 1963.
49. "We paid him the current Norfolk labourer's wage of 32/6d for a 48 hour week". Williamson, *op. cit.*, p. 129.
50. Aldcroft & Richardson, *The British Economy 1870–1939*, *op. cit.*, p. 233. quoting K. S. Lomax
51. Matthews et. al., *op. cit.*, p. 277.
52. Deane & Cole, *op. cit.*, pp. 330–31 show rise in income per head in 1930s of nearly 20%.
53. G.A. Phillips & R.T. Maddock, *The growth of the British Economy, 1918–68*, Allen & Unwin, 1973, p. 54.
54. Aldcroft & Richardson, *op. cit.*, p. 229.
55. In 1933 I.C.I. discovered polythene and by 1939 the first polythene unit was in production, *ibid.*, p. 273.
56. *New Statesman & Nation*, 27.7.1935, p. 143.
57. *Report of Commissioner for special Areas, Year to 30.9.1938*, pp. 65 and 108–10.
58. *Report of Special Areas Commissioner, 1938*, *op. cit.*, p. 38.
59. McCrone, *op. cit.*, p. 96.

Chapter 12.   Society between the wars

1. Quoted by A. Briggs in ed. Floud & McCloskey, *op. cit.*, p. 350.
2. V. Brittain, *Testament of Experience*, Fontana, 1980, p. 123.
3. P. Street, *Arthur Bryant*, Collins, 1979, p. 99.
4. *Report of an enquiry into the effects of existing economic circumstances on the health of the community in the County Borough of Sunderland and certain districts of C. Durham.*, Cmd, 4886, H.M.S.O., 1935.
5. J. Stevenson and C. Cook, *The Slump*, Cape, 1977, pp. 136, 217.
6. N. Mitchison, *You may well ask. A memoir 1920–40*, Gollancz, 1979, p. 19.
7. Ethel Mannin, *Young in the Twenties*, Hutchinson, 1971, p. 17.
8. Pay Taylor, "Daughters and mothers – maids and mistresses: domestic service between the wars", in ed. Clarke et al. *op. cit.*, p. 121. One who experienced service between the Wars was Margaret Powell, *Below Stairs*, Peter Davis, 1968. "I've often wondered why the status of our work was so low" – p. 159.

9. N. Nicolson, *Portrait of a marriage*, Weidenfeld & Nicolson, 1973, pp. 83, 225.

10. Blythe, *op. cit.*, p. 116, et seq.

11. ed. J. Burnett, *Useful Toil*, *op. cit.*, p. 324, et seq.

12. Robertson Scott, *op. cit.*, p. 33.

13. Williamson, *op. cit.*, p. 280.

14. Russell Braddon, *The Naked Island*, Pan, 1955, p. 40. et seq.

15. A. Powell, *Memoirs, 2, Messengers of Day*, Heinemann, 1978, p. 153, describing a 1930 happening.

16. A. Boyle, *Only the wind will listen, Reith of the B.B.C.*, Hutchinson, 1972, p. 290.

17. A. Bell, *Corduroy*, publ. 1930, O.U.P., 1982, e.g. p. 131.

18. Mitchison, *op. cit.*, pp. 25–6.

19. Priestley, *English Journey*, *op. cit.*, p. 372.

20. Durham County Record Office, *Files on Lord Mayor's Distress Fund*. Subsequent quotations are taken from these.

21. *Reports of the School Medical Officers* in 1920, e.g. Gateshead, 1921, p. 5.

22. H.A. Mess, *Voluntary Social Services since 1928*, Kegan Paul, 1947, pp. 53–5.

23. G. Orwell, *The Road to Wigan Pier*, first published 1937. Penguin, 1962, p. 12.

24. *ibid.*, p. 67.

25. Ministry of Labour, *Reports of Investigations into the Industrial Conditions in certain depressed areas*. H.M.S.O., 1934, p. 71.

26. Sunderland, *Health Report 1936*, p. 132, et seq.

27. Ed. Beales & Lambert, *op. cit.*, Subsequent quotations are from this book. The radio talks and "Listener" articles called forth a large response of practical offers of help.

28. Even on this not all agreed. "Dr. Watts said he was continually struck by the objections to putting in more hours of labour in a healthy occupation such as that of mining. Mining was with one exception the healthiest occupation in the country. It was second only to that of the agricultural labourer. There were very few diseases to which miners were specially prone. . . ." *Lancet*, 2, 1926, p. 732.

29. Sir Thomas Oliver, *Medical Officer*, 12.5.1928, p. 212.

30. B. Grainger and J. Hurst, *Report on the Incidence of Disability amongst Durham Miners*, Durham University, 1969.

31. Garside, *op. cit.*, p. 255.

32. *Northern Echo*. 14.1.1927, p. 5.

33. *Report of Chief Inspector of Factories*, 1934, p. 7 (graph).

34. Oliver, *op. cit.*, p. 212.

35. *Sunderland Echo*, 19.8.1975, p. 6.

36. Cheap cigarettes.

37. F.C. Kelly, "Fifty years of progress in nutritional science", *Medical Officer*, 16.2.1935, p. 65.

38. J. Burnett, *Plenty and Want*, Penguin, 1968, p. 319.

39. J. Boyd Orr, *Food, Health & Income*, Macmillan, 1931. As the words of a song exprssed it, "The rich get richer and the poor get children".

40. G.M.C. M'Gonigle and J. Kirby, *Poverty and Public Health*, Gollancz, 1936, p. 188.
41. Newcastle, *Health Report 1933*, Appendix A.
42. F.C.S. Bradbury, *Causal Factors in Tuberculosis*. National Association for Prevention of Tuberculosis, 1933.
43. *The Health of the School Child. Annual Report of the Chief Officer, Board of Education for 1936*, H.M.S.O. 1937, p. 30.
44. *Lancet*, 2, 1939, p. 442.
45. Newcastle upon Tyne, *Study of the Diet of 69 working class families*, 1934.
46. *Registrar-General's Decennial Supplement. England and Wales, 1921*, H.M.S.O., 1927. Part 1 Life table.
47. *Registrar-General's Decennial Supplement, 1931*, H.M.S.O., p. 23.
48. *ibid.*, p. 164.
49. *On the State of the Public Health, Annual Report of Chief Medical Officer, Min. of Health for 1932*, H.M.S.O. 1933, p. 41.
50. *New Statesman and Nation*, 23.11.1935, p. 759.
51. Quoted by E. Wilkinson, *The town that was murdered*, Gollancz, 1939, p. 253.
52. ed. M. Ginsberg, *Law and opinion in England in the 20th century*, Stevens, 1959, p. 11.
53. *ibid*, p. 20.
54. A T.V. series, produced in 1975, by B.B.C. was called "Days of Hope" – it dealt with these years.
55. Williamson, *op. cit.*, p. 281: "his whole life from the Somme onwards was one long wound. . . . . He was not killed . . . . but he was certainly maimed, crippled and wounded. . ." ed. B. Sewell, Henry Williamson, *The Man. The writings*, Padstow, 1980, p. xiii.
56. *Medical Officer*, 18.8.1928, p. 69.
57. *Medical Officer*, 29.5.1937, p. 215 (words underlined in italics in original).
58. "Observations of Chorea; The Environmental Factor", *Lancet*, 1935, 2, p. 553. (Chorea is often known as St. Vitus' Dance).
59. F.R. Seymour in *Medical Officer*, 2.2.1935, p. 45.
60. D.R. Laurence, *Clinical Pharmacology*, Churchill Livingstone. 4 ed. 1973, Section 7.2.
61. Gateshead, *Health Report, 1938*, p. 121 (the nine year old son of Naomi Mitchison died of meningitis in 1927).
62. Calculated from local *Health Reports*.
63. Mannin, *Young in the Twenties*, *op. cit.*, pp. 56, 44.
64. Mitchison, *You may well ask*, *op. cit.*, p. 34.
65. Co. Durham, *Health Report 1938*, p. 47.
66. J. Fenton and Violet Russell, "Report of an investigation into the question of contraception and abortion", *Medical Officer*, 16.7.1938, pp. 29–30.
67. *Listener*, 1.10.1981, p. 371.
68. *Registrar-General's Statistical Review for 1938 and 1939*, p. 192.
69. Cole and Postgate, *op. cit.*, p. 626.
70. Priestley, *English Journey*, *op. cit.*, p. 122.
71. John Hilton in ed. T.H Marshall, *Class conflict and social stratification*, Le Play House Press, 1938, pp. 68–9.

72. Prais, *op. cit.*, pp. 4, 51, 55.
73. G.C. Allen, *The structure of industry in Britain*, Longmans, 3 ed. 1970, pp. 32–33.
74. Miss Strachey, *Our Freedom*, 1936, quoted by Hamilton, *op. cit.*, p. 339.
75. Hamilton, *op. cit.*, p. 338.
76. Marsh, *op. cit.*, p. 145.
77. B. Abel-Smith, *A History of the Nursing Profession*, Heinemann, 1960, p. 257, et. seq.
78. Hamilton, *op. cit.*, p. 340.
79. B. Seebohm Rowntree and G.R. Lavers, *Poverty and the Welfare State*, Longmans, 1951, p. 7.
80. J. Boyd Orr, *Food, Health and Income*, Macmillan, 2 ed. 1937, p. 24.
81. Pollard, *op. cit.*, p. 294.
82. Mitchell and Deane, *op. cit.*, p. 355 et seq.
83. *Ibid*, p. 253, et seq.
84. Newcastle, *Journal*, 20.5.1933, p. 9.
85. *J.S. 100*, *op. cit.*, p. 44.
86. Jeffreys, *op. cit.*, p. 131, et seq.
87. Newcastle upon Tyne, *School Medical Report, 1921*, p. 34.
88. J.M. Mackintosh, *Trends of opinion about the Public Health 1901–51*, O.U.P., 1953, pp. 107–8.
89. Ruth Inglis, "The gospel according to St. Michael", *Sunday Times Magazine*, 27.3.1966, p. 66.
90. P. Wild in ed. J. Clarke et al., *op. cit.*, p. 148.
91. *Journal*, 13.7.1926.
92. Pollard, *op. cit.*,. p. 260.
93. Quoted by B.B. Gilbert, *British Social Policy*, *op. cit.*, p. 203.
94. *Medical Officer*, 12.2.1938, p. 112.
95. Gateshead, *Health Report, 1936*, p. 83.
96. Priestley, *English Journey*, *op. cit.*, p. 10.
97. G. Orwell, *Coming up for air*, pub. 1939, Penguin, 1962, p. 180.
98. G.F. McCleary, *The Maternity and Child Welfare Movement*, King & Son 1935, p. 20.
99. Newcastle, *Health Report 1938*, p. 62.
100. Co. Durham, *Health Report 1921*, p. 19.
101. Newcastle, *Report of School Medical Officer, 1921*, p. 17.
102. *ibid*, p. 33.
103. Gateshead, *School Medical Report 1939*, pp. 10–11.
104. H. Levy, *National Health Insurance. A critical study*, C.U.P., 1944, p. 97.
105. R. Pinker, *English Hospital Statistics 1861–1838*, Heinemann, 1966, p. 112.
106. *ibid*, p. 49.
107 E.G.J.S. Collings "General Practice in England today; A Reconnaissance". *Lancet*, 1950, I, pp. 555–585. Conditions were no better before the Second War.
108. H. Eckstein, *The English Health Service*, Harvard, 1959, p. 168 (footnote).
109. Gateshead, *Health Report 1938*.
110. e.g. Obituary of Dr. J. Wilkie Smith of Ryton on Tyne in *Medical Officer*, 1.12.1928.

111. Sunderland P.A.C. *Minutes*, 4.12.1933.
112. e.g. J. & A. Jewkes, *The Genesis of the British Health Services*, Basil Blackwell, 1962, defend the pre-war medical system from charges of inadequacy.
113. K. Jones, *Mental Health and Social Policy 1845–1959*, Routledge & Kegan Paul, 1960, p. 73.
114. Gilbert, *British Social Policy*, *op. cit.*, p. 308.
115. ed. A.H. Halsey, *Trends in British Society since 1900*, Macmillan, 1972, p. 158.
116. J. Stevenson, *Social Conditions in Britain between the Wars*, Penguin, 1977, p. 36.
116a One working class girl's schooling is described in: Phyllis Willmott, *A Green Girl*, Peter Owen, 1983.
117. E. Waugh, *A Little Learning*, Chapman & Hall, 1964, p. 208.
118. A. Bullock, *The Life and Times of Ernest Bevin, ii*, Heinemann, 1967, p. 281.
119. Trevelyan, *op. cit.*, p. 586 (footnote).
120. A. Briggs, in ed. Floud & McCloskey, *op. cit.*, p. 363.
121. J. Sykes, *British Public Expenditure, 1921–31*, P.S. King & Son, 1933, pp. 12, 17.
122. Sunderland, *Abstract of the Treasurer's Accounts 1930–31*, 1938–9.
123. W. Holtby, *South Riding*, pub. 1939, Fontana 1954, Prefatory letter to Alderman Mrs. Holtby, p. 6.

Chapter 14. The Second War

1. From a huge literature, the following books are selected. They describe experiences, (J. Ellis, *The sharp end of war*, Corgi, 1982, p. 386 et seq. lists very many books and articles on the war).

(i) Of airmen:
R. Hillary, *The last enemy*, Macmillan, 1943.
R. Clostermann, *The big show*, Penguin, 1958.
G. Gibson, *Enemy coast ahead*, Pan, 1955.

(ii) Of soldiers:
R.L. Crimp, *The diary of a desert rat*, Leo Cooper, 1971.
J. Horsfall, *The wild geese are flighting*, Roundwood, 1976.
K. Douglas, *Alamein to Zem Zem*, Penguin, 1976.
K. Tout, *Tank! 40 hours of battle*, R. Hale, 1985.

(iii) Of sailors:
R. Hill, *Destroyer Captain*, Granada, 1979.
J.P.W. Mallalieu, *Very ordinary seaman*, Panther, 1956.
M. Middlebrook, *Convoy*, Allen Lane 1976.

(iv) Of women's services:
Mary Lee Settle, *All the brave promises*, Heinemann, 1962.

(v) Of civilians:
T. Harrison, *Living through the blitz*, Collins, 1971.

ed. P. Donnelly, *Mrs. Milburn's diaries*, Fontana,. 1986.

(vi)   Of those "out of step"
       P. Grafton, *You, you and you*, Pluto, 1981.

2.   See, for example, the amazing story of 13 Bn King's Liverpool Regt. Many
     of the men were aged over 30, from Lancashire cities. They were drafted
     into Wingate's Chindits to fight behind Japanese lines in Burma. 721 went
     in 384 came out. L. Allen, *Burma, The Longest War, 1941–45,* Dent, 1986.

3.   E. Bowen, *The heat of the day*, Reprint Soc., 1950, p. 87.

4.   "The Air Ministry never lost its conviction that gentlemen made the best
     aircrew . . . . . a . . . memorandum in . . . . 1942 suggested 'that we are
     not getting a reasonable percentage of the young men of the middle and
     upper classes' ". M. Hastings, *Bomber Command*, Pan, 1981, p. 254.

4a. Margaret Powell found during the war that formerly wealthy families had
     only a "daily". M. Powell, *The Treasure Upstairs*, Peter Davies, 1970, e.g.
     p. 2.

5.   *Times*, 1.7.1940.

6.   Bullock, *op. cit.*, p. 137. (Bullock dated Labour's effective victory in 1940
     not 1945. Economic came before political power).

7.   *ibid.*, p. 62.

8.   A.S. Milward, *The economic effects of two World Wars on Britain*,
     Macmillan, 1970, p. 26.

9.   J.C.R. Dow, *The Management of the British Economy*, 1945–60, C.U.P.,
     1964, p. 7.

10. A. Price, *The Hardest Day*, Granada, 1980, p. 62.

11. An example of shattered lives was revealed in a conversation reported in
     1978. An elderly lady told how she had struggled to bring up her two
     children. "My husband committed suicide after the war, it just unbalanced
     him. He was never strong, but that was the finish of him. He was in a
     prisoner of war camp in Japan. He was not the man who went away. . . ."
     J. Seabrook, *What went wrong?*, Gollancz, 1978, p. 203.

12. Winston Churchill, quoted by A. Mars, *British submarines at war 1939–45*,
     W. Kimber, 1911 (dedication).

13. Hastings, *op. cit.*, p. 9, 169–70.

14. M. Middlebrook, *The Nuremburg Raid*, A. Lane, 1973, p. 57.

15. D. Wood and D. Dempster, *The Narrow Margin*, Arrow, 1967, pp. 496 et
     seq.

16. M. Lindsey, *So Few Got Through*, Arrow, 1968, p. 255.

17. W. Sargant, *The Unquiet Mind*, Heinemann, 1967, p. 86, et seq.

18. For example, 1,179 civilians were killed and over 3,000 injured in
     Plymouth, A.L. Cramp and H.P. Twyford, *The blitz on Plymouth,
     1940–44*, P.D.S. Printers, Plymouth.

19. R.M. Titmuss, *Problems of Social Policy*, H.M.S.O., Longmans, 1950,
     p. 139.

20. *ibid.*, p. 414.

21. *ibid.*, p. 211 (footnote).

22. *ibid.*, pp. 307–13.

23. G. Perry, *Boy in the Blitz*, Colin A. Perry Ltd, 1980.

24. Irene Thomas, *The Bandsman's Daughter*, Futura, 1980, p. 38.
25. *Times*, 16.1.1941, quoted in Titmuss, *op. cit.*, p. 135.
26. *ibid*. (Titmuss), p. 393 (footnote) and 394.
27. R. Trevelyan, *The Fortress*, Penguin, 1958, p. 107.
28. W.K. Hancock and M.M. Gowing, *British War Economy*, H.M.S.O. and Longmans, 1949, p. 548.
29. Titmuss, *op. cit.*, p. 435 (footnote, quoting article in *Social Work*, April, 1946.
30. *ibid.*, pp. 405–9.
31. Quoted Hancock & Gowing, *op. cit.*, p. 519.
32. *Our Towns – A close-up*, Women's Group on Public Welfare. O.U.P. 2 ed. 1944, p. 3.
33. Titmuss, *op. cit.*, p. 388.
34. *ibid.*, p. 208.
35. White paper, *Employment Policy*, H.M.S.O., 1944, Foreword.
36. Titmuss, *op. cit.*, p. 521, et seq.
37. Ministry of Health, *Report on the incidence of rickets in war-time*, H.M.S.O., 1914, prefatory note, and Titmuss, *op. cit.*, p. 535.
38. Hancock & Gowing, *op. cit.*, p. 366, et seq. and p. 455 (footnote).
39. Bullock, *op. cit.*, p. 25.
40. Hastings, *op. cit.*, p. 445.
41. Hancock & Gowing, *op. cit.*, p. 373.
42. Bullock, *op. cit.*, p. 161.
43. Hancock & Gowing, *op. cit.*, p. 479 (abbreviated).
44. *ibid.*, p. 465.
45. *ibid.*, p. 76.

Chapter 14.   Britain in a changed and changing world

1. ed. C. Allen, *Tales from the Dark Continent*, A. Deutsch and B.B.C. 1979, p. 149.
2. P. Oppenheimer, "Europe and the Common Market", *Nat. West, Bank Quarterly Review*, Feb. 1971, p. 16.
3. D. Swann, *The Economics of the Common Market*, Penguin 4 ed. 1978, p. 162, et seq.
4. M. Featherston, B. Moore, J. Rhodes, "What happened to Britain's trade since entry into the EEC". *Times*, 28.1.1980.
5. Lord Thomson, "The European Community: the Tortoise that moves!" *Lloyds Bank Review*, July, 1977, pp. 1, 3.

Chapter 15.   The post-war consensus

1. A. Leijonhufvud, *Keynes and the Classics*, Institute of Economic Affairs, 1969, p. 8.
2. See Keynes, *General Theory*, p. 129 for a teasing passage on the solution of

the unemployment problem by burying bank notes in bottles in disused coalmines.

3.   Beatrice Webb thought, "The better you treat the unemployed in the way of means, without service, the worse the evil becomes: because it is better to do nothing than to work at low wages and conditions", quoted Harris, *op. cit.*, p. 424.

4.   e.g. among widely read works were Joan Robinson, *The Problem of Full Employment*, W.E.A., 1943, often reprinted: Beveridge, *Full Employment in a Free Society*, 1944, much dependent on Keynesians ideas and material supplied by N. Kaldor and others, R. Meade, *Economic Analysis and Policy*, O.U.P. 2 ed 1937 (a most lucid introduction to economics).

5.   Cripps, 1949, quoted by "Economist" 1949 and reprinted in Dow, *op. cit.*, pp. 34–5.

6.   Except in very exceptional circumstances in the harsh winter months of early 1947.

7.   G.C. Allen, *The structure of industry in Britain*, Longman 3 ed 1970, p. 252.

8.   *A National Health Service*, 1944, quoted *Report of Royal Commission on the National Health Service*, H.M.S.O., 1979, p. 10.

9.   *Report of Royal Commission*, *op. cit.*, p. 431.

10.   Quoted *History of the T.U.C. 1868–1968*, *op. cit.*, p. 136.

11.   The phrase "age of clatter and buzz, of gape and gloat", surely deserves preservation.

12.   *Report of the Committee on the Working of the Monetary System* (Chairman Lord Radcliffe) H.M.S.O., 1959, p. 22.

13.   Reproduced in S. Brittan, *Steering the Economy*, Secker and Warburg, 2 ed., 1969, p. 204.

14.   *Employment Policy*, H.M.S.O., 1944 foreword.

15.   Until the late 1950s, National Service i.e. service in the Armed Forces for 18 months or two years was clearly a large demand on manpower.

16.   *Joint Statement of Intent, 1964, op. cit.*

17.   The National Plan, H.M.S.O., 1965, p. 1.

18.   e.g. L.A. Dicks-Mireaux, *Cost or Demand Inflation?* Woolwich Polytechnic, 1965.

19.   A.W. Phillips, "The Relation between Unemployment and the Rate of Change of Money Wage Rates in the United Kingdom, 1861–1957", *Economica*, Nov. 1958 reprinted in ed. M.G. Mueller, *Readings in Macroeconomics*, Holt, Rinehart and Winston, 1966, p. 245.

20.   Judith Marquand, *Wage Drift: Origins, measurement and behaviour*, Woolwich Polytechnic, 1967, p. 3.

21.   M. Panic, "Why the UK's propensity to import is high", *Lloyds Bank Review*, Jan. 1975, p. 1.

22.   Dow, *op. cit.*, p. 178.

23.   *Radcliffe Report*, *op. cit.*, pp. 132, 133, 337.

24.   ed. R.E. Caves, *Britain's Economic Prospects*, Allen & Unwin, 1968, p. 196.

25.   Matthews et al., *op. cit.*, pp. 28, 126, 171, 277, 128.

26.   C.S.O., *Annual Abstract of Statistics 1980*, H.M.S.O., p. 249.

27. P. Wormell, *Anatomy of Agriculture*, Harrap, 1978, p. 366.
28. Blythe, *op. cit.*, p. 31, describes increased output in one East Anglian village.
29. *Annual Abstract of Statistics, 1980*, p. 254.
30. Wormell, *op. cit.*, p. 171.
31. Pollard, *op. cit.*, p. 410 (footnote).
32. *J.S. 100*, *op. cit.*, pp. 68 and 72.
33. Ruth Inglis, *op. cit.*, p. 67, "No one has ulcers here", an executive told her. "No, they wouldn't" said a retired fashion designer, "they haven't time – they just keel over and die directly".
34. Chairman's statement, *Times*, 2.7.1980.
35. W.W. Rostow, *The Stages of Economic Growth*, C.U.P., 1963, p. 73, et seq. (it must be pointed out that 19th century sewing machines and bicycles were articles of mass-consumption too.)
36. A. Sillitoe, *Saturday Night and Sunday Morning*, pub. 1960, pp. 21 & 20. This novel contains excellent descriptions of conditions and attitudes in a mass-production factory.
37. As described in e.g. P. Townsend, *Poverty in the United Kingdom*, Penguin, 1979.
38. E.F. Denison in ed. Caves *op. cit.*, p. 232.
39. *Bank of England Quarterly Bulletin*, Dec. 1979, p. 362.
40. *Daily Telegraph*, 27.8.1979.
41. Panic, *op. cit.*, p. 3.
42. R. Rose and G. Peters, *Can Government go Bankrupt?* Macmillan, 1978, pp. 252–3.
43. ed. Caves, *op. cit.*, p. 34.
44. Letter to *Times*, 11.7.1980 from Mr. W.I. Webb.
45. ed. Caves, *op. cit.*, p. 3.

Chapter 16.   Society

1. *Social Trends 1979*, H.M.S.O., p. 35.
2. *ibid.*, p. 37.
3. *Registrar-General's Statistical Review for 1971*, H.M.S.O. 1973, part I, Table 3.
4. *Times*, 30.7.1980, p. 16.
5. *ibid.*
6. *Social Trends 1979*, H.M.S.O., p. 53.
7. *British Medical Journal*, 19.4.1980, p. 1061.
8. *Social Trends 1979*, p.38.
9. ed. House, *op. cit.*, p. 122.
10. *ibid.*, p. 144, 146.
11. *ibid.*, p. 191.
12. *New Society*, 13.9.1979, referring to K. Dunnell, *Family Formation*, 1976, H.M.S.O.
13. R. Fletcher, *The Family and Marriage in Britain*, Penguin, 3 ed, 1973, p. 118.

14. Quoted *ibid.*, p. 121.
15. Thus Molly Hughes waited 10 years before marrying in 1897, M.V. Hughes, *A London Family 1870–1900*, O.U.P., 1981, p. 509.
16. *Social Trends, 1979*, p. 51.
17. J. Dominian, *Marriage in Britain 1945–80*. Study Commission on the Family, 1980, p. 18.
18. Fletcher, *op. cit.*, p. 173, quoting *Sunday Times*, Survey, 1970.
19. P. Manley and D. Sawbridge "Women at Work". *Lloyds Bank Review*, Jan. 1980, p. 29.
20. *Social Trends, 1979*, p. 45.
21. M. Young and P. Willmott, *Family and Kinship in East London*, Penguin, 1962, pp. 46–49.
22. P. Townsend, *The family life of Old People*, Penguin, 1963, p. 103.
23. J. Seabrook, *What went wrong?*, Gollancz, 1978, pp. 40, 203, 221.
24. The Select Committee on Race Relations and Immigration reported in 1978: "There are no reliable figures about immigrants now resident in the United Kingdom: no reliable statistics which can be described as indicators of immigration. . .". Quoted in Runnymede Trust and Radical Statistics Race Group, *Britain's Black Population*, Heinemann, 1980, p. 123.
25. A.M. Richmond, *Colour Prejudice in Britain*, Routledge & Kegan Paul, 1954.
26. *ibid.*, p. 145.
27. *ibid.*, p. 86.
28. J. Conrad, *The Nigger of the Narcissus, Typhoon and other Stories*, Penguin, 1963, p. 249.
29. Diana Spearman, "Enoch Powell's Postbag", *New Society*, 9.5.68.
30. Seabrook, *op. cit.*, gives many examples of strongly expressed feelings against immigrants, e.g. p. 160, et seq.
31. *Time*, 20.8.1979.
32. *Britain's Black Population*, *op. cit.*, p. 9.
33. *Times*, 20.5.1981.
34. *Social Trends, 1980*, p. 103 (Diagram).
35. *Peterborough Standard*, 26.10.1979.
36. *Britain's Black Population*, *op. cit.*, p. 114–115.
37. *Social Trends, 1980*, diagrams pp. 198, 201.
38. *New Society*, 23.8.1979, p. 399.
39. *Britain's Black Population*, *op. cit.*, p. 58.
40. *Report of the Royal Commission on the N.H.S.*, H.M.S.O., 1979, pp. 217–18, 195, 251 (footnote).
41. *The Brixton Disorders 10–12 April, 1981, Report by Lord Scarman*, H.M.S.O. Cmnd 8427, 1981. Lord Scarman reported that: while whites and blacks had common difficulties, in the inner cities, there were "three areas of disadvantage for black people – Housing, Education, Employment" (p. 103). Much of his evidence pointed to inner city deprivation. But, "Social Services expenditure by Lambeth Borough Council in 1979–80 at £117.39 per capita was the highest in England. . . Total revenue expenditure by the Local Area Health Authority in the same period was also among the highest in England at £243. . . ." (p. 7). Much of the report

deals with the riots themselves and with policing. In this brief note, emphasis is given to social and economic factors.

41a. R. Dahrendorf, *On Britain*, B.B.C., 1982, p. 67.

42. B. Seebohm Rowntree and G.R. Lavers, *Poverty and the Welfare State*, Longmans, 1951, p. 46.

43. *Social Trends, 1979*, p. 84.

44. A.M. Carr-Saunders, D. Caradog Jones, C.A. Moser, *A Survey of Social Conditions in England and Wales*, Oxford, 1958, p. 84.

45. ed. Halsey, *op. cit.*, p. 97.

46. Reference has been made to Abrams, *op. cit.*, p. 69, et seq. in this section.

47. *Social Trends, 1979*, p. 99.

48. Central Statistical Office, *National Income and Expenditure*, 1979, H.M.S.O., p. 5.

49. Deane & Cole, *op. cit.*, p. 247.

50. M. Paldam, "Towards the Wage-earner State", *International Journal of Social Economics*, 6.1.1979, p. 55.

51. *New Society*, 1.11.1979, p. 258. Comment on *Final Report of Royal Commission on Distribution of Income and Wealth*, H.M.S.O., 1980.

52. Routh, *op. cit.*, p. 147.

53. Graph in *A to Z of Income and Wealth, Royal Commission on Distribution of Income and Wealth*, H.M.S.O., 1980, p. 11.

54. Routh, *op. cit.*, p. 104.

55. *A to Z of Income and Wealth, op. cit.*, pp. 12, 4, 5, 16.

56. H. Lydall, "The economics of inequality" *Lloyds Bank Review*, July, 1975, p. 35.

57. *A to Z of Income and Wealth, op. cit.*, p. 6.

58. *ibid.*, p. 21.

59. C.D. Harbury and P.C. McMahan, "Inheritance and the characteristics of top wealth receivers in Britain". *Economic Journal*, Sept. 1973, p. 832.

60. "The myth of Self-made man", *New Statesman*, 15.2.1980, a brief version of C.D. Harbury and D.W.M. Hitchens, *Inheritance and Wealth Inequality in Britain*, Allen & Unwin, 1979.

61. J. Westergaard and H. Resler, *Class in a Capitalist Society*, Penguin, 1976, p. 112.

62. *A to Z of Income and Wealth, op. cit.*, pp. 22–27.

63. N. Mitchison, *You may well ask*, Gollancz, 1979, p. 206.

64. Department of Employment, *Family Expenditure Survey, 1975*, H.M.S.O., p. 17.

65. Carr-Saunders et al., *op. cit.*, p. 205.

66. *Social Trends, 1980*, pp. 21–2.

67. Brewers' Society, *Beer Facts, 1980*.

68. *Brewing Review*, Oct. 1977.

69. *Social Trends, 1980*, p. 30.

70. "Housing Policy, a consultative document" 1977, quoted in N. Clarke, "Too much housing?" *Lloyds Bank Review*, Oct. 1977, p. 17.

71. In 1977/8 in the London Borough of Lambeth, there was an estimated shortage of about 20,000 dwellings. Some 12,000 households lived in overcrowded conditions, *Scarman Report of Brixton Disorders*, 1981,

H.M.S.O., p. 5.

72. B. Kilroy, "Housing Finance" – Why so privileged?", *Lloyds Bank Review*, July 1979, p. 40.

73. *Social Trends, 1980*, p. 29.

74. ed. Abrams, *op. cit.*, p. 31.

75. *Annual Abstract of Statistics, 1980*, p. 278.

76. Letter, *Times*, 20.11.1979.

77. A. Peaker, "Holiday spending by the British at home and abroad", *Nat. West. Quarterly Review*, Aug. 1973, pp. 47–55.

78. *Poverty and the Welfare State, 1961,op. cit.*

79. Carr-Saunders, et. al., *op. cit.*, p. 203.

80. P. Corrigan, in ed. Abrams, *op. cit.*, p. 271, his figures taken from B. Abel Smith and P. Townsend, *The Poor and the Poorest*, Bell, 1965.

81. P. Townsend, *Poverty in the United Kingdom*, Penguin, 1979, p. 31.

82. A. Marwick, *Class Image and Reality in Britain, France and the U.S.A. since 1930*, Collins, 1980, p. 19.

83. Buchan, *op. cit.*, pp. 40–41, and 248–249. His biographer writes of Ernest Bevin "he was unashamedly himself on all occasions, entirely without class consciousness (that special English vice. . .)". A. Bullock, *Ernest Bevin – Foreign Secretary 1945–51*, Heinemann, 1983, p. 856.

84. V. Sackville West, *The Edwardians*, Hogarth Press, 1960, p. 79.

85. O. Chadwick, *Victorian Miniature*, Hodder and Stoughton, 1960.

86. *Times*, 23.6.1980, 27.6.1980.

87. e.g. A. Giddens, *The Class Structure of the Advanced Societies*. Hutchinson, 2 ed 1981 – excellent analysis of modern class structure. Westergaard and Resler, *op. cit.*, e.g. p. 117 ("Class inequality is not withering away"). R. Dahrendorf, *On Britain*, p. 78 ("So does class matter? The answer is clearly yes"). Jilly Cooper, *Class*, Corgi, 1980, p. 11 ("Three years of research later, I can assure you that the class system is alive and well and living in people's minds in England").

I. Thomas, *op. cit.*, p. 9 ("It is class rather than sex, or money or football, which is the great British secret obsession").

88. Dahrendorf, *op. cit.*, p. 55.

89. R.H. Tawney: quoted by Giddens *op. cit.*, p. 166.

90. After the Second War, when Geoffrey Keynes stayed at Balcarres, his shoes were cleaned by the 28th Earl.

Later Keynes visited famous Holkham Hall. Lord Leicester, alone in the great house, could not ask him to lunch and could not find the key to a box containing a Leonardo da Vinci manuscript. (G. Keynes, *The Gates of Memory*, Oxford, 1981, pp. 312, 352).

91. J.H. Goldthorpe, *Social Mobility and Class Structure in Modern Britain*, O.U.P., 1980, p. 60.

92. T. Noble, *Modern Britain: Structure and Change*, Batsford, 1975, p. 168.

93. quoted Cooper, *op. cit.*, p. 12.

94. I. Reid, *Social Class differences in Britain,* Open Books, 1977, p. 15 et seq.

95. G. Orwell, *The Lion and the Unicorn*. 1941, in *Collected Essays, etc.*, 2. Penguin, 1970, p. 98.

96. J.H. Goldthorpe and D. Lockwood, *The Affluent Worker*, C.U.P.

97. A. Heath, *Social Mobility*, Fontana, 1981, p. 75.

98. *ibid*, p. 54.

99. *ibid*., p. 107 et seq.

100. M. Young, *The Rise of the Meritocracy*, Penguin, 1961, p. 53.

101. C.D. Cohen, "The Social Contract and the Standard of Living", *Nat. West. Quarterly Review*, Aug. 1975, p. 54.

102. ed. Halsey, *op. cit.*, p. 167.

103. *National Income and Expenditure, 1979*, p. 68.

104. A.J. Halsey, *Origins and destinations. Family Class and Education in Modern Britain*, Oxford, 1980, p. 184 (Slightly adapted).

105. *ibid*., p. 172.

106. Quoted *ibid*., p. 203.

107. *Annual Abstract of Statistics, 1980*, p. 22 et seq.

107a. Thus, young designers took advantage of opportunities not previously available to those without money and went on grants to institutions such as the Royal College of Art. Janey Ironside, *Janey*, Michael Joseph, 1973, p. 113.

108. *Social Trends, 1980*, p. 113.

109. G. Simenon, *When I was old*, Penguin, 1973, p. 43.

110. *Report of Royal Commission on National Health Service*, 1979, p. 127.

111. *ibid*., p. 252.

112. *ibid,*. pp. 356, 355.

113. *ibid*., pp. 431, 432, 209, 194, 243.

114. N. Fairbrother, *op. cit.*, p. 208.

115. *National Income and Expenditure, 1979*, p. 68.

116. N. Bosanquet and P. Townsend, *Labour and Equality*, Heinemann, 1980, p. 179.

117. *Social Trends, 1979*, p. 177, et seq.

118. Brewers' Society, *Brewing Review*, Oct. 1977.

119. M. Shulman, Letter to *Times*, 26.9.1980 (abbreviated).

120. *Penal Practice in a Changing Society*, 1969, quoted in D. Thomson, *England in the 20th century*, Penguin, 1965, p. 274.

121. B. Whitaker, *The Police*, Eyre & Spottiswoode, 1964, p. 45, et seq.

122. *Social Trends, 1979*, p. 199.

123. P. Corrigan in ed. Abrams, *op. cit.*, p. 249.

124. *Social Trends, 1979*, p. 199, referring to Sparks, Genn and Dodd, *Surveying Victims, A Study of criminal victimisation*, Wiley, 1977.

125. J.A. Mack, "The Able Criminal" in ed. E. Butterworth and D. Weir, *Social Problems of Modern Britain*, Fontana, 1972, p. 277.

126. An account of police work and problems on Merseyside is in J. McClure, *Spike Island*, Pan, 1981.

127. ed. Abrams, *op. cit.*, p. 288.

128. J. Barron Mays, *Crime and its treatment*, Longmans, 1970, p. 107.

Chapter 17.   Aspects of the 1970s

1. N. Kaldor, "Inflation and recession in the World Economy" *Economic Journal*, Dec., 1976, p. 704.
2. *Annual Abstract of Statistics, 1980*, p. 310.
3. *Bank of England Quarterly Bulletin*, March, 1980, p. 12.
4. ed. R.E. Cales and L.B. Krause, *Britain's Economic Performance*, Brookings Institution, 1980, p. 5.
5. *Annual Abstract of Statistics, 1980*, p. 342 (Footnote).
6. *ibid.*, p. 168, et seq.
7. *Times*, 3.9.1980 referring to J. Alexander and Susan Toland, "Measuring the public sector borrowing requirement", *Economic Trends*, Sept. 1980.
8. ed. Caves and Krause, *op. cit.*, p. 3 (abbreviated).
9. *Social Trends, 1979*, p. 89.
10. *Annual Abstract of Statistics, 1980*, p. 146.
11. A.P. Thirlwall, "*Deindustrialisation* in the United Kingdom", *Lloyds Bank Review*, Apr. 1982, p. 22.
12. S. Moore and B. Rhodes, "The relative decline of the U.K. manufacturing sector", *Economic Policy Review*, Cambridge Dept. of Applied Economis, Mar. 1976, p. 36, et seq.
13. C.F. Pratten, "Mrs. Thatcher's Economic Experiment", *Lloyds Bank Review*, Jan. 1982, p. 37.
14. S.J. Prais, in ed. Caves and Krause, *op. cit.*, p. 193.
15. *Times*, 13.11.1970.
16. *Guardian*, 26.8.1980.
17. *Annual Abstract of Statistics, 1980*, p. 166.
18. *Britain 1977*, Central Office of Information, H.M.S.O., 1977, p. 228, et seq.
19. *Annual Abstract of Statistics, 1980*, p. 300.
20. *ibid*, p. 251 et seq.
21. *National Income and Expenditure, 1979*, p. 62 et seq.
22. R. Rose and G. Peters, *Can Government go Bankrupt?* Macmillan 1979, pp. 64, 252, 253.
23. e.g. ed. P. Townsend and N. Davidson, *Inequalities in Health, The Black Report*, Penguin, 1982.
24. D.C. Hague quoted *Times*, 20.6.1980.
25. R. Clutterbuck, *Britain in agony*, Penguin, 1980, p. 152, et seq.
26. *ibid.*, pp. 158–59.
27. Joe Gormley, *Battered cherub*, Hamish Hamilton, 1982, e.g. p. 144.
28. *New Society*, 29.11.1979.
29. J. Seabrook, *What went wrong?* Gollancz, 1978m, p. 13. Among working class, says Seabrook, "Despite spectacular material improvements there persists . . . . a malaise, an anger, a bitterness".
30. Quoted in *Listener*, 1.10.1981, p. 365.
31. "Within the intelligentsia a derisive and mildly hostile attitude towards Britain is more or less compulsory". G. Orwell, "Notes on nationalism", 1945, in *Decline of the English murder and other essays*, Penguin, 1965, p. 173

32. M. Friedman, *The Counter Revolution in Monetary Theory*, I.E.A., 1970, pp. 24, 22.
33. Sir John Hicks, "What is wrong with Monetarism?" *Lloyds Bank Review*, Oct. 1975, p. 2, et seq.

Chapter 18. Conclusion

1. Shils, *op. cit.*, p. 321, et seq.
2. Roberts, *A ragged schooling*, *op. cit.*, p. 157.
3. *ibid.*, p. 156.
4. e.g. Jean Robin, *Elmdon. Continuity and change in a North-west Essex village, 1861–1964, C.U.P., 1980.*
5. *Annual Abstract of Statistics, 1986*, H.M.S.O., p. 237.
6. G.C. Fiegehen, "Income after retirement", *Social Trends 1986*, H.M.S.O., p. 13.
7. *Social Trends, 1986*, p. 161.
8. *ibid.*, p. 175.
9. Thus, after a horrendous mass killing at Hungerford in Aug. 1987, a "Times" headline on 24.8.1987 was: "Churches attempt to rekindle faith".
10. "London in crisis", *Illustrated London News*, Sept. 1980.
11. *Social Trends, 1987*, p. 32.
11a. *Listener*, 3.9.1987 (Article by P. Hay).
12. Diana Spearman, "Enoch Powell's Postbag", *New Society*, 9.5.68.
13. Escott, *op. cit.*, p. 129.
14. *Times*, 29.7.87.
15. A.H. Halsey, "Social Trends since World War II", *Social Trends 1987*, p. 15.
16. *Social Trends 1987*, p. 139.
17. *Times*, 18.8.1987.
18. *Social Trends, 1987*, p. 16.
19. Smout, *op. cit.*, p. 214, et seq.
20. F. Donaldson, *Edward VIII*, Weidenfeld & Nicolson, 1974, p. 42.
    (It is interesting to note that the Prince was surprised to be sent to Oxford, since he knew that his father "distrusted scholarship and, like many other Englishmen regarded intellectual capacity and attainments almost as a handicap to sound judgement". *ibid.*, p. 38. Does this illustrate one more reason for our relative national decline?
21. *Social Trends, 1987*, p. 18.
22. M. Nissel, *People count. A history of the General Register Office*, H.M.S.O., 1987, pp. 139, 121.
23. E. Bishop, *The debt we owe*, Allen & Unwin, 2 ed. 1979, p. 60.
24. At Kohima, in Burma.

INDEX